Assessing Vulnerability to Global Environmental Change

Assessing Vulnerability to Global Environmental Change

Making Research Useful for Adaptation Decision Making and Policy

Edited by
Anthony G. Patt, Dagmar Schröter, Richard J. T. Klein and Anne Cristina de la Vega-Leinert

London • Washington, DC

First published by Earthscan in the UK and USA in 2009
Moved to digital printing 2010

ISBN: 978-1-84407-697-0

Typeset by MapSet Ltd, Gateshead, UK
Cover design by Susanne Harris

For a full list of publications please contact:

Earthscan Ltd, Dunstan House, 14a St Cross Street, London EC1N 8XA, UK
Earthscan LLC, 1616 P Street, NW, Washington, DC 20036, USA
Earthscan publishes in association with the International Institute for Environment and Development

For more information on Earthscan publications, see www.earthscan.co.uk or write to earthinfo@earthscan.co.uk

A catalogue record for this book is available from the British Library

Library of Congress Cataloging-in-Publication Data

Assessing vulnerability to global environmental change : making research useful for adaptation decision making and policy / edited by Anthony G. Patt … [et al.] ; with forewords by Hans Joachim Schellnhuber and Rik Leemans.
p. cm.
ISBN 978-1-84407-697-0 (hardback)
1. Global environmental change. 2. Environmental policy. 3. Environmental risk assessment. I. Patt, Anthony G.
GE149.A88 2008
363.7'0561–dc22

2008033032

At Earthscan we strive to minimize our environmental impacts and carbon footprint through reducing waste, recycling and offsetting our CO_2 emissions, including those created through publication of this book. For more details of our environmental policy, see www.earthscan.co.uk.

Printed and bound in the UK by
CPI Antony Rowe.
The paper used is FSC certified.

Contents

List of Figures and Tables

Figures

Tables

List of Contributors

Lilibeth Acosta-Michlik

Lilibeth Acosta-Michlik is an adjunct professor at the School of Environmental Science and Management (SESAM) in the University of the Philippines and senior researcher at the Centre for the study of Environmental Change and Sustainability (CECS) in the University of Edinburgh in the United Kingdom and at the Unité d'économie rurale in the Université Catholique de Louvain (UCL) in Belgium. She is currently coordinating and participating in various interdisciplinary research projects with funding from international organizations such as the European Commission and Asia Pacific Network. Her research focuses on the application of quantitative analyses including application of agent-based models, fuzzy logic, econometric analysis and others to assess the impacts of globalization and climate change on vulnerability, adaptation and sustainability in Europe and Asia. She has worked on development and policy issues for agricultural and environmental sectors in different institutions abroad including the National Economic Development Authority in the Philippines, University of Bonn in Germany, University of Kyoto in Japan and Potsdam Institute for Climate Impact Research in Germany. She received her degrees from the University of the Philippines (BSc agricultural economics), the University of Cambridge in England (MPhil economics of development) and the University of Bonn in Germany (PhD agricultural policy).

Antonella Battaglini

Antonella Battaglini is the Managing Director of the European Climate Forum, an organization carrying out research in the field of climate change risks management and stakeholder dialogues. Since 2001 she has worked as scientist at the Potsdam Institute for Climate Impact Research where she leads the research group 'Innovative Stakeholders Dialogue'. The group, led by Antonella, tries to identify options for a transition towards a decarbonized economy and brings together relevant actors for developing pathways and implementing them. Her research group is particularly focused on the Mediterranean region, the role Europe and individual member states need to play for fostering energy and climate security in the region. The SuperSmart Grid process is at the centre of her interests. It aims at advancing policy-oriented discussions and at drawing the political roadmap for linking the MENA region's renewable resources to Europe. Antonella is the co-founder of The Compensators and member of the EU ad hoc advisory group on ICT and energy security.

A. Cristina de la Vega-Leinert

A. Cristina de la Vega-Leinert is a trained geographer and completed in 1998 her PhD at the Centre for Quaternary Research, Coventry University (UK) on Holocene coastal palaeoecology on Mainland Orkney, Scotland. Until 2001 she worked at the Flood Hazard Research Centre (UK) as the scientific coordinator of the SURVAS (Synthesis and Upscaling of Relative Sea-Level Vulnerability Assessment Studies) EU Project. Until 2005, Cristina was the scientific coordinator of the EU project DINAS-COAST (Dynamic and Interactive Assessment of National, Regional and Global Vulnerability of Coastal Zones to Climate Change and Sea-Level Rise) and of the stakeholder dialogue within ATEAM (Advanced Terrestrial Ecosystem Analysis and Modelling) at the Potsdam Institute for Climate Impact Research, Germany. Since 2006, Cristina has collaborated with the GoBi (Governance of Biodiversity) project on success factors in the management of UNESCO Biosphere Reserves worldwide. Cristina moreover recently completed a Master of Arts in Intercultural Conflict Management at the Alice-Salomon University for Applied Sciences, Berlin (Germany), with a thesis on the human right to food in Mexico City in the context of economic liberalization. Cristina is currently a senior researcher and lecturer at the Institute of Geography, Ernst-Moritz-Arndt-University Greifswald, Germany. Her teaching has focused on integrated coastal zone management, (coastal) vulnerability and adaptation to global change, science-stakeholder dialogues in sustainability sciences, participative research and regional geography of Latin America. Her current research interests are to explore synergies between biodiversity management, sustainable development and food issues in the context of global change.

Kristie Ebi

Dr Kristie L. Ebi is an independent consultant (ESS, LLC) who has been conducting research on the impacts of and adaptation to climate change for more than a decade, primarily on extreme events, thermal stress, food-borne diseases and vector-borne diseases. She has worked with WHO, UNDP, USAID and others on implementing adaptation measures in low-income countries and is working with some US states on identifying adaptation options to address health vulnerabilities. She was a lead author for the Human Health chapter of the IPCC Fourth Assessment Report, and was lead author for Human Health for the US Synthesis and Assessment Product 'Analyses of the Effects of Global Change on Human Health and Welfare and Human Systems'. She has edited three books on climate change and health and is responsible for more than 80 publications. Dr Ebi's scientific training includes an MS in toxicology and a PhD and MPH in epidemiology, and two years of postgraduate research at the London School of Hygiene and Tropical Medicine (see www.essllc.org).

Siri Eriksen

Siri Eriksen is a post-doctoral researcher in the Department of Sociology and Human Geography at the University of Oslo. She has a PhD in Environmental Sciences from University of East Anglia. She has done research for the past 12 years on climate change and development, with particular attention paid to household-level vulnerability and adaptation to climate variability and change in Africa. Recent projects focus on the impact of conflict on vulnerability to climate change among dryland populations in Kenya; the effect of market integration on household responses to droughts and floods in Mozambique; and identifying critical linkages between adaptation and poverty reduction efforts in development policy. She has also studied vulnerability and adaptation to climate change in Norway.

Evan D. G. Fraser

With a BA in anthropology, an MSc in forestry and a PhD in environmental studies (thesis on sustainable agriculture), Evan has a multidisciplinary background that has allowed him to use both qualitative and quantitative tools to assess the social and environmental impact of global change on regional food systems. His research interests focus on food security and sustainable agriculture in a world buffeted by major environmental and economic changes. Specifically, he is interested in the resilience of community food systems in light of climate change and economic globalization, and how farm management responds to these different types of risks. Thus far, Evan has focused on case studies in Europe, North America, South-east Asia and Central America, and has studied how increased trade in agricultural commodities affects farm management and how this in turn affects the environment. He is also interested in how community participation can meet these challenges and result in both social and environmental benefits.

Hans-Martin Füssel

Dr Hans-Martin Füssel is a senior research fellow in the Research Domain Sustainable Solutions at the Potsdam Institute for Climate Impact Research (Potsdam, Germany) and a professor by special invitation at the Ritsumeikan Research Center for Sustainability Science (Ritsumeikan University, Kyoto, Japan). He holds a PhD in physics and Masters degrees in applied systems science and computer science. His main research interests include climate impacts modelling, adaptation planning for climate change, comparative assessment of vulnerability to climate change, equity implications of climate change impacts and policies, and probabilistic integrated assessment of climate change. Dr Füssel has served as author, review editor and expert reviewer for the IPCC Fourth Assessment Report. He has advised the UNDP, UNFCCC, WHO and the European Commission on climate change.

Jochen Hinkel

Jochen Hinkel is a senior research fellow at the Potsdam Institute for Climate Impact Research (PIK) where he leads a research group on climate change vulnerability and adaptation. He holds a PhD in environmental sciences (Wageningen University, The Netherlands) and a Masters in geo-ecology (Karlsruhe University, Germany). His PhD thesis developed and applied methods for facilitating the integration of knowledge from natural and social sciences in the context of transdisciplinary assessments. Hinkel coordinated the development of the tool DIVA (Dynamic and Interactive Vulnerability

Assessment), an integrated coastal vulnerability assessment tool that has been applied widely in the context of the United Nations Framework Convention on Climate Change (UNFCCC) for the preparation of National Communications and the assessment of coastal adaptation. Further research activities include mathematical formalization of vulnerability and related concepts as well as meta-analysis of vulnerability and adaptation case studies. Prior to his academic engagement he was working as a development practitioner, software developer and information technology consultant.

Stefan Hochrainer

Stefan Hochrainer is a research scientist at the International Institute for Applied System Analysis (IIASA) and lecturer at the University of Vienna. He holds a PhD in statistics from the University of Vienna and a Masters degree in sociology. His main research interests include decision support under uncertainty and quantitative risk management against extreme risks. He has worked extensively on extreme value theory topics, rare events estimation, catastrophe risk management strategies, natural disaster events in developing countries to and statistical modelling of rare events. He has held invited presentations in major (re)insurance meetings and scientific conferences. He has also contributed to and facilitated a number of workshops with senior representatives of ministries of finance and planning in the Caribbean countries, as well as Madagascar, Turkey, Philippines, India and Mexico.

Ian Holman

Dr Ian Holman gained his PhD investigating the linkage between land management and saline intrusion of the Crag aquifer in Norfolk, UK. The integration of spatial landscape properties, human activities, weather, hydrological response and ecosystem or species impacts has been the core of his research for a range of clients over the past 15 years at the Soil Survey and Land Research Centre (now the National Soil Resources Institute) and the Natural Resources Department at Cranfield University. He was lead author and project manager of the RegIS and RegIS2 projects, respectively, which developed the first integrated approach to investigating the regional impacts of climate and socioeconomic change on the regional landscape of the UK. He is also Co-chairman of the International Association of Hydrogeologists' Commission on Groundwater and Climate Change

Carlo C. Jaeger

Professor Dr Carlo Jaeger is Department Head for Transdisciplinary Concepts and Methods, at the Potsdam Institute for Climate Impacts Research in Germany, as well as Professor for Modelling Social Systems at the University of Potsdam. He is an honorary professor at the Beijing Normal University, the Chair of the European Climate Forum, and Co-chair of the Integrated Risk Governance Project, a proposed new core activity for the International Human Dimensions Programme on Global Environmental Change. He has written or edited 11 books on economics, sociology, risk and the environment, as well as countless peer-reviewed papers.

Richard Klein

Richard J. T. Klein is a geographer with over 15 years of research experience on human vulnerability and adaptation to climate variability and change. He is a leading expert on adaptation science and climate policy and has been involved in the Intergovernmental Panel on Climate Change since 1993, most recently as coordinating lead author in the Fourth Assessment Report. He also contributed to the Millennium Ecosystem Assessment, the Stern Review on the Economics of Climate Change, and Tony Blair's report 'Breaking the climate deadlock'. His current research interests include methodological aspects of vulnerability assessment, societal adaptation to climate change, and integration of climate and development policy. Richard co-directs the Climate and Energy programme at the Stockholm Environment Institute (SEI) and coordinates climate policy research across all SEI centres. In addition, he is the editor-in-chief of the international journal *Climate and Development*. Before joining SEI, he spent almost eight years at the Potsdam Institute for Climate Impact Research (PIK), where he was group leader and deputy head of the Department of Global Change and Social Systems. He has been a principal investigator in a number of large collaborative research and capacity-building projects, and has provided consultancy and advisory services to a range of governments, UN agencies and non-governmental organizations.

Robin Leichenko

Dr Robin M. Leichenko is Associate Professor and Graduate Director in Geography at Rutgers University. Leichenko's current research programme emphasizes economic vulnerability to climate change and globalization in both advanced and developing countries. Her new book, co-authored with Dr Karen O'Brien, is titled *Environmental Change and Globalization: Double Exposures* (Oxford University Press, 2008).

Reinhard Mechler

Reinhard Mechler is an economist at the International Institute for Applied Systems Analysis (IIASA) and leads the research group on *Disasters and Development*. Specific interests of his include catastrophe risk modelling, the longer-term impacts of extreme events and climate change on development, the use of novel risk-financing mechanisms for sharing disaster risks, and the assessment of the efficiency and equity of risk management and adaptation measures. He has published in journals such as *Science, Climate Policy, Atmospheric Environment* and *Natural Hazards*. He acted as a reviewer of the Fourth Assessment Report of the Intergovernmental Panel on Climate Change and has been leading and contributing to projects for organizations including the European Commission, DFID, the UN, ProVention Consortium, World Bank, Inter-American Development Bank, Caribbean Development Bank and GTZ. Reinhard Mechler studied economics, mathematics and English and holds a diploma in economics from the University of Heidelberg and a PhD in economics from the University of Karlsruhe in Germany.

Florence Nazare

Florence Nazare is a Zimbabwean development researcher. She has been enrolled as a PhD candidate at the University of Witwatersrand in South Africa, and holds a Masters degree in environmental policy and an honours degree in sociology from the Universities of Zimbabwe and Fort Hare. She has worked as a researcher with the Southern African Regional Institute for Policy Studies and Ministries of Industry and Commerce and Community Development, and as Coordinator of the NEPAD (New Partnership for African Development) Capacity Development Initiative.

Karen O'Brien

Karen O'Brien is a professor in the Department of Sociology and Human Geography at the University of Oslo, Norway and chair of the Global Environmental Change and Human Security (GECHS) project. Her current research focuses on adaptation to environmental change as a social process. She has recently published a book with Robin Leichenko entitled *Environmental Change and Globalization: Double Exposures* (Oxford University Press, 2008).

Lars Otto Næss

Lars Otto Næss is a PhD candidate in environmental sciences at the Tyndall Centre for Climate Change Research, University of East Anglia, UK. He was formerly a research fellow at the Center for International Climate and Environmental Research – Oslo (CICERO), and worked for three years on gender, biodiversity and local knowledge issues with the UN Food and Agriculture Organization (FAO). Climate change has been a focus of his work for over ten years, particularly the social and institutional dimensions. His research has concentrated on local aspects of vulnerability and adaptation, in developed as well as developing country contexts. Projects relating to Norway include 'Climate change in Norway: Analysis of economic and social impacts and adaptation' (2002–2004), funded by the Norwegian Research Council. He was also lead author of a scoping study on a national climate adaptation strategy for the Norwegian Ministry of the Environment.

Anthony Patt

Anthony Patt leads the Decisions and Governance research group in the Programme on Risk and Vulnerability at the International Institute for Applied Systems Analysis (IIASA) in Austria. Before that, he was Assistant Professor of Environmental Policy at Boston University. He holds doctoral degrees in law (Duke University) and public policy (Harvard University). His research focuses on individual and collective decision making, especially in the context of climate- and environmentally-related choices. He has conducted extensive research on the use of seasonal climate forecasts in Africa, as well as climate adaptation choices more generally. His research also investigates the factors accounting for new investment in renewable energy, both in Europe and Africa. He is on the editorial board of the journal *Global Environmental Change*, and an associate editor of the journals *Regional Environmental Change* and *Climate and Development*. He was a contributing author to Working Group II of the IPCC.

Mark Rounsevell

Mark Rounsevell is Professor of Rural Economy and Sustainability within the School of GeoSciences at the University of Edinburgh and is Director of the School's Centre for the study of Environmental Change and Sustainability (CECS). His research focuses on the effects of environmental change on rural and urban landscapes with particular emphasis on the development and application of social simulation techniques such as agent-based models. Model applications include the exploration of alternative futures of climate and other environmental change drivers and the response of individual people and society to these changes. He was a lead author to Working Group II of the IPCC Second, Third and Fourth Assessment Reports, notably as an expert on climate change impacts, adaptation and vulnerability methodologies and the effects on ecosystems. He participates in several European Commission projects that are evaluating the impacts of climate change on land use and ecosystems and the potential for adaptation to these impacts. He is the Leader of the Society Theme of the Scottish Alliance for Geosciences, Environment and Society (SAGES).

Dagmar Schröter

Dagmar Schröter is an expert on global change and ecosystem services in the Department of Environmental Impact Assessment and Climate Change of the Federal Environment Agency in Vienna, Austria. From 2005–2008 she was research fellow at Clark University's George Perkins Marsh Institute (Worcester, USA), which is dedicated to research on the fundamental question: what is and ought to be our relationship with nature? Prior to this she was visiting research fellow at Harvard University in the Science, Environment and Development Group at the Center for International Development (CID, Cambridge, MA). From 2001–2004, Dagmar was affiliated with the Potsdam Institute for Climate Impact Research (PIK), Department of Global Change and Natural Systems (Potsdam, Germany). She directed the European Vulnerability Assessment Project ATEAM, a European Union funded large-scale research initiative led by PIK that was completed in 2005. Dagmar obtained her PhD in ecosystems research in 2001 at Gießen University, Department of Animal Ecology, Germany, combining field research and numerical modelling. Prior to this she studied biology at the Technical University, Aachen, Germany. Her research interests are human–environment interactions, global change vulnerability assessment, ecological food web modelling and the carbon and nitrogen cycle. Her ultimate research goal is to make environmental sciences useful in interdisciplinary dialogues on sustainable management of the human–environment system.

Franziska Steinbruch

Franziska Steinbruch is Manager of Scientific Services of Gorongosa National Park in Mozambique, where she is responsible for the coordination of research and monitoring activities. She assists the Gorongosa National Park restoration project in the establishment of the Scientific Service and provides scientific advice to the park management. Her professional background is in hydrogeology, GIS and remote sensing, with experience in the development of technical facilities and research capacity in Mozambique. She has previously worked at the Center for Geographic Information at the Catholic University, Beira, Mozambique, where she focused specifically on GIS in disaster risk management in Mozambique.

Coleen Vogel
Professor Coleen Vogel holds the BMW Chair of Sustainability at the School of Geography, Archaeology and Environmental Studies at the University of the Witwatersrand, South Africa. Her research interests are in environmental change, extreme events, disaster risk reduction and the role of science in policy and decision making. Her publications include *Coping with Climate Variability: The Use of Seasonal Climate Forecasts in Southern Africa*, co-edited with Karen O'Brien. She is the former Chair of the Scientific Committee of the International Human Dimensions Programme on Global Environmental Change.

Martin Welp
Professor Dr Martin Welp is engaged at the University of Applied Sciences Eberswalde (near Berlin) in the Faculty of Forest and Environment. He heads the recently launched International Master Study Programme 'Global Change Management'. Before his appointment as Professor of Socioeconomics and Communication, he was a senior researcher at the Potsdam Institute for Climate Impact Research (PIK). He has headed research projects on public participation and stakeholder dialogues in various fields of environmental management, including forest management, coastal management and protected area management.

Gina Ziervogel
Gina Ziervogel is a lecturer in the Department of Environmental and Geographical Science at the University of Cape Town and a Research Fellow at the Stockholm Environment Institute. Gina's work focuses on how people, particularly the poor, interact with their social and physical environment in order to pursue their livelihoods and develop adaptation responses in the context of environmental change. Currently she is focusing on ways of integrating scientific information in planning strategies in light of climate change across a number of scales. Gina completed her PhD in geography at the University of Oxford, she has been involved in numerous projects in southern Africa and internationally and is a South African citizen.

Foreword 1

It might seem a banality to state that targeted, efficient and – above all – successful adaptation strategies to global environmental change require sound information on the vulnerability of the human–environment system affected. However, many recent lessons teach us that this prerequisite is not such a banal requirement after all. With the operationalization of the United Nations Framework Convention on Climate Change (UNFCCC) Adaptation Fund at the Bali Conference in December 2007, intended to finance adaptation projects in developing countries that are Parties to the Kyoto Protocol (UNFCCC, 2002), the question of how to define which countries are 'particularly vulnerable to the adverse effects of climate change' (UNFCCC, 1998) is due to be asked again. And it is likely to generate a lively debate.

As the reduction of vulnerability is seen as one of the crucial targets of any adaptation action, the logical consequence is that resources should be distributed in such a manner that those most in need receive the assistance they require. And here, we are already about to get ourselves into the first predicament. Should this assistance include funds purely for adapting to climate change or will it also provide resources for combating the root of vulnerability, that is, poverty? A large amount of literature is currently being compiled to answer some of these essential questions, but I will abstain from projecting the potential outcomes. Instead, I will focus on the tools that can contribute to making such a decision an educated one: vulnerability assessments. By bringing together information on the exposure and sensitivity of a particular population or environment to change, and assessing its adaptive capacity to deal with this change, vulnerability analyses can succeed in highlighting areas of concern and accordingly inform political decision-making processes. Consequently, as vulnerability assessments do play an integral role in facilitating adaptation activities, their use is clearly not limited to this outcome alone. Taken in a much broader context, vulnerability assessments can also highlight the far-reaching impacts of environmental change and thus help to trigger political action in order to avoid these.

An example to illustrate the clout such exercises can have is recognizable in the vulnerability maps produced by the United Nations Scientific Expert Group (UNSEG) for their report on Climate Change and Sustainable Development in 2007 (SEG, 2007). Outlining the ecological, agroeconomic and social vulnerability to future climate change on a global scale, developing countries were clearly identified as the most vulnerable. However, these maps also highlighted the existence of particularly vulnerable regions in industrialized countries such as coastal or alpine areas. In addition, major parts of eastern Europe were shown to have a high agroeconomic vulnerability due to the projected loss of agricultural productivity. The visualization of such risks is an important part of 'bringing home the message', that is, the need for stringent mitigation targets since there are clearly limits to adaptation, even for industrialized countries.

This message was further supported by our recently published assessment of potential tipping elements in the Earth system (Lenton et al, 2008). Contrary to the public notion of climate change presenting a gradually intensifying – and thus manageable – risk, these tipping elements carry the potential to provide us with nasty surprises. Pushed past a critical point through anthropogenic activities, several Earth system components could enter into a qualitatively very different state of operation. Examples are the much-debated collapse of the thermohaline circulation, the irreversible melting of the Greenland ice sheet or the potential dieback of the Amazon rainforest. Each of these transitions would entail serious consequences, not only for the environmental systems concerned, but even more so for human society. To get an idea of the probability of these events occurring we recently examined a number of possible tipping elements in an expert elicitation exercise (Kriegler et al, 2008). From the list of tipping elements considered, the Arctic sea ice and the Greenland ice sheet were identified as those closest to reaching a critical tipping point within this century as a consequence of anthropogenic climate change. Just thinking of the 7m sea-level rise that a complete melting of the Greenland ice sheet would lead to points to the urgency of keeping global average temperature from exceeding 2°C above pre-industrial levels.

And via this telling detour on some of the consequences of unhalted climate change, let us return to the focus of this book. As outlined in the introductory sentences above, vulnerability research does serve an important purpose in political decision making. This exciting research field, squeezed between the disciplines of the natural and social sciences, therefore needs to face up to the responsibility it carries and be aware of its political impacts. The demand on the methodical practices and methodological standards in vulnerability research is accordingly high. This book makes a valuable contribution to the ongoing debate regarding these issues. Written not with the sole intention of excelling in the scientific debate but rather with the aim of making vulnerability research a domain of policy analysis, it marks the continuation of the so-called Potsdam Process: a new methodological approach, map-based, multiple scenario, stakeholder participation and ecosystem service oriented. It deploys a geographically explicit viewpoint on the human–environment system, with ecosystem services seen as its vital connecting links. It specifically addresses the human component in this system, its individual and value-based character, and thus highlights the indispensible necessity for a coherent stakeholder dialogue. Anyone interested in this rapidly developing discipline will be thankful for this book, the critical review it presents and its broad collection of practical examples in vulnerability research.

Hans Joachim Schellnhuber
Professor of Physics (Potsdam & Oxford)
Director, Potsdam Institute for Climate Impact Research (PIK)
Potsdam, March 2008

References

Kriegler, E., Hall, J., Dawson, R., Held, H. and Schellnhuber, H. J. (2008) 'Imprecise probability of crossing tipping points in the Earth system elicited from experts', *Proceedings of the National Academy of Sciences of the United States of America*, forthcoming

Lenton, T. M., Held, H., Kriegler, E., Hall, J. W., Lucht, W., Rahmstorf, S. and Schellnhuber, H. J. (2008) 'Tipping elements in the earth's climate system', *Proceedings of the National Academy of Sciences of the United States of America*, vol 105, p1786

SEG (Scientific Expert Group on Climate Change) (2007) 'Confronting climate change: Avoiding the unmanageable and managing the unavoidable', Report prepared for the United Nations Commission on Sustainable Development, Bierbaum, R. M., Holdren, J. P., MacCracken, M. C., Moss, R. H., Raven, P. H. (eds) Sigma Xi, Research Triangle Park, NC, and the United Nations Foundation, Washington DC

UNFCCC (1998) 'Text of the Kyoto Protocol, 1998', http://unfccc.int/resource/docs/convkp/kpeng.pdf

UNFCCC (2002) 'Marrakesh Accords', FCCC/CP/2001/13/Add.1, 21 January 2002, http://unfccc.int/resource/docs/cop7/13a01.pdf

Foreword 2

We are now living in a 'risk society' as Beck (1982) already stated 25 years ago. Although hardships and fortuities are part of everybody's life, of the functioning of ecosystems, of the climate system and of the dynamics of the whole Earth system, we now try to manage all hazards and to minimize negative impacts. However, the dangers threatening society are no longer dominated by natural forces alone, but also by humans. Depletion of resources, decline of biodiversity, the ozone hole and climate change are globally significant phenomena caused by human activities. These global changes require different coping and managing strategies. Many communities therefore focus on reducing vulnerability, enhancing resilience and reducing risks.

Scientific research has thrived on these changes. The first disciplines that picked up these new concepts were related to disaster studies and ecology. Part of that history is illustrated in the seminal books by Clark and Munn (1986) and Blaikie et al (1994). A decade ago, the Intergovernmental Panel on Climate Change (IPCC) redirected its impact assessment towards a more comprehensive vulnerability assessment with chapters on different regions, sectors and natural ecosystems. In its latest Fourth Assessment Report (Parry et al, 2007) the term vulnerability was used 1166 times, resilience 230 times and risk 1789 times. IPCC defined 'vulnerability' as the degree to which a system is susceptible to, and unable to cope with, adverse effects of climate change, including climate variability and extremes. Vulnerability is a function of the character, magnitude and rate of climate change and variation to which a system is exposed, the sensitivity and adaptive capacity of that system (Parry et al, 2007). Unfortunately, this definition is not employed in a very strict way, mainly because of the many different definitions used in the scientific literature feeding into the IPCC assessment. This makes the interpretation of the results intricate or even fuzzy and therefore less useful to inform policy makers. This is unfortunate because providing guidance to climate change decision making is one of the major objectives of IPCC.

This book has taken a different approach. It discusses vulnerability as the central theme and brings together many different applications from disaster studies, from climate change impact studies and several other fields. The book provides the most comprehensive synthesis of definitions, theories, formalization and applications, illustrated with examples from different disciplines, regions and periods. This is one of the strengths of the book. Most of its examples illustrate how the differences are elaborated in real applications. Several chapters present new transdisciplinary approaches. Most of the authors have ample experience in accomplishing state-of-the-art research projects with different science–policy dialogues and stakeholder involvements at local, regional, national and international levels. Some of the chapters clearly stress that these dialogues must be transparent to be effective and concentrate on a mutual understanding of the concepts used. Many of these points are obvious, but they are rarely implemented in practice. The book ends with a unifying framework for analysing integrated methodologies of vulnerability assessment.

This book is highly recommended for everyone trying to elaborate and quantify relatively fuzzy concepts like vulnerability, but it is definitely a must-read for all researchers in the climate-change community who want to develop a broader perspective. In a recent workshop of the international research programmes for global environmental change (Sydney, September 2007) on further developing their research agenda on the basis of the results of IPCC's Fourth Assessment Report, it was concluded that the approaches applied by the climate modellers, scenario developers and vulnerability assessors were incompatible. These research communities should collaborate more closely and develop appropriate interfaces. When some of the insights and recommendations from this book are implemented or when the unifying framework is applied in their research, results will be much more comparable and compatible. This will make a future IPCC assessment less ambiguous, more comprehensive and quantitative and therefore much more valuable for the policy community.

In the coming years, the Earth System Science Partnership will take a lead to connect the vulnerability research community with others in the Global Change Research programmes. This book sets the scene onto which future research can build. I thank all the authors but also the editors for their efforts to compile this impressive compendium on vulnerability research and its applications.

Rik Leemans
Chair Earth System Science Partnership (www.essp.org)
Professor of Environmental Systems Analysis, Wageningen University
Wageningen, March 2008

References

Beck, U. (1982) *Risikogesellschaft: auf dem Weg in eine andere Moderne Edition*, Surkamp, Frankfurt Am Main

Blaikie, P. M., Cannon, T., Davis, I. and Wisner B. (eds) (1994) *At Risk: Natural Hazards, People's Vulnerability, and Disasters*, Routledge, New York

Clark, W. C. and Munn, R. E. (eds) (1986) *Sustainable Development of the Biosphere*, Cambridge University Press, Cambridge

Parry, M. L., Canziani, O. F., Palutikof, J. P., Hanson, C. E. and Van der Linden, P. J. (eds) (2007) 'Climate Change 2007: Impacts, adaptation and vulnerability', Contribution of Working Group II to the Fourth Assessment Report of the Intergovernmental Panel on Climate Change, Cambridge University Press, Cambridge

List of Acronyms and Abbreviations

ACIA	Arctic Climate Impact Assessment
ATEAM	Advanced Terrestrial Ecosystem Analysis and Modelling
CAN	Climate Action Network
CatSim	Catastrophe Simulation model
CAP	Common Agricultural Policy
cCASHh	Climate Change and Adaptation Strategies for Human Health
CCD	colony collapse disorder
CCRIF	Caribbean Catastrophe Risk Insurance Facility
CDB	Caribbean Development Bank
CZMS	Coastal Zone Management Subgroup
DALY	disability adjusted life year
Defra	Department for Environment, Food and Rural Affairs
DFID	Department for International Development
DFNK	German Research Network for Natural Disasters
DINAS-COAST	Dynamic and Interactive Assessment of National, Regional and Global Vulnerability of Coastal Zones to Sea-Level Rise
DIVA	Dynamic and Interactive Vulnerability Assessment
DOA	Department of Agriculture
DPCCN	Department for the Prevention and Combat of Natural Disasters
DRM	disaster risk management
ECF	European Climate Forum
FANRPAN	Food, Agriculture and Natural Resources Policy Analysis Network
FAO	Food and Agriculture Organization
FEWS-NET	Famine Early Warning System Network
FIVIMS	Food Insecurity and Vulnerability Information Mapping System
FSTAU	Food Security and Technical Administration Unit
GBD	Global Burden of Disease 2000
GCM	general circulation model
GDP	gross domestic product
GHG	greenhouse gas
GIS	geographical information system

GPS	global positioning system
GTZ	German Technical Cooperation Agency
GUI	graphical user interface
IA	Integrated Assessment
IDB	Inter-American Development Bank
IIASA	International Institute for Applied Systems Analysis
IFPRI	International Food Policy Research Institute
INGC	National Institute of Disaster Management
IPCC	Intergovernmental Panel on Climate Change
ISO	International Organization for Standardization
LFA	less favoured area
MA	Millennium Ecosystem Assessment
MICOA	Ministry for Coordination of Environmental Affairs
MoE	Ministry of the Environment
MPF	Mozambique, Ministry of Planning and Finance
NEPAD	New Partnership for Africa's Development
NGO	non-governmental organization
NVAC	National Vulnerability Assessment Committee
NVE	Norwegian Water Resources and Energy Directorate
ODI	Overseas Development Institute
OECS	Organisation of Eastern Caribbean States
PDPMCN	*Plano Director para Prevenção e Mitigação das Calamidades Naturais* (Plan for the Prevention and Mitigation of Natural Disasters)
PIK	Potsdam Institute for Climate Impact Research
PPS	Planning Policy Statement
PRSP	poverty reduction strategy
RegIS	Regional Climate Change Impact and Response Studies in East Anglia and North West England
RIVM	National Institute of Public Health and Environment (Netherlands)
RVAC	Regional Vulnerability Assessment Committee
SADC	Southern Africa Development Community
SARPN	Southern African Regional Poverty Network
SAVI	Southern Africa Vulnerability Initiative
SES	socioeconomic scenario
SETSAN	National Executive Secretary of Food Security and Nutrition
SIAM	Scenarios, Impacts and Adaptation Measures
SRES	Special Report on Emission Scenarios
SURVAS	Synthesis and Upscaling of Sea-Level Rise Vulnerability Assessment Studies
UCM	Catholic University of Mozambique
UEM	Eduardo Modlane University
UKCIP	United Kingdom Climate Impacts Programme

UNDP-GEF	United Nations Development Programme – Global Environment Facility
UNEP	United Nations Environment Programme
UNFCCC	United Nations Framework Convention on Climate Change
UNRAVEL	Understanding Resilient and Vulnerable Livelihoods
UNSEG	United Nations Scientific Expert Group
VA	vulnerability assessment
VAC	Vulnerability Assessment Committee
VAM	Vulnerability Analysis and Mapping
VISTA	Vulnerability of Ecosystem Services to Land Use Change in Traditional Agricultural Landscapes
WBGU	German Advisory Board on Global Change
WFP	World Food Programme
WHO	World Health Organization
WWF	World Wide Fund for Nature
XML	extensible mark-up language

Chapter 1

Vulnerability Research and Assessment to Support Adaptation and Mitigation: Common Themes from the Diversity of Approaches

Anthony G. Patt, Dagmar Schröter, A. Cristina de la Vega-Leinert and Richard J. T. Klein

The vulnerability trap

In the last ten years, the study of vulnerability has mushroomed. The Intergovernmental Panel on Climate Change (IPCC), for example, shifted the focus of their second working group from one studying climate change impacts, to one studying climate change vulnerability in their Third Assessment Report (McCarthy et al, 2001), and by their Fourth Assessment Report have cited scores of vulnerability assessments (Parry et al, 2007). Recently, the term vulnerability has increasingly been used in environmental sciences, ecology, resource management and development, in particular concerning the phenomena of global change and the Earth system. In this book we focus on vulnerability to global environmental change. There have been a growing number of local and regional assessments of vulnerability, particularly to climate change, or a combination of climate change and other factors. We try to answer the question: what makes an assessment of global change vulnerability useful?

Probably the most important cause of the attention to vulnerability is the recognition that global changes of important magnitude, in particular climate and land-use change, are already taking place, and that the nature and magnitude of potential impacts, according to modelling exercises, could be dramatic (Schröter et al, 2005a). Since the 1980s, scientists and policy makers have debated how much effort should be spent to stop or limit climate change, and what policy instruments would be the best tools to use. But as these debates have been going on, it has increasingly been recognized that a certain amount of climate change has already occurred, and that no matter what policies come into place, an ever-greater amount of climate change will occur in the future (McCarthy et al, 2001). In the last 100 years, global mean temperatures have risen approximately 0.6°C, with evidence of corresponding changes in precipitation, sea-level rise and occurrence of extreme events (Folland et al, 2001). But these have been simply the transient responses to the change in greenhouse gas concentrations that have already occurred, meaning that the planet has not yet come into equilibrium. Should we stop increasing the atmospheric concentration of CO_2 and other greenhouse gases now, one recent modelling study suggests we could still experience at least another 0.5°C of warming, potentially much more, and a degree of sea-level rise several times what we have already experienced (Meehl et al, 2005). In the more likely case that society reduces its CO_2 emissions neither completely nor immediately, these changes will be even greater. On top of this, there is the threat that important thresholds could be passed, leading to irreversible changes in the basic states of several global systems, such as the North Atlantic thermohaline circulation (Broeker, 1997), the Amazon basin rainfall regime (Laurance and Williamson, 2001) or the Asian monsoon (Gupta et al, 2003). The apparent inevitability of future climate change of a magnitude greater than society has ever experienced, coupled with other global-scale changes such as population growth, land degradation and nitrification, makes it increasingly important to anticipate and adapt. For the first time in human history, policy makers are now trying to manage, at a global scale, the long-term consequences of gradual change.

Science plays a vital function not only in suggesting but also in justifying policy decisions. Ezrahi (1990) argues that modern systems of governance rely on science for their very legitimacy, much as past monarchies relied on claims of divine right. Policy makers need to show that their decisions are supported by sound scientific theory. In recent decades, there have been several cases where the public has not only called into question the validity of the science on which policy makers relied, but also succeeded in revealing its shortcomings (Wynne, 1996). The result, many scholars suggest, is a public that is rightfully sceptical of the claims that scientists make, and less than willing to trust them (Freudenberg, 1996; Hoffman-Reim and Wynne, 2002). If scientists cannot demonstrate the validity of their knowledge to the people who will be affected, they will not only be ignored (Michael, 1996), but their future reputation will be harmed (Glantz, 2000). Scientists involved in the policy-making process, whether willingly or not, now carry the burden of proof for the knowledge claims they make. Those who fail to do so risk harming not only their own credibility, but also the credibility of their colleagues.

The onus is especially difficult to bear in the realm of vulnerability. Scientists conducting vulnerability assessment gather a great deal of important and reliable information about the various factors that probably give rise to vulnerability, such as the direction and magnitude of future climate change, the existing stresses on the human environment system, and economic indicators that may increase or lessen adaptive capacity. None of these factors is a measure of vulnerability itself, but rather is an indicator that, when combined with other indicators according to one or more theoretical models, contributes to an overall picture. However, because of the lack of precedent for the current combination of global environmental changes, scientists need to wait 20, 50 or 100 years to validate those very theoretical models. There are now many competing models, rooted in different scientific traditions, each suggesting that it is a slightly different combination of factors that leads to increased vulnerability. By calling on scientists to assess vulnerability, and to use a theoretical model to aggregate their data into a form that is useful, policy makers are setting an unwitting trap. This trap can lure scientists into simplifying complexity and uncertainty too much in order to be helpful, funded or famous. Scientists are drawn to assess vulnerability, either out of a desire to save the world or else out of simple vanity and, given the importance of their work, this lands them squarely in the limelight. In this process, they can easily make statements that they are unable to support with credible theory, or to defend against competing claims. Having their advice ignored is not the worst that can happen.

The purpose of this book is to suggest how scientists conducting vulnerability assessment can avoid falling into this trap, and how policy makers and stakeholders can avoid setting it in the first place. The thesis of this book is that, at least for now, the study of vulnerability to global environmental change can and should fall within the domain of policy analysis – engineering practical solutions to pressing problems – rather than within the much broader discourse of natural, social and systems science. While scientists can offer an abundance of valuable information on vulnerability to stakeholders and policy makers, no *single* indicator or *single* theory of vulnerability will be helpful or credible for the purpose of understanding and lessening the vulnerability of a specific place or system. Instead we must engage in an open dialogue relying on the best available science and inviting the participation of all relevant stakeholders, in a way that promotes effective policy or decision making.

In this introductory chapter, we will lay out our argument, first by discussing the basis for theory on vulnerability, second by describing the various reasons to assess vulnerability and third by describing the ways to conduct vulnerability assessment such that it is useful. We introduce the remaining chapters of the book, each of which tells a different story about vulnerability and vulnerability assessment, told from a different perspective, and each of which suggests that the thesis of this book – the study of vulnerability should fall within the domain of policy analysis, that is, engineering practical solutions to pressing problems – holds.

Vulnerability research

Several review articles document the development of vulnerability within the social and environmental sciences. We briefly summarize this history here, in order to set the stage for our discussions of the purpose of vulnerability research.

Global environmental-change vulnerability assessments are rooted in three traditions of research: risk/hazard research, food security studies and, most recently, climate impact assessment. The first of these grew out of efforts to identify the potential effects of acute pressures on a system. The focus is on vulnerability to a single cause of harm, and how other features of a system could exacerbate or mitigate that harm (Cutter, 2001). For example, an earthquake might damage a human settlement. The extent and form of the damage can depend on physical features of the system, such as the construction of buildings. How quickly the system can recover from the damage, in turn, depends on institutions: emergency teams take care of the injured and the dead, and insurance and financing mechanisms facilitate rapid rebuilding (Freeman and Kunreuther, 2002). The second of these is centred not on a single cause, but a single effect, namely hunger and famine (Ribot et al, 1996). While it was initially attractive to lay the blame for hunger on a particular cause, such as a drought, the theory of economic entitlements, propounded by Amartya Sen, convincingly demonstrated that people's physical or latent resources play at least as great a role (Sen, 1981). In researching the vulnerability to a single outcome (rather than a source of harm), these researchers attempt to examine the interactions of multiple stresses, often building over time.

The third tradition, climate impact assessment, initially focused on determining the marginal damages associated with the human choice to place additional greenhouse gases in the atmosphere. Like hazard assessment, this strand of vulnerability assessment concerns itself primarily with a single driver of harm. However, just as vulnerability to food security increases slowly over time as entitlements erode, so too will climate impacts accumulate gradually over long timescales. It thus becomes necessary, in assessing climate change impacts, to consider other causes or adaptations that may develop over the same time span, and which will either exacerbate or lessen the harm. For this reason, the field of climate change impact assessment has evolved into that of global environmental-change vulnerability assessment. Since the publication of its First and Second Assessment Reports, the Intergovernmental Panel on Climate Change (IPCC) has contributed considerably to the increased usage of the vulnerability concept. In its Third Assessment Report the IPCC moved from a climate impact-oriented view to a broader, more integrated and less climate-focused perspective on vulnerability. The Fourth Assessment Report continues this focus. The concept of global environmental change vulnerability embraces multiple causes and multiple effects of global change for a single but highly complex concern: human well-being.

Development of theory

The critical feature of vulnerability, whether it is vulnerability to a hazard, vulnerability to famine or global change vulnerability, is that it cannot be observed or measured directly, but rather must be deduced. Vulnerability is not a feature of how a system functions in the present, but rather of how it is likely to function in the future, and in particular of the ways in which it will not function as well in the future as it does today. To surmise that a system is vulnerable, one has to combine projections of what events the future will bring with a theory of how these events will make the system under study worse off.

For many simple systems, describing vulnerability is trivially easy. A pumpkin that is thrown from the top of the Eiffel Tower is obviously in a highly vulnerable state (as are those walking under it!): it is fairly easy to predict that the pumpkin will crash against the ground, rather hard. Most human environment systems, however, are far more complex, and reasonable minds can differ as to whether they are headed for a crash, or will discover an appropriate parachute to ensure a soft landing. For example, consider the interaction of climate change and deforestation in the Amazon, factors that may lead to irreversible transformation (Laurance and Williamson, 2001). Not only did it take decades to recognize that such an outcome was possible, but how the future will unfold is still subject to a great amount of uncertainty. Whether a system is vulnerable today to a future event can only be known for sure once that future event has come and gone, but by then any assessment of today's system vulnerability is too late to be useful.

One response to this problem is to employ the precautionary principle in areas where irreversibility may occur (Dovers and Handmer, 1995). Another is to engage in developing robust theory about the relationships between current system state variables and the likelihood of future collapse. In the areas of hazards and famines, theory has been built on the analysis of past crises. For example, Sen grounded his theory of entitlements in an analysis of the past famines, such as that occurring in Bengal in 1941–1943 (Sen, 1981). Some measure of historical analysis is also appropriate to study global change vulnerability, as several authors in this volume (e.g. Fraser, Chapter 2, and Schröter, Chapter 6) demonstrate.

Increasingly, archaeologists are able to connect the decline and collapse of ancient societies to changes in their natural environments. For example, consider the story of the Norse settlers in Greenland, as told by Diamond (2004). These people depended on a limited supply of land, lying along coastal inlets, to sustain their farming livelihoods. Unfortunately, they degraded that land through many of their traditional practices, which in retrospect appear unsustainable. They used turf, valuable as farmland and in far more limited supply in Greenland than it had been in Norway, as a building material for their houses. This in turn increased the pressure they placed on the remaining land, and their sensitivity to changes that might make that land less productive. It was just a matter of time before they overgrazed that land, caused erosion, and then entered a cycle of decline, as they depended on an ever-shrinking area to supply them with their livelihoods. This was made worse by a gradual change in climate, over which they had no control. They had arrived in Greenland during a relatively warm period but, over the coming decades, the winters became longer and colder, and the summers less life-sustaining. Eventually, as a combination of local environmental degradation and regional climate change made a farming lifestyle impractical on Greenland, they turned to eating fish and seals. By analysing the elemental isotopes in their bones, it is possible to identify a shift in their foodstuff from terrestrial to marine. But here another issue becomes important. Unlike the nearby Inuit people, who had long hunted on the sea and been able to survive on Greenland, the Norse did not have these skills or traditions. Moreover, many of their own traditions, including their religious practices and a fundamental lack of respect for the Inuit, left the Norse unwilling or unable to learn from the Inuit. Rather than adapt their ways and copy the Inuit, such as by adopting the kayak and the harpoon as tools, the Norse remained poor at hunting seals. Ultimately, as Diamond chronicles, the Norse settlement on Greenland died completely.

From case studies such as this one it can be seen quite clearly that vulnerability is a consequence of multiple factors. Diamond proposes, for a first order analysis, to look to five factors to understand what made past societies vulnerable to collapse: environmental damage, climate change, hostile neighbours, the loss of friendly trading partners and the society's responses to its environmental challenges. Furthermore, case studies show what can be at stake: some past cultures did not simply suffer minor declines in their standard of living, a small risk they may have voluntarily taken in exchange for the short-term benefits their unsustainable behaviour probably brought them. Rather, the worst-case scenario eventually occurred, and they all died, something that probably seemed as out of the question to them then as our own civilization's demise seems to us today. Other societies, like the Maya in Central America and the inhabitants of Easter Island, did not all die, but their civilization went into an irreversible decline of prosperity. The case studies also show how hard it can be to predict events that will lead to a society's demise. For example, the Norse were among the best boatbuilders in the world, and had launched successful expeditions across the Atlantic, setting up temporary outposts on the North American mainland, hundreds of years before the Spanish, English and Portuguese were to do the same. Yet part of their downfall in Greenland was their failure to make use of the simple Inuit kayak for hunting seals. They probably had the skill to copy the Inuit design, but Diamond suggests that they refused to do so because they viewed the Inuit as morally inferior. The Norse proved to be remarkably un-adaptive, but it was not because they lacked technology.

Case studies such as that of the Norse can contribute to the theory of vulnerability in important ways, but they cannot complete it. We live in a global society where no single group of people need ever be out of contact, for more than a few hours or days, with the rest of civilization. The modern social context for vulnerability is fundamentally more complex than that of the isolated Greenland settlement. Moreover, the current environmental threats are unlike any that have been experienced in the past. If current estimates of climate sensitivity are correct, the magnitude of climate change, all across the globe, will dwarf any that has occurred since the dawn of human civilization (Solomon et al, 2007; Stern, 2007). Theory on the vulnerability of contemporary human environment systems to global change must be extrapolated from studies of societies facing far less significant stress. Exactly how best to extrapolate is the subject of vigorous academic debate, which we turn to next.

Current debates

At the level of language, researchers argue whether we should describe a system as being vulnerable to an external stressor (e.g. an earthquake, or climate change), or an outcome (e.g. famine) (Suarez and Ribot, 2003). Those arguing the former suggest that a focus on a limited number of stressors is essential to link vulnerability assessment to the decisions of real people and government agencies (Dilley and Boudreau, 2001). Those arguing the latter suggest that it is essential to remain open to the multiple interacting sources of harm (Ribot et al, 1996).

At the level of definition, there are debates about what are the features of a system that give rise to vulnerability, what should be the scale of the study, what are the appropriate indicators of vulnerability and whether indicators are even appropriate. There have been numerous competing frameworks and flow charts suggesting the pathways by which a system becomes more or less vulnerable (Kasperson et al, 1995; Jones, 2001; Turner et al, 2003; Patt et al, 2005a; Füssel and Klein, 2006; Metzger and Schröter, 2006). Some have suggested that for information about vulnerability and environmental threats to influence decision makers, it is vital that it should 'fit' the temporal and spatial scale at which decisions can be made (Orlove and Tosteson, 1999). Others, however, suggest that one needs to analyse nested scales (e.g. Stephen and Downing, 2001), both spatial (O'Brien et al, 2004) and temporal (Schröter et al, 2004). With respect to indicators, there have been several propositions, each weighing a different set of features of the system, and based on a slightly different model of vulnerability. The IPCC, for example, proposed the idea that vulnerability is a function of exposure, sensitivity and adaptive capacity (McCarthy et al, 2001), although exactly what form that function should take remains vague (Füssel and Klein, 2006). Many researchers have proposed quantitative indicators, which then allow mapping to reveal relative levels of vulnerability. Luers et al (2003) suggest an indicator that takes into account how far a spatial grid cell is from a threshold value of environmental stress. O'Brien and colleagues (2004) suggest a very different indicator that highlights the interaction of two quite different stressors. Schröter et al (2005a) settled on mapping a set of indicators, each corresponding to a different environmental stress. Additionally, despite producing a generic-based aggregated indicator of adaptive capacity, they concluded that this was too broad to be meaningfully included within their indicators of environmental stress. Others, however, argue that the very idea of vulnerability indicators is flawed. First, they suggest that few if any decisions will be based on indicators of relative vulnerability, but that the focus of analysis needs to be on how to make each element of the system less vulnerable. Moreover, any indicator will fail to take into account the tremendous heterogeneity of vulnerability even within the smallest of scales (Suarez and Ribot, 2003). Finally, many of the current indicators of vulnerability are deceptive because they fail to convey the unavoidable uncertainty they contain (Patt et al, 2005a).

Perhaps nowhere is the debate stronger than in the issue of adaptive capacity. What is it, what causes it, and when does it express itself? If one measures vulnerability by the loss of life that occurs in the wake of disaster, and adaptive capacity can avoid that loss of life, then financial wealth is a clear and simple indicator of adaptive capacity (Yohe and Tol, 2002). If one measures vulnerability by total damages, and includes in the analysis not just wealth but also the factors that are precursors to wealth, then money loses its place of importance compared to transportation infrastructure and other physical system features (Brooks and Adger, 2004). If adaptive capacity includes not just the ability to change, but also the willingness to (something the Greenland Norse apparently lacked), then psychological indicators prove to be far more predictive than economic ones (Grothmann and Patt, 2005; Grothmann and Reusswig, 2006). Other studies suggest that it is not simply the agents who do the adapting that matter, but also their relationship to the communicators of the information on which they would act (Patt et al, 2006), how organizations that communicate this knowledge are structured (Cash et al, 2003), and in what form they present it (Patt et al, 2005b). Adaptive capacity is an intellectual quagmire. This is not surprising, since adaptive systems change the way they respond to a stimulus over time (Bradbury, 2002). Numerical models of adaptive systems are simple, if they exist, and do not take into account the multitude of actors and factors needed to represent most real-world systems.

Vulnerability assessment

The resolution to these debates lies not in working harder to develop a better theory of vulnerability, but in better recognizing that work on vulnerability is driven primarily by policy needs, rather than scientific curiosity. Many of the disputes about global change controversy evaporate when one sees it as a proper subject not of scientific research, but of scientific assessment.

Scientific research and scientific assessment are different beasts. The goal of scientific *research* is primarily to develop general theory, which can be applied in places and contexts other than where the research took place. Hence, social scientists interested in the causes of vulnerability can study the collapse of ancient societies, and learn something that may be useful to our own society. The selection of case studies, of the temporal and spatial scale of analysis, and indeed of the methods for collecting and analysing data, needs to be made in order to yield results that are of as general validity as possible. By definition the goal of scientific *assessment* is quite different, namely to make scientific knowledge useful and accessible, in order to help actual stakeholders to design better strategies and policies to cope with a particular problem (Farrell et al, 2001). While scientific assessment includes elements of research, the design of assessment has to respond to the needs of the particular stakeholders who might use it, assuming they are known, rather than the 'virtual stakeholder' that scientists imagine will use the information (Farrell and Jäger, 2005), and hence has to include such stakeholders as integral collaborators. Since, even for a particular place, different stakeholders will want to know different things, the task can become every bit as challenging as that of designing scientific research (Schröter et al, 2005b; Chapter 11 in this volume: de la Vega-Leinert and Schröter).

Scholars describe assessment primarily as the social process, one that links scientific knowledge to policy making (Mitchell et al, 2006). As has become clear through numerous case studies, the processes that help to give rise to a successful assessment – one that actually has an impact on the policy-making process – are not necessarily the same as those that give rise to high quality scientific research (Cash, 2000). Assessments are more likely to be influential when they meet three criteria: they must provide information that is *salient* to decision makers, they must be *credible*, and they must be socially and politically *legitimate* (Cash et al, 2003, 2006). Salient information is that which matters to decision makers. Thus, the temporal and spatial scale of the assessment must fit the temporal and spatial scale of decisions available to specific actors. In the case of Peruvian fisheries, for example, information about an approaching El Niño was extremely salient to banks that provided loans to operators of fishing boats, since it informed them that the risks for the coming season had changed. For the operators of the fishing boats themselves, however, the information was not salient, since there was nothing they could do with it; it was too late to find alternative sources of income (Broad, 1999). Information becomes credible when people believe both the messenger and the message. Often, organizations with personal ties, not just to the scientific community, but also to the user community, can help maintain credibility of an assessment, even when users have reason to disbelieve it (Guston, 2001). Finally, users often only accept information when it comes from a socially and politically legitimate source. In debates during the 1980s on acid rain in Europe, for example, an integrated model developed at the International Institute for Applied Systems Analysis (IIASA) in Austria, not closely linked with any country either substantially causing or suffering from transboundary air pollution, was seen as more legitimate a tool for policy makers than one developed in England, a major exporter of pollution (Patt, 1999b).

Global change vulnerability assessment highlights the need for a user- and purpose-driven process, because there are many different questions that the process can raise and answer. The commonly assumed goal of vulnerability assessment is to inform the decision making of specific stakeholders about options for adapting to the effects of global change (Metzger and Schröter, 2006). However, this is not always the only goal, and other objectives may also be in focus. We identify four typical reasons that people conduct vulnerability assessment, which we describe below as ideal types. In reality, of course, the boundary between the different goals is likely to be blurred, and one assessment will be undertaken for more than one purpose.

Assessing vulnerability to improve adaptation

The main goal of vulnerability assessment often is to help policy makers minimize harm by adapting to ongoing or anticipated changes. Depending on the scale at which the policy makers are acting, assessment of this sort can potentially be useful in two ways. First, if the spatial scale of the decision makers is the same as that of the basic type of vulnerability, then the assessment can be useful by describing the elements of the system that are sensitive to change or may exacerbate harm, and by exploring the potential consequences of specific interventions to modify these elements (Parson et al, 2003). For example, one can describe the elements of coastal communities, including their systems of governance and social division of labour and responsibility, that make such communities more or less vulnerable to potential flooding (Adger, 2000). In this case, comparing the relative vulnerability of the place under study with that of other locations becomes useful when it illustrates the potential for making improvements. For example, following the hurricanes of 2005 that destroyed much of New Orleans and the United States Gulf Coast, there were many newspaper stories illustrating how other industrialized coastal regions, such as in The Netherlands, had made themselves less vulnerable through better-functioning infrastructure. These reports allow decision makers to learn from the experiences of other communities that are similarly situated with respect to the same type of environmental risk.

Second, the spatial scale of the vulnerability assessment that seeks to promote adaptation may be aimed at decision makers operating at a spatial scale that is larger than that of the basic type of vulnerability. These assessments are about comparing different places, and, in theory, should help decision makers to prioritize efforts, directing resources at the places that are most vulnerable. To return to the example of New Orleans, maps prepared in advance of the storms indicated those neighbourhoods that would be most severely flooded, and where the residents would be least likely to evacuate on their own. Such maps, if they had been used, could have allowed first evacuation teams and then rescue teams to direct a larger share of their efforts at these neighbourhoods. At a much larger spatial scale, studies of entire countries can indicate which regions are most vulnerable to the effects of climate change and other social stressors, to help national-level decision makers make decisions to assist the most vulnerable regions (O'Brien et al, 2004; Zebisch et al, 2005; Schröter et al, 2005a). This type of assessment often requires the development of vulnerability indicators, which can be communicated via maps, charts or tables, identifying places or sectors that are most vulnerable (Metzger et al, 2004, 2006; Metzger and Schröter, 2006).

Within the class of vulnerability assessment targeted towards improving adaptation, there are thus two very different criteria for judging success. In the case of that aimed at local-level decision makers, did the assessment provide them with the information about the system that they needed in order to make preparations or changes? Did the assessment offer them examples of successful policies, perhaps those implemented in other communities, which could be useful? Did the assessment adequately explore the uncertainties associated with trying to predict the consequences of interventions to a complex adaptive system? In the case of those assessments aimed at mapping relative vulnerability, it is valid to ask whether governments actually engage in prioritizing one community over another based on scientifically derived, and very uncertain, indicators (Patt et al, 2005a). Hence, what are the decisions that policy makers, embedded in a contested political space, actually would take in response to a comparative assessment of vulnerability? Is the information provided by the vulnerability assessment useful to prioritize different regions' concerns in a fair and reliable way? Are the risks potential adaptation strategies carry with them adequately portrayed (Patt and Schröter, 2008)?

Assessing vulnerability to frame the climate change mitigation problem

At the international level, humankind must decide what degree of climate change to create, through the emission of greenhouse gasses (GHGs). To some extent this decision hinges on an assessment of the damages that climate change would create, weighed against the economic growth that GHG emissions, unencumbered by mitigation policies, create (Stern, 2007). Thus, it is important to assess damages that may occur to human–environment systems from continued climate change.

Traditionally, this assessment of damages was within the scope of impact assessment (Kates et al, 1985; Carter et al, 1994). Climate change impact assessment is the natural cousin of the ubiquitous Environmental Impact Statement, whereby economic actors project the consequences of their actions. The target audience for impact assessment is the policy-making community concerned with climate mitigation. Although large countries such as the United States have commissioned their own domestic impact assessments (National Assessment Synthesis Team, 2001), mitigation is usually seen as a global problem, and hence the scale of impact assessment is typically seen as global (Schröter et al, 2005b). The goal of climate change impact assessment is to develop estimates of the total and marginal costs arising from various levels of global climate change, assuming various sets of background conditions.

The line between vulnerability assessment and impact assessment is fuzzy. Vulnerability assessment, one may argue, ought to be more precise about the potential for adaptation (Füssel and Klein, 2006), about the risks of extreme events that could overwhelm local communities, the interconnections between human systems and environment systems (Turner, 1991; Turner et al, 2003) or the potential for harm flowing from multiple causes. In practice, however, impact assessment often does many of these (Jones, 2001), and vulnerability assessment often does not (Downing, 2000). It is not surprising, then, that many assessments claim to be of both impacts and vulnerabilities, and do not draw a sharp distinction between them (McCarthy et al, 2001).

A successful vulnerability assessment of this type, then, is one that manages to present credible estimates of aggregate societal damages to climate change, in such a way as to influence policy makers concerned with global mitigation targets. Indeed, it can be a valid criticism of this type of assessment that it provides too much detail on local-scale impacts or opportunities, such that policy makers lose the forest for the trees.

Assessing vulnerability to address social injustice

A third reason to assess vulnerability is to address social injustice, by exposing the degree to which global forces are negatively affecting the plight of the poor (Kasperson and Kasperson, 2001). Most researchers expect climate change to have the greatest impacts on developing countries, for several reasons (Kasperson, 2001; McCarthy et al, 2001). First, people in developing countries are far more reliant on agriculture for their livelihoods, compared to people in industrialized countries. In the United States, for example, less than 3 per cent of the population is engaged in farming, whereas in most developing countries the majority of people earn their livelihood from the land (Ribot et al, 1996; National Assessment Synthesis Team, 2001). Agriculture, especially rain-fed agriculture, is extremely sensitive to changes in temperature, precipitation and other climatic factors (Antle, 1995). Second, many developing countries already have unsustainable patterns of land use. In rural areas, erosion from drought, wind and rain is already a problem, something that climate change could exacerbate (Downing, 1991; Luers et al, 2003). In urban areas, millions of people live in poorly planned peri-urban settlements where flooding, landslides and other risks are a frequent problem (Kasperson et al, 1995; Boullé et al, 1997; Smyth and Royle, 2000). Third, developing countries are often in a state of rapid social change, meaning that they do not have the social institutions to maintain stability in society when physical harm occurs (Adger, 1999). Fourth, developing countries often lack the capital – physical, human or financial – to invest in adaptation to changing conditions (Brooks and Adger, 2004).

Given that the people who are already the worst off are likely to suffer disproportionately, and that those perceived as causing the harm in the first place – through the emission of GHGs – are relatively wealthy, there is a strong moral argument for rich countries assisting poorer ones to adapt to climate change, or providing them with reparations (Kasperson and Kasperson, 2001). Some have suggested, based on these moral arguments, that part of the international policy response ought to be in providing economic relief to developing countries hardest hit by climate change, above and beyond that already provided in the area of disaster assistance, development assistance and the Clean Development Mechanism to assist in creation of low-emissions energy projects (Müller, 2002). Even though such a funding mechanism does not yet exist, one potential goal of comparative vulnerability assessment is prioritizing regions that may be in particular need for such a programme.

Evaluating the success of such an assessment is difficult, since it is not clear who the audience is, and what decisions an assessment of this type is trying to influence. Even though the primary stakeholders are the poor themselves, the assessments may mostly be communicated to outsiders that feel a sense of responsibility or a strategic need to act upon vulnerability of others, and that may have the means to make a difference. We may expect this type of vulnerability assessment to be prepared by advocacy organizations, where the audience for the assessment is the general public in wealthy countries, and the purpose is to build awareness of the injustice flowing from climate change (Patt, 1999a). More often, examining social justice would be the collateral purpose of an assessment aimed at helping specific stakeholders to adapt, namely also giving them the political arguments to ask for assistance with that adaptation (Suarez and Ribot, 2003; O'Brien et al, 2004). The success of such assessments then needs to be judged by the question whether they actually shed light on the causalities resulting in vulnerability. Such assessments should point out the responsibility or capacity of actors both outside and within the system to improve the situation, and ideally make suggestions on which strategies to follow.

Assessing vulnerability to conduct scientific research

The fourth reason to conduct a vulnerability assessment is to learn about the system. In this case, the vulnerability assessment becomes the vehicle to conduct basic scientific research, creating value not just for the relevant stakeholders, but also for the scientific community in general. As Chapter 4 by Eriksen and co-authors in this volume makes clear, the practical fact is that vulnerability assessment often is the process through which the scientific community begins to understand the root causes of vulnerability, especially in developing countries where the level of scientific research funding is low. The boundary between scientific assessment and scientific research is necessarily fuzzy.

There are three reasons for trying to conduct basic research in the context of a vulnerability assessment. The first is that the vulnerability assessment provides the resources to conduct research. For example, vulnerability assessment allows for access to stakeholders. Since they will hopefully benefit from the assessment they have an incentive to work with the scientists who are involved. In a study on the use of seasonal climate forecasts in southern Africa to reduce vulnerability, researchers organized community workshops to explore the usefulness of the forecasts. The stakeholders attended the workshops over multiple years, because they felt that they benefited from the information being communicated there (Patt and Gwata, 2002). Ultimately, however, one of the strongest research findings of that project was not on the uses of the forecast, but on the benefits of the communication method used in the workshops, a valid social science research question (Patt et al, 2005b). The vulnerability assessment had provided the opportunity to compare people hearing the same information in different forms. Furthermore, in order to conduct a good local vulnerability assessment, it is necessary to collect a great deal of data about the current practices and historical conditions in a particular place or set of places. While one use of this information can certainly be to estimate present and future vulnerability, the information in general, in particular the historical or comparative information, can often be of general use in the study of historical vulnerability trends (Ribot et al, 1996). Similarly, the methods used to assess vulnerability, including spatial analysis, modelling and mapping, often overlap with the same tools used in basic scientific research. A recent assessment of the vulnerability of European terrestrial ecosystem services, for example, made heavy use of a variety of downscaled climate, land-use and environmental models

(Schröter et al, 2005a). The development of these models for the purpose of the assessment, which was funded by the European Union and which fed into vulnerability-related decision making, also was beneficial for basic scientific research using the same modelling tools.

The second reason to conduct scientific research within the context of a vulnerability assessment can be to learn generalizable knowledge about vulnerability. The exercise of mapping vulnerability to multiple threats, as described in this volume and in O'Brien et al (2004), is often both an assessment and a research exercise. In this case, the interesting hypotheses are whether the projections of increased vulnerability made because of climate change overlap spatially with similar projections made on account of globalization and trade liberalization. To the extent they do, it alerts other assessment teams, working elsewhere, to pay attention to similar patterns where they are working. Hence, it potentially adds to the understanding of vulnerability and its root causes.

The third reason is to improve the practice of vulnerability assessment. For example, many assessments of vulnerability that are published in the primary scientific literature are first attempts at using new methodologies to assess vulnerability (Luers et al, 2003; O'Brien et al, 2004; Metzger and Schröter, 2006; Metzger et al, 2006, 2008). Only by going through the process of testing new methods in the process of an actual vulnerability assessment can researchers learn whether the methods work, hopefully in satisfaction of one of the other three purposes already listed. In such pilot projects, one benefit is the information about the assessment methodology, while the immediate value to stakeholders becomes a data point in that study. The primary question to judge success of such projects is then whether they increased our understanding of vulnerability, or any components of vulnerability, and whether they have helped us learn about appropriate methods to undertake vulnerability assessment.

Common denominators for vulnerability assessment

Vulnerability assessments can be most salient, legitimate and credible to policy makers, and hence most successful at productively influencing decision making, when they fulfil the specific purpose or purposes for which they were undertaken. The information that is sought from the vulnerability assessment should determine the methodology for undertaking it, such as what data the scientists choose to examine, and how they examine them. Since there are a range of different purposes for undertaking vulnerability assessment, each with a different set of information needs, the methods that are appropriate for a particular vulnerability assessment are necessarily highly variable. Moreover, in almost all cases the information that fulfils the purpose of the assessment is only a subset of potential exposure, sensitivity and adaptive capacity.

Consider briefly each of the four purposes already listed. The first kind of assessment is there to guide the first efforts at adaptive changes. In this case stakeholders need a rich description of the changes, with the focus of comparing alternative potential adaptive changes against each other, along with the challenges involved in undertaking each one. Stakeholders need information about multiple adaptive strategies, which they would begin now or later, and how to implement these. The second kind of assessment answers the question: What will be the effects of climate change given different mitigation options, and hence which mitigation options are better than others? The purpose of the assessment may be to inform global-scale policy makers, or to persuade individual citizens that their own self-sacrifice is worthwhile. In either case, the relevant question is the extent to which people's lifestyles will be affected; changes of any sort – whether mitigation today or adaptation in the future – are costly, and apparently many people would like to change as little as possible. The challenge for assessment is to juxtapose descriptions of the mitigative or adaptive changes society will have to make, one way or another, so that the choice of which to engage in becomes clearer. What is needed is a rich description, and in some cases quantification, of those changes. The third kind of assessment, revealing social inequity as a result of climate change, needs to focus on who is able to make, request or force what changes, and comparing these with the responsibilities each group of people has had in the past. Again a rich description of adaptation is required, but the focus of comparison is between groups of people. The fourth type of assessment – undertaking scientific research – is not really assessment at all, since it will not necessarily benefit the people in the place of study, but rather the scientific community and humanity in general. If scientific research is the sole purpose of the assessment, which may be rarely the case, a rich description of the particular adaptations that the local people will make is not called for. The goal is rather a description that is general enough to be applied to other locations, times and circumstances. Clearly, each of these types of assessment requires collecting and communicating a different set of information, through a different method. Even in a single geographical region, it is likely that several different vulnerability assessments will be necessary, in order to answer different sets of questions.

Outline for the book

We are proposing a model of vulnerability assessment that contains great diversity in its definition, formalization and use of indicators of vulnerability. Rather than suggest a single set of guidelines to follow that applies a general theory of vulnerability, we suggest that there are many different kinds of assessment and indicators that are appropriate, each for a specific set of questions.

Against this backdrop of diversity in the concept of global change vulnerability, there are some general lessons to be learned for the practice of vulnerability assessment. The successful assessments are those where the scientists are able to focus on the specific questions their stakeholders need answered, in an organic ad hoc manner. Doing so, we suggest, requires paying attention to several points. First, the study of contemporary global change vulnerability can best be seen as an act of policy analysis, rather than an exercise of social and systems science research. Being within the domain and discourse of policy analysis eliminates the need for generalizable and broadly applicable results, but it does mean that discussions of vulnerability constantly raise questions that involve both facts and values. Second, scientific assessment, compared to scientific research, requires a continual open dialogue involving not only scientists but all relevant stakeholders. The legitimacy of the vulnerability assessment depends on the transparency of the process by which this dialogue takes place. Third, vulnerability assessments must be practical. In particular, the spatial and temporal scale of the assessment needs to match the scale of decision making. This, in turn, has implications for the choice of indicators used to describe vulnerability.

Each of these points may seem rather obvious, but actually putting them into practice raises a number of design issues for vulnerability assessments. What we offer in the remainder of the book are examples of how other assessments, serving a wide diversity of stakeholders and their respective purposes, have succeeded or failed in implementing them; each of the chapters illustrates at least one of the issues that we have raised in this introduction. In sum, they illustrate both the diversity of methods needed for vulnerability assessment and the presence of some common denominators.

Evan Fraser demonstrates, in Chapter 2, how the study of an historical case can improve our theory of vulnerability. The study applies a social concept (the theory of entitlement, (Sen, 1981)) and an ecological concept (the theory of panarchy (Gunderson and Holling, 2002)), to analyse Irish historical vulnerability and to identify the multiple social and environmental causes and intertwined processes that led to suffering. The theory of panarchy is an attempt to capture the likelihood of a non-linear shift in ecosystems that is currently being tested by application in a series of case studies undertaken by a research network known as the Resilience Alliance (Ostrom, 2004). The author shows that the theory of vulnerability to climate change can learn from both of these theories (and hence, implicitly, from the Irish case study), and that these theories suggest a set of features of a system that may be useful indicators for assessing vulnerability. The author proposes ways in which the resulting theory can guide the practice of vulnerability assessment to spur adaptation to global change.

Ian Holman and Lars Otto Næss, in Chapter 3, compare assessments of vulnerability that took place in Norway and the United Kingdom. Rather than comparing vulnerability in these two places, the chapter compares the approaches taken, and evaluates their effectiveness. It suggests that the UK assessments may have been more successful, partly because they engaged stakeholders, and partly because the degree to which stakeholders recognized global change as an area of concern was already quite advanced. In Norway, by contrast, the idea that the country could be vulnerable to global change was still new, and the assessments there have been driven by the curiosity of scientists, rather than by the government and local stakeholders. Partly as a consequence, the authors suggest, the level of government action is significantly lower in Norway than in the UK, despite the fact that at particular scales the basis for adaptive action ought to be as great.

Siri Eriksen, Coleen Vogel, Gina Ziervogel Franziska Steinbruch and Florence Nazare describe, in Chapter 4, a variety of efforts to assess vulnerability in South

Africa and Mozambique, two bordering countries. First, the chapter describes the common features of vulnerability in the two countries. Next, the chapter presents several different assessments that were made, and how each responded to stakeholder needs at a variety of scales, including a multi-stressor approach to vulnerability. Importantly, the assessments dealt explicitly with issues of development, as an essential element of global change and adaptation. However, the assessments also illustrate how a variety of approaches was needed, even within a limited geographical area, requiring a diversity of indicators to answer stakeholders' respective questions.

Richard J. T. Klein and Jochen Hinkel, in Chapter 5, describe the evolution of coastal vulnerability assessment and how it has increasingly combined knowledge from different scientific disciplines. They describe the global-scale simulation model DIVA (Dynamic and Interactive Vulnerability Assessment), the development of which presented a number of challenges to the project team. An important challenge was the design of a method that allowed for the integration of natural and social sciences and for the collaborative model development by a group of geographically distributed experts.

Dagmar Schröter, in Chapter 6, identifies ecosystem services, which are vital to the function of a human–environment system, as an important subunit of analysis. The author provides historical examples of times when societies have been vulnerable due to a loss in ecosystem services, and the reasons for their mismanagement. The chapter then turns to a recent European project studying terrestrial ecosystem services. The author shows that the focus on ecosystem services served two purposes: providing a rationale to mitigate, and the basis of understanding to guide adaptation. In some cases, there were identifiable actors who could respond to the information to adapt, such as forest managers and agriculture planners, whose time horizon matched that of the assessment. For other ecosystem services or vulnerabilities (e.g. water stress) there was no limited group of stakeholders, and in this case the assessment was taken up by the media for its implications for mitigation.

Hans-Martin Füssel and Kristie L. Ebi, in Chapter 7, show that global change vulnerability assessment often focuses on a particular outcome – loss of health. Health is an area of concern that has an entire policy community and infrastructure already established. In order to assess global change vulnerability with respect to health, it is important to link the work to other health related work in non-global-change related contexts. This is consistent with other chapters in this volume, in particular Chapter 4, which demonstrate the importance of relating outcome-oriented assessments to pre-existing concerns about development.

Robin Leichenko and Karen O'Brien, in Chapter 8, describe an assessment undertaken in India. By mapping indicators of vulnerability, the assessment raises the issues of differential vulnerability, the potential of some communities to suffer great harm and the injustice associated with various aspects of global change. Such a mapping exercise does not necessarily assist local communities to adapt, nor does it suggest particular mitigation targets, but rather serves to build awareness of the risks many people may face unless proactive steps are taken.

Lilibeth Acosta-Michlik and Mark Rounsevell, in Chapter 9, describe a project that links vulnerability assessment with advanced theoretical research. One of the cutting edge areas of scientific research is the study of complex adaptive systems, and an important tool to develop and test hypotheses about their functioning is the agent-based model. A case study of a Portuguese village's potential responses to climate change and globalization shows how a vulnerability assessment, undertaken with stakeholders, can be an effective vehicle for parameterizing an agent-based model, and carrying out basic research on the functioning of complex adaptive systems.

Stefan Hochrainer and Reinhard Mechler, in Chapter 10, describe the process of assessing the vulnerability, not of physical and human systems, but of financial and economic systems. The difference is important, as the robustness of financial systems in a place suffering from a natural hazard can depend in large part on its integration into a global financial and economic framework, including having potential risk-spreading mechanisms in place. Assessment not just of local exposure, but of the integration into the global system, can help offer policy makers important information about the options they face. While deploying resources to make physical systems – bridges and buildings – more robust and reduce direct losses, preparing financial systems can allow reconstruction to occur much faster, and reduce the indirect losses suffered when an economy is operated without critical infrastructure.

Anne de la Vega-Leinert and Dagmar Schröter, in Chapter 11, offer insights into the crucial role of stakeholder participation in a regional assessment. The authors first present the methodology applied to engage a diverse group of stakeholders from the onset of a European vulnerability assessment project. They then offer lessons learned and explore questions like the following: what pieces of information were most useful to the stakeholders, and what were the critical challenges in engaging their participation? How did the participation of stakeholders change (1) the assessment project and (2) the business of the stakeholders?

Martin Welp, Antonella Battaglini and Carlo Jaeger, in Chapter 12, examine the use of vulnerability assessment in the process of building broad-based consensus around mitigation goals. In this case, the focus was truly global, without need for fine-scale local investigation, matching the global scale at which consensus was sought. The role of vulnerability information and regional representation was in helping to build consensus that would be later seen as legitimate. In reaching consensus, anecdotal information played at least as important a role as aggregate indicators and uncertainty ranges.

Jochen Hinkel, in Chapter 13, proposes a framework for tackling some of the confusion that the diversity of approaches toward vulnerability and vulnerability assessment creates. Vulnerability assessments are almost always ad hoc, responding to particular stakeholder needs. They also contain a great number of separate tasks and pieces of analysis, and often bridge national and scientific cultures. Participants in such projects need to clarify what their own roles are, even if they have participated in other vulnerability assessments in the past. Given constrained project budgets and timelines, this limits the effectiveness of assessments.

Vulnerability assessments could thus benefit from describing their own structure and process with a common syntax, such as the one the author proposes in this chapter. This would better allow all participants to understand their respective roles, allow for more effective and rapid integration, and ultimately more effective assessment.

The selection of chapters is neither complete nor representative. We have chosen them first because we believe they paint a rough sketch of the diversity of vulnerability assessment, and in doing so offer the reader numerous hooks onto which to latch. Second, we have chosen them because the authors were able to spare the time to write them. The point is, the demand for useful knowledge about how to cope with the unprecedented changes taking place on the planet far outstrips the supply of people to research and convey that knowledge. Every vulnerability assessment is undertaken with a conviction that it is necessary, and a hope that it can make a difference to real people, and the work needed to translate conviction and hope into reality often seems endless. Our hope is that by taking a minute to come up for air, we can reinvigorate the practice.

Conclusion

The current debates about global change vulnerability reflect two important points. First, as we have already shown, there is a paucity of data to guide our study of global change vulnerability. Researchers may suggest alternative models and indicators, and need to rely on a combination of logical argument and an extrapolation of pre-existing models far beyond their boundary conditions in order to support their propositions. Second, and more importantly, research on global change vulnerability is driven more by the needs of policy makers than by curiosity about unanswered riddles within the scientific community. Many vulnerability studies, such as those that Diamond so well describes, are fuelled by the desire to understand why past societies have collapsed, and here they stand on the firmest ground. But more often, they are fuelled by the legitimate desire of a broad range of policy makers and concerned scientists to avoid imminent harm. In this case, not only are the factors that may lead to harm very heterogeneous, but so too are the types of harm that concern them. Some may legitimately be worried about the entire collapse of their society. Others fear the loss of human life and infrastructure. Still others care about the disruption of historical patterns of social and environmental functioning. The debates around how exactly to quantify or even describe vulnerability represent an attempt to pin the word down to a particular technical and legalistic definition. Yet as long as the word 'vulnerability' is spoken by those feeling exposed and fearing loss, it will continue to mean very different things to very different people, and any debates about how exactly to define it will not cease. Instead of hiding our perceptions and values in discussions about definitions, it makes sense to communicate openly what we value and why as part of any discourse on vulnerability. Some would argue that this then is the very point of departure of vulnerability assessment from a purely scientific exercise. Others feel that the distinction between facts and values is less clear, and that values should be a matter of open discourse as much as facts (Putnam, 2002).

If an assessment is the most useful when it describes the different threats to the elements of society that people value, it can become the most confusing, can lose the most credibility and can generate the most controversy when it delivers aggregate indicators, claiming these to represent measures of vulnerability itself. Indicators can be very useful, but will be ones most closely suited to the specific questions posed by stakeholders and interpreted by scientists. Since the questions and their interpretations differ from assessment to assessment, the necessary indicators must as well. Each of these indicators serves a valuable purpose, but the purposes are different. We have already seen that it generates a great deal of confusion when different assessment teams report a variety of indicators, each of which is suitable for the specific questions they are answering, and yet call all of these different indicators by the same name, namely 'vulnerability'. Successful vulnerability assessments can avoid confusion and conflict by labelling their output something other than vulnerability itself. Being careful about assigning numbers to vulnerability goes beyond the need to avoid confusion. Vulnerability assessment needs to survive in a world where stakeholders differ in their world-views. Policies that succeed in such a world are ones that different people support for different reasons (Verweij and Thompson, 2006). In the area of vulnerability assessment, rarely will any single indicator's quantitative value match the emotional sense of vulnerability that many stakeholders feel, or deny. But vulnerability assessment can offer different reasons for a variety of actors to coalesce around a particular policy.

We can ask ourselves: if the Norse Greenlanders were to commission a vulnerability assessment, what would they have needed to know in order to survive? What they probably did not need was a single number indicating the summation of threats to their livelihoods. But they did need help from natural and social scientists: a collection of knowledge about ongoing climate changes, the fragility of Greenland soils and hints about how to learn to live with the Inuit as good neighbours. Modern people, facing an uncertain future, need something of the same.

References

Adger, W. N. (1999) 'Social vulnerability to climate change and extremes in coastal Vietnam', *World Development*, vol 27(2), pp249–269

Adger, W. N. (2000) 'Institutional adaptation to environmental risk under transition in Vietnam', *Annals of the Association of American Geographers*, vol 90(4), pp738–758

Antle, J. M. (1995) 'Climate change and agriculture in developing countries', *American Journal of Agricultural Economics*, vol 77, pp741–746

Boullé, P., Vrolijks, L. and Palm, E. (1997) 'Vulnerability reduction for sustainable urban development', *Journal of Contingencies and Crisis Management*, vol 5(3), pp179–188

Bradbury, R. (2002) 'Futures, predictions, and other foolishness', in Janssen, M. A. (ed) *Complexity and Ecosystem Management*, Edward Elgar, Cheltenham, pp48–62

Broad, K. (1999) 'Climate and society: The case of the Peruvian fisheries', in Potter, T. and Coleman, B. (eds) *Weather, Climate, and Water: Handbook of Atmospheric Sciences, with Related Topics from Hydrology and Oceanography*, McGraw Hill, New York

Broeker, W. (1997) 'Thermohaline circulation, the Achilles Heel of our climate system: Will man-made CO_2 upset the current balance?' *Science*, vol 278, pp1582–1588

Brooks, N. and Adger, W. N. (2004) 'Assessing and enhancing adaptive capacity', *Adaptation Policy Framework*, United Nations Development Programme, Geneva, pp165–181

Carter, T., Parry, M., Harasawa, H. and Nishioka, S. (1994) *IPCC Technical Guidelines for Assessing Climate Change Impacts and Adaptations*, Department of Geography, University College London, London

Cash, D. (2000) 'Distributed assessment systems: An emerging paradigm of research, assessment, and decision-making for environmental change', *Global Environmental Change*, vol 10(4), pp241–244

Cash, D., Clark, W., Alcock, F., Dickson, N., Eckley, N., Guston, D., Jäger, J. and Mitchell, R. (2003) 'Knowledge systems for sustainable development', *Proceedings of the National Academy of Sciences of the United States of America*, vol 100(14), pp8086–8091

Cash, D., Borck, J. and Patt, A. G. (2006) 'Countering the "loading dock" approach to linking science and decision making: A comparative analysis of ENSO forecasting systems', *Science, Technology, and Human Values*, vol 31, pp465–494

Cutter, S. (2001) 'A research agenda for vulnerability science and environmental hazards', *International Human Dimensions Program Update*, vol 1(2), pp8–9

Diamond, J. (2004) *Collapse: How Societies Choose to Fail or Succeed*, Viking, New York

Dilley, M. and Boudreau, T. E. (2001) 'Coming to terms with vulnerability: A critique of the food security definition', *Food Policy*, vol 26, pp229–247

Dovers, S. R. and Handmer, J. W. (1995) 'Ignorance, the precautionary priniciple and sustainability', *Ambio*, vol 24(2), pp92–97

Downing, T. E. (1991) 'Vulnerability to hunger in Africa: A climate change perspective', *Global Environmental Change*, vol 1, pp365–380

Downing, T. E. (2000) 'Human dimensions research: Toward a vulnerability science?', *International Human Dimensions Program Update*, vol 00(3), pp16–17

Ezrahi, Y. (1990) *The Descent of Icarus: Science and the Transformation of Contemporary Democracy*, Harvard University Press, Cambridge, MA

Farrell, A. and Jäger, J. (eds) (2005) *Assessments of Regional and Global Environmental Risks: Designing Processes for Effective Use of Science in Decisionmaking*, Resources for the Future, Washington DC

Farrell, A., VanDeveer, S. and Jäger, J. (2001) 'Environmental assessments: Four under-appreciated design elements', *Global Environmental Change*, vol 11(4), pp311–333

Folland, C. K., Karl, T., Christy, J., Clarke, R., Gruza, G., Jouzel, J., Mann, M., Oerlemans, J., Salinger, M. and Wang, S. (2001) 'Observed climate variability and change', in Houghton, J. T. and Ding, Y. (eds) *Climate Change 2001: The Scientific Basis*, Cambridge University Press, Cambridge

Freeman, P. K. and Kunreuther, H. (2002) 'Environmental risk management for developing countries', *The Geneva Papers on Risk and Insurance*, vol 27(2), pp196–214

Freudenberg, W. (1996) 'Risky thinking: Irrational fears about risk and society', *Annals of the American Academy of Political and Social Science*, vol 545, pp44–53

Füssel, H.-M. and Klein, R. (2006) 'Climate change vulnerability assessments: An evolution of conceptual thinking', *Climatic Change*, vol 75(3), pp301–329

Glantz, M. (2000) *Once Burned, Twice Shy? Lessons Learned from the 1997–98 El Niño*, UNEP/NCAR/UNU/WMO/ISDR, Tokyo, Japan

Grothmann, T. and Patt, A. (2005) 'Adaptive capacity and human cognition: The process of individual adaptation to climate change', *Global Environmental Change*, vol 15, pp199–213

Grothmann, T. and Reusswig, F. (2006) 'People at risk of flooding: Why some residents take precautionary action while others do not', *Natural Hazards*, vol 38, pp101–120

Gunderson, L. and Holling, C. S. (2002) *Panarchy: Understanding Transformations in Human and Natural Systems*, Island Press, Washington DC

Gupta, A., Anderson, D. and Overpeck, J. (2003) 'Abrupt changes in the Asian southwest monsoon during the Holocene and their links to the North Atlantic ocean', *Nature*, vol 421, pp354–357

Guston, D. H. (2001) 'Boundary organizations in environmental policy and science: An introduction', *Science, Technology, and Human Values*, vol 26(4), pp399–408

Hoffman-Reim, H. and Wynne, B. (2002) 'In risk assessment, one has to admit ignorance', *Nature*, vol 416, p123

Jones, R. N. (2001) 'An environmental risk assessment/management framework for climate change impact assessments', *Natural Hazards*, vol 23(2/3), pp197–230

Kasperson, R. (2001) 'Vulnerability and global environmental change', *International Human Dimensions Program Update*, vol 01(2), pp2–3

Kasperson, R. and Kasperson, J. X. (2001) *Climate Change, Vulnerability, and Social Justice*, Stockholm Environment Institute, Stockholm

Kasperson, J. X., Kasperson, R. and Turner, B. L. I. (eds) (1995) *Regions at Risk: Comparisons of Threatened Environments*, United Nations University Press, Tokyo

Kates, R. W., Ausubel, J. H. and Berberian, M. (eds) (1985) 'Climate impact assessment: Studies of the interaction of climate and society', *SCOPE 27*, Wiley, Chichester

Laurance, W. and Williamson, G. B. (2001) 'Positive feedbacks among forest fragmentation, drought, and climate change in the Amazon', *Conservation Biology*, vol 15(6), pp1529–1535

Luers, A. L., Lobell, D. B., Sklar, L. S., Addams, C. L. and Matson, P. (2003) 'A method for quantifying vulnerability, applied to the agricultural system of the Yaqui Valley, Mexico', *Global Environmental Change*, vol 13, pp255–267

McCarthy, J. J., Canziani, O. F., Leary, N. A., Dokken, D. J. and White, K. S. (eds) (2001) *Climate Change 2001: Impacts, Adaptation, and Vulnerability*, published for the Intergovernmental Panel on Climate Change, Cambridge University Press, Cambridge, 1032 pp

Meehl, G., Washington, W., Collins, W., Arblaster, J., Hu, A., Buja, L., Strand, W. and Teng, H. (2005) 'How much more global warming and sea level rise?', *Science*, vol 307, pp1769–1772

Metzger, M. and Schröter, D. (2006) 'Towards a spatially explicit and quantitative vulnerability assessment of environmental change in Europe', *Regional Environmental Change*, vol 6, pp201–216

Metzger, M. J., Leemans, R., Schröter, D., Cramer, W. and ATEAM consortium (2004) 'The ATEAM vulnerability mapping tool', *Quantitative Approaches in Systems Analysis*, No. 27, CD-ROM publication, Office C. T. de Wit Graduate School for Production Ecology & Resource Conservation (PE&RC), Wageningen, The Netherlands

Metzger, M. J., Rounsevell, M. D. A., Acosta-Michlik, L., Leemans, R. and Schröter, D. (2006) 'The vulnerability of ecosystem services to land use change', *Agriculture, Ecosystems & Environment*, vol 114, pp69–85

Metzger, M. J., Schröter, D., Leemans, R. and Cramer, W. (2008) 'A spatially explicit and quantitative vulnerability assessment of ecosystem service change in Europe', *Regional Environmental Change*, vol 8, pp91–107

Michael, M. (1996) 'Ignoring science: Discourses of ignorance in the public understanding of science', in Irwin, A. and Wynne, B. (eds) *Misunderstanding Science? The Public Reconstruction of Science and Technology*, Cambridge University Press, Cambridge, pp107–125

Mitchell, R., Clark, W., Cash, D. and Alcock, F. (eds) (2006) *Global Environmental Assessments: Information, Institutions, and Influence*, MIT Press, Cambridge

Müller, B. (2002) *Equity in Climate Change: The Great Divide*, Oxford Institute for Energy Studies, Oxford

National Assessment Synthesis Team (2001) *Climate Change Impacts on the United States*, Cambridge University Press, Cambridge

O'Brien, K., Leichenko, R., Kelkar, U., Venema, H., Aandahl, G., Tompkins, H., Javed, A., Bhadwal, S., Barg, S., Nygaard, L. and West, J. (2004) 'Mapping vulnerability to multiple stressors: Climate change and globalization in India', *Global Environmental Change*, vol 14, pp303–313

Orlove, B. and Tosteson, J. (1999) 'The application of seasonal to interannual climate forecasts based on El Niño – Southern Oscillation (ENSO) events: Lessons from Australia, Brazil, Ethiopia, Peru, and Zimbabwe', Working Papers in Environmental Policy, Institute of International Studies, University of California, Berkeley

Ostrom, E. (2004) 'Panarchy: Understanding transformations in human and natural systems', *Ecological Economics*, vol 49(4), pp488–491

Parry, M. L., Canziani, O. F., Palutikof, J., van der Linden, P. and Hanson, C. (eds) (2007) 'Climate change 2007: Impacts, adaptation and vulnerability', Contribution of Working Group II to the Fourth Assessment Report of the Intergovernmental Panel on Climate Change, Cambridge University Press, Cambridge, 976pp

Parson, E., Corell, R., Barron, E., Burkett, V., Janetos, A., Joyce, L., Karl, T., Maccracken, M., Melillo, J., Morgan, M. G., Schimel, D. and Wilbanks, T. J. (2003) 'Understanding climatic impacts, vulnerabilities, and adaptation in the United States: Building a capacity for assessment', *Climatic Change*, vol 57, pp9–42

Patt, A. G. (1999a) 'Assessing extreme outcomes: The strategic treatment of low probability impacts in scientific assessment', *Risk Decision and Policy*, vol 4(1), pp1–15

Patt, A. G. (1999b) 'Separating analysis from politics: Acid rain in Europe', *Policy Studies Review*, vol 16(3–4), pp103–137

Patt, A. G. and Gwata, C. (2002) 'Effective seasonal climate forecast applications: Examining constraints for subsistence farmers in Zimbabwe', *Global Environmental Change*, vol 12(3), pp185–195

Patt, A. G. and Schröter, D. (2008) 'Perceptions of climate risk in Mozambique: Implications for the success of adaptation and coping strategies', *Global Environmental Change* (in press)

Patt, A. G., Klein, R. and de la Vega-Leinert, A. (2005a) 'Taking the uncertainties in climate change vulnerability assessment seriously', *Comptes Rendus Geosciences*, vol 337, pp411–424

Patt, A. G., Suarez, P. and Gwata, C. (2005b) 'Effects of seasonal climate forecasts and participatory workshops among subsistence farmers in Zimbabwe', *Proceedings of the National Academy of Sciences of the United States of America*, vol 102, pp12623–12628

Patt, A. G., Bowles, H. R. and Cash, D. (2006) 'Mechanisms for enhancing the credibility of an advisor: Prepayment and aligned incentives', *Journal of Behavioral Decision Making*, vol 19(4), pp347–359

Putnam, H. (2002), *The Collapse of the Fact/Value Dichotomy and Other Essays*, Harvard University Press, Cambridge

Ribot, J. C., Magalhaes, A. and Panagides, S. (eds) (1996) *Climate Variability, Climate Change, and Social Vulnerability in the Semi-Arid Tropics*, Cambridge University Press, Cambridge

Schröter, D., Acosta-Michlik, L., Arnell, A. W., Araújo, M. B., Badeck, F., Bakker, M., Bondeau, A., Bugmann, H., Carter, T., Vega-Leinert, A. C. de la, Erhard, M., Espiñeira, G. Z., Ewert, F., Fritsch, U., Friedlingstein, P., Glendining, M., Gracia, C. A., Hickler, T., House, J., Hulme, M., Kankaanpää, S., Klein, R. J. T., Krukenberg, B., Lavorel, S., Leemans, R., Lindner, M., Liski, J., Metzger, M. J., Meyer, J., Mitchell, T., Mohren, F., Morales, P., Moreno, J. M., Reginster, I., Reidsma, P., Rounsevell, M., Pla, E., Pluimers, J., Prentice, I. C., Pussinen, A., Sánchez, A., Sabaté, S., Sitch, S., Smith, B., Smith, J., Smith, P., Sykes, M. T., Thonicke, K., Thuiller, W., Tuck, G., Werf, G. van der, Vayreda, J., Wattenbach, M., Wilson, D. W., Woodward, F. I., Zaehle, S., Zierl, B., Zudin, S. and Cramer, W. (2004) *ATEAM (Advanced Terrestrial Ecosystem Analysis and Modelling) Final Report*, Potsdam Institute for Climate Impact Research (PIK), Potsdam

Schröter, D., Cramer, W., Leemans, R., Prentice, I. C., Araújo, M. B., Arnell, N. W., Bondeau, A., Bugmann, H., Carter, T. R., Gracia, C. A., Vega-Leinert, A. C. de la, Erhard, M., Ewert, F., Glendining, M., House, J. I., Kankaanpää, S., Klein, R. J. T., Lavorel, S., Lindner, M., Metzger, M. J., Meyer, J., Mitchell, T. D., Reginster, I., Rounsevell, M., Sabaté, S., Sitch, S., Smith, B., Smith, J., Smith, P., Sykes, M. T., Thonicke, K., Thuiller, W., Tuck, G., Zaehle, S. and Zierl, B. (2005a) 'Ecosystem service supply and vulnerability to global change in Europe', *Science*, vol 310(5752), pp1333–1337

Schröter, D., Polsky, C. and Patt, A. G. (2005b) 'Assessing vulnerabilities to the effects of global change: An eight step approach', *Mitigation and Adaptation Strategies for Global Change*, vol 10(4), pp573–595

Sen, A. K. (1981) *Poverty and Famines: An Essay on Entitlements and Deprivation*, Oxford University Press, Oxford

Smyth, C. G. and Royle, S. A. (2000) 'Urban landslide hazards: Incidence and causative factors in Niteroi, Rio de Janeiro State, Brazil', *Applied Geography*, vol 20(2), pp95–118

Solomon, S., Qin, D., Manning, M., Chen, Z., Marquis, M., Averyt, K. B., Tignor, M. and Miller, H. L. (eds) (2007) 'Climate change 2007: The physical science basis', Contribution of Working Group I to the Fourth Assessment Report of the Intergovernmental Panel on Climate Change, Cambridge University Press, Cambridge, UK, and New York, USA, 996pp

Stephen, L. and Downing, T. E. (2001) 'Getting the scale right: A comparison of analytical methods for vulnerability assessment and household-level targeting', *Disasters*, vol 25(2), pp113–135

Stern, N. (2007) *The Economics of Climate Change*, Cambridge University Press, Cambridge, 712pp

Suarez, P. and Ribot, J. (2003) 'The political economics of climate change vulnerability', IIASA Working Papers, Laxenburg, Austria

Turner, B. L. (1991) 'Opinion: Thoughts on linking the physical and human sciences in the study of global environmental change', *Research and Exploration*, Spring, pp133–135

Turner, B. L. II., Matson, P., McCarthy, J. J., Corell, R., Christensen, L., Eckley, N., Hovelsrud-Broda, G., Kasperson, J. X., Kasperson, R., Luers, A. L., Martello, M. L., Mathiesen, S., Naylor, R., Polsky, C., Pulsipher, A., Schiller, A., Selin, H. and Tyler, N. (2003) 'Illustrating the coupled human–environment system for vulnerability analysis:

Three case studies', *Proceedings of the National Academy of Sciences of the United States of America*, vol 100(14), pp8080–8085

Verweij, M. and Thompson, M. (eds) (2006) *Clumsy Solutions for a Complex World: Governance, Politics, and Plural Perceptions*, Palgrave Macmillan, New York

Wynne, B. (1996) 'Misunderstood misunderstandings: Social identities and the public uptake of science', in Irwin, A. and Wynne, B. (eds) *Misunderstanding Science? The Public Reconstruction of Science and Technology*, Cambridge University Press, Cambridge, pp19–46

Yohe, G. and Tol, R. S. J. (2002) 'Indicators for social and economic coping capacity: Moving toward a working definition of adaptive capacity', *Global Environmental Change*, vol 12, pp25–40

Zebisch, M., Grothmann, T., Schröter, D., Hasse, C., Fritsch, U. and Cramer, W. (2005) *Klimawandel in Deutschland Vulnerabilität und Anpassungsstrategien klimasensitiver Systeme*, Forschungsbericht 201 41 253 UBA-FB 000844, Umweltbundesamt, Berlin

Chapter 2

The House is Both Empty and Sad: Social Vulnerability, Environmental Disturbance, Economic Change and the Irish Potato Famine

Evan D. G. Fraser

Kilkelly Ireland 18 and 50 my dear and loving son John,
Your good friend the school master, Patrick O'Donnel, is so good to write these words down.
Your brothers have all gone to find work in England; the house is both empty and sad,
And the crop of potatoes is sorely infected, a third to half of them bad.

(Excerpt from a traditional song about the Irish Potato Famine based on a series of letters between a father in Ireland and his son, who emigrated to the USA during the Great Irish Potato Famine)

Introduction

Between 1845 and 1850, famine, pestilence and death descended on Ireland. These five years reduced the population from 8 to 6.5 million and set off a tidal wave of emigration that was to last for decades. The catastrophe began in September 1845, when a disease caused by the fungal pathogen *Phytophthora infestans* destroyed the crop that the vast majority of people depended on. The blight returned in the following year. 1847 saw a reprieve, but people did not have seed potatoes to plant. It then reappeared in 1848, 1849 and 1850. By the time the blight subsided, it left a path of destruction that changed Ireland forever. Approximately 2 million people lost their lives, families and homes during these years. The population of Ireland continued to fall until it reached just 2 million in the early 20th century (Allen Figgis Publishers, 1968).

One of the interesting features of the blight is that fungal pathogens regularly caused the potato crop to fail in the 17th and 18th centuries. Indeed, *Phytophthora infestans* is still a serious pest today (Scholte, 1992; Kabaluk and Vernon, 1999). However, previous outbreaks in Ireland (and subsequent outbreaks in the rest of the world) caused nothing like the suffering wrought in Ireland between 1845 and 1850. This suggests that something made Irish society in the 1840s vulnerable. So, aside from its considerable historical and cultural significance, the Irish Potato Famine provides a stark example of a collision between human society and environmental conditions. It illustrates how social and economic forces made the population dependent on the potato and vulnerable to anything that disrupted this one crop. It also illustrates how agricultural management made the potato crop itself vulnerable to a pest outbreak. Looked at in this way, the famine is a case study that can contribute to the ongoing academic debate on vulnerability and the relationship between society and the environment (Fraser, 2003).

The path to the famine

The road to the famine began in 1815. With the fall of Napoleon, the socioeconomic context changed for the rural poor throughout Europe. First, Europe's military powers decommissioned, causing an influx of rural labour as men who had been employed for decades of fighting flooded back onto the land in search of livelihoods (Holmes, 2002). Second, the war ensured that the international price of grain had been high for decades. The Governments of England, France, Spain, Belgium and Prussia needed vast quantities of food to keep troops fed and were willing to pay to do so. The end of the war spelled an end to these high prices. Faced with a decline in the price of wheat, and a sharp increase in the demand for livestock products caused by the emerging middle class, landlords found it uneconomical to maintain large areas of land under continuous cultivation and began switching to livestock production causing large-scale evictions as the best land was turned into sheep pastures (Foster, 1988).

Upheaval in the agricultural economy was only one change that the Irish peasant needed to adapt to. Another hallmark of this period was the massive advance in England's industrial sector. Oddly, Ireland, Britain's closest neighbour, actually de-industrialized during this time. The 1821 UK census shows that 41.2 per cent of Ireland's population was involved in the industrial or commercial sector, and 40.1 per cent was involved primarily in agriculture. By 1841, only 30 per cent of Ireland was considered industrial or commercial, while 53 per cent found their livelihood in agriculture (Mokyr, 1987). The primary reason for this decline is that the 'industry' in Ireland almost entirely referred to cottage industries such as linen production that would have taken place on the farm. These firms were simply unable to compete with the large textile mills from northern England. For example, in 1825, the town of Bandon had an excess of 2000 private, self-employed weavers. By 1840, fewer than 100 remained (Foster, 1988).

Over this time Ireland also experienced significant population growth, exploding from 2.2 million in 1600 to somewhat over 8 million on the eve of the Famine (Daly, 1986). By European standards, this was unusually high: in the 1840s Ireland's growth rate was 1.3 people per 1000 people while France had a much more modest growth rate of 0.4 per 1000 people. This led to the situation where Ireland, with 700 people per square mile of arable land, boasted the highest rural population densities in Europe (O'Grada, 1989).

Thoughts on why Ireland was different from the rest of Europe differ. One possibility is the tradition of partible inheritance, where each son was given a parcel of land to use upon reaching maturity. This led to younger marriages and larger families (Kinealy, 1994). Second, cottage industries provided an income that was not tied to the farm and also helped younger people to marry. The cultural influence of the Catholic Church may have played a role. Finally, there were incentives to have numerous children as a supply of labour that helped individual families intensify food production and cottage industries. Elsewhere in Europe, specifically in places where industrialization provided new economic opportunities, this logic did not apply.

The land tenure system created another important complication (Ross, 1986). Generally, the people working the land did not own it; rather, they rented it under a number of possible agreements from an agent of the landlord. Woodham-Smith (1962) argues that peasants often generated their rent by growing cash crops that were never used as food. For the small farmer who failed in his rent payments the consequence was immediate eviction by landlords who were often ignorant of the local situation, and thus unsympathetic to their plight.

Faced with these social, economic and demographic pressures, there were only three choices for the poor of Ireland: become wholly dependent on agricultural production, become a landless labourer or emigrate. For those who stayed in Ireland, it was vital to obtain any scrap of land on which to eke out a meagre existence. This meant that marginal land was brought into cultivation where only the hardiest of crops could survive. It also meant that the poor found themselves geographically isolated, far away from urban centres where they could participate in trade or commerce.

For those who clung to Ireland, the potato, a remarkably hardy crop that can grow on even the most marginal of soil, seemed a God-send. Compared to other crops, the potato is an extremely efficient source of nutrition, and O'Grada comments that '... an acre of land could feed 2.08 people on wheat or 4.18 people on potatoes.' (1989, p62) Very quickly, therefore, the potato became the only viable crop for the poorest, most marginal and remotest communities.

Earlier in Irish history, however, potatoes had not been seen as fit for regular human consumption but were used as source of animal feed, and only eaten by people if cereal crops failed and there was no money to buy food (Bourke, 1993). By 1845, however, much of the country, especially the west, had switched over entirely to potato subsistence. Not only that, the strains of potato changed over time, and, starting in the 1730s, the most commonly grown varieties degenerated as quality and nutrition were replaced by productivity and tolerance to poor soils.

For example, the Black potato was used extensively in the 1700s and was reported to be the first 'outstanding variety' of potato. It kept throughout the year and '... its pulp affords a strong invigorating diet to the labourer ...' (Rye, *Considerations on Agriculture*, in Bourke, 1993, p32) The Apple, which was first described in the 1770s, also was highly praised, despite not being particularly productive. Rye, in *Considerations on Agriculture*, declared that: '... [the apple] should be called the poor man's potato, because Providence has, in a most kind and benign manner, withheld its shoots till he has time to begin his tillage.' (quoted in Bourke, 1993, p33)

The Cup, which was widespread in the first decades of the 1800s, was notable only for productivity and its ability to grow in adverse conditions as '... [the Cup was] more productive, but very inferior in every other quality [to the apple] ...' (Bourke, 1993, p34) The Lumper, however, was by far the most common variety grown in Ireland just before the Famine. The Drummond Report (a report for the Irish railway which was written in 1838) describes the Lumper as:

> *A species of potato ... [that] ... has been brought into general cultivation, on account of its great productiveness, and the facility with which it can be raised from an inferior soil and with a comparatively small portion of manure. The root, at its first introduction, was scarcely considered food enough for swine; it neither possesses the farinaceous qualities of the better varieties of the plant, nor is it as palatable as any other, being wet and tasteless, and in point of substantial nutriment, little better as an article of human food, than a Swedish turnip.* (Drummond report, 1838 quoted in Bourke, 1993, p34)

Even worse, the Lumper could not be stored for a full year. As a result, many people went hungry every summer, between the time when the last year's crop was no longer fit to eat, and the new crop was ready. This situation accentuated the differences between social classes. A well-established farming family would have been unaffected by the seasonal hunger, and would also have been in a position to sell their surplus to the peasants whose potatoes did not sustain them.

Thus, beginning about 100 years before the Famine, poorer communities sacrificed quality of food for productivity, to the point that some regions – the west coast in particular – depended on one poor cultivar that was unable even to provide food throughout the year. When this supply of food was eliminated by the blight there was no realistic alternative as a food supply.

Using theory to help explain famine

When it comes to trying to explain the causes of the famine, a number of theoretical frameworks can be employed. There are deterministic theories, based on large-scale generalizations such as Malthus's assertion that population growth inevitably leads to a situation where the land is over-taxed (Malthus, 1976 edition). This theory has often been employed to explain the Potato Famine, though modern scholarship suggests that there was little correlation between population density, growth or size and the effect of the blight (Mokyr, 1987). Another argument against applying Malthusian theory to Ireland lies in Irish grain exports. Ireland was a net exporter of grain in 1845 and 1846, and although it had a grain deficit by 1847, it still continued to export sizeable amounts of corn (284,146 and 314,000 tonnes of grain were exported in 1847 and 1848, respectively). The fact that in 1847 Ireland imported six times more grain than it exported shows the magnitude of the supply failure, but the continued exportation of food during the leanest years indicates that distribution problems and a failure of local demand went hand in hand with a diminishing supply.[1]

There are also sweeping 'political' theories that focus on the role of the international economy and British colonial rule. This includes those like the playwright G. B. Shaw, who viewed the famine as caused by UK economic policies that made British politicians ideologically opposed to intervening:

> *Malone: Me father died of the starvation in the Black 47 ...*
>
> *Violet: The Famine?*
>
> *Malone: No, the Starvation. When a country is full of food and exporting it, there can be no famine ...*
>
> (Shaw, 1911, p196)

This theory has also been largely dismissed by modern scholars who point out that the British government provided a number of different types of famine relief, mostly by selling low-priced grain to the Irish market and by employing people on public works projects (750,000 people were employed at the height of the famine in 1847). Although these were hampered by a host of bureaucratic problems, they illustrate that the famine was caused by more than just colonial exploitation.

Other theories focus on local issues. Most notably, the economist Amartya Sen provides a valuable conceptual framework for understanding the problems of food availability. Sen's (1981) work on poverty and famines led him to coin the phrase *Food Entitlements* to refer to all the various ways that people access food at the local scale. Famines, in Sen's conceptualization, are not a result of there being insufficient food, but in individuals not having access to adequate entitlement. Entitlements can come from either direct sources (e.g. a farming family that grows its own food) or indirect sources (e.g. a labouring family who exchanges money for food), or be transferred from one person to another (often in the form of charity, gifts or food aid). Starvation and famine happen when a person's or community's entitlements are disrupted for some reason. This can be an indirect or demand-side failure, which can occur when a group of people lose their purchasing power through unemployment, falling wages, rising food prices or inflation. Alternatively, a population may experience a direct entitlement failure when a crop fails and there is a shortage in the supply of food. In this way, one can understand how poverty may play the key role in a famine. Under conditions of prosperity, people whose food supply is destroyed (a loss of direct entitlement), may still have enough money to purchase food, thus switching to an indirect food entitlement. Poverty, however, prevents those who lose direct entitlements from switching to indirect ones.

The situation in Ireland leading up to the famine can be characterized as a society slowly losing food entitlement options. The English Industrial Revolution and a shift in agricultural management practices made it impossible for large parts of the population to participate in the cash economy. This constituted a loss of indirect entitlements. Population growth and landlords evicting peasants to make room for livestock meant that increased rural congestion affected direct entitlements by forcing families to exist on very small landholdings. Economic and geographic isolation meant that transfer entitlements were unavailable to the most vulnerable members of society. This made subsistence agriculture, based around the potato, the only viable way that poor members of this society could obtain food entitlements.

Despite its considerable merits, the entitlement framework only explains some of the causes that led to the Irish Potato Famine. While it provides valuable insights into the socioeconomic characteristics of those communities who were vulnerable to collapse, it does not provide any real insight into the sorts of environmental conditions that precipitated the spread of the fungus itself. For example, historically, many subsistence agricultural communities and hunter–gatherer societies have flourished for long periods despite having few entitlement options (McMichael, 2001): what was different about Ireland in the 1840s that made it more vulnerable than these other communities who also depended directly on the environment for sustenance?

To address this lacuna, and add an explicit environmental dimension into the entitlements framework, some propose that resource-dependent communities use an 'environmental entitlement' just as they access the direct and indirect entitlements (Mearns, 1996). This focuses on the rights and resources people have and how they can use these rights and resources to enhance well-being (Leach et al, 1999). Although this approach shows progress in that it helps highlight the role of institutions in facilitating or inhibiting access to natural capital (Post and Snel, 2003), it reduces the environment to a static and unchanging resource base and ignores the fact that precipitation variation, pest outbreaks and temperature extremes may cause a resource-plenty environment to become impoverished very quickly. Environmental entitlements, therefore, ignore multiple equilibrium ecology (Behnke and Scoones, 1993) and do not help us assess whether agricultural practices themselves contribute to increased or decreased food security.

The field of landscape ecology provides some insight into the characteristics of ecosystems that may collapse due to an environmental shock like the outbreak of a pest. For example, the 'Panarchy' framework proposed by Gunderson and Holling (2002) holds that all ecosystems cycle through periods of resource accumulation and collapse based on three key characteristics: the resilience of the ecosystem, the connectedness of individuals in the ecosystem and the potential for change in the ecosystem. The first two characteristics – resilience and connectedness – are relatively simple. Gunderson and Holling define resilience as the adaptive capacity of an ecosystem, which can be measured as the diversity in that system. Diverse systems are better able to tolerate a wide range of environmental conditions and disturbances than are simple systems (Altieri, 1990; Gliessman, 1998). For example, the native prairie in North America is made up of a mixture of plants that use slightly different photosynthetic pathways. There are the 'C4' plants (like big bluestem – *Andropogon gerardii*) where the receptive carbohydrate in photosynthesis has an extra carbon molecule making them more drought tolerant than the 'C3' plants like Mammoth wild rye (*Elymus racemosus*) that are highly productive but do not tolerate dry conditions so well. Together, communities of C3 and C4 plants provide the drought-resistant and productive ecosystem that evolved in the US and Canadian Great Plains (Soule and Piper, 1992).

For the landscape ecologists, connectedness is an assessment of whether individuals in the ecosystem are closely crowded together over both space and time.[2] This provides an indication of the degree to which a system can be controlled by external forces. A dense forest would have more connectivity and be more vulnerable to external forces than a loosely stocked plantation, and disturbances (such as windstorms, fires and pest outbreaks) generally have a bigger impact in tightly connected ecosystems (Attiwill, 1994).

The third characteristic, potential for change, is slightly more complex. Gunderson and Holling define 'potential' as the amount of biological wealth in an ecosystem that can be released in the event of a disturbance. A mature boreal forest, with a closed canopy of spruce and pine trees, and a thick duff layer of pine needles, would have a large amount of biological wealth and, therefore, be vulnerable to fires or pest outbreaks. Similarly, an agricultural field, with abundant (and rich) biomass is extremely vulnerable to outbreaks of opportunistic pests.

According to the Panarchy model, after a disturbance, an ecosystem accumulates biomass, thereby increasing the wealth available in the system and the potential for change. As this happens, new species fill available ecological niches and connectivity increases. Simultaneously, more competitive species outcompete less successful species, and diversity dwindles. As ecosystems move through this process, they reach a point when the potential for change is high, connectivity is high, and resilience is low, becoming '... accidents waiting to happen' (Holling, 2001). At this stage, a system is vulnerable to disturbances and external shocks, such as pest outbreaks. A disturbance then releases accumulated resources and returns the system to a state of higher diversity, less connectivity and less wealth.

Many of the characteristics of the agro-ecosystem in Ireland in the decades leading up to the famine conform to the trajectory described by Panarchy. We can assess the resilience of the Irish agricultural landscape in terms of crop diversity. As already discussed, the agro-ecosystem in Ireland progressed from a relatively complex system of mixed livestock, grain and potato production to a system that was wholly based on one cultivar of potato. This offered no opportunities for crop rotation, which even today is essential to keep pests out of potato crops worldwide. We can also infer that the connectivity of the Irish agricultural landscape increased as the famine approached by considering the already-cited figures on rural population density. This meant that, once established, the blight was able to spread quickly through the entire countryside and quickly devastate huge areas. Finally, from the perspective of the organism that caused the blight, these tightly packed potato fields represented a very wealthy system, full of resources that could support a massive, virulent and devastating outbreak of this disease. Therefore, leading up to the famine the agro-ecosystem in the west of Ireland moved from a state of low connectivity to high connectivity, low wealth to high wealth, and diversity to specialization. In doing so, it became vulnerable to a trigger or disturbance such as the potato blight.

Synthesizing theory for policy makers

To move forward, we need a way of combining a socially driven framework such as Entitlements with Panarchy, a tool of landscape ecology, to help explain both the social and environmental characteristics of vulnerability. If possible, this could provide a significant tool to help identify regions today that are vulnerable to climate change and could help shape policy proactively before problems emerge.

There are some hints that the characteristics of the Panarchy framework could form the basis of such a tool and be applied directly to social systems. However, this would lead us to expect that rich, connected and specialized communities would be the most vulnerable to environmental problems. The evidence from Ireland refutes this. In reality, the hardest hit communities in Ireland were poor and economically isolated. Indeed, around the world it seems to be the poor and isolated who are most at risk (Fraser et al, 2005). Various chapters in the book *Panarchy* edited by Gunderson and Holling (2002) acknowledge this complexity by suggesting that, under certain circumstances, poverty (not wealth) creates vulnerability in human systems. However, with the exception of a brief note by Berkes and Folke (2002), little work has been done to understand under what conditions a poverty trap exists and to what extent the Panarchy model provides useful insights. Both ecological and social systems in Ireland, however, were simple systems, lacking resilience and diversity. This suggests that although an ecologically fragile system may be characterized as simple, wealthy and connected, socially vulnerable systems may more commonly be simple, poor and isolated.

Leaving the Panarchy model aside for the moment, there are a number of other attempts to integrate social–environmental models of vulnerability that are based on 'meta-indicators' of social and environmental variables. These efforts often propose that vulnerability is a function of things like the 'ability to adapt', 'environmental sensitivity', or the concept of 'environmental criticality' that is supposed to capture the point at which ecosystems can no longer function (see Kasperson et al, 1995; Alcamo et al, 2001; Fraser et al, 2003). Similarly, Chambers (1989) argues that vulnerability in food systems is a result of large-scale or external forces (for example, being exposed to problems such as climate change), as well as local or internal causes like the ability to adapt to these problems. Watts and Bohle (1993) echo this conclusion when they define vulnerability as the outcome of environmental and socioeconomic forces. They then present one of the most cited conceptual models of food insecurity, which they break into three elements: the exposure to a risk or hazard, the capacity to adapt to this hazard, and the potential of the problem to have severe consequences. Turner et al (2003a, b) take only a slightly different approach with their recently published framework where they nest vulnerability within a complex flow chart of social, economic and ecological forces.

Although these efforts all provide extremely interesting insights, it is difficult to see how to operationalize concepts like 'environmental criticality' or 'the ability to adapt' so that they can provide guidance for proactive policy. Similarly, it is difficult to see how a complex flow chart of social, political, economic and ecological factors can easily help highlight vulnerable regions. Policy makers need more concrete indicators on which to base decisions and need a list of variables that are easy to measure and relatively simple (though not simplistic). The Entitlement framework and the Panarchy theory together may help meet this challenge and provide a more useful integration between social and environmental factors.

First, the tools of Entitlement Theory can be applied to assess the extent to which communities have the assets they need to command different forms of entitlement. These assets include human capital (often measured through assessing health or education) social capital (kinship and community networks), human-made or economic capital (represented by the build infrastructure as well as financial assets), institutional capital (government support) and natural capital (natural resources such as soil fertility) (Pretty, 2003). This assessment would also build on the tools of 'sustainable livelihoods analysis' that provides guidance to development workers on how to work with local residents in a participatory fashion to contextualize local socioeconomic conditions and prioritize development projects (Morse and Fraser, 2005). If engaged in this sort of livelihoods assessment, it is extremely important for any work to be sensitive to inequalities within communities and households. For example, empirical research on food and education budgets of female- versus male-headed households show that assets are not always equally shared (Haddad et al, 1997).

Second, the tools of landscape ecology can help assess the ecological wealth, diversity and connectivity of different agro-ecological landscapes. This can be done at a number of scales. For example, national-level data (such as that freely available on the Food and Agricultural Organization's homepage, www.fao.org) shows the extent to which a country's agricultural production is specialized on a narrow range of crops. Crop harvests and yield per hectare can provide an assessment of the biological wealth present in these systems. Data on the quantity of agricultural land, the amount of land every year left fallow and the size and density of farms can provide insight in the connectivity of landscape. Data can be also used at smaller spatial scales when available (Bradshaw, 2004; Fraser, 2006). If an assessment of wealth, connectivity and diversity shows agro-ecosystems becoming more biologically productive, specialized and connected, then it may be reasonable to infer that these landscapes are also becoming more vulnerable to environmental shocks.

Third, to link these two sets of tools, it would be necessary to assess the extent to which people without assets depend on vulnerable landscapes. This could be determined economically, by looking at the proportion of the economy that comes from subsistence agriculture. Trends over time will also be extremely important and, if there is a gradual erosion of non-farm employment options, then it may be inferred that people are relying more heavily on a narrow range of natural resources. Finally, it would also be important to assess this dependence spatially. If a community's food supply comes from a large area, then it may be less vulnerable to environmental disruptions than if all the food came from a single region or a tightly packed and homogeneous landscape.

Fourth, the story of the Irish Potato Famine hints that there is at least one other important dimension to vulnerability that lies outside either the Entitlement or Panarchy frameworks. The famine occurred during a period of rapid socioeconomic change, when social relations and traditional coping strategies were breaking down. A brief survey of other environmentally induced famines suggests that environmental changes seem to cause serious havoc during such times. For example, El Niño droughts precipitated massive famines in India, Brazil, the Philippines and China during the late 19th and early 20th centuries. Many scholars, both modern and those who witnessed these events, have concluded that the suffering was at least partly as a result of the loss of traditional communities that became unviable due to emerging global trade networks (Davis, 2001). This point is supported more generally by Polany (1944) who suggests that a simple view of famine as a result of colonial exploitation hides the greater issue of cultural degeneration that makes regions vulnerable.

These four characteristics (a lack of assets, fragile agro-ecosystems, a dependence on specialized environmental entitlements, and rapid socioeconomic changes) offer a suggestive and intuitively simple list of indicators that link social and biophysical variables to highlight vulnerability to environmental changes. However, it is inappropriate to propose a new model of vulnerability based on just one case study. The next step is to further refine and test these characteristics through additional historic cases in order to determine if they are indeed common to other situations where environmental problems triggered a wholesale collapse in human systems. Ultimately, and with enough refinement, this sort of list could form the basis of a series of diagnostic tools that should be combined with community participation to help target climate adaptation strategies. For example, the results hinted at through this case study might lead a policy maker to work with local communities to diversify assets in times of economic turmoil. It could also highlight the need to work with communities to maintain diverse agro-ecosystems in the face of international market pressures that may create incentives for farmers to create more economically efficient, but ecologically fragile, monoculture landscapes. A third implication might be to highlight the need to reduce the physical connectivity of the landscape while increasing social connectivity and the range of assets communities can draw upon. Whatever way results point, as these indicators of vulnerability are refined, the ultimate goal will be to generate a simple set of concrete indicators that help identify regions or communities that are at risk of changes in the environment.

Conclusions

As the world wakes up to the realities of climate change, it is worth remembering that the climate has always changed, and that human society has had to cope with fluctuations in precipitation, outbreaks of pests and extreme storms in the past. Most of the time, we have managed to adapt, and the presence of human civilization in most of the planet's ecosystems shows that our ability to adapt and innovate is enormous. Sometimes, however, environmental change knocks us off our stride. Either the change is too large, or our ability to adapt is constrained, and suddenly we find ourselves facing a big problem. Occasionally, the change is so big, the problem so enormous, that entire societies teeter on the edge of oblivion: little is known about Ancient Sumeria (Wright, 2004) or the Mayans who inhabited the ruined cities of Tikal and Palenque (Haug et al, 2003). However, evidence now suggests that climate change played a major role in their collapse. In other cases, we have direct evidence about the role of climate change. The *Vineland Sagas* describe how the Vikings farmed Greenland during a warm period. These farms were later abandoned once icebergs reinvaded the North Atlantic. Therefore, as we stand on the edge of an uncertain future, where increased climatic variability seems inevitable, it is helpful to cast our eye back to see what can be learned by studying the way that past cultures failed to adapt to these same sorts of problem.

The challenge is to determine what lessons to draw from the past for the study of contemporary vulnerability. One lesson is to look for parallels between past and present. For example, the tragedy outlined in this chapter occurred at a point in history when rapid economic growth in one part of the world disenfranchised poor communities in remote locations. As traditional social and economic structures collapsed, some people adapted by moving in search of work. In other places, people adapted to these changes by extracting every possible calorie from the soil. Intensifying agricultural production through specializing production made the Irish vulnerable to changes in the environment. In our own world of rapid financial growth, economic marginalization and rapid environmental change, there is some urgency to identify regions that may be responding to these challenges in the same way as the Irish peasant responded.

A second lesson from this story is more general. Policy makers need tools to fuse an understanding of social adaptability alongside models of environmental change in order to identify regions where small changes in the environment may have big changes in human communities. The approach proposed here is to use history to search out the common denominators that link social adaptability and environmental change in order to determine diagnostic characteristics that may identify places unlikely to adapt to climate change. The four characteristics identified in this historic analysis provide a starting point for this. The next step will be to better understand how assets, fragile agro-ecosystems, a dependence on specialized environmental entitlements, and rapid socioeconomic changes have affected other communities' ability to adapt in other periods of environmental change.

Notes

1 Interestingly, Malthus himself did not apply the Irish Famine to his theory; rather, he predicted a slow and gradual stop to Ireland's population growth:

Although it is quite certain that the population of Ireland cannot continue permanently to increase at its present rate, yet it is as certain that it will not suddenly come to a stop… Both theory and experience uniformly instruct us, that a less abundant supply of food operates with a gradually increasing pressure for a long time before its progress is stopped… (Quoted in O'Grada (1989) The Great Irish Famine, Macmillan, London)

2 Connectedness in this case is used in a slightly different sense than in 'food web theory', where connectedness refers to the number of possible predators an individual may be consumed by. See Jordan et al (2002).

References

Alcamo, J., Endejan, M., Kaspar, F. and Rosch, T. (2001) 'The GLASS model: A strategy for quantifying global environmental security', *Environmental Science and Policy*, vol 4, pp1–12

Allen Figgis Publishers (ed) (1968) *Encyclopaedia of Ireland*, Allen Figgis Publishers, Dublin

Altieri, M. (1990) 'Why study traditional ecology?', in Carroll, R., van der Meer, J. and Rossett, P. (eds) *The Ecology of Agricultural Systems*, McGraw Hill Publishers, New York

Attiwill, P. (1994) 'The disturbance of forest ecosystems: The ecological basis for conservative management', *Forest Ecology and Management*, vol 63, pp247–300

Behnke, R. and Scoones, I. (1993) *Range Ecology at Disequilibrium*, Overseas Development Institute, London

Berkes, F. and Folke, C. (2002) 'The Hindu cast system and the hierarchy trap', in Gunderson, L. and Holling, C. (eds) *Panarchy: Understanding Transformations in Human and Natural Systems*, Island Press, Washington DC

Bourke, A. (1993) *The Visitation of God? The Potato and the Great Irish Famine*, Lilliput Press, Dublin

Bradshaw, B. (2004) 'Plus c'est la meme chose? Questioning crop diversification as a response to agricultural deregulation in Saskatchewan, Canada', *Journal of Rural Studies*, vol 20, pp25–48

Chambers, R. (1989) 'Vulnerability, coping and policy', *IDS Bulletin*, vol 20, pp1–7

Daly, M. (1986) *The Famine in Ireland*, Dublin Historical Association, Dublin

Davis, M. (2001) *Late Victorian Holocausts: El Niño Famines and the Making of the Third World*, Verso, London

Foster, R. F. (1988) *Modern Ireland*, Penguin Books, New York

Fraser, E. (2003) 'Social vulnerability and ecological fragility: Building bridges between social and natural sciences using the Irish Potato Famine as a case study', *Conservation Ecology*, vol 7(2), art 9, www.consecol.org/vol7/iss2/art9/

Fraser, E. (2006) 'Crop diversification and trade liberalization: Linking global trade and local management through a regional case study', *Agriculture and Human Values*, vol 23, pp271–281

Fraser, E., Mabee, W. and Slaymaker, O. (2003) 'Mutual dependence, mutual vulnerability: The reflexive relation between society and the environment', *Global Environmental Change*, vol 13, pp137–144

Fraser, E., Mabee, W. and Figge, F. (2005) 'A framework for assessing the vulnerability of food systems to future shocks', *Futures*, vol 37, pp465–479

Gliessman, S. (1998) *Agroecology*, Ann Arbour Press, Chelsea

Gunderson, L. and Holling, C. S. (2002) *Panarchy: Understanding Transformations in Human and Natural Systems*, Island Press, Washington DC

Haddad, L., Hoddinott, J. and Alderman, H. (1997) *Intra-household Resource Allocation in Developing Countries*, John Hopkins University Press, London

Haug, G. H., Gunther, D., Peterson, L. C., Sigman, D. M., Hughen, K. A. and Aeschlimann, B. (2003) 'Climate and the collapse of Maya civilization', *Science*, vol 299, pp1731–1735

Holling, C. (2001) 'Understanding the complexity of economic, ecological, and social systems', *Ecosystems*, vol 4, pp390–405

Holmes, R. (2002) *Wellington: The Iron Duke*, Harper Collins, London

Jordan, F., Scheuring, I. and Vida, G. (2002) 'Species positions and extinction dynamics in simple food webs', *Journal of Theoretical Biology*, vol 215, pp441–448

Kabaluk, J. and Vernon, R. (1999) 'The effect of crop rotation on tuber flea beetle *Epitrix tuberis Gentner* populations in Potato', Pacific Research Centre, Agriculture and Agri-food Canada, Summerland, BC

Kasperson, J., Kasperson, R. and Turner, B. (1995) *Regions at Risk*, United Nations University Press, Tokyo

Kinealy, C. (1994) *The Great Calamity*, Gill & MacMillan, Dublin

Leach, M., Mearns, R. and Scoones, I. (1999) 'Environmental entitlements: Dynamics and institutions in community-based natural resource management', *World Development*, vol 27, pp225–247

Malthus, T. (1976 edition) *An Essay on Population*, Norton Books, New York

McMichael, T. (2001) *Human Frontiers, Environments and Disease*, Cambridge University Press, Cambridge

Mearns, R. (1996) 'Environmental entitlements: Pastoral natural resource management in Mongolia', *Cahiers des Sciences Humaines*, vol 32, pp105–131

Mokyr, J. (1987) *Why Ireland Starved*, George Allen & Unwin, London

Morse, S. and Fraser, E. (2005) 'Making "dirty" nations clean: The nation state and the problem of selecting and weighing indices as tools for measuring progress towards sustainability', *Geoforum*, vol 36(5), pp625–640

O'Grada, C. (1989) *The Great Irish Famine*, Macmillan, London

Polany, K. (1944) *The Great Transformation*, Beacon Press, Boston

Post, J. and Snel, M. (2003) 'The impact of decentralised forest management on charcoal production practices in Eastern Senegal', *Geoforum*, vol 34, pp85–98

Pretty, J. (2003) 'Social capital and the collective management of resources', *Science*, vol 302, pp1912–1914

Ross, E. (1986) 'Potatoes, population, and the Irish famine: The political economy of demographic change', in Handwerker, W. (ed) *Culture and Reproduction*, Westview Press, Boulder

Scholte, K. (1992) 'Effect of crop rotation on the incidence of soil-borne fungal diseases of potato', *Netherlands Journal of Plant Pathology*, supplement 2, pp93–102

Sen, A. (1981) *Poverty and Famines*, Clarendon Press, Oxford

Shaw, G. (1911) *Man and Superman*, Constable, London

Soule, J. and Piper, J. (1992) *Farming in Nature's Image*, Island Press, Washington DC

Turner, B. L., Kasperson, R. E., Matson, P. A., McCarthy, J. J., Corell, R. W., Christensen, L., Eckley, N., Kasperson, J. X., Luers, A., Martello, M. L., Polsky, C., Pulsipher, A. and Schiller, A. (2003a) 'A framework for vulnerability analysis in sustainability science', *Proceedings of the National Academy of Sciences of the United States of America*, vol 100, pp8074–8079

Turner, B. L., Matson, P. A., McCarthy, J. J., Corell, R. W., Christensen, L., Eckley, N., Hovelsrud-Broda, G. K., Kasperson, J. X., Kasperson, R. E., Luers, A., Martello, M. L., Mathiesen, S., Naylor, R., Polsky, C., Pulsipher, A., Schiller, A., Selin, H. and Tyler, N. (2003b) 'Illustrating the coupled human–environment system for vulnerability analysis: Three case studies', *Proceedings of the National Academy of Sciences of the United States of America*, vol 100, pp8080–8085

Watts, M. and Bohle, H. (1993) 'The space of vulnerability: The causal structure of hunger and famine', *Progress in Human Geography*, vol 17, pp43–67

Woodham-Smith, C. (1962) *The Great Hunger*, Penguin Books, London

Wright, B. (2004) *A Short History of Progress*, Anansi, Toronto

Chapter 3

Vulnerability Assessments in the Developed World: The UK and Norway

Ian Holman and Lars Otto Næss

Introduction

The United Kingdom and Norway both completed their first national efforts to assess the potential impacts of climate change in 1991. Since then, developments in the two countries have diverged considerably. In Norway, a number of studies of climate change impacts have been carried out, and regionally downscaled climate change scenarios have been developed and used for further analysis. However, there has been no comprehensive follow-up to the 1991 report and there is as yet no national programme for assessment of vulnerability and adaptation. Further, most research to date has taken place without extensive involvement of stakeholders. In contrast, an updated assessment of potential impacts and a new evaluation of possible adaptive responses was carried out and published in the UK in 1996 (UKCCIRG, 1996). This national overview report has since been augmented by regional scoping studies and national sectoral assessments of potential impacts and adaptation responses. Stakeholder engagement has been a key component of most UK research. This chapter provides a critical review of these contrasting approaches to vulnerability assessments in the UK and Norway, in order to analyse lessons learned and provide recommendations for the way forward.

Vulnerability assessments in the UK and Norway

This section traces the history of vulnerability assessments in the two countries, which include, among others, vulnerability mapping, analyses of social and economic effects and discussions of adaptation processes. Three overlapping issues are addressed: first, we discuss what types of information have been developed, and for which target audience; second, the choice of methods, and their application across scales are elaborated; and finally, the utility of vulnerability assessments to reduce vulnerability in the two countries, and the barriers to adaptation, are discussed.

Information and audience

Norway

The first Norwegian assessment of the consequences of climate change (Ministry of the Environment (MoE), 1991) was based on about 40 individual reports. The scale of the effort reflected the country's ambitious environment policy in the early 1990s. A number of subsequent research projects have assessed potential responses to factors such as elevated CO_2 levels and increased temperature. Examples include whole-ecosystem responses, effects of rapid climate change on biodiversity in boreal and montane ecosystems, effects on soils and studies of effects on species (e.g. Hill and Hodkinson, 1995; Wright, 1998; Dalen et al, 2001). The commencement of regional climate change scenario development by the RegClim Project in 1997 allowed more detailed studies at sub-national levels.[1] Norway participated in the Arctic Climate Impact Assessment (ACIA, 2004), and funding from the Norwegian Research Council on consequences of climate change in the country was consolidated in 2004 under the NORKLIMA programme (2004–2013). Up to now, the main focus of studies has been climate change impacts on sectors and ecosystems, with some regional and local-level studies (Sygna et al, 2004). The majority of the work has been undertaken by, and for, the research community, with little participation of other stakeholders, and until recently little focus on issues of vulnerability and adaptation (Sygna et al, 2004).

The first national-level effort to map vulnerability to climate change in Norway was conducted by O'Brien et al (2003). Their purpose was to illustrate differential vulnerability in municipalities across the country. The authors developed maps intended for stakeholder dialogue, to raise awareness of potential areas for concern and in turn to develop a mutual understanding between researchers and users at various levels of the factors that influence vulnerability to climate change in a real-world context. The work focused on three sectors that were locally important and, at the same time, considered to be particularly sensitive to climate change, namely agriculture, forestry and winter tourism. Table 3.1 shows a description of the vulnerability indicators selected for the agricultural sector, including a justification for their choice. Values for each of the indicators were calculated from a RegClim regional climate change scenario under 2 × CO_2 conditions for the 2030–2050 period, compared to a 1980–2000 baseline (O'Brien et al, 2006). The average values of all indicators then formed a composite vulnerability indicator, shown in Figure 3.1 for the agricultural sector. The map thus shows how exposure of the agricultural sector to climate change may change in different regions in Norway,

Table 3.1 *Agriculture: Indicators for vulnerability*

Indicator	*Description*	*Justification*
Spring precipitation	Monthly precipitation in April and May (mm change)	Increased spring precipitation assumed negative as it may cause delayed sowing, rot/fungus attack on seeds and soil erosion.
Autumn precipitation	Monthly precipitation in August and September (mm change)	Increased autumn precipitation assumed negative as it may cause delayed harvesting, rain and wind damage rot and less time for soil preparation before the winter.
Length of growing season	Number of days per year with average temperature above 5°C (no. of days change)	Longer growing season assumed beneficial as it may give higher yields, possibly more harvests, opportunities for new crop types, and longer pasture seasons.
Frost/thaw days, spring	No. of days per month in April and May with min. temperature below 0°C and max. temperature above 0°C in April and May (no. of days change).	Increased number of days in April–May with frost–thaw fluctuations assumed negative as it may cause soil disruptions and damage to yields.
Frost/thaw days, autumn	No. of days in September with min. temperature below 0°C and max. temperature above 0°C (no. of days change).	Increased number of days in September with frost–thaw fluctuations assumed negative as it may cause soil disruptions and damage to yields.
Average snow depth January, February, March	Average snow depth in January, February and March (no. of cm change)	Reduced snow depth assumed negative as it may lead to soil erosion, incomplete isolation for winter harvests (e.g. winter wheat) and it exposes plants to frost. Snow cover of 20cm or less assumed insufficient.

Source: O'Brien et al (2003)

based on one climate model. The map for exposure (left) shows the biophysical aspects of vulnerability, emphasizing the degree to which areas are susceptible from a resource management perspective. A gridded surface was created for each indicator, which was then interpolated to political boundaries for the municipal level. The adaptive capacity map shows a composite index based on an average of figures for the key factors shown in Table 3.2. The second map (right) shows the social aspects of vulnerability, indicating the degree to which the society is sensitive to climatic changes as well as its capacity to adapt.

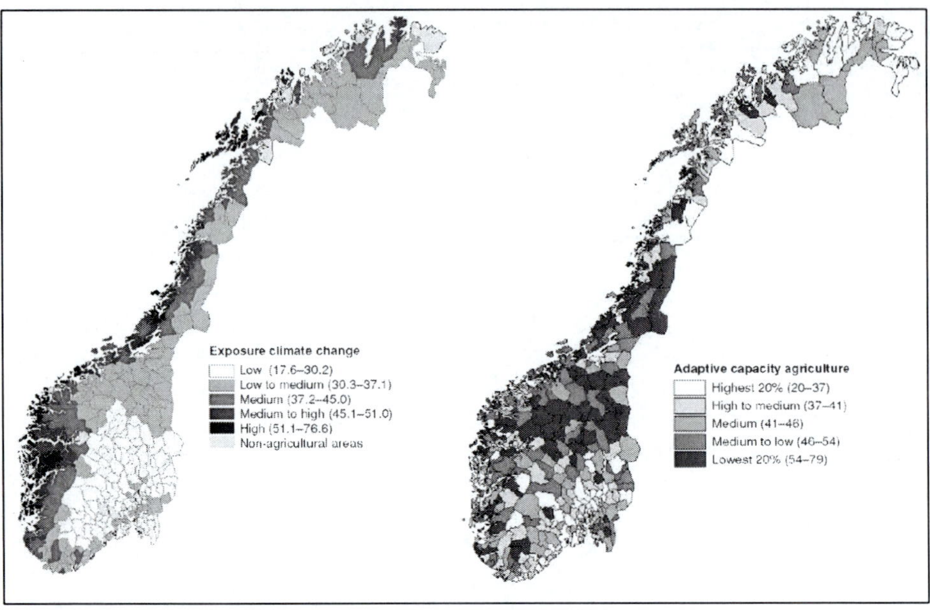

Source: Adapted from O'Brien et al (2003)

Figure 3.1 *Examples of maps for exposure (left) and adaptive capacity (right) in the agricultural sector in Norway*

UK

Since the second report on the potential effects of climate change in the UK (UKCCIRG, 1996), a series of regional studies have been carried out covering the whole of England and the devolved administrations of Wales and Scotland. These studies have been of two types:

1. Regional scoping studies – commissioned by regional stakeholder groups and coordinated by the United Kingdom Climate Impacts Programme (UKCIP). These initial studies have used expert judgement and literature review methods to provide a qualitative overview of climate change impacts on a range of sectors. A range of vulnerability issues have been identified:
   - sub-regional vulnerability, e.g. areas prone to flooding or subsidence due to clay-rich soils, or cities with significant urban heat island affects;
   - sectoral vulnerability, e.g. transport and energy infrastructure, winter sports, manufacturing and insurance industries;
   - social vulnerability, e.g. vulnerable social groups (based on income, language, age, mobility, health) or workers (e.g. outdoor workers);
   - factors which may act so as to increase vulnerability – e.g. identifying 'ill-informed and ill-prepared industries' and developments which increase vulnerability due to their location in floodplains.
2. Regional and national modelling studies – e.g. the Regional Climate Change Impact and Response Studies in East Anglia and North West England

Table 3.2 *Indicators of adaptive capacity*

Social sensitivity	*Economic factors*	*Demographic factors*
Employment in the sector	Tax base Government transfers Employment forecasts	Age distribution Migration Dependency rate

Source: O'Brien et al (2003)

(RegIS) Integrated Assessment (IA) (Holman et al, 2005a, b) which investigated the effects of regional climate and socioeconomic change on flooding, agriculture, water resources and biodiversity in East Anglia and north-west England, and MONARCH (Harrison et al, 2001) which provided quantitative evidence to complement previous UKCIP biodiversity assessments.

RegIS was funded by, what is now, the Department for Environment, Food and Rural Affairs (Defra) and UK Water Industry Research, who facilitate collaborative research for UK water operators. Additional support was provided by the Environment Agency (national environmental regulator) and English Nature (national nature conservation organization). As the funders of the study, these organizations would be regarded as the target audience, although the project contained important wider stakeholder engagement activities (Holman et al, 2005a).

As the vulnerability to climate change of a sector is a function of exposure, sensitivity and adaptive capacity, it is intrinsically linked to the future social, political and economic systems which, more likely than not, will be different to our current systems, behaviour and policies. To assume that vulnerability will, in the future, solely change as a result of climate change is to ignore the importance of non-climate (socioeconomic) factors in shaping our futures. The RegIS study therefore investigated the effects of climate and socioeconomic change in isolation and combination. Regional UKCIP98 climate (Hulme and Jenkins, 1998) and socioeconomic (Shackley and Deanwood, 2002) scenarios provided the quantitative inputs to a series of linked numerical models. The two climate change scenarios used for the 2050s were a 'Low' scenario constructed from the HadCM2 GGd experiment – 0.5 per cent per annum increase in greenhouse gases (GHGs) – scaled to the IS92d emissions scenario and a low climate sensitivity of 1.5°C, and a 'High' scenario constructed from the HadCM2 GGa experiment (1 per cent per annum increase in GHGs) scaled to the IS92a emissions scenario and a high climate sensitivity of 4.5°C, hereafter referred to as the 2050s Low and 2050s High scenarios, respectively. The quantitative and qualitative outputs identified a range of vulnerability issues:

- Areas within the regions are prone to fluvial and coastal flooding, but the vulnerability of these areas depends on societal approaches to flood management and spatial planning. The methodology developed in RegIS for

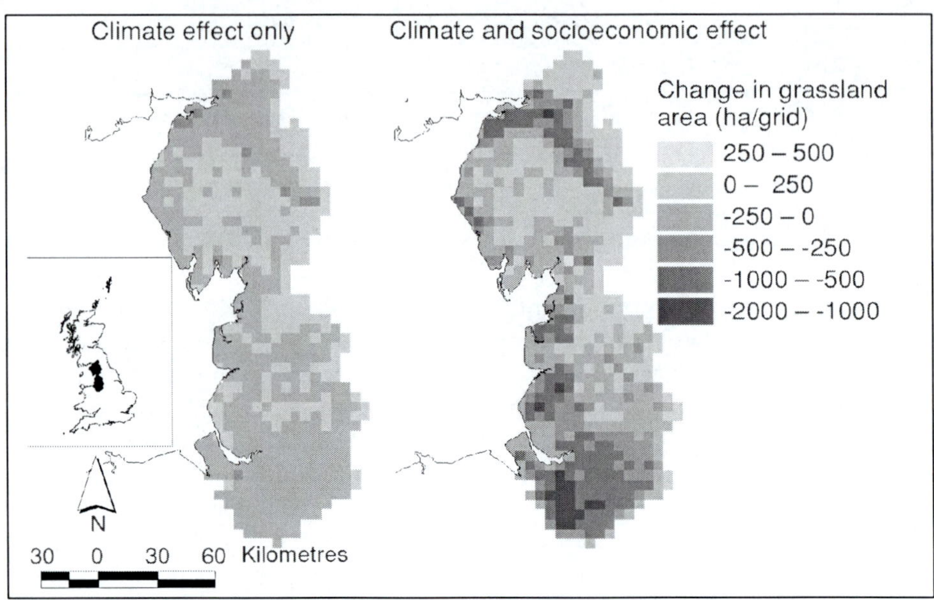

Note: 'High' scenario from HadCM2 using 1 per cent p.a. increase in GHGs, scaled to the IS92a emissions scenario and a high climate sensitivity of 4.5°C.

Figure 3.2 *Example of the changes in the area of managed grassland in north-west England under a 2050s High climate scenario, without and with socioeconomic change*

assessing changes in future flood frequency was subsequently developed further for the national Foresight flooding study (Foresight, 2004).

- Agricultural systems are vulnerable to change associated with changing profitability owing to socioeconomic and policy change. Expansion of the areas where arable crops are viable due to a warmer climate will put pressure on livestock systems. Periods of low prices for grass-based products, combined with quality-of-life considerations, will thus inevitably cause a gradual change from grass to arable in the north-west (Figure 3.2).
- Species (and habitats) vulnerable to climate change and to changes in agricultural practices associated with socioeconomic change were identified (Figure 3.3). The SPECIES model developed in RegIS for identifying vulnerable species on the basis of their bioclimatic envelope has been used in further stakeholder-funded projects (e.g. MONARCH).
- Catchments vulnerable to reducing low flows and water availability were identified, although the vulnerability of the water supply system will depend on future water allocation policy, regional population trends and implementation of demand- and supply-side adaptation.

Methods and scales

In simple terms, success for vulnerability assessments can be understood as the ability to facilitate adaptation and justify climate change mitigation efforts. This

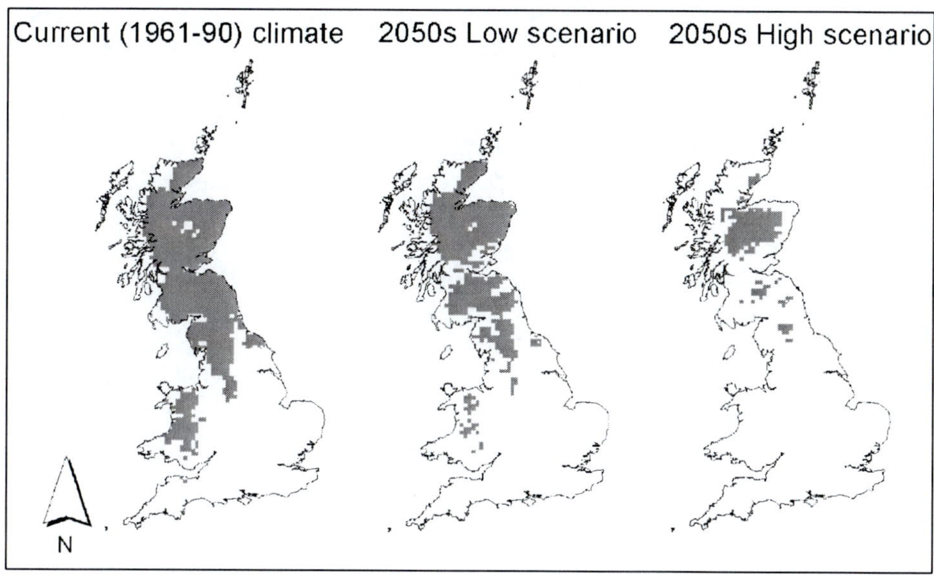

Note: 'Low' scenario = 0.5 per cent p.a. increase in GHGs scaled to the IS92d emissions scenario and a low climate sensitivity of 1.5°C; 'High' scenario = as in Figure 3.2.

Figure 3.3 *The area of bioclimatic suitability for* Geranium sylvaticum *(shown in grey) shows that it is sensitive to climate change, but will it become even more vulnerable due to socioeconomic-induced changes to its managed grassland habitat?*

depends, among other factors, on assessments being scientifically valid, understood and deemed valid by stakeholders at different levels, as well as being relevant to existing decision-making frameworks at different scales. Anecdotal feedback from stakeholders in the UK and Norway indicates that there is still some way to go until these criteria are fulfilled. This section discusses the methods used in vulnerability assessments in this light.

Norway

The late attention to research on vulnerability and stakeholder involvement in Norway compared to the UK may at least partly be ascribed to a perception of national resilience to climate variability (O'Brien et al, 2004; 2006). Indeed, Norway scores high on indicators for adaptive capacity such as economic resources, technology, information and skills, infrastructure, institutions and equity (Smit et al, 2001). However, the situation changes as scale is taken into account. Synthesizing and framing studies of climate change impacts in Norway in the context of vulnerability, O'Brien et al (2004) argue that vulnerability becomes more evident as one moves from the national to regional to local scales, where changes in snow cover, rainfall intensities and wind frequency may have significant impacts. Recent climate-related hazards such as storms and floods have resulted in extensive damages at the local level, leading to institutional changes to planning guidelines, such as regulations for building in hazard-prone areas (Næss et al, 2005). They have also led to increased awareness of changes in patterns of vulnerability: for example, most of the damages caused by a severe hurricane in western Norway in 1992 would not have occurred if buildings had been constructed according to existing building codes and regulations (National Office of Building Technology and Administration, 1993, cited by Lisø et al, 2003). Lisø et al (2003) suggest that people's concern for climate risks have been reduced due to factors such as well-developed insurance schemes, increased land pressure, increased private wealth and loss of traditional knowledge.

The recognition of the importance of scale has prompted further research into indicators for vulnerability at the local level, which incorporate both scientific validity and relevance to a local policy context. Aall and Norland (2004) argue that the vulnerability mapping developed by O'Brien et al (2003) needs to be complemented by analyses of what vulnerability means in a local context. The authors propose a stepwise approach to assessing vulnerability by combining nationally available indicators with indicators tailored to a local context. Ultimately, the goal would be to make assessments more relevant to current decision-making processes and to give feedback to regional and national levels of governance. A national mapping exercise could be used to select geographic areas for further research, while local analyses would involve assessing vulnerability within a municipality, that is, more detailed than the unit of the analysis for O'Brien et al (2003).

Following this, a key outstanding challenge in Norway is to develop assessment methods and indicators that reflect local realities while at the same time being applicable for the whole country (O'Brien et al, 2003; Aall and Norland, 2004; Næss et al, 2006). Considerable climatic and land-use differences throughout the country make this a daunting task. For example, while the timing of the first autumn frost can be represented based on minimum temperatures in September for much of southern Norway, this indicator is meaningless in northern Norway, where the first frost occurs much earlier. In some cases, important factors influencing vulnerability cannot easily be captured by climate-related indicators. For example, for the agricultural sector, factors such as exposure of soils throughout the year and changes in production patterns may be as important as changes in temperature and precipitation. Less explored, yet potentially important, are discrepancies between assessments by researchers and factors of most concern for various stakeholders in a given community, as perceptions and local interpretations of vulnerability are likely to differ across and within municipalities.

UK

The credibility of the RegIS assessment was underpinned by a suite of highly regarded public-domain data sets and tools provided by the UKCIP. The approach of UKCIP has been to place emphasis on providing the tools and defining the methodologies which in themselves provide the basis from which organizations should be able to reach their own conclusions or decisions to carry out assessments:

- *Climate change scenarios.* The UKCIP02 scenarios (Hulme et al, 2002) present monthly climate data for four possible future climates, based on differing levels of GHG emissions. The scenarios are based upon the 50km HadRCM, and have been downscaled to 10km resolution. The UKCIP02 scenarios supersede the UKCIP98 scenarios (Hulme and Jenkins, 1998) which provided period mean data at 10km resolution based on HadCM2.
- *Socioeconomic scenarios.* A social/economic framework (UKCIP, 2001) has been developed considering four potential futures depending upon future trajectories of social and governance values.

The approach taken in RegIS was in keeping with the contention that a regional, as opposed to a national, focus is of more relevance to stakeholders. In a regional study, particularly one in which contrasting regions are being studied, international-scale (Nakicenovic and Swart, 2000) and national-scale (UKCIP, 2001) socioeconomic scenarios cannot be used directly, but have to be modified such that they discriminate between and within regions. The use of regional quantified socioeconomic scenarios was therefore dictated by the needs of the models and the scale of assessment, despite the risk that the development of local socioeconomic determinants of particular impacts might be seen as a highly complex and indefensibly arbitrary exercise (Parson et al, 2003). However, RegIS has demonstrated that the continual effort of stakeholder engagement can render sufficient credibility to the resulting scenarios to provide far more defensible results than implicitly or explicitly assuming that the present socioeconomic conditions will continue unchanged.

The modelling scale was chosen to balance the detailed spatial resolution desired by stakeholders against the data and model run-time constraints that result from an integrated, multi-sectoral modelling approach. A 5km × 5km grid was chosen for both data input and model output, except for the hydrological modelling, where catchments and water resource units were also used. This scale ensured that stakeholders were presented with information that was of sufficient detail for use in regional decision support, while limiting misuse or over-interpretation of model results at very local scales (Holman et al, 2005a). Nevertheless there was significant demand for finer resolution local information from stakeholders, many of whom are operating (or have responsibility for implementation) at the local level (Shackley and Deanwood, 2002).

Although socioeconomic scenarios are only illustrative and deliberately intended to demonstrate the potential for divergent futures and associated changes, the necessarily precise (given the need for quantification) nature of the downscaled scenarios means they are contentious and inevitably subject to some disagreement. The level of spatial detail portrayed can render them, in the eyes of some stakeholders, as unacceptable predictions. For example, one scenario for East Anglia contained significant urban development along the scenically attractive North Norfolk coast due to a desire within the affluent storyline for second homes. However, it was considered by a number of stakeholders that this would not be allowed to happen under any circumstances. If the 'same' scenario (in terms of overall numbers of new homes within the region) had been shown at a lower spatial resolution, such strong opposition is less likely to have emerged.

Application of results and barriers to adaptation

Norway

The Norwegian climate policy is set out in Government White Papers 54 (MoE, 2001) and 15 (MoE, 2002). Many of the references to vulnerability and adaptation in these documents relate to supporting vulnerable regions and countries to tackle climate change. For Norway, the main emphasis is on the link between adaptation and civil protection. This link is also highlighted in Government White Paper 39, 2003–2004 (Ministry of Justice and the Police (MoJP), 2004). In practice, attention to adaptation has remained low, however, with little consideration within government institutions (Aall and Groven, 2003). Attention to adaptation has been notably absent at the regional and local level, where climate change continues to be framed mainly as a mitigation issue.

At the same time, an increasing number of sector agencies have over the last few years taken up adaptation as a topic of concern, including water resource management, the building sector, the public road administration, national civil protection and emergency planning, and municipal planning, and some municipalities have made efforts to consider adaptation in their plans (e.g. Norwegian Water Resources and Energy Directorate (NVE), 2003; Lisø et al, 2003; Steen, 2003; Næss et al, 2005). The above still remain fragmented examples, however, typically relating to geographic areas, government agencies and economic sectors exposed to recent climate-induced events such as floods and storms.

The MoE organized a seminar for central government ministries and agencies in August 2005. A parliamentary bill about a year later (MoE, 2006) referred to efforts by the Ministry to prepare for a national strategy for adaptation in Norway, linked to civil protection and in close cooperation with the MoJP, which is still (March 2007) in the planning stages. Thus, compared to the UK and a number of other European countries, Norway is late in setting up a government strategy or body to coordinate efforts on adaptation to climate change. O'Brien et al (2006) argue that this lack of national leadership may signify a case of complacency towards climate change, shaped by a notion that, as a wealthy country, Norway is robust and can easily tackle climate change. This echoes recent experiences within other areas, notably Local Agenda 21, where municipalities have complained of a lack of national facilitation of local initiatives and for being left to their own devices (Lindseth, 2003).

At the local level, recent studies suggest that institutional set-up and local power relations are key factors for determining the extent to which vulnerability assessments may be integrated in decision-making processes. For example, while there have been changes in national-level regulations to prevent natural hazard damages based on floods and storms over the last decade, there has been a reduction in local-level institutional capacity on environmental issues, and there are few institutional incentives for proactive measures at the local level (Aall and Groven, 2003; Næss et al, 2005). Among others, generous compensation schemes for natural hazards damages have contributed to a common perception among local actors that the national government will intervene and cover climate-related damages.

Another challenge is communication with stakeholders at different levels, which so far has been more or less absent in Norwegian climate-impact studies. The RegClim project had no clear mandate or mechanism for communicating climate scenario information to various potential users, beyond making downscaled climate change scenarios available for further studies and assessments by impact researchers. Studies focusing on sectors, ecosystems and regions have likewise up to now largely been undertaken without consultation with decision makers at regional or local levels.[2] As of 2007, several new studies are under way that seek active engagement with decision makers. The needs and challenges of such stakeholder dialogue were highlighted by O'Brien et al (2003) through focus group discussions in two municipalities. The municipalities (Voss and Oppdal) had been identified by the maps as having high vulnerability to climate change. The discussions showed that several of the indicators needed adjustment to a local setting. Moreover, they highlighted the challenge of communicating climate scenarios, initially perceived by participants as the most likely outcome, rather than one possible outcome based on one climate scenario. They also demonstrated that vulnerability mapping cannot be seen isolated from its social connotations. Some participants protested against their municipality being labelled as vulnerable, arguing that their area was robust and that there were other, more important, concerns for them than climate change. Beyond this, the above also highlight the present disconnect between the available information and decision-making processes at various levels. Arguably, most information on vulnerability to climate change in Norway is supply-based, in the sense that it has reflected researchers' interests and what they perceive to be important for various users more than the same users' information needs and demands.

UK

In the RegIS stakeholder workshops and interviews, the reality of climate change was rarely questioned. This suggests that a consensus has emerged among a wide range of local and regional UK environmental and resource policy makers and stakeholders that climate change has been sufficiently demonstrated (Shackley and Deanwood, 2002) and that credible data sets and tools have been developed on which to base assessments.

Despite this suite of expanding data sets and methodologies, the long timescales involved with climate change make it difficult to identify instances whereby the findings of individual studies have been materially used by UK stakeholders to change practice or justify expenditure. Nevertheless, the combined results of the many studies on the potential impacts of, and adaptation to, climate change are being mainstreamed into policy and practice in a range of arenas:

- Planning guidance in England, Wales and Scotland explicitly states that the planning system should act so as not to increase the vulnerability of developments to climate change: 'The planning system should take the possible impacts of climate change, for example greater rainfall and increased risk of flooding, into account when taking decisions on the location of new development and other changes in land use' (Scotland) and '... should consider their regions' vulnerability to climate change ...' (England). A Planning Policy Statement (PPS) on 'Planning and Climate Change', which sets out how planning should help to shape places with lower carbon emissions and resilience to climate change, was published in December 2007.

- Climate change impacts on water resources are taken into account in the rolling 25-year Water Resource Planning process which the water industry in England and Wales has to undertake for the Environment Agency.
- Biodiversity-modelling results have contributed to the debate on the challenges posed to nature conservation policy by climate change acting upon the location of species and habitats (Hossell et al, 2000).
- An allowance for sea-level rise is included within guidance for the planning and design of coastal flood defence infrastructure (Ministry of Agriculture, Fisheries and Food (MAFF) 1999; Defra, 2006).
- The findings of UKCIP studies are used by Defra, the government's lead department on climate change, to inform policy.

It is apparent that the greatest success is in those sectors (planning, water supply and flood defence) that have existing institutional and decision-making frameworks with long time horizons. Sectors with shorter planning horizons are less inclined to consider climate change. Nevertheless the provision by UKCIP of a decision-making framework for adaptation (Willows and Connell, 2003) and a costing methodology (Metroeconomica, 2004) to provide a method for valuing the impacts of climate change, and for comparing these to the costs of adaptation, may increase the adoption of win–win or 'no regrets' adaptation measures.

Within the RegIS IA, the climate and socioeconomic scenarios (SESs) were treated as formally independent, so that the SESs do not take any account of climate change. This differs from the co-evolutionary approach (e.g. Lorenzoni et al, 2000a) in which there are interactions between climate change and socioeconomic change, which may be more realistic of social systems (Shackley and Deanwood, 2003). The use of non-climate change socioeconomic scenarios is more conceptually straightforward to stakeholders, in that the assumptions underpinning the description and quantification of each storyline are explicit. The model results can be viewed, therefore, in light of these assumptions. Transparency of the RegIS outputs was further increased as the scenarios were based not only on integrated (internally consistent) visions of the future (where the emissions, climate and socioeconomic scenarios were all consistent) but also because of the disaggregation of the resulting impacts into their constituent climate and socioeconomic components. Compared to modelling studies using a 'co-evolutionary' scenario approach, this has allowed a comparison of the relative sensitivity of the key impacts to variation in climate and socioeconomic conditions, and to interactions between them (as recommended by Parson et al, 2003).

Table 3.3 *Overview of vulnerability assessments: Norway and the UK*

Issue	Norway	UK
Key research areas	– National vulnerability maps – Local vulnerability indicators – Sector studies	– Regional vulnerability assessments – Local case studies
Involvement of stakeholders	Low	High
Funders	National Government/ Research Council	Stakeholders/National Government
Main target group(s)	Researchers	Stakeholders
Key geographical focus	National and local	National, regional and local
Scenarios	Climate change only	Climate ± non-climate (socioeconomic) change
Application of results and barriers to adaptation	– So far little interaction with stakeholders – Need to resolve gap between local and national levels	– Insufficient technical detail for implementation – Highlighted importance of future non-climate change

Lessons learned

The following two key lessons can be identified from the UK and Norwegian experiences (summarized in Table 3.3) which have wider applicability to inform future assessments.

First, there is the need to resolve the current methodological differences between sectoral, regional and ecosystem-based studies aiming to assess impacts of climate change and those seeking to address societal vulnerability to climate change as one of many processes of change. Most of the research to date has been aimed at mapping potential impacts and then identifying possible adaptation options, with little focus on adaptation as a process in either country. Consideration of adaptation typically appears as an afterthought with little analysis of how it might take place. While there is clearly no right or wrong approach, O'Brien et al (2006) argue that the dominance of the former leads to an implicit assumption that adaptation is inevitable as soon as climate change is deemed 'real'. Hence, studies and assessments have, explicitly or implicitly, been seen as *products* that would be able directly to assist stakeholders in assessing vulnerability and planning adaptation to climate change. This runs contrary to many studies highlighting that adaptation is not inevitable or 'automatic', that communication is key to making studies relevant and operational, and that studies need to understand and relate to decision-making processes at various levels (Lorenzoni et al, 2000a, b; Berkhout et al, 2002; O'Brien et al, 2006). O'Brien et al (2004) and other authors argue that comprehensive vulnerability assessments are a necessary first step in a situation with great uncertainty and little predictive capacity at the local level. In complex integrated systems, the complexity should be within the integration and cross-sectoral linkages, rather than in the models (Holman et al, 2005a). Hence, vulnerability assessments are as much a process as a product.

This leads to a *second* and related issue, namely managing the interface between the available climate-impact information provided by the scientific community and the needs and demands of those from the stakeholder community who might ultimately use it. This involves the need to address the questions of why vulnerability assessments are undertaken, who are the providers of different types of information and who the users are. Næss et al (2006) argue that vulnerability assessments risk being marginalized if they are not integrated in a decision-making context. Experiences show that stakeholder contact from an early stage of assessments is key for developing locally relevant and valid indicators.

The experiences of stakeholder engagement from the two countries are very different. So far, research in Norway has been initiated and implemented with little involvement of stakeholders, and few efforts have been made to test the real-world validity and relevance with stakeholders. In effect, one could argue that studies in Norway have served the need to assess the seriousness of the climate change issue, rather than to assess what is needed to enable stakeholders to make necessary adjustments and adaptations. In contrast, regional studies in the UK have been partly or wholly stakeholder-led, on the premise that climate-impacts research driven by stakeholders will provide information that meets their needs and helps them to plan how to adapt (McKenzie-Hedger et al, 2000). Many of these studies have been facilitated by UKCIP, an organization whose remit is to provide information on climate change and help stakeholders to identify the relevant implications. UKCIP does not commission research, but rather facilitates the stakeholders or partners to commission the research and determine the research agenda, ensuring that the end products of the research meet their needs.

Identification of, and engagement with, the target stakeholder audience(s) at the outset is essential for designing a successful stakeholder-focused study, as the appropriate scale of indicators or assessment approaches is a function of the stakeholder audience. Stakeholders who have a very local perspective or requirement for information will inevitably not be satisfied with regional indicators or assessment methods, but these may be appropriate for policy-oriented stakeholders. For example, the need for, and scope of, RegIS were dictated by earlier stakeholder analysis (Science and Policy Associates and ESYS, 1996), ensuring that the project was designed to deliver identified needs. The approaches taken were not dictated by the tools available to the research team, but rather the research team was chosen to deliver the desired tools. As the complexity of the representation of the natural and human systems within such studies increases, it becomes more difficult for the results to be transparent, and therefore credible, to stakeholders. Although there are many benefits of integrating models to describe complex systems, in that a much wider range of processes and process interactions can be considered, it can become difficult to identify a link between cause and effect as there may be several interacting processes contributing to the result.

Integrated Assessment approaches are needed that allow (multiple) cause and effect relationships to be identified, and the ensuing results explained. This will inevitably require a modelling system that allows the user to iteratively interact with, and explore, the system (Holman et al, 2005a) such as the Regional Impact Simulator (Holman et al, 2008).

Finally, a successful vulnerability assessment needs to identify the target audience's information requirements in order to produce stakeholder-relevant literature. For example, the contractual reporting requirement for the RegIS study was a detailed scientific report, but this was unacceptable to many stakeholders who wanted a short, easily digestible summary highlighting the main findings. The compromise was a colourful, 20-page plain English summary report (Holman et al, 2002). We may not like to admit it, but the success of a scientific vulnerability assessment in the eyes of stakeholders may depend as much on the appropriateness of the communication techniques employed as on the quality of the science.

Conclusions

It is apparent that, since their first reports in 1991, the approaches taken in Norway and the UK have diverged, but most fundamentally with regard to stakeholder engagement. In Norway, the majority of studies on vulnerability, impacts and adaptation have up to now arguably been undertaken by, and for, the research community, with little participation outside the research community. Unlike the UK, no government department, organization or research programme has been given the specific mandate for communication with end-users, and there is as yet no comprehensive strategy for integrating climate change concerns within government departments at different levels. Challenges remain both in terms of how and for what purpose the information is generated, and how it may be used by different stakeholders.

In contrast in the UK, a subsequent national overview report has been augmented by regional scoping studies and national sectoral assessments in which stakeholder participation is a continual key component. Coordinated stakeholder-led research has allowed the issue cycle to develop further in the UK and enabled stakeholders and government to develop a focused research agenda. As a result, consensus has emerged among a wide range of environmental and resource policy makers and stakeholders that climate change and its impacts have been sufficiently demonstrated, allowing it to be mainstreamed into policy and practice in a range of arenas.

It is therefore apparent that identification of, engagement with, and communication strategies for, the target stakeholder audience(s) are essential for designing a successful stakeholder-focused research agenda.

Acknowledgements

The contributions of the RegIS team, in particular Peter Loveland, Eric Audsley, Paula Harrison, Robert Nicholls, Simon Shackley, Pam Berry, Mark Rounsevell and Robert Wood are gratefully acknowledged. For the information on Norway, the authors would like to thank Karen O'Brien for extensive comments and data, and the contributions from the vulnerability mapping team, including Guro Aandahl, Bård Romstad, Heather Tompkins and Anders Underthun. The sections on Norway have benefited greatly from the author's collaboration with Ingrid Thorsen Norland and William M. Lafferty at ProSus, University of Oslo, and Carlo Aall at the Western Norway Research Institute, Sogndal.

Notes

1 The RegClim project closed at the end of 2006, but most of its activities are to be continued in the new NorClim project (Grønås et al, 2007).

2 See, for example, the project portfolio of the NORKLIMA programme funded by the Norwegian Research Council (The Research Council of Norway, 2006).

References

Aall, C. and Groven, K. (2003) 'Institutional response to climate change: Review of how four institutional systems can contribute in efforts for societal adaptation to climate change', in Norwegian, English summary, VF Report 3/03, Western Norway Research Institute, Sogndal

Aall, C. and Norland, I. T. (2004) 'Indicators for assessing local climate vulnerability' (Indikatorer for vurdering av lokal klimasårbarhet), in Norwegian, Report 2/04, ProSus, University of Oslo, Oslo

ACIA (2004) *Arctic Climate Change Impact Assessment: Scientific Report*, Cambridge University Press, http://amap.no/acia/

Berkhout, F., Hertin, J. and Jordan, A. (2002) 'Socio-economic futures in climate change impact assessment: Using scenarios as "learning machines"', *Global Environmental Change*, vol 12(2), pp83–95

Dalen, L. S., Johnsen, O. and Ogner G. (2001) 'CO_2 enrichment and development of freezing tolerance in Norway spruce', *Physiologia Plantarum*, vol 113(4), pp533–540.

Defra (Department for Environment, Food and Rural Affairs) (2006) 'Supplementary note to operating authorities: Climate change impacts', supplement to *Flood and Coastal Defence Appraisal Guidance FCDPAG3 Economic Appraisal*, www.defra.gov.uk/environ/fcd/pubs/pagn/climatechangeupdate.pdf

Foresight (2004) *Future Flooding: Executive Summary*, Office of Science and Technology, London; also at www.foresight.gov.uk

Grønås, S., Iversen, T. and Martinsen, E. (2007) 'Ten years of research on Norway's climate' (Ti år med forskning på Norges klima), in Norwegian, *Cicerone*, vol 1/2007, pp24–26

Harrison, P. A., Berry, P. M. and Dawson, T. P. (eds) (2001) *Climate Change and Nature Conservation in Britain and Ireland: Modelling Natural Resource Responses to Climate*

Change (the MONARCH project), UKCIP Technical Report, Oxford, www.ukcip.org.uk

Hill, J. K. and Hodkinson, I. D. (1995) 'Effects of temperature on phenological synchrony and altitudinal distribution of jumping plant lice (Hemiptera, psylloidea) on dwarf willow (*Salix lapponum*) in Norway', *Ecological Entomology*, vol 20(3), pp237–244

Holman, I. P., Loveland, P. J., Nicholls, R. J., Shackley, S., Berry, P. M., Rounsevell, M. D. A., Audsley, E., Harrison, P. A. and Wood, R. (2002) *RegIS – Regional Climate Change Impact Response Studies in East Anglia and North West England*, Defra, London, 20pp

Holman, I. P., Rounsevell, M. D. A., Shackley, S., Harrison, P. A., Nicholls, R. J., Berry, P. M. and Audsley, E. (2005a) 'A regional, multi-sectoral and integrated assessment of the impacts of climate and socio-economic change in the UK: Part I. Methodology', *Climatic Change*, vol 71, pp9–41

Holman, I. P., Nicholls, R. J., Berry, P. M., Harrison, P. A., Audsley, E., Shackley, S. and Rounsevell, M. D. A. (2005b) 'A regional, multi-sectoral and integrated assessment of the impacts of climate and socio-economic change in the UK: Part II. Results, *Climatic Change*, vol 71, pp43–73

Holman, I. P., Rounsevell, M. D. A., Cojacaru, G., Shackley, S., McLachlan, C., Audsley, E., Berry, P. M., Fontaine, C., Harrison, P. A., Henriques, C., Mokrech, M., Nicholls, R. J., Pearn, K. R. and Richards, J. A. (2008) 'The concepts and development of a participatory regional integrated assessment tool', *Climatic Change*, vol 90(1–2), pp5–30

Hossell, J. E., Briggs, B. and Hepburn, I. R. (2000) *Climate Change and UK Nature Conservation: A Review of the Impact of Climate Change on UK Species and Habitat Conservation Policy*, Defra, London

Hulme, M. and Jenkins, G. J. (1998) *Climate Change Scenarios for the United Kingdom: Scientific Report*, UK Climate Impacts Programme Technical Report No. 1, Climatic Research Unit, Norwich, p80

Hulme, M., Jenkins, G. J., Lu, X., Turnpenny, J. R., Mitchell, T. D., Jones, R. G., Lowe, J., Murphy, J. M., Hassell, D., Boorman, P., McDonald, R. and Hill, S. (2002) *Climate Change Scenarios for the United Kingdom: The UKCIP02 Scientific Report*, Tyndall Centre for Climate Change Research, School of Environmental Sciences, University of East Anglia, Norwich, p120

Lindseth, G. (2003) *Addressing Climate Adaptation and Mitigation at the Local and Regional Level: Lessons for Norway*, ProSus rapport no. 3/03, Program for Research and Documentation for a Sustainable Society, University of Oslo www.prosus.uio.no/publikasjoner/Rapporter/2003-3/r3-03.pdf

Lisø, K. R., Aandahl, G., Eriksen, S. and Alfsen, K. H. (2003) 'Preparing for climate change impacts in Norway's built environment', *Building Research and Information*, vol 31(3–4), pp200–209

Lorenzoni, I., Jordan, A., Hulme, M., Kerry Turner, R. and O'Riordan, T. (2000a) 'A co-evolutionary approach to climate change impact assessment: Part I. Integrating socio-economic and climate change scenarios', *Global Environmental Change*, vol 10(1), pp57–68

Lorenzoni, I., Jordan, A., O'Riordan, T., Kerry Turner, R. and Hulme, M. (2000b) 'A co-evolutionary approach to climate change impact assessment: Part II. A scenario-based case study in East Anglia (UK)', *Global Environmental Change*, vol 10(2), pp145–155

MAFF (Ministry of Agriculture, Fisheries and Food) (1999) *Flood and Coastal Defence Project Appraisal Guidance*, MAFF Flood and Coastal Defence Division, London

McKenzie-Hedger, M., Gawith, M., Brown, I., Connell, R. and Downing, T. (eds) (2000) *Climate Change: Assessing the Impacts – Identifying Responses. The First Three Years of the UK Climate Impacts Programme*, UKCIP and DETR, Oxford

Metroeconomica (2004) 'Costing the impacts of climate change in the UK: Overview of Guidelines', UKCIP Technical Report, UKCIP, Oxford

MoE (Ministry of the Environment) (1991) 'The Greenhouse effect, impacts and measures' (Drivhuseffekten, virkninger og tiltak), Report from an interdepartmental working group (in Norwegian), Ministry of the Environment, Oslo.

MoE (2001) 'Norwegian Climate Policy' (Norsk klimapolitikk), White Paper 54 (2000–2001) (in Norwegian), Ministry of the Environment, Oslo

MoE (2002) 'Amendment to White Paper 54 (2000–2001), Norwegian Climate Policy' (Tilleggsmelding til St.meld. nr. 54 (2000–2001) Norsk klimapolitikk), White Paper 15 (2001–2002) (in Norwegian), Ministry of the Environment, Oslo

MoE (2006) Parliamentary Bill 1 (2006–2007) (Stortingsproposisjon nr. 1 (2006–2007) for budsjettåret 2007) (in Norwegian), Ministry of the Environment, Oslo

MoJP (Ministry of Justice and the Police) (2004) 'Civil Protection and Civil-Military Cooperation' (Samfunnssikkerhet og sivilt-militært samarbeid), White Paper 39 (2003–2004) (in Norwegian), Ministry of Justice and the Police, Oslo

Nakicenovic, N. and Swart, R. (eds) (2000) *Special Report on Emissions Scenarios. A Special Report of Working Group III of the Intergovernmental Panel on Climate Change*, Intergovernmental Panel on Climate Change, Cambridge University Press, Cambridge

Næss, L. O., Bang, G., Eriksen, S. and Vevatne, J. (2005) 'Institutional adaptation to climate change: Flood responses at the municipal level in Norway', *Global Environmental Change*, vol 15(2), pp125–138

Næss, L. O., Norland, I. T., Lafferty, W. and Aall, C. (2006) 'Data and processes linking vulnerability assessment to adaptation decision-making on climate change in Norway', *Global Environmental Change*, vol 16(2), pp221–233

NVE (2003) 'The "water country" in 2050: Water, nature and society in a changed climate' (Vannlandet i 2050: Vann, natur og samfunn i et endret klima), in Norwegian, Norwegian Water Resources and Energy Directorate, Oslo, www.nve.no/FileArchive/224/Vannlandet-M.pdf

O'Brien, K. L., Aandahl, G., Orderud, G. I. and Sæther, B. (2003) 'Vulnerability assessment: A starting point for dialogue' (Sårbarhetskartlegging – et utgangspunkt for klimadialog), in Norwegian, *Plan*, vol 5 pp12–17

O'Brien, K., Sygna, L. and Haugen, J. E. (2004) 'Vulnerable or resilient? A multi-scale assessment of climate impacts and vulnerability in Norway', *Climatic Change*, vol 64(1–2), pp193–225

O'Brien, K., Eriksen, S., Sygna, L. and Næss, L. O. (2006) 'Questioning complacency: Climate change impacts, vulnerability, and adaptation in Norway', *Ambio*, vol 35(2), pp50–56

Parson, E. A., Corell, R. W., Barron, E. J., Burkett, V., Janetos, A., Joyce, L., Karl, T. R., MacCracken, M. C., Melillo, J., Morgan, M. G., Schimel, D. S. and Wilbanks, T. (2003) 'Understanding climatic impacts, vulnerabilities, and adaptation in the United States: Building a capacity for assessment', *Climatic Change*, vol 57, pp9–42

Science and Policy Associates Inc and ESYS (1996) 'Proposal for a UK integrated climate change impacts assessment', report prepared for the Department of the Environment and the Environment Agency, Department of the Environment, London

Shackley, S. and Deanwood, R. (2002) 'Stakeholder perceptions of climate change impacts at regional scale: Implications for the effectiveness of regional and local responses', *Journal of Environmental Planning and Management*, vol 45(3), pp381–402

Shackley, S. and Deanwood, R. (2003) 'Constructing social futures for climate change impacts and response studies: Building qualitative and quantitative scenarios with the participation of stakeholders', *Climate Research*, vol 24(1), pp71–90

Smit, B., Pilifosova, O., Burton, I., Challenger, B., Huq, S., Klein, R. J. T., Yohe, G., Adger, N., Downing, T., Harvey, E., Kane, S., Parry, M., Skinner, M., Smith, J. and Wandel, J. (2001) 'Adaptation to climate change in the context of sustainable development and equity', in McCarthy, J. J., Canziani, O. F., Leary, N. A., Dokken, D. J. and White, K. S. (eds) *Climate Change 2001: Impacts, Adaptation, and Vulnerability. Contribution of Working Group II to the Third Assessment Report of the Intergovernmental Panel on Climate Change*, Cambridge University Press, Cambridge

Steen, R. (2003) 'Climate change: Is the emergency management in place?' (Klimaendringer – er beredskapen på plass?), in Norwegian, *Plan*, vol 5, pp18–23

Sygna, L., Eriksen, S., O'Brien, K. and Næss, L. O. (2004) 'Climate change in Norway: Analysis of economic and social impacts and adaptations', Report 2004, p12, CICERO, Oslo

The Research Council of Norway (2006) *Project Catalogue 2006, NORKLIMA – Climate Change and Impacts in Norway. Programme Period 2004–2013*, The Research Council of Norway, Division for Strategic Priorities, Oslo, http://program.forskningsradet.no/norklima/

UKCCIRG (United Kingdom Climate Change Impacts Review Group) (1996) *Review of the Potential Effects of Climate Change in the United Kingdom*, HMSO, London

UKCIP (United Kingdom Climate Impacts Programme) (2001) *Socio-economic Scenarios for Climate Change Impacts Assessment: A Guide to Their Use in the UK Climate Impacts Programme*, UKCIP, Oxford

Willows, R. I. and Connell, R. K. (eds) (2003) 'Climate adaptation: Risk, uncertainty and decision-making', UKCIP technical report, UKCIP, Oxford

Wright, R. F. (1998) 'Effect of increased CO_2 and temperature on runoff chemistry at a forested catchment in southern Norway' (CLIMEX project), in *Ecosystems*, vol 1(2) (1998) No 1, pp 216–225, ISSN 1435-0629

Chapter 4

Vulnerability Assessments in the Developing World: Mozambique and South Africa

Siri Eriksen, Coleen Vogel, Gina Ziervogel, Franziska Steinbruch and Florence Nazare

Introduction

There has been an increasing number of policy-driven vulnerability assessments in southern Africa over the past five years (see for example www.wahenga.net and www.sarpn.org.za). As pointed out by Patt et al (this volume, Chapter 1), vulnerability assessments encompass a very diverse set of purposes and conceptual and methodological approaches. Stakeholders, whose needs to which assessments are designed to respond, are often concerned with very specific development issues, sectors or institutional purposes. It has been suggested, however, that vulnerability, that is, the inability of groups or individuals to secure well-being in the face of climatic stress, is best understood in terms of the totality of interacting environmental, social, economic and political stressors rather than through a focus limited to single stressors (Leichenko and O'Brien, 2001). Food insecurity in southern Africa is, for example, driven not only by failing food production, but also by threats to livelihoods derived from multiple non-agricultural sources, such as social networks, employment, forest products, trade and migration (Scoones et al, 1996; Ellis, 2003; O'Brien and Vogel, 2003; Wiggins, 2005). How does one ensure that assessments driven by diverse and sometimes relatively isolated development concerns generate sound understanding of vulnerability, including the interaction between multiple dimensions of vulnerability? Such understanding is critical to formulating holistic, rather than piecemeal, adaptation measures that may effectively address the causes of vulnerability.

In this chapter, we investigate the implications of development concerns and institutional setting for the purpose and focus of different vulnerability assessments. Southern Africa provides a particularly useful case study in which to investigate these issues. First, a relatively large number of vulnerability studies, driven by diverse policy concerns, have been carried out in this region (Southern African Regional Poverty Network (SARPN), 2004; Food Insecurity and Vulnerability Information Mapping System (FIVIMS), 2005; Babugura, 2005; Gandure, 2005; Reid and Vogel, 2005; Eriksen and Silva, O'Brien et al , 2009; various Vulnerability Assessment Committee (VAC) activities). Place-based investigation of present-day vulnerability to a variety of stresses, the focus of many of these assessments, has been identified as important for the purpose of better understanding future vulnerability to longer-term changes (Vogel and Smith, 2002; Eriksen and Kelly, 2007). An examination of assessments undertaken in the policy and development arena in southern Africa may provide useful lessons to other developing regions as well as to industrialized countries that have comparatively little experience with such assessments.

Second, southern Africa provides a stark example of a situation where immediate development concerns are central in shaping both the vulnerability context and the institutional settings of vulnerability assessments. Global warming may potentially impact the southern African region by influencing rainfall through likely decreases, particularly in much of the winter rainfall region and western margins. Drier subtropical areas could also warm more than moister areas. Detailed assessments of the incidences of tropical cyclones are limited but some assessments show possible increased precipitation in east Africa extending into southern Africa under climate change (Hulme et al, 2001; Hewitson et al, 2005; Boko et al, 2007; Christensen and Hewitson, 2007). There are, however, other important potential stressors in the region that are often shouldered by the poor, including the unprotected economic liberalization of emerging local markets (such as for sugar, cashew and textile) and the spread of infectious diseases such as AIDS (Mozambique, Ministry of Planning and Finance/Eduardo Modlane University/International Food Policy Research Institute (MPF/UEM/IFPRI), 1998; National Directorate of Planning and Budget et al, 2004; O'Brien et al, 2009). Arndt (2003), for example, estimated an average reduction due to AIDS in per capita growth rates of between 0.3 per cent and 0.1 per cent (period 1997–2010) in Mozambique, with the most notable impacts expected to occur in the latter half of the period 2003–2010 (National Directorate of Planning and Budget et al, 2004).

We examine the diverse ways that vulnerability information is produced, understood and used in the southern African region. In the next section, we start by investigating how regional concerns regarding drought and food security have formed the framework for many assessment efforts. We then focus in more detail on two countries, Mozambique and South Africa. Key characteristics of vulnerability assessments, including their objectives, methods and data, are investigated for a total of four assessments, selecting assessments in which the authors have been involved and which represent the range of assessment types undertaken in the region.

Mozambique and South Africa have been chosen because they illustrate two very different development and institutional contexts in the region. Both, however, experience macro-structural influences on vulnerability, including changing policies and biophysical stresses, as well as various local factors that help to configure vulnerability, such as erosion of kinship networks (Drinkwater, 2003; SARPN, 2004). Mozambique is one of the poorest countries in Africa, and institutional frameworks have been focused on emergencies such as war, floods and droughts. In contrast, South Africa is the economic engine in the region. Social inequality remains large, however, with some rural populations being particularly exposed to food insecurity in areas of Limpopo Province, parts of KwaZulu-Natal, and parts of Western and Eastern Cape. Efforts to address these inequities and long-term vulnerability, rather than emergency responses, have played a large role in driving vulnerability assessments. Importantly, both Mozambique and South Africa illustrate governments supporting vulnerability assessments via legislation, policies and plans at both national and local levels as part of institutionalizing vulnerability and disaster risk management approaches (Selvester and Castro, 2003; Republic of South Africa, 2003; Drimie, 2005; Arlindo, 2006; Drimie and Ziervogel, 2006).

We then profile some of the policy implications that emerge from the different assessments. Lessons for how the reduction of vulnerability can best be addressed through improved vulnerability assessments are drawn out in the following section. We argue that the assessments illustrate a diversity of focus and scope. Multiple issues of development are an essential element of global change and the investigation of each of these dimensions is important in its own right, however. Rather than selecting one method or focus for a definitive vulnerability assessment methodology, therefore, we suggest that a variety of approaches is needed, even within a limited geographical area, requiring a diversity of data, both qualitative and quantitative. Close interaction across development sectors and between policy makers and various stakeholders (including the wider practitioner community) becomes critical in the assessment effort in order to generate adaptation measures that address vulnerability in a holistic manner (Vogel et al, 2007).

Evolution of vulnerability assessments in southern Africa

In this section, we first present regional vulnerability assessments, which have been an important influencing factor on national vulnerability assessments carried out in southern African countries. We then compare the context of vulnerability and institutional frameworks for assessments in Mozambique and South Africa. The social context of the two countries is described in Table 4.1.

Regional vulnerability assessments

The past few years have seen region-wide humanitarian crises triggered by

Table 4.1 *Profile of Mozambique and South Africa*

	Mozambique	*South Africa*
Total population in 2005	20.5 million	47.9 million
Urban population (% of total) in 2005	34.5	59.3
Life expectancy at birth (2000–2005)	42.8 years	50.8 years
Adult literacy rate (1995–2005)	38.7%	82.4%
GDP per capita (PPP US$) in 2005	1242	11,110
Population living below $1/day 1990–2005	36.2%	10.7%
Share of income/consumption by richest 10% (2002–2003)	39.4%	44.7% (in 2000)
HIV prevalence (% of ages 15–49) in 2005	12.5-20.0	16.8–20.7

Source: UNDP Human Development Statistics (2008) http://hdr.undp.org/statistics

climatic stressors in southern Africa. The poor rainfall and harvests in the early part of this decade heightened into a food and humanitarian crisis and threatened the lives of several million people in the countries of Malawi, Swaziland, Zambia, Mozambique, Lesotho and Zimbabwe (Wiggins, 2005). In July 2002, the UN issued a consolidated appeal for US$611 million to address the crisis (SARPN, 2004). There are fears that such regional crises may be further adversely impacted by climate change. The recent Intergovernmental Panel on Climate Change (IPCC) Fourth Assessment Report of 2007 suggests that observed drying in southern Africa is likely to continue under climate change, and heavy precipitation events may become more frequent (Christensen and Hewitson, 2007).

Such region-wide food crises have triggered the establishment by donor and humanitarian organizations of an increasing number of assessment systems aimed at monitoring food security and vulnerability, such as those carried out by the Food and Agriculture Organization of the UN (FAO), FEWS-NET (USAID-funded Famine Early Warning System Network), the World Food Programme (WFP) – Vulnerability Analysis and Mapping (VAM) and Save the Children (UK). Each have used different methods, ranging from agricultural production and climatic and satellite data, to market data, socioeconomic indicators and a household economy approach (Moseley and Logan, 2001; Marsland, 2004). This plethora of systems has led to a demand for a coordinated vulnerability assessment system using harmonized methodologies across the southern African region.

The crisis in the southern African region which was prompted by stresses associated with climate variability but also by weaknesses in regional governance, the influence of HIV and AIDS and the long-term decline in livelihood resulted in the initiation of a number of vulnerability assessments (Maunder and Wiggins, 2007). A multi-agency committee, called the Regional Vulnerability Assessment Committee (RVAC)[1] was tasked with developing coordinated regional mechanisms for vulnerability assessments and strengthening the capacity of member states to undertake and utilize vulnerability assessments in both emergency and non-emergency situations. The National Vulnerability Assessment Committees (NVACs) are responsible for undertaking the vulnerability assessments at the country level. These are under the leadership of national governments and involve government agencies, non-governmental organizations (NGOs) and international and humanitarian organizations. The assessments, the first starting in August 2002, include Lesotho, Malawi, Zambia and Zimbabwe as well as Mozambique. Coordinating overlapping assessments by different institutions and avoiding duplication of efforts has remained a challenge. Despite this and other problems, they have succeeded in providing information on food needs and security to relief organizations and governments. In several Southern Africa Development Community (SADC) countries, including Mozambique, these regularly updated regional assessments are a major source of information for national contingency planning.

A lesson that soon emerged, however, was that food insecurity and vulnerability associated in part with climatic variability, are also the result of longer-term societal and development challenges and cannot be addressed in a once-off and reactive manner when a crisis emerges (Tschirley et al, 2004). Throughout the region, there is a growing consensus to have vulnerability assessment information better linked with longer-term livelihood programmes that address related issues of poverty and food security planning. There has thus been a shift from an initial focus on a food crisis to the incorporation of a range of stresses that compromise livelihoods, such as poverty and HIV and AIDS (Drinkwater, 2003; Marsland, 2004).

Despite this widening of scope, in practice the tendency has been to use the information for justifying emergency measures and improving the targeting of food assistance. Initiatives beyond short-term relief have been rather limited (Mano et al, 2003; SARPN, 2004; Tschirley et al, 2004; Wiggins, 2005). The historic dichotomy between relief and longer-term development, as described in Christoplos et al (2001), still prevails in many instances.

The Mozambique case: Institutional responses to natural disasters, war and food insecurity

Civil war, floods and drought have fundamentally shaped the context of vulnerability as well as institutional responses in Mozambique (Hanlon, 1996; Christie and Hanlon, 2001). A series of floods in the late 1970s triggered the establishing of the Department for the Prevention and Combat of Natural Disasters (DPCCN) in 1980. The outbreak of civil war then changed the role of the DPCCN from relief to logistical operations of food aid for victims of the war. The end of the war in 1992 led to a shift in focus to short-term vulnerability to natural disasters. The DPCCN was drastically cut back in staff and infrastructure and in 1999 its functions were replaced by the National Institute of Disaster Management (INGC). The INGC became a platform for the coordination of emergency activities between ministries and among national and international agencies during food crises. Its influence on measures centres around advising on quantities of food and non-food aid for distribution in emergencies (Selvester and

Castro, 2003). The INGC has been restructured over the past couple of years to create a greater focus on longer-term development and now includes a directorate for development in semi-arid areas. In recognition that longer-term vulnerability needs to be reduced as part of poverty reduction strategies (PRSPs) and that natural disasters can aggravate poverty, the Plan for the Prevention and Mitigation of Natural Disasters (*Plano Director para Prevenção e Mitigação das Calamidades Naturais*, PDPMCN) includes many dryland development measures in addition to short-term emergency measures (Republic of Mozambique, 2007).

There has been increasing policy attention paid to climate-related disasters, but emergency management approaches continue to dominate responses. The effects of floods and cyclones in 2000, 2001 and 2007 in southern and central Mozambique were very severe. The floods in 2000, for example, caused considerable damage to property and infrastructure, and reduced Mozambique's annual growth rate from 8 per cent to 2 per cent (Washington et al, 2004). Policies triggered by these events, including the Law on Disaster Management, ratified in August 2003, and the National Strategic Long-term Plan of the INGC, approved in 2004, primarily provide an instrument for the management of emergencies rather than longer-term measures to address social causes of vulnerability. Effects of droughts have also been severe; the 2001–2003 drought, for example, put 659,000 people in need of food aid (FEWS-NET, 2004). An increased focus on food security and the Millennium Development Goals during the 1990s occasioned the setting up of institutional frameworks with a stronger inter-ministerial and inter-sectoral approach. A group on food and nutrition security consisting of technicians from government ministries and institutions as well as universities was created in 1997, motivated by the goal of halving the number of malnourished by 2015 (Selvester and Castro, 2003). The current operational group, known as SETSAN (the Technical Secretariat) coordinates and brings together information and analyses from all relevant agencies. This is the institutional framework under which the Vulnerability Assessment Committee (VAC, see Table 4.2) operates, as a working group.

While institutional responses in this way are integrated in a multi-sectoral framework that could, in principle, facilitate a multi-stressor approach to addressing longer-term causes of vulnerability, the findings of VAC assessments have been guided by the immediate need to identify specific groups and areas that were vulnerable at a specific point in time. The VAC survey in Mozambique in March 2004, for example, found that 187,000 people would require 49,000 tonnes of cereal relief food aid in marketing year 2004/2005 (April–March), in order to recover from droughts and floods of previous years as well as the impact of HIV and AIDS (FAO/WFP, 2004). The links with broader and longer-term policy measures, such as adaptation to climate change (Ministry for Coordination of Environmental Affairs (MICOA), 2000), have in practice been weak.

Donor agencies have played an increasing role in shaping vulnerability assessments. The end of the civil war, as well as the dramatic floods in 2000 and 2001, contributed to a huge increase in aid to Mozambique from bilateral as well as UN and other multilateral agencies. In some areas, massive funds were made available for interventions related to disaster. The realization among these donors that such interventions need to contribute to preparedness for any future events, has triggered a set of assessments analysing sources of vulnerability to natural hazards. These assessments have been initiated by non-Mozambican bilateral and multilateral organizations,[2] often implemented as conjunctive efforts between donor, academic, government and NGO institutions (Steinbruch, 2003; Eriksen and Silva, 2009; Dantas, unpublished). Two such vulnerability assessments for Mozambique are summarized in Table 4.2.

This set of assessments has revealed that vulnerability in Mozambique, though manifested as food insecurity triggered by droughts and floods in the short term, is caused by a number of longer-term social and development factors. A donor-initiated planning workshop with representatives of governmental institutions, Mozambican NGOs and the Catholic University of Mozambique (UCM) spurred a risk assessment in Búzi District, a district just south of Beira town, exposed to both floods and droughts. A detailed risk assessment was elaborated within the German-supported 'Disaster Risk Management (DRM) project of the Búzi River Basin in central Mozambique', forming part of a rural development programme.[3] Methods focused on identifying sources of vulnerability in a local context and involved investigating a broad set of variables using qualitative as well as quantitative methods. Hazard risk, the level of vulnerability to natural disasters and the existing coping mechanisms were analysed in order to derive a list of short- to long-term activities to be supported by donor assistance. The study revealed that poverty is a major impediment to establishing community- and household-level disaster management structures. It also found that people's high vulnerability was due not only to floods, but also due to a number of small daily 'disasters' that occur throughout the year. Main social factors driving vulnerability included HIV and malaria.

The second assessment examined here, the World Bank-funded assessment called 'Economic Impact of Climate Change' (2002–2004), was carried out by Mozambican and foreign university institutes. The study exemplified assessments aimed at enhancing understanding of how multiple stressors shape longer-term vulnerability and using this information to inform policy making in general rather than place specific food aid or development interventions. Like the DRM study, data collection focused on a smaller targeted geographic area (two villages in the Limpopo River Valley exposed to the 2000 floods and the 2001–2003 drought). It investigated how market integration affected the social and geographic differentiation of household vulnerability. Data were collected over time in order to gauge changes in coping strategies and market participation during increasing climatic stress.

The assessment found that the manifestations of floods and drought are diverse. While destroying agricultural land for many households, the flood also left fertile soil on other people's land. The flood also triggered massive aid and rehabilitation of irrigation infrastructure in one of the villages. At the same time, a process of marginalization may be driving vulnerability in other, dryland rainfed farming areas. Such small-scale agricultural villages received little donor and

Table 4.2 *Key characteristics of examined assessments*

Country	*Types of assessments*	*Name of study*	*Actors*	*Objectives*	*Methods and data*
Southern Africa	Mapping, gathering data on vulnerability and livelihoods.	VAC	SADC, WFP, DFID (UK aid), FEWS-NET, food relief organizations, government departments.	Develop a coordinated system to monitor food security and vulnerability in southern Africa.	Food crop production, food supply and livelihoods data, household surveys.
Mozambique	Interaction between stressors: Linkage between market integration and climate vulnerability.	Economic Impacts of Climate Change Vulnerability	World Bank, CICERO (Oslo), University of Oslo, Rutgers University (US), University of Eduardo Mondlane (Mozambique).	Enhance understanding of how economic liberalization and climate vulnerability interact. Increase understanding of how farmer responses to increasing climatic variability are affected by economic changes.	Comparative analysis of two villages exposed to drought and floods, with differing levels of market integration. Household-level, focus group and key informant interviews.
Mozambique	Community risk mapping, gathering data on local context of disaster risks.	Disaster Risk Management	Donors and organizations active in rehabilitation after disaster: PRODER (Rural development prog), NGC, GTZ (German Technical Cooperation), CVM (Red Cross Mz), Catholic University (Mozambique).	Establish household- and community-level structures for risk management. Identify sources of vulnerability to natural disasters. Identify safe havens and evacuation routes based on community-mapping exercise.	Vulnerability assessment for Búzi River Basin, production of risk, land-use and community infrastructure maps.
South Africa	Interaction between stressors: Linkage between food security and HIV/AIDS.	UNRAVEL	Developed by Univerity of Cape Town (South Africa) and donors, Trocaire and UNISDR, developed at NGO level.	Identify everyday threats to livelihoods as well as sudden-onset and creeping threats and understand household responses. Understand temporal dynamics of food security.	Comparison of HIV/AIDS-affected household with non-affected household during an agricultural cycle.
South Africa	Vulnerability and food security assessments.	FIVIMS-ZA	A consortium of partners including University of Cape Town, University of the Witwatersrand, University of Western Cape, larger research NGOs, Department of Agriculture (South Africa)	Begin to develop a comprehensive system that enables possible identification of vulnerable and food-insecure groups.	Modelling approaches and detailed surveys using PRA and other methods.

government attention, affecting recovery and consecutive harvests. Furthermore, the 2001–2003 drought revealed that the opening up of market opportunities with increased trade and liberalization of the economy is having very unequal benefits. Market-based economic activities, such as cultivation of vegetables and trade, were profitable and robust in the face of drought only for a few commercial farmers and only in areas where access to regional and national markets was fairly good. For most small-scale farmers, market-based coping strategies proved unviable as the drought intensified. Such farmers saw their livelihood options dwindle, and were pushed into activities that yielded marginal income and put pressure on household labour availability, such as casual employment or production of sweet potato and pumpkin leaves in the river bed.

The South African case: Institutional responses to multiple stressors

Natural disasters have also played a role in shaping the vulnerability context in South Africa. The development of comprehensive and longer-term vulnerability assessments in South Africa is fairly recent; several efforts are being undertaken, however, to enhance the understanding and capacity requirements for improved vulnerability assessments. Methodological approaches are being designed to capture the impacts of multiple rather than singular stressors, supported by an understanding of ongoing local processes (Drinkwater, 2003; Mano et al, 2003; Vogel and Smith, 2002; Marsland, 2004; Wiggins, 2005; Ziervogel and Taylor, 2008). Two South African vulnerability assessments are summarized in Table 4.2.

Unlike Mozambique, the establishing of an information system that would enable the government to better target food and other development interventions was not driven by the regional VAC process, although agencies active in regional VACs have also been brought in for technical expertise, such as Save the Children (UK). The FIVIMS process in South Africa was set up in late 2003 within the Department of Agriculture (DOA). A large consortium, including university research teams drawn from the University of Cape Town, the University of the Witwatersrand and the University of Western Cape, as well as larger research NGOS, were tasked by the DOA to undertake a large and detailed vulnerability assessment, with a focus on food insecurity in the Limpopo Province, with a view to wider roll-out of such an approach across the country (Drimie and Ziervogel, 2006). South Africa sees FIVIMS growing into a 'process and system that helps to facilitate better analysis and assessment of food insecurity and vulnerability to food insecurity at various levels in the country'.[4]

FIVIMS has found that vulnerability at the local level in South Africa is generated by a range of factors, including access to resources, health status, poverty and past socioeconomic policy. In order to capture how such factors change over time for different stakeholders, contextual qualitative and quantitative data at various levels, national as well as household, have been required. FIVIMS uses various modelling, interview and participatory techniques to develop a 'pilot' system that tracks vulnerability to a range of factors (Drimie,

2005). The need for capturing context has also led to various place-based initiatives including piloting of the methods in a limited geographic area (Sekhukuneland in the Limpopo province).[5]

A number of social factors determining household vulnerability were also identified by the UNRAVEL (Understanding Resilient and Vulnerable Livelihoods) project, the second South African assessment examined here. These factors include availability of medical services, distance to medical services, transport costs, access to grants, access to labour and inputs for agriculture, and social networks. The aim of the UNRAVEL study in South Africa and related studies undertaken in Malawi, Zambia, Zimbabwe and Botswana (Babugura, 2005; Gandure, 2005; Ziervogel and Drimie, 2008) was to identify the 'everyday' threats as well as other sudden-onset and 'creeping' threats faced in rural villages. Different at-risk and affected households were monitored during the course of a full agricultural cycle (12 months) to determine the type and level of support required by those individuals most vulnerable to a range of stressors. The responses of individuals and households to chronic illness, the death of a household member and the consequences for household and community well-being were examined.

The UNRAVEL project was developed at the University of Cape Town in conjunction with donors (Trócaire, Ireland, with back-funding from Development Cooperation Ireland and the United Nations International Strategy for Disaster Reduction, Nairobi). Like Mozambique, South Africa exemplifies donor needs for assessments using a longer-term perspective. The findings illustrate that non-climate stressors, including HIV and AIDS and social policies, are critical in shaping vulnerability and food insecurity in South Africa. Where there are sick members, access to cash through social grants has enabled households to redirect attention away from physically exhausting activities and focus on activities they could not afford to undertake otherwise. The increase in transport costs, an important funeral expense in households with AIDS-related deaths, has also impacted households negatively as they have less money to spend on other essential products such as food. An important methodological lesson from the assessment was that although an initial baseline survey provides a type of snapshot information that can be entered into the database, ongoing monitoring is critical for uncovering the dynamics of household vulnerability.

Empirical use of vulnerability assessments: Policy implications and barriers to adaptation

The assessments examined in the previous section have shown that the factors that shape vulnerability in southern Africa are diverse. It follows that the various dimensions of vulnerability cannot be addressed by a 'one size, fits all' framework or plan. Interventions will also need to be diverse, as reflected in policy implications identified by the assessments (see Table 4.3).

The threat to life and property during floods or droughts requires specific sets of measures in the short term. The food requirement in the 2004/2005 season

Table 4.3 *Comparative analysis of selected vulnerability assessments*

Country	*Name of study*	*Findings*	*Policy implications*	*Lessons*
Southern Africa	VAC	Numbers of people and amount of food aid needed. Initially – drought as trigger contributing to food insecurity. Later – crisis found to be the result of multiple stressors.	Targeting of food and non-food aid. Later findings, a developmentally linked response is required in addition to a food-relief programme.	Need to incorporate information on multiple stressors, use for medium- and long-term planning. Multiple-sectoral coordination at various scales essential.
Mozambique	Economic Impact of Climate Change	Marginalization of rainfed farming. Unequal benefits from market integration. Lack of integration of local coping and production into formal market structures. Shift from formal employment to poorly paid casual employment, endangering household food security.	The most vulnerable unlikely to be assisted by technology-intensive interventions. Enhance position of rainfed farming in market, investments. Niche products, local knowledge, market information important to improve bargaining power of the vulnerable in market exchanges.	Effective adaptation policies need to address the way that long-term societal processes driving vulnerability, such as economic liberalization, affect different groups.
Mozambique	Disaster Risk Management	Poverty is a major impediment to establishing community- and household-level disaster management structures. People are highly vulnerable because of a number of small daily 'disasters' that occur throughout the year. HIV and AIDS are important factors.	Vulnerability can to a large extent be targeted by poverty alleviation. Vulnerability reduction requires long-term investments and engagements in education and economic diversification.	Multiple responses necessary. Methodological challenges: local expertise needed to collect reliable local contextual, often qualitative data.
South Africa	UNRAVEL	Cash grants important. Food security programmes have not made significant difference to those most vulnerable.	Food for work and conventional emergency programmes to support vulnerable people do not assist those weak/sick. Need to support community-initiated projects that support livelihoods.	Combination of stresses create situations of high vulnerability (including climate, economic, cultural practices).
South Africa	FIVIMS-ZA	Vulnerability generated by a range of factors including access to resources, health status, poverty and past socioeconomic policy.	Multiple and cross-sectoral approach required to address vulnerability to a range of stressors.	Vulnerability to multiple stressors requires a multiple response approach, solution and implementation (e.g. multiple-sectoral responses and improved institutional design).

identified by the Mozambique VAC, for example, was to be met through carry-over stocks, local purchases of maize, as well as the distribution of relief food aid. However, a different set of measures is required to address the inherent and chronic vulnerability, which is compounded by multiple stresses such as poverty, liberalization of markets and past socioeconomic policies, decline in formal employment, loss of livelihoods, lack of access to key resources with which to manage variability, and poor health and the spread of HIV and AIDS. A critical lesson common to all the examined assessments is that investigating such stressors can enhance the policy relevance due to the need to address longer-term causes of vulnerability. The DRM study in Mozambique, for example, resulted in multiple-response type recommendations. An evaluation of VACs yielded the need to incorporate information on multiple stressors, to use for medium- and long-term development planning, and that multiple-sectoral coordination of measures at various scales was essential. The 'Economic Impacts of Climate Change' vulnerability assessment in Mozambique suggested that policies aiming to reduce long-term vulnerability to a range of risks could focus on reversing marginalization of small-scale rainfed farming, making market opportunities available to vulnerable groups, as well as improving infrastructure and social services. In South Africa, the FIVIMS pilot programme found that addressing identified 'chronic' vulnerable groups required a multiple-response approach spanning different development sectors. UNRAVEL found that conventional food security programmes, such as food for work, did not support the most vulnerable people such as the weak and sick. The emerging policy implication appears to be that reducing long-term vulnerability involves diverse responses and sectors.

Making the shift to address longer-term and multi-sectoral policy objectives is not unproblematic, however. In Mozambique, demand for vulnerability information stems from institutions with much of their traditional funding and capacity centred on disaster management, and findings have most effectively been translated into action within this sphere. Participatory elaborated community maps resulting from the DRM project assessment in Mozambique served as a basis for disaster-simulation exercises and the identification of evacuation routes and 'safe havens', in case of future floods. The findings also led to the establishment of community emergency committees and a disaster preparedness component was implemented and budgeted within the district development plan (Steinbruch, 2003). Different institutions often focus on isolated components of what comprises local vulnerability. Thus in Mozambique, the WFP and the INGC coordinate massive efforts related to emergency management and food distribution during droughts and floods. Drought resistance and diversification of farming in general fall within the sphere of the Department of Agriculture and rural development programmes; however, multi-sectoral issues such as people's capacity to access non-agricultural sources of food and income during harvest failure are more difficult to fit in within the current institutional framework of vulnerability interventions.

Despite the conceptual developments illustrated by UNRAVEL and FIVIMS, practical interventions for reducing vulnerability in South Africa, too, remain constrained. Their findings, supported by other studies such as Reid and Vogel (2005), Wiggins (2005), Maunder and Wiggins (2007), Vogel et al (2007) and O'Brien et al (2009), show that vulnerability depends on interaction between local phenomena and more national and global phenomena as well as a range of institutional and governance challenges. Climate variability is just one group of stressors. Yet many interventions remain sector specific, both because of funding support and government and other stakeholders' capacity. For example, FIVIMS highlighted that water stress was a key constraint in the pilot study area. The district municipality is supporting agricultural development options even though this might put further pressure on water resources; developing alternative water-saving livelihoods such as small industry instead would require the integration of DOA food insecurity efforts with other departments, however.

The studies illustrate the difficulties in making the institutional transitions from short-term emergency responses to longer-term food security perspective, and from operational aid distribution to longer-term development and interventions to reduce vulnerability. The rich information derived from vulnerability assessments can serve as an important source of developing effective adaptation measures; however, difficulties in achieving multi-sectoral responses and management in practice, even if outlined at a strategy level such as SETSAN, may be one of the main barriers to adaptation.

Lessons learned and the way forward

This investigation shows that the different institutional starting points lead to assessments investigating very different dimensions of vulnerability, both in terms of timescale (short term and long term), stressor (e.g. natural disasters, economic liberalization) and focus (e.g. food security, health, economic activity). The assessments illustrate that no single definitive assessment or method exists, or can be developed, despite the initial appeal of such unifying methodologies and assessment approaches. Instead there is emerging, even within a limited geographical area such as southern Africa, a diversity of methods to answer stakeholders' respective questions. This observation underscores the need to examine carefully the institutional basis and fundamental motivation of an institution carrying out vulnerability assessments (Darcy and Hofmann, 2003; Wiggins, 2005).

Particular lessons can be drawn from this analysis of vulnerability assessments that are useful to other developing regions and to industrial country contexts. First, conducting assessments to improve emergency response alone is insufficient to effectively address vulnerability. There is a trend towards trying to link vulnerability data to longer-term policy processes and to twin development and adaptation (Huq and Reid, 2004; Nazare and Drimie, 2005). Identifying ways in which recent successes in institutional collaboration in VAC can be channelled into collaboration with long-term development and vulnerability-reduction interventions and, more concretely, adaptation measures, is a critical area in further work.

A second lesson is that in order to identify longer-term policies and interventions that target the causes of vulnerability, a different set of methods needs to be used from those assessments tailored for emergency response. Vulnerability assessments both in Mozambique and South Africa show that a focus on the household level is critical to understand which are the most vulnerable groups. In addition, broadening the scope beyond agricultural production and food security to detailed contextual, often qualitative data for a smaller geographic area, improves information on what factors policies should target. Another important methodological consideration is the need to go beyond short-term emergency food needs to track long-term household vulnerability dynamics over time.

A third lesson, supported by all assessments examined here, is that vulnerability cannot be addressed by using a single-stressor perspective. A single response reacting only to climate stress is inappropriate in the region. It may be necessary to tackle issues often thought of as outside the narrow range of climate-related adjustments, such as poverty alleviation, as part of adaptation to global environmental change. Inter-sectoral collaboration between institutions at different scales is important in developing such an approach.

How can one make sure that vulnerability assessments and measures address the above lessons? Difficulties in crossing the traditional spheres of work of different institutions, which is sectoral and often focused on emergencies in the short term, is one of the major challenges to improving vulnerability assessments. Institutional frameworks that were initially aimed at addressing two pressing concerns – natural disasters and food security – have played a large part in shaping vulnerability assessments in many southern African countries (Dilley and Boudreau, 2001; Darcy and Hofmann, 2003), as exemplified by Mozambique. Although assessment methodologies are beginning to be linked to longer-term development priorities in South Africa, implementing cross-sectoral collaboration and interventions is still hampered by institutional inertia and capacity challenges.

It may well be that policy and practitioner stakeholders, driven by institutional dynamics, normally are confined to addressing a specific dimension of vulnerability pertinent to their sphere of operations. Their question posed in assessments may therefore differ from that posed by academic stakeholders: the former asking what they can do to take account of vulnerability within their existing framework; the latter asking what needs to be done to address the causes of vulnerability more holistically, which frequently involves changing the institutional framework within which practitioners and policy makers operate (Vogel et al, 2007). All the examined assessments, however, including those assessments driven by more specific policy concerns, consistently identify a need for information regarding multiple stressors on livelihoods and the links between adaptation and development. These lessons point to the fundamental point in vulnerability science that in order to identify adaptation options, studying the why, or causes of vulnerability (Cutter, 2003), is critical. In order to respond to this need, the interaction of producers and users of 'science' is key. The distinction between scientific research and scientific assessment as identified by Patt et al (this volume, Chapter 1) is therefore not always clear-cut. While the design of the assessments studied here responds to the need of a particular stakeholder, many of the assessments are carried out through academic–donor–NGO–government institution collaboration via a 'consortia' model. In such consortia, the academic is a stakeholder informing assessments.

An important way of improving vulnerability assessments in Africa is forging stronger links between assessment efforts driven by specific sectoral or government institution needs and academic-driven efforts to understand the causes of vulnerability. The Southern African Vulnerability Initiative (www.savi.org.za) represents one such initiative, bringing together practitioners and researchers from different fields relevant to different dimensions of vulnerability. Given that vulnerability to change in the southern African region is *multidimensional* and occurs at *various scales*, interventions and management options, therefore, require more *flexible institutional responses and design*. It follows that a more nuanced set of vulnerability assessments as well as institutional links therefore will need to be developed. Despite their limitations and difficulties, vulnerability assessments in southern Africa provide useful data for a range of purposes, including insights critical to supporting more sensitive adaptation interventions in future.

Notes

1 Through a partnership with the Department for International Development (DFID), FEWS-NET and WFP.

2 Such as FEWS-NET, German Technical Cooperation Agency (GTZ), Red Cross Mozambique (CVM), World Health Organization.

3 This project is a component of a GTZ-supported rural development programme (PRODER).

4 Quote from Dr Scott Drimie, Human Science Research Council, who was the Coordinator of the first phase of FIVIMS in South Africa.

5 For further details and various papers see www.agis.agric.za

References

Arlindo, P. (2006) 'Knowledge review and gap analysis report: Hunger and vulnerability in Mozambique', RHVP (Regional Hunger and Vulnerability Programme), www.wahenga.net

Arndt, C. (2003) *HIV/AIDS, Human Capital and Economic Growth Prospects for Mozambique*, Africa Region Working Paper Series, No.48, The World Bank, Washington DC

Babugura, A. (2005) 'Vulnerability to climate variability in Botswana, 1972–2002', unpublished PhD thesis, University of the Witwatersrand, Johannesburg

Boko, M., Niang, I., Nyong, A., Vogel, C., Githeko, A., Medany, M., Osman-Elasha, B., Tabo, R. and Yanda, P. (2007) 'Africa. Climate change 2007: Impacts, adaptation and vulnerability', Contribution of Working Group II to the Fourth Assessment Report of the Intergovernmental Panel on Climate Change, in Parry, M. L., Canziani, O. F., Palutikof, J. P., van der Linden, P. J. and Hanson, C. E. (eds) Cambridge University Press, Cambridge, pp433–467

Christensen, J. H. and Hewitson, B. (2007) 'Regional climate projections', in Solomon, S., Qin, D., Manning, M., Marquis, M., Averyt, K., Tognor, M. M. B., Le Roy Miller Jnr, H. and Chen, Z. (eds) *Climate Change 2007: The Physical Science Basis. Contribution of Working Group I to the Fourth Assessment Report of the Intergovernmental Panel on Climate Change*, Cambridge University Press, Cambridge, pp847–940

Christie, F. and Hanlon, J. (2001) *Mozambique and the Great Flood of 2000*, James Currey, Oxford

Christoplos, I., Liljelund, A. and Mitchell, J. (2001) 'Re-framing risk: The changing context of disaster mitigation and preparedness', *Disasters*, vol 25, pp185–198

Cutter, S. L. (2003) 'The vulnerability of science and the science of vulnerability', *Annals of the Association of American Geographers*, vol 93(1), pp1–12

Dantas, V. (unpublished) 'Save Basin Disaster Risk Assessment: A district level analysis, in Mozambique', Disaster Mitigation for Sustainable Livelihoods Programme (DiMP), University of Cape Town

Darcy, J. and Hofmann, C.-A. (2003) 'According to need? Needs assessment and decision-making in the humanitarian sector', Humanitarian Policy Group Report 15, Overseas Development Institute, London

Dilley, M. and Boudreau, T. (2001) 'Coming to terms with vulnerability: A critique of the food security definition', *Food Policy*, vol 26, pp229–247

Drimie, S. (2005) 'Monitoring food security in South Africa: The FIVIMS-ZA experience', a paper for the SARPN Workshop, 'Civil Society Experiences of Monitoring Food Security Issues in Southern Africa', Birchwood Conference Centre, Johannesburg, 24 May

Drimie, S. and Ziervogel, G. (2006) 'Food insecurity in South Africa: Monitoring and managing the realities of integrating local information and experience into national policy and practice', Case Study for Vulnerability and Resilience in Practice (VARIP), 21–22 June, Oxford

Drinkwater, M. (2003) 'HIV/AIDS and agrarian change in southern Africa', paper presented at the United Nations Regional Inter-agency Coordination and Support Office Technical Consultation on Vulnerability in the light of an HIV/AIDS Pandemic, 9–11 September 2003, Johannesburg, www.sarpn.org.za

Ellis, F. (2003) 'Human vulnerability and food security: Policy implications', Forum for Food Security in Southern Africa, ODI, London, www.odi.org.uk/food-security-forum

Eriksen, S. and Kelly, P. M. (2007) 'Developing credible vulnerability indicators for policy assessment', *Mitigation and Adaptation Strategies*, vol 12(4), pp495–524

Eriksen, S. and Silva, S. (2009) 'The vulnerability context of a savanna area of Mozambique: Household drought coping strategies and responses to economic change', *Environmental Science and Policy*, vol 12, forthcoming

FAO/WFP (2004) *Special Report, FAO/WFP Crop and Food Supply Assessment Mission to Mozambique*, July 2004, www.fao.org/giews

FEWS-NET (2004) 'Fears of third consecutive drought year', Mozambique Monthly Report, Food Security Update, January 2004, www.fews.net/centers/current/monthlies/report/?f=mz&m=1001144&l=en

Gandure, S. (2005) 'Coping with and adapting to drought in Zimbabwe', unpublished PhD thesis, University of the Witwatersrand, Johannesburg

Hanlon, J. (1996) *Peace Without Profit: How the IMF Blocks Rebuilding in Mozambique*, James Currey, Oxford

Hewitson, B., Tadross, M. and Kack, C. (2005) 'Scenarios developed with empirical and regional climate model-based downscaling', in Schulze, R. (ed) *Climate Change and Water Resources in Southern Africa*, WRC Report, 1430/1/05

Hulme, M., Doherty, R. M., Ngara, T., New, M. G. and Lister, D. (2001) 'African climate change: 1900–2100', *Climate Research*, vol 17, pp145–168

Huq, S. and Reid, H. (2004) 'Mainstreaming adaptation in development', *IDS Bulletin*, vol 35(3), pp15–21

Leichenko, R. and O'Brien, K. (2001) 'The dynamics of rural vulnerability to global change: The case of southern Africa', *Mitigation and Adaptation Strategies for Global Change*, vol 7, pp1–18

Mano, R., Isaacson, B. and Daardel, P. (2003) 'Identifying policy determinants of food security and recovery in the SADC region: The case of the 2002 Food Emergency', Food, Agriculture and Natural Resources Policy Analysis Network (FANRPAN), Policy Paper prepared for the FANRPAN Regional Dialogue on Agricultural Recovery, Food Security and Trade Policies in Southern Africa, Gaborone, Botswana, 26–27 March 2003.

Marsland, N. (2004) *Development of Food Security and Vulnerability Information Systems in Southern Africa: The Experience of Save the Children, UK*, Consultant for Save the Children, Save the Children-UK, www.sarpn.org.za

Maunder, N. and Wiggins, S. (2007) 'Food security in southern Africa: Changing the trend? Review of lessons learnt on recent responses to chronic and transitory hunger and vulnerability', *Natural Resource Perspectives*, 106, www.odi.org.uk/resources/specialist/natural-resource-perspectives/106-food-security-southern-africa.pdf

MICOA (2000) *Vulnerability of the Economy of Mozambique to Potential Climate Changes*, Ministry for Co-ordination of Environmental Affairs, Maputo

Moseley, W. G. and Logan, B. I. (2001) 'Conceptualising hunger dynamics: A critical examination of two famine early warning methodologies in Zimbabwe', *Applied Geography*, vol 21, pp223–248

MPF/UEM/IFPRI (1998) *Understanding Poverty and Well-Being in Mozambique: The First National Assessment (1996–97)*, Mozambique, Ministry of Planning and Finance/Eduardo Modlane University/International Food Policy Research Institute, Washington DC

National Directorate of Planning and Budget, MPF, IFPRI, Purdue University (2004) *Poverty and Well-Being in Mozambique: The Second National Assessment*, www.sarpn.org.za/documents/d0000777/P880-Mozambique_032004.pdf

Nazare, F. and Drimie, S. (2005) 'Key food and nutrition security policy–process issues in southern Africa', a discussion paper for the SARPN/ODI/FARNPAN Inaugural Meeting, 'The Use of CSOs' "Evidence" in Policies for Food Security in Southern Africa', Birchwood Conference Centre, Johannesburg, 25 May

O'Brien, K. and Vogel, C. (2003) *Coping with Climate Variability: The Use of Seasonal Climate Forecasts in Southern Africa*, Athenaeum Press, Ashgate

O'Brien, K., Quinlan, T. and Ziervogel, G. (2009) 'Vulnerability interventions in the context of multiple stressors: Lessons from the Southern Africa Vulnerability Initiative', *Environmental Science and Policy*, vol 12, forthcoming

Reid, P. and Vogel, C. (2005) 'Living and responding to multiple stressors in South Africa: Glimpses from KwaZulu-Natal', *Global Environmental Change*, vol 16(2), pp195–206.

Republic of Mozambique (2007) *Plano Director para Prevenção e Mitigação das Calamidades Naturais*, INGC, Maputo, www.ingc.gov.mz

Republic of South Africa (2003) 'No. 57 of 2002: Disaster Management Act, 2002', *Government Gazette*, vol 451, Cape Town, 15 January 2003

SARPN, Southern African Regional Poverty Network (2004) 'Scoping study towards DFIDSA's regional hunger and vulnerability programme', abridged version, Department for International Development, London, www.sarpn.org.za, accessed 9 September 2008

Scoones, I., with Chibudu, C., Chikura, S., Jeranyama, P., Machaka, D., Machanja, W., Mavedzenge, B., Mombeshora, B., Mudhara, M., Mudziwo, C., Murimbarimba, F. and Zirereza, B. (1996) *Hazard and Opportunities: Farming Livelihoods in Dryland Africa: Lessons from Zimbabwe*, Zed Books and International Institute for Environment and Development, London

Selvester, K. and Castro, M. A. (2003) 'Mozambique food security issues', paper for Forum for Food Security in Southern Africa, ODI, London, www.odi.org.uk/food-security-forum

Steinbruch, F. (2003) *Hazard Risk and Vulnerability Assessment for the Búzi River Basin/Central Mozambique*, GTZ, PRODER-Sofala, Mozambique

Tschirley, D., Nijhoff, J., Arlindo, P., Mwinga, B., Weber, M. T. and Jayne, T. S. (2004) 'Anticipating and responding to drought emergencies in southern Africa: Lessons from the 2002–2003 experience', prepared for the New Partnership for Africa's Development (NEPAD) Regional Conference on Successes in African Agriculture, 22–25 November 2004, Nairobi, Kenya

Vogel, C. and Smith, J. (2002) 'The politics of scarcity: Conceptualising the current food security crisis in southern Africa', *South African Journal of Science*, vol 98, pp315–317

Vogel, C., Moser, S., Kasperson, R. and Dabelko, G. (2007) 'Linking vulnerability, adaptation and resilience science to practice: Pathways, players and partnerships', *Global Environmental Change*, vol 17, pp349–364

Washington, R. W., Harrison, M. and Conway, D. (2004) 'African Climate Report', commissioned by the UK government to review African climate science, policy and options for action, www.britishembassy.gov.uk/Files/kfile/africa-climate.pdf

Wiggins, S. (2005) 'Southern Africa's food and humanitarian crisis of 2001–4: Causes and lessons', discussion paper, Agricultural Economic Society Annual Conference, Nottingham, 4–6 April 2005

Ziervogel, G. and Drimie, S. (2008) 'The integration of support for HIV and AIDS and livelihood security: District level institutional analysis in southern Africa', *Population and Environment*, vol 28, pp3–4

Ziervogel, G. and Taylor, A. (2008) 'Feeling stressed: Integrating climate adaptation with other priorities in South Africa', *Environment*, vol 50(2), pp32–41

Chapter 5

Global Assessment of Coastal Vulnerability to Sea-Level Rise: Experience from DINAS-COAST

Richard J. T. Klein and Jochen Hinkel

Introduction

Knowledge of coastal vulnerability to sea-level rise and other effects of climate change is helping scientists and policy makers to identify and prioritize management efforts that can be undertaken to minimize risks to, or reduce possible impacts on, people and ecosystems. Before climate change emerged as an academic focus, vulnerability as such was not an important concept in coastal research. Research in coastal zones has traditionally been conducted mainly by geologists, ecologists and engineers, roughly as follows (Klein, 2002):

- Geologists study coastal sedimentation patterns and the consequent dynamic processes of erosion and accretion over different spatial and temporal scales.
- Ecologists study the occurrence, diversity and functioning of coastal flora and fauna from the species to the ecosystem level.
- Engineers take a risk-based approach, assessing the probability of occurrence of storm surges and other extreme events that could jeopardize the integrity of the coast and the safety of coastal communities.

The challenge of climate change has spurred the collaboration between these three groups of coastal scientists; vulnerability has become the integrating focus of this research collaboration. Since the early 1990s efforts have been made to develop guidelines and methodologies that combine the expertise of the three disciplines, as well as economics, in assessing coastal vulnerability to climate change. Many involved in these efforts were unaware of the history of vulnerability assessment in other disciplines, particularly the social sciences, where studies tend to focus in more depth on particular groups and communities within a society and on the variety of social, cultural, economic, institutional and other factors that define their vulnerability. These studies do not rely on global or regional models to inform the analysis; instead the major source of information is the vulnerable community itself (see, for example, Chapters 2 and 4, this volume).

In 1992 the former Coastal Zone Management Subgroup (CZMS) of the Intergovernmental Panel on Climate Change (IPCC) published the latest version of its Common Methodology for Assessing the Vulnerability of Coastal Areas to Sea-Level Rise (IPCC CZMS, 1992). It comprises seven consecutive analytical steps that allow for the identification of populations and physical and natural resources at risk, and of the costs and feasibility of possible responses to adverse impacts. Results can be presented for seven vulnerability indicators:

1 People affected (the people living in the hazard zone affected by sea-level rise);
2 People at risk (the average annual number of people flooded by storm surge);
3 Capital value at loss (the market value of infrastructure which could be lost due to sea-level rise);
4 Land at loss (the area of land that would be lost due to sea-level rise);
5 Wetland at loss (the area of wetland that would be lost due to sea-level rise);
6 Potential adaptation costs, with an overwhelming emphasis on protection;
7 People at risk, assuming the adaptation considered in indicator 6.

The Common Methodology has been used as the basis of assessments in at least 46 countries; quantitative results were produced in 22 country case studies and eight sub-national studies (for an overview see Nicholls, 1995). Studies that used the Common Methodology were meant to serve as preparatory assessments, identifying priority regions and sectors and providing an initial screening of the feasibility and effect of coastal protection measures. They have been successful in raising awareness of the potential magnitude of climate change and its possible consequences in coastal zones. They have thus provided a motivation for implementing policies and measures to control greenhouse gas emissions. In addition, they have encouraged long-term thinking and they have triggered more detailed local coastal studies in areas identified as particularly vulnerable, the results of which would contribute to coastal planning and management. For example, El-Raey et al (1999) carried out a follow-up study on the Port Said Protectorate in Egypt.

Nonetheless, a number of problems with the Common Methodology have been identified, which mainly concern its data intensity and its simplified approach to assessing biogeophysical and socioeconomic system response (for a more detailed discussion see Klein and Nicholls, 1999). Alternative assessment methodologies have been proposed, but they have generally not been applied by anyone but their developers. A semi-quantitative methodology proposed by Kay and Hay (1993) was applied in a number of South Pacific island countries, where it was felt that the Common Methodology put too much emphasis on market-based impacts. An index-based approach proposed by Gornitz et al (1994) included the risk of hurricanes and was developed for use along the east coast of the United States. However, it does not consider socioeconomic factors.

The relative success of the Common Methodology led the IPCC to adopt its approach as a model for assessing the vulnerability of other, non-coastal systems to climate change. The top–down approach of the Common Methodology was intuitively attractive to the wider climate change community, which is strongly model-oriented. In 1994 the IPCC published its *Technical Guidelines for Assessing Climate Change Impacts and Adaptations* (Carter et al, 1994), which provide system-independent guidance to countries that wish to assess their vulnerability to climate change. The Technical Guidelines are outlined in a similar fashion to the Common Methodology, but fewer analytical steps are implied and less prior knowledge is assumed. In addition, the Technical Guidelines are not prescriptive in the choice of scenarios, tools and techniques to conduct the analysis. For a range of socioeconomic and physiographic systems, the United Nations Environment Programme (UNEP) Handbook on Methods for Climate Change Impact Assessments and Adaptation Strategies (Feenstra et al, 1998) offers a detailed elaboration of the IPCC Technical Guidelines, including for coastal zones (Klein and Nicholls, 1998). The UNEP Handbook has been used in a range of developing countries under the UNEP Country Studies Programme and the first phase of the Netherlands Climate Change Studies Assistance Programme. The United States Country Studies Program used similar guidance, provided by Benioff et al (1996).

Global assessment of coastal vulnerability to sea-level rise

In the late 1990s the EU-funded project SURVAS (Synthesis and Upscaling of Sea-Level Rise Vulnerability Assessment Studies) aimed to synthesize and upscale all available coastal vulnerability studies and to develop standardized data sets for coastal impact indicators suitable for regional and global analysis (de la Vega-Leinert et al, 2000a, b; see also www.survas.mdx.ac.uk/). However, this effort was only partially successful: synthesis and upscaling was impeded by the fact that studies had used different methodologies, scenarios and assumptions. As a result, until recently the global assessment by Hoozemans et al (1993) and its updates by Baarse (1995) and Nicholls (2002, 2004) remained the only sources of global information on coastal vulnerability to sea-level rise.

These global assessments played an important part in the preparation of the World Coast Conference 1993 and several IPCC reports. They have also been used extensively for further academic analyses, including integrated assessment modelling. However, with the widespread use of the global assessments, their limitations have become increasingly apparent. These limitations include:

- the obsolescence and low spatial resolution of underlying data sources;
- the reliance of global mean sea-level rise as the only driver of coastal vulnerability;
- the non-consideration of biogeophysical and socioeconomic dynamics and feedback; and
- arbitrary and rather simplistic assumptions regarding adaptation.

The increased research focus on global change and the availability of faster computers created an opportunity to combine improved data, scenarios and assessment modules into a new integrated modelling activity to assess coastal vulnerability to sea-level rise: the project DINAS-COAST (Dynamic and Interactive Assessment of National, Regional and Global Vulnerability of Coastal Zones to Sea-Level Rise). DINAS-COAST built on methods and expertise developed in a range of scientific-technological disciplines to produce the simulation model DIVA (Dynamic and Interactive Vulnerability Assessment; Hinkel and Klein, 2007). DIVA enables its users to produce quantitative information on a range of coastal vulnerability indicators, for user-selected climatic and socioeconomic scenarios and adaptation strategies, on national, regional and global scales, covering all coastal nations. The multitude of scenarios, adaptation options, impact indicators and spatial scales that can be considered with DIVA means that a vast amount of data can be produced. To publish only a limited number of model runs in a printed report would therefore be a strong limitation; by making available the model itself, users can explore their own questions. The latest version of DIVA was released on a CD-ROM in December 2006 (DINAS-COAST Consortium, 2006) and is available for free download from the DIVA website (www.pik-potsdam.de/diva/). Further upgrades will follow.

DIVA has been developed to meet the demand for new information on coastal vulnerability on a global scale while addressing important limitations of the earlier global studies. Important improvements are the inclusion of feedbacks within the combined natural and socioeconomic coastal system and the more explicit and realistic representation of adaptation. Making these improvements required integrating natural and social science knowledge in a much more comprehensive way than had ever been done for coastal vulnerability assessment. Adding to this challenge was the fact that it had to be done by a geographically distributed group of scientists with a relatively limited budget (€1.4 million). A second challenge was that DIVA needed to be developed in a form that would enable its distribution to a broad community of users. The first challenge called for an innovative, modular approach to model development. The second challenge required the development of a powerful yet user-friendly graphical user interface and a computationally efficient (i.e. fast) model. In the remainder of this chapter we present in detail the systematic approach by which the DINAS-COAST consortium has addressed these challenges. In so doing we hope to provide the rapidly growing number of researchers active in interdisciplinary integrative science with insights and tools that would enable them to tackle similar challenges.

Requirements for DIVA

The integration of knowledge

The first set of requirements for DIVA relates to the integration of knowledge, which has social, cognitive and technical dimensions. Integrative research is a social activity, in which researchers, policy makers and other stakeholders meet and work together. Different interests, motivations and goals are discussed and need to be harmonized. Cognitive integration refers to the knowledge that people possess; the heterogeneous knowledge of project partners must be integrated in a meaningful way to address a particular problem. Technical integration concerns the artefacts produced by a collaborative team of people. For example, experiments are set up jointly, databases or computer models must be coupled, papers are written collectively. These three dimensions of integration are interrelated and every problem of integrative research has aspects that fall into each of the dimensions.

In this chapter we focus on the cognitive and technical dimensions of integration, acknowledging that they presuppose the social integration of people with the relevant knowledge and producing the necessary artefacts. The social dynamics in a collaborative research team are an important factor determining the quality of a project's outcome. A common identification with the objectives and the final product, the will to invest time and energy in mutual learning, and good communication skills are essential. These issues are not further addressed here because any lessons learned are highly project-specific. To generalize the lessons from DINAS-COAST would be unacademic, to discuss them in detail inappropriate.

At the cognitive level, the development of DIVA required the integration of knowledge from various natural and social science disciplines. Each project consortium member provided unique knowledge about a specific coastal subsystem or process in the form of concepts, data, models and relevant questions to be addressed. Incompatible conceptualizations (terminologies) had to be harmonized and different model types (e.g. discrete, continuous and optimization models) had to be incorporated. For example, the concept 'land loss' was understood differently by different project partners: as an area (m^2), a rate (m^2/year) and a fraction (%).

As is frequently the case in integrative research, the interactions between the various subsystems were not fully understood at the start of the project; instead, such understanding typically develops during the project and then becomes an outcome of the project itself. The process of integration was also complicated by the fact that project partners were distributed over various institutes in different countries. As a result, frequent project meetings were not possible, and most of the model development was coordinated using email, the internet and telephone calls.

At the technical level, the choice of software technology and development techniques was important, ensuring that DIVA could be produced efficiently by the project participants. Since several people were involved in developing the tool, a component-based approach was needed, in which the tool's individual components could be developed and validated separately. The development of the database and the model had to take place simultaneously because no existing database was suitable for use in DIVA. A modular architecture was required for the model, whereby individual project participants represented their subsystem knowledge in the form of self-contained modules. It was necessary to provide support to assist participants with little programming and modelling experience.

User interaction

The second set of requirements comes from the user's perspective. The goal of DINAS-COAST was not only to integrate knowledge but also to make available this knowledge to a wider audience. To this end, a graphical user interface (GUI) is required that recognizes the specific information needs of the users. The GUI must be intuitive and user-friendly, but also allow for advanced interactions for more professional users. At the basic level, users must be able to select climate and economic scenarios, choose from a set of adaptation strategies, run the model and analyse the results. A question frequently asked by policy makers is which country or region is more or most vulnerable, so the GUI puts special emphasis on enabling comparative analyses of impacts under different scenarios and for different adaptation strategies. At the advanced level, users should also be able to edit the data, use their own scenarios and possibly even alter the model's algorithms. Furthermore, experiences in software engineering have shown that it is difficult to specify all user requirements at the start of a project. It is therefore necessary to consult frequently with the user, invite their comments on GUI prototypes, and use their feedback to refine the specifications. Finally, making the model available for user interaction requires a fast model.

Both sets of requirements called for the possibility of project partners to make changes to data, algorithms, subsystem interactions (interfaces) and GUI during the tool's development phase. But how does one design a product that is essentially a moving target? The answer was that rather than designing the product, the DINAS-COAST consortium designed the process of developing it (Hinkel, 2005). Put differently, instead of presenting a rigid specification of the final product at the outset of the project, a process was initiated that allowed for the refinement of DIVA in any number of iterative steps. This means that requirements had to be addressed both at the process level and at the product level. To do so, DINAS-COAST produced two separate results: a method, called the DIVA method, to organize the model and tool development process and the actual DIVA tool, which has been built using the DIVA method. While the DIVA tool is specific to DINAS-COAST, the DIVA method is generic and could easily be re-used in other vulnerability contexts with similar requirements.

The DIVA method

The DIVA method is a method for building modular integrated computer models by distributed partners. The method addresses both cognitive and technical integration. At the cognitive level, interdisciplinary communication and harmonization of terminology are facilitated. At the technical level, the DIVA method provides software tools for writing and analysing integrated computer models. For a detailed presentation of the DIVA method see Hinkel (2005).

The straightforward way of developing an integrated modular model would be to define the linkages between the modules at the beginning of the project (i.e. one specialized interface for each module). However, as stated in the previous section, a distinguishing feature of interdisciplinary research is that linkages between subsystems are usually not fully understood at the start of the project; such understanding is a result of the project itself. Thus, general interfaces are required (i.e. all modules have the same interface), leaving the developers of modules with more freedom to define subsystem linkages. The flexibility offered by general interfaces thus facilitates the interdisciplinary learning process. However, it does have implications for the model development process. While specialized interfaces would not require extensive collaboration between partners developing the individual modules, general interfaces do. To facilitate such collaboration, the process of model development must be rigorously defined.

The DIVA method therefore consists of two parts: a modelling framework and a semi-automated development process. A modelling framework is a partial software architecture that frames the model to be built by providing a general *a priori* conceptualization of the system of interest. This means that only those phenomena that can be expressed using the framework's concepts can in fact be modelled. The semi-automated development process of the DIVA tool facilitates integration at the process level. It structures and facilitates the iterative specialization of the framework's general concepts to the needs of the specific problem addressed.

The modelling framework provides concepts for expressing static information about the system, as well as concepts for representing the system's dynamics. The statics of the system are represented by a data model consisting of geographical features, properties and relations, which follows the OpenGIS Abstract Specification of the OpenGIS Consortium (www.opengeospatial.org/standards). The geographical features represent the real-world entities, such as regions, countries and river basins. Properties capture the quantitative information about the features. For example, a country might have the property 'area' or a river the property 'length'. Finally, relations describe how the features are structured. For example, the feature 'region' might contain several 'country' features. The dynamics of the system are represented in the form of first-order difference equations, in which the state of the system is a function of its state in the previous time step and of the drivers. For example, the surface area of coastal wetlands in a country might be a function of the wetland surface area in the previous time step and of the value of the sea-level rise scenario driving the model in the current time step.

The development process organizes the integration of knowledge, based on the *a priori* conceptualization provided by the modelling framework. Knowledge about the system to be modelled enters the process in four ways (Hinkel, 2005):

1 the ontology, which is a shared language to talk about the system to be modelled;
2 the algorithms, which represent the system's dynamics;
3 the data, which represent the initial (observed) state of the system and the scenarios that represent the system's possible future evolutions; and
4 the use-cases, which specify how the user can interact with the model via the GUI.

The first task of any iteration of the development process is the elaboration of the shared ontology. An ontology is a specification of a conceptualization (Gruber, 1993), that is, a list of terms and their definitions. In the case considered here this means that the specific features, properties and relations that constitute the modelled system must be specified in accordance with the general framework. According to the role they have in the system's dynamics, all properties of the features must be classified into one of four categories: driver, state variable, diagnostic variable and parameter. For example, the country's area is static (a parameter), while its population might be a driver. The compilation of the ontology is a joint responsibility of the entire project consortium and forms the basis for all discussions about the system. The ontology is stored in a central repository as an XML (extensible mark-up language) document.

Once the knowledge has entered the development process, most subsequent processes are automated and model development proceeds in three parallel tracks: the database development, the GUI development and the algorithm development. The ontology feeds into all three tracks. The database development consists of two steps. First, raw data must be pre-processed to fit the ontology. Second, the pre-processed data is automatically converted into the DIVA database format. The GUI is automatically generated using the XML document, which also specifies the description of the properties, the units, the minimum and maximum values, and so on.

The ontology is also used to generate automatically Java source code, which then is used by the project partners to code the algorithms. Since the model's ontology is then hard-coded in Java, an algorithm will only compile if it is consistent with the ontology. Related algorithms are grouped into modules. For example, a project partner could write a module called CountryDynamics, which simulates how the properties of the feature 'country' evolve over time. Before a module is submitted for inclusion into the integrated model it is run and validated in stand-alone mode.

The last step of an iteration of the development process involves the analysis of the modules and their linkages, and the validation of the complete model. Whenever a new version of a module is submitted, the project's internal tool development website is automatically updated, offering documentation and the

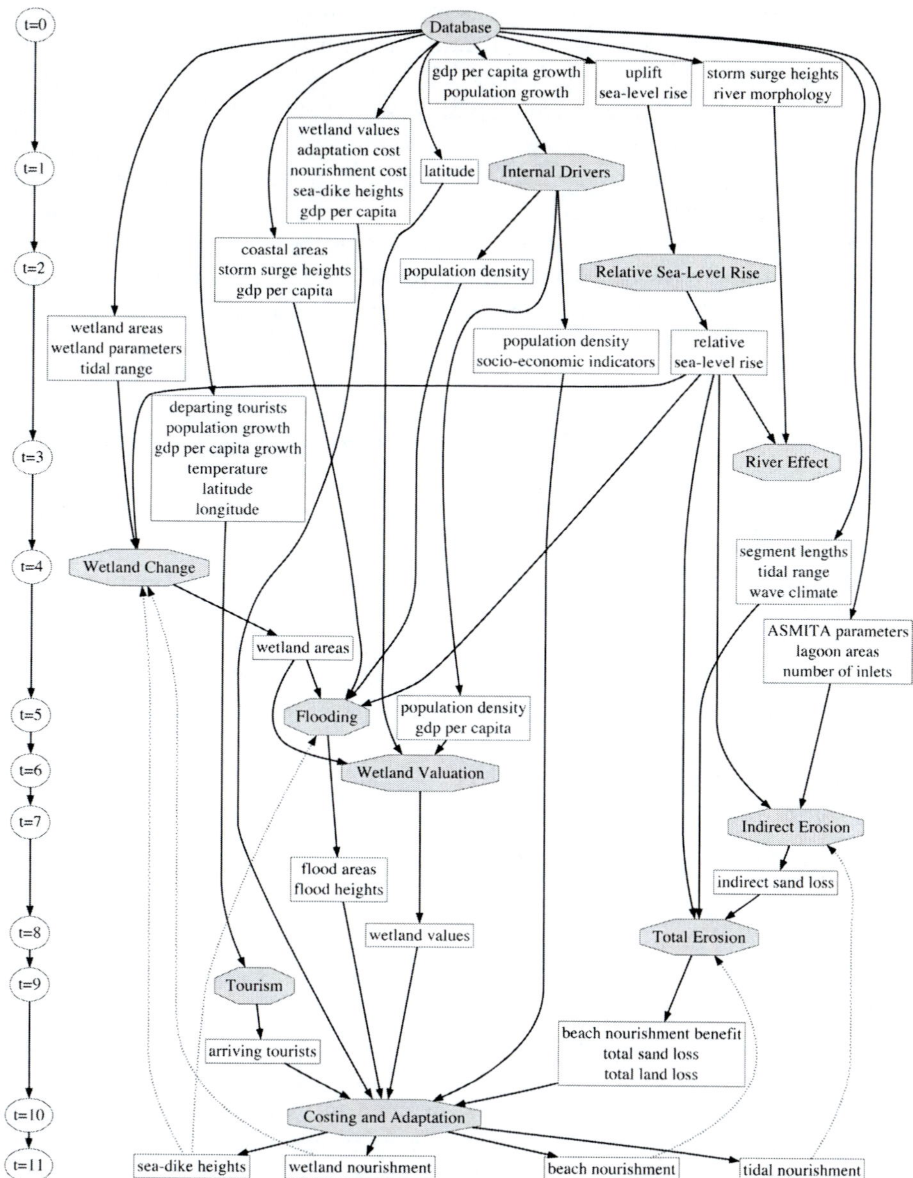

Note: Octagons represent the modules, rectangles represent data, the solid arrows represent the flow of data during one time step, and the dotted arrows represent the data fed into the next time step

Figure 5.1 *Module linkages in DIVA 1.5.5*

new integrated model for download. An important document that is automatically generated is a graph that visualizes the flow of data through the modules (see Figure 5.1). Module developers can use this graph to analyse the interactions between the modules and decide whether any changes need to be made in the next iteration of the development process. This may then create the need to update the ontology, change the algorithms, incorporate new data and adjust the GUI's functionality.

The principal advantage of this iterative approach to model development is that the interfaces between the subsystems modules do not have to be specified before the coding can start. The module developers can start coding their knowledge before analysing which information they need to take from and provide to other modules. The development process can be iterated as many times as necessary. At any stage new knowledge in the form of data, algorithms or linkages between the modules can be incorporated, yet there is always a complete model available.

The DIVA tool

The DIVA tool built by applying the DIVA method comprises four components:

1. a detailed global database with biophysical and socioeconomic coastal data;
2. global and regionalized sea-level and socioeconomic scenarios until the year 2100;
3. an integrated model, consisting of interacting modules that assess biophysical and socioeconomic impacts and the potential effects and costs of adaptation; and
4. a graphical user interface for selecting data and scenarios, running model simulations and analysing the results.

The database of the DIVA tool is a collection of data and coverage files. Following the development process outlined in the previous section, raw data was pre-processed to fit DIVA's ontology, which contains the following seven types of features: coastline segments, administrative units, countries, rivers, tidal basins, world heritage sites and CLIMBER grid cells. Most data are attributed to the coastline segments. These coastline segments were developed by decomposing the world's coastline into variable-sized segments. The segmentation was performed on the basis of a series of physical, administrative and socioeconomic criteria that influence impacts and vulnerability; a new segment was started whenever one (or several) of the criteria changed, producing 12,148 coastline segments in total. The average length of a coastline segment is 70km. The choice to represent data this way was motivated by the requirement to have a fast model. Attributing the information to this 'one-dimensional grid' of coastline segments simplifies the calculations of the model because all expensive GIS (geographical information system) operations have already been performed as part of the data pre-processing (Vafeidis et al, 2008).

The scenarios that drive the model contain information about sea-level rise, land-use change and socioeconomic development (i.e. population and economic growth), all of which was consistent with the IPCC Special Report on Emission

Scenarios (SRES) (Nakicenovic and Swart, 2000). The sea-level rise scenarios were produced with the climate model of intermediate complexity, CLIMBER-2 of the Potsdam Institute for Climate Impact Research (Germany). For each SRES emission scenario six different sea-level rise scenarios, assuming three different climate sensitivities, as well as uniform and regionalized sea-level rise, were produced. For further information see Petoukhov et al (2000) and Ganopolski et al (2001).

The model of the DIVA tool consists of a model kernel and a number of modules. The model kernel is responsible for data input and output, and invokes the modules for each time step. The modules, developed by the various project partners, represent the coastal subsystems and compute the impacts of sea-level rise on natural and human systems, as well as the effects of human adaptation on these impacts. Table 5.1 lists all modules in DIVA 1.5.5 and Figure 5.1 shows the flow of data through the modules. The first modules to be invoked compute the effects of sea-level rise on the coastal natural systems, including direct coastal erosion, erosion within tidal basins, changes in wetlands and the increase of the backwater effect in rivers. This is followed by an assessment of socioeconomic impacts, either directly due to sea-level rise or indirectly via the impacts on the natural systems. The last module is the Costing and Adaptation Module, which implements adaptation options according to the user-selected strategy. The adaptation options then influence the calculations of the natural and socioeconomic impacts of the next time step.

The explicit incorporation of adaptation is an important innovation that DIVA contributes to vulnerability research and modelling. The impacts calculated do not only depend on the user-selected scenarios but also on the user-selected adaptation strategy. The adaptation options considered in the model are (i) do nothing, (ii) build dikes, (iii) move away and (iv) nourish the beach, tidal basins or wetlands. Any combination of these options is valid. For each time step the model selects an adaptation option according to the following adaptation strategies:

- No adaptation: the model only computes potential impacts.
- Full protection: raise dikes or nourish beaches as much as is necessary to preserve the status quo.
- Optimal protection: optimization based on the comparison of monetary costs and benefits of adaptation options and potential impacts.
- User-defined protection: the user sets a protection standard by defining a return period against which to protect.

DIVA does not produce a single measure or indicator of vulnerability. The model's output (see Table 5.2) has many components that are not comparable and therefore unsuitable for aggregation into a single measure. Only the monetary components of the output can be readily compared and added up, which is the basis for the optimal protection adaptation strategy. The comparison of the other output is left to the user's own judgement. For this purpose, DIVA is equipped with a powerful graphical user interface.

Table 5.1 *The modules in DIVA 1.5.5*

Module Name	*Author(s)*	*Description*
Relative sea-level rise	Robert Nicholls, Loraine McFadden	Creates relative sea-level rise scenarios by adding vertical land movement to the climate-induced sea-level rise scenarios.
River effect	Rob Maaten	Calculates the distance from the river mouth over which variations in sea level are noticeable.
Indirect erosion	Luc Bijsterbosch, Zheng Bing Wang, Gerben Boot	Calculates the loss of land, the loss of sand and the demand for nourishment due to indirect erosion in tidal basins. This is a reduced version of the Delft Hydraulics ASMITA model (Stive et al, 1998).
Total Erosion	Robert Nicholls, Loraine McFadden	Calculates direct erosion on the open coast based on the Bruun rule. Sums up direct erosion and indirect erosion for the open coast, including the effects of nourishment where applied.
Wetland change	Loraine McFadden, Robert Nicholls, Tom Spencer, Jochen Hinkel	Calculates area change due to sea-level rise, sea dike construction and possible wetland nourishment for six types of wetlands.
Flooding	Robert Nicholls	Calculates flooding due to sea-level rise and storm surges, taking into account sea dikes.
Wetland valuation	Luke Brander, Onno Kuik, Jan Vermaat	Calculates the value of different wetland types as a function of GDP, population density and wetland area.
Tourism	Jacqueline Hamilton, David Maddison, Richard Tol	Calculates number of tourists per country.
World heritage sites	Marilena Pollicino, Richard Tol	Calculates whether a UNESCO world heritage site is threatened by sea-level rise.
Costing and adaptation	Gerben Boot, Poul Grashoff, Jacqueline Hamilton, Oliver Hansen, Jochen Hinkel, Maren Lau, Loraine McFadden, Robert Nicholls, Christine Schleupner, Richard Tol	Calculates socioeconomic impacts of the geodynamic effects, taking into account pre-set and/or user-defined adaptation options.

The GUI of the DIVA tool enables users to choose scenarios and adaptation strategies, to run the model, and to analyse and compare the results for different regions, time steps, scenarios and adaptation strategies. The GUI was built on the basis of the Delft Tools (www.demis.nl/home/pages/products.htm), which is a collection of software components for decision support and temporal–spatial data analysis. Input and output data can be visualized in forms of tables, graphs, charts and maps. In so doing, the user creates cases (each of which consists of a selected scenario and adaptation strategy, as well as the initial values), runs simulations for

Table 5.2 *The output of DIVA 1.5.5*

Aspect	*Output Variable*
Erosion	Wetland loss, erosion of the coastline, sand loss in tidal basins
Flooding	Dike height, people at risk, people actually flooded, area influenced by salt water intrusion
Wetlands	Area of different types of wetlands, monetary value of wetlands
Costs	Adaptation cost, cost of nourishment, cost of building dikes, cost of salt water intrusion, cost of migration, cost of residual damage

each case and compares their results. All data used by the model can be edited, imported from spreadsheets and exported to standard Office formats.

Discussion

The development of the DIVA tool involved making two major trade-offs. First, there was an academic trade-off between the wish to represent disciplinary state-of-the-art knowledge in great detail and the wish to integrate the disciplinary knowledge into a consistent whole. Integration was achieved through modularity: encapsulating expert knowledge in the form of self-contained modules and making them available to others via well-defined interfaces. Modularity enables experts with different disciplinary backgrounds to integrate their knowledge without the need to understand the details of each other's knowledge domains. An irresolvable drawback of the modular approach is that none of the module developers has a comprehensive understanding of the complete model. Semantically, this means that there could be conflicting assumptions underlying the modules. Algorithmically, this means that it is difficult to debug or simplify the algorithmic structure across several modules. Since no complete specification of the mathematical problem is available, numerical artefacts could be introduced and more efficient numerical solutions are difficult to find.

A second trade-off to be made was between the overall scientific complexity represented in the model and the communicability of results to users. While one aim of DINAS-COAST was to improve on previous global assessment efforts by including more realistic scenarios and by representing the dynamic interactions between natural and social coastal subsystems, at the same time the wish was to make the model itself available to a broad audience. The more comprehensive and complex the model, the smaller would be the audience that can use the model and the more difficult it becomes to communicate model results. The GUI has been designed in such a way that a user, while confronted with much more information than in previous assessments, should be able to handle the information in ways that provide more insights than a published text can give. In hindsight, the development of the GUI might have benefited from greater interaction with potential users. However, given the limited time and financial resources a conscious decision was made not to include users so as to be able to focus on the interdisciplinary knowledge integration described above.

Note that the DIVA tool is not explicit about the exact meaning of vulnerability. There are two reasons for this. First, there is no accepted definition of vulnerability, or a single way of making it operational (e.g. Brooks, 2003; O'Brien et al, 2004; Patt et al, 2005; Adger, 2006; Eakin and Luers, 2006; Füssel and Klein, 2006). Second, we view vulnerability as having a strong subjective dimension, that is, statements about the vulnerability of an entity depend on the personal preferences one has on the state of that entity (Ionescu et al, 2008). It is therefore left to the user to decide how to value the individual components of DIVA's output (see Table 5.2).

DIVA has so far been used in a number of scientific activities. It contributed to the development of the Special Report *The Future Oceans: Warming Up, Rising High, Turning Sour* by the German Advisory Council on Global Change (WBGU, 2006). It has been used in the EU-funded PESETA and BRANCH projects to estimate the costs of climate change in Europe and to assess the role of climate change in European spatial planning, respectively. Further scientific applications of DIVA include its use as a component in the Community Integrated Assessment System of the Tyndall Centre for Climate Change Research and the exploration of differential impacts due to different global patterns of sea-level rise at the Met Office Hadley Centre for Climate Change. Currently DIVA is applied in an integrated vulnerability assessment of coastal areas in the South-east Asia and East Asian Region, funded by the Asian Pacific Network. Interest in the DIVA database, an output of DINAS-COAST in its own right, has been expressed by the Massachusetts Institute of Technology and the Land-Ocean Interactions in the Coastal Zone project of the International Geosphere-Biosphere Programme and the International Human Dimensions Programme on Global Environmental Change. DIVA has also been used in a series of regional workshops organized by the Secretariat of the United Nations Framework Convention on Climate Change (UNFCCC), which aimed to familiarize national policy makers with methods for assessing impacts, vulnerability and adaptation in preparation of their National Communications to the UNFCCC. At several universities, including those of Delft, Barcelona and Southampton, DIVA is used in the education of undergraduate and graduate students.

Conclusions and outlook

The project DINAS-COAST has developed a new model to conduct assessments of vulnerability to sea-level rise on national, regional and global scales, motivated by the demand for updated information and the limitations of previous assessments. The approach taken was innovative in two respects. First, any stakeholder can conduct their own assessment interactively by using the software tool DIVA (as opposed to model developers running their own model and publishing a selection of the results in a report). Second, the requirements for producing the DIVA tool have led to the development of a second product, the DIVA method. The DIVA method represents a new approach to building an integrated model by geographically distributed partners. It provides scientists with different backgrounds with a way to harmonize their conceptualizations of the system to be modelled and with an intuitive interface to express their knowledge about it. The process of model development is well defined and automatically documented, providing a basis for the efficient communication and collaboration between project partners.

The applications of DIVA to date have made apparent a number of limitations. While DIVA was never meant as a decision-support tool for coastal planners and managers, there is a high demand for DIVA-like tools that operate at a resolution that is high enough for decision making in the face of sea-level rise and associated hazards. Another limitation is that the DIVA GUI does not provide GIS functionality at the expert level and does not support standard GIS file formats. It is technically a minor operation to import and export to and from standard GIS tools, yet this functionality is not currently available via the GUI. Finally, the use of DIVA by people with detailed local knowledge of particular coastal areas has also revealed inconsistencies in the data (all data in DIVA have been derived from global databases).

As a result of its modular structure and the flexible development process, the DIVA tool can easily be extended to address some limitations and to incorporate new knowledge and insights. For example, work has started to develop an index module that can aggregate the multidimensional output of DIVA into a single user-defined index of vulnerability, producing a scalar measure of vulnerability for each administrative unit. In addition, the possibility of adding a module to assess the impacts of rising sea level and sea-surface temperature on coral reefs and atolls is currently being examined. Extensions to the adaptation modules also appear possible. Additional adaptation strategies could be added and the interdependence of adaptation actions could be explored with a multi-agent adaptation module.

Further applications of the DIVA method are intended as well. It is conceivable to develop regional versions of the DIVA tool, such as a DIVA-Europe, a DIVA-South Asia and a DIVA-Caribbean. Increasing the spatial resolution of the analysis would increase the model's usefulness to coastal management. As part of the ongoing application of DIVA in South-east and East Asia, the database is updated with local data provided by local experts. In addition, a number of smaller-scale coastal vulnerability assessments are conducted and compared in order to identify the processes and subsystem linkages that need to be considered in regional versions of DIVA. These include:

- impacts of changing river sediment discharge on coastal erosion/sedimentation;
- impacts of changing river sediment discharge, sea-surface temperature rise and acidification on aquatic ecosystems (e.g. coral reefs);
- impacts of tourism on coastal ecosystems;

- impacts of regional climate processes such as changing monsoon circulation, El Niño, La Niña and the Indian Ocean Dipole Mode; and
- coastal development and urbanization.

In conclusion, DINAS-COAST has led to the development of the DIVA tool and the DIVA method, both of which are innovative and have the potential to be further developed and applied in the coming years.

Acknowledgement

DINAS-COAST was funded by the European Commission's Directorate-General Research under contract number EVK2-2000-22024.

References

Adger, W. N. (2006) 'Vulnerability', *Global Environmental Change*, vol 16(3), pp268–281

Baarse, G. (1995) *Development of an Operational Tool for Global Vulnerability Assessment (GVA): Update of the Number of People at Risk Due to Sea Level Rise and Increased Flooding Probability.* CZM Centre Publication No. 3, Ministry of Transport, Public Works and Water Management, The Hague, The Netherlands, 17pp

Benioff, R., Guill, S. and Lee, J. (1996) *Vulnerability and Adaptation Assessments: An International Handbook*, Version 1.1, Kluwer Academic Publishers, Dordrecht, The Netherlands

Brooks, N. (2003) *Vulnerability, Risk and Adaptation: A Conceptual Framework*, Working Paper 38, Tyndall Centre for Climate Change Research, University of East Anglia, Norwich, 16pp

Carter, T. R., Parry, M. L., Nishioka, S. and Harasawa, H. (eds) (1994) *Technical Guidelines for Assessing Climate Change Impacts and Adaptations*, Report of Working Group II of the Intergovernmental Panel on Climate Change, University College London, and Centre for Global Environmental Research, Tsukuba, Japan, x+59pp

de la Vega-Leinert, A. C., Nicholls, R. J. and Tol, R. S. J. (eds) (2000a) *Proceedings of the SURVAS Expert Workshop on European Vulnerability and Adaptation to Accelerated Sea-Level Rise*, Hamburg, Germany, 19–21 June 2000, Flood Hazard Research Centre, Middlesex University, Enfield, viii+152pp

de la Vega-Leinert, A. C., Nicholls, R. J., Nasser Hassan, A. and El-Raey, M. (eds) (2000b) *Proceedings of the SURVAS Expert Workshop on African Vulnerability and Adaptation to Accelerated Sea-Level Rise*, Cairo, Egypt, 5–8 November 2000, Flood Hazard Research Centre, Middlesex University, Enfield, vi+104pp

DINAS-COAST Consortium (2006) *DIVA 1.5.5*, Potsdam Institute for Climate Impact Research, Potsdam, Germany, CD-ROM, www.pik-potsdam.de/diva/

Eakin, H. and Luers, A. L. (2006) 'Assessing the vulnerability of social-environmental systems', *Annual Review of Environment and Resources*, vol 31, pp365–394

El-Raey, M., Frihy, O., Nasr, S. M. and Dewidar, Kh. (1999) 'Vulnerability assessment of sea-level rise over Port Said Protectorate', *Environmental Monitoring and Assessment*, vol 56(2), pp113–128

Feenstra, J., Burton, I., Smith, J. B. and Tol, R. S. J. (eds) (1998) *Handbook on Methods for Climate Change Impact Assessment and Adaptation Strategies*, Version 2.0, United Nations

Environment Programme and Institute for Environmental Studies, Vrije Universiteit, Nairobi, Kenya and Amsterdam, The Netherlands, xxvi+422pp

Füssel, H.-M. and Klein, R. J. T. (2006) 'Climate change vulnerability assessments: An evolution of conceptual thinking', *Climatic Change*, vol 75(3), pp301–329

Ganopolski, A., Petoukhov, V., Rahmstorf, S., Brovkin, V., Claussen, M., Eliseev, A. and Kubatzki, C. (2001) 'CLIMBER-2: A climate system model of intermediate complexity. Part II: model sensitivity', *Climate Dynamics*, vol 17(10), pp735–751

Gornitz, V., Daniels, R., White, T. and Birdwell, K. (1994) 'The development of a coastal risk assessment database: Vulnerability to sea-level rise in the U.S. Southeast', *Journal of Coastal Research*, special issue, no 12, pp327–338

Gruber, T. R. (1993) 'A translation approach to portable ontology specifications', *Knowledge Acquisition*, vol 5(2), pp199–220

Hinkel, J. (2005) 'DIVA: An iterative method for building modular integrated models', *Advances in Geosciences*, vol 4, pp45–50

Hinkel, J. and Klein, R. J. T. (2007) 'Integrating knowledge for assessing coastal vulnerability to climate change', in McFadden, L., Nicholls, R. J., and Penning-Rowsell, E. C. (eds) *Managing Coastal Vulnerability*, Elsevier Science, Amsterdam, The Netherlands, pp61–77

Hoozemans, F. M. J., Marchand, M. and Pennekamp, H. A. (1993) *Sea Level Rise: A Global Vulnerability Assessment – Vulnerability Assessments for Population, Coastal Wetlands and Rice Production on a Global Scale*, second revised edition, Delft Hydraulics and Rijkswaterstaat, Delft and The Hague, The Netherlands, xxxii+184pp

Ionescu, C., Klein, R. J. T., Hinkel, J., Kavi Kumar, K. S. and Klein, R. (2008) 'Towards a formal framework of vulnerability to climate change', *Environmental Modeling and Assessment*, in press

IPCC CZMS (1992) 'A common methodology for assessing vulnerability to sea-level rise', second revision, in *Global Climate Change and the Rising Challenge of the Sea*, Report of the Coastal Zone Management Subgroup, Response Strategies Working Group of the Intergovernmental Panel on Climate Change, Ministry of Transport, Public Works and Water Management, The Hague, The Netherlands, Appendix C, 27pp

Kay, R. C. and Hay, J. E. (1993) 'A decision support approach to coastal vulnerability and resilience assessment: A tool for integrated coastal zone management', in McLean, R. F. and Mimura, N. (eds) *Vulnerability Assessment to Sea-Level Rise and Coastal Zone Management*, Proceedings of the IPCC/WCC'93 Eastern Hemisphere Workshop, Tsukuba, Japan, 3–6 August 1993, Department of Environment, Sport and Territories, Canberra, Australia, pp213–225

Klein, R. J. T. (2002) *Coastal Vulnerability, Resilience and Adaptation to Climate Change: An Interdisciplinary Perspective*, PhD thesis, Christian-Albrechts-Universität zu Kiel, Kiel, Germany, x+133pp

Klein, R. J. T. and Nicholls, R. J. (1998) 'Coastal zones', in Feenstra, J. F., Burton, I., Smith, J. B. and Tol, R. S. J. (eds) *Handbook on Methods for Climate Change Impact Assessment and Adaptation Strategies*, Version 2.0, United Nations Environment Programme and Institute for Environmental Studies, Vrije Universiteit, Nairobi, Kenya and Amsterdam, The Netherlands, pp7.1–7.35

Klein, R. J. T. and Nicholls, R. J. (1999) 'Assessment of coastal vulnerability to climate change', *Ambio*, vol 28(2), pp182–187

Nakicenovic, N. and Swart, R. (eds) (2000) *Emissions Scenarios*, Special Report of Working Group III of the Intergovernmental Panel on Climate Change, Cambridge University Press, Cambridge, x+599pp

Nicholls, R. J. (1995) 'Synthesis of vulnerability analysis studies', in Beukenkamp, P. C., Günther, P., Klein, R. J. T., Misdorp, R., Sadacharan, D. and de Vrees, L. P. M. (eds)

Preparing to Meet the Coastal Challenges of the 21st Century, Proceedings of the World Coast Conference, Noordwijk, The Netherlands, 1–5 November 1993, Coastal Zone Management Centre Publication 4, The Hague, The Netherlands, pp181–216

Nicholls, R. J. (2002) 'Analysis of global impacts of sea-level rise: A case study of flooding', *Physics and Chemistry of the Earth, Parts A/B/C*, vol 27(32), pp1455–1466

Nicholls, R. J. (2004) 'Coastal flooding and wetland loss in the 21st century: Changes under the SRES climate and socio-economic scenarios', *Global Environmental Change*, vol 14(1), pp69–86

O'Brien, K., Eriksen, S., Schjolden, A. and Nygaard, L. (2004) *What's In a Word? Conflicting Interpretations of Vulnerability in Climate Change Research*, Working Paper 2004:04, Centre for International Climate and Environmental Research Oslo, University of Oslo, Norway, iii+16pp

Patt, A. G., Klein, R. J. T. and de la Vega-Leinert, A. C. (2005) 'Taking the uncertainty in climate-change vulnerability assessment seriously', *Comptes Rendus Geoscience*, vol 337(4), pp411–424

Petoukhov, V., Ganopolski, A., Brovkin, V., Claussen, M., Eliseev, A., Kubatzki, C. and Rahmstorf, S. (2000) 'CLIMBER-2: A climate system model of intermediate complexity. Part I: Model description and performance for present climate', *Climate Dynamics*, vol 16(1), pp1–17

Stive, M. J. F., Capobianco, M., Wang, Z. B., Ruol, P. and Buijsman, M. C. (1998) 'Morphodynamics of a tidal lagoon and the adjacent coast', in Dronkers, J. and Scheffers, M. (eds) *Physics of Estuaries and Coastal Seas*, Balkema, Rotterdam, The Netherlands, pp397–407

Vafeidis, A. T., Nicholls, R. J., McFadden, L., Tol, R. S. J., Hinkel, J., Spencer, T., Boot, G. and Klein, R. J. T. (2008) 'A new global coastal database for impact and vulnerability analysis to sea-level rise', *Journal of Coastal Research*, vol 24(4), pp917–924

WBGU (2006) *The Future Oceans: Warming Up, Rising High, Turning Sour*, German Advisory Council on Global Change, Berlin, Germany, xii+110pp

Chapter 6

Our Vulnerability to Changes in Ecosystem Services

Dagmar Schröter

Introduction: The environmental dimension of human vulnerability

Vulnerability is immediately and intuitively understood as the risk of harm and, consequently, suffering. The complexity of this widely used concept arises when we think about who is vulnerable to what, and why? Humans cause or influence their own vulnerability in a complex manner. We have short- and long-term, linear and non-linear, direct and indirect influences on a multitude of contributing factors, and vice versa. We are an inseparable part of our environment through our dependence on ecosystems and the services they provide. Our understanding of our own and other people's vulnerability influences whether or not we take action to prevent threatening events from happening (mitigation) or to alleviate their effects (adaptation). We may think of sustainable management as a luxury for environmentalists, if we fail to recognize our dependence on ecosystems. In this chapter I will argue that the mismanagement of ecosystem services increases *human* vulnerability. I will give examples of how unsustainable management of ecosystem services led to vulnerability in the past. I then present some future projections of ecosystem service supply and vulnerability in Europe. Finally, I discuss three general reasons for unsustainable management of ecosystem services, and explore how environmental sciences can facilitate sustainable management.

Ecosystems, ecosystem services and human well-being

In the recent decades we have moved from understanding humans as being reactive to their environment (pre-1980s), to thinking of *environmental crises* as being caused by humans (1980s), to thinking of *environmental crises* as being caused by *socio-natural interaction* (1990s, van der Leeuw, 2001). In the present decade, we begin to understand *human crises* as caused by socio-natural interaction. Surely not every human crisis is rooted in an environmental crisis – we refer to a change in our environment as a crisis, when it threatens our livelihood or well-being. However, often environmental crisis leads to human crisis. Humans rely on ecosystems, because they depend on ecosystem services (de Groot, 1992; Daily, 1997). Ecosystems offer provisioning services (e.g. food, fresh water, fuelwood, biochemicals), regulating services (e.g. climate and disease regulation, pollination), cultural services (e.g. spiritual, recreational and aesthetic value, inspiration) and supporting services (e.g. soil formation, nutrient cycling, primary production) (Millennium Ecosystem Assessment, 2005). They are important for our security, basic material for a good life, health, good social relations and ultimately our freedoms and choices, in short our well-being (Millennium Ecosystem Assessment, 2003). We are bound to the human perspective, even if we recognize the intrinsic value in ecosystems and biodiversity.

Ecosystem services weave people into ecosystems (Daily and Ellison, 2002). Social systems and natural systems are inseparable. The recognition of this fact is evident in new terms, such as 'human–environment system' (Turner et al, 2003, Schröter et al, 2005b), 'socioecological system' (Palmer et al, 2004), 'nature–society system' (Kates et al, 2001), 'eco-social system' (Waltner-Toews et al, 2003), 'linked social-ecological system' (Holling, 2001; Walker et al, 2002), and 'combined human–nature system' (Gunderson et al 1995). In this chapter I understand ecosystems as follows: ecosystems are environments of interacting animals (including humans), plants and microbes. In doing so I risk oversimplifying human interactions within ecosystems, because currently our models of ecosystems represent complex social interactions as poorly as economic and social models represent complex ecological interactions. The ultimate goal is to construct models that represent ecosystems adequately, including all relevant social, economic and environmental elements and interactions.

Global change, ecosystem services and vulnerability

During the present century society will increasingly be confronted with global changes such as population growth, pollution, climate and land-use change. By 2050, the human population will probably be larger by 2 to 4 billion people (Cohen, 2003). Anthropogenic warming and sea-level rise would continue for centuries due to the timescales associated with climate processes and feedbacks, even if greenhouse gas concentrations were to be stabilized (Intergovernmental Panel on Climate Change (IPCC), 2007). Land-use changes will have an immediate and strong effect on agriculture, forestry, rural communities, biodiversity and amenities such as traditional landscapes, especially in a continent as

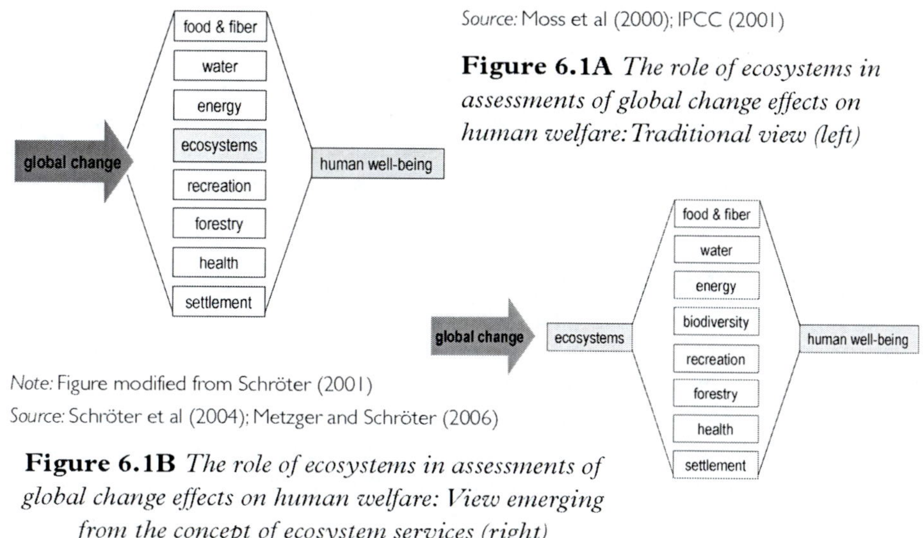

Source: Moss et al (2000); IPCC (2001)

Figure 6.1A *The role of ecosystems in assessments of global change effects on human welfare: Traditional view (left)*

Note: Figure modified from Schröter (2001)

Source: Schröter et al (2004); Metzger and Schröter (2006)

Figure 6.1B *The role of ecosystems in assessments of global change effects on human welfare: View emerging from the concept of ecosystem services (right)*

densely populated as Europe (Watson et al, 2000). Plausible scenarios of severe changes like these, as well as evidence of past anthropogenic impacts on the environment have led to a growing awareness of potential impacts of global change (cf. Smith et al, 1999; Sala et al, 2000; Stenseth et al, 2002; Walther et al, 2002; Parmesan and Yohe, 2003; Root et al, 2003). Traditionally, this effect on the environment has been seen as an additional effect of global change, besides its effects on, for example, food and fibre production, health, recreation and settlement (Figure 6.1A). In contrast to this view, the ecosystem service concept leads to the recognition that ecosystems mediate global change (Figure 6.1B). Therefore, environmental impacts of global change can add to human vulnerability by altering the supply of ecosystem services, which lie at the base of human well-being (Schröter et al, 2004, 2005a; Metzger and Schröter, 2006).

Cases of vulnerability

Examples from the past and present

Global change vulnerability is the likelihood that a specific coupled human–environment system will experience harm from exposure to stresses associated with alterations of societies and the environment, accounting for the process of adaptation (Schröter et al, 2005b). Vulnerability assessments aim to inform decision making *today* by estimating the likelihood of adverse *future* outcomes given a range of socioeconomic and environmental assumptions. Because of these assumptions about the future, the validity of vulnerability assessments can only be empirically tested in hindsight. Since vulnerability is a fairly young concept, to date, no vulnerability assessment has become of age so that it could be validated. An analysis of past damage events based on the vulnerability concept can demonstrate its usefulness, as shown by the insightful vulnerability study of the Irish Potato Famine 1845–1850 (Fraser, 2003). Another goal of this exercise is to identify adaptive actions that could have lessened vulnerability before the damage occurred in order to shed light on adaptation processes today. Which types of information would have been useful to which agents and could have altered the outcome of the historical event (see also Fraser, Chapter 2, this volume)?

The Canadian dust bowl: Fertility gone with the wind

The following example is taken from *An Environmental History of the Twentieth-Century World* (McNeill, 2001), which analyses historical cases of environmental exploitation. The case illustrates how agricultural livelihood depends on both providing and supporting ecosystem services.

The arrival of the Canadian Pacific Railway initiated settlement of the Palliser Triangle of western Canada at the end of the 19th century. In 1857 the Triangle had been considered unsuitable for human settlement by early enquiry of the Royal Geographical Society. However, after 1897 the prairies enjoyed a run of rainy and therefore fertile years, and its farming population grew tremendously in consequence. Additionally, high wheat prices around the world during World War I enhanced the trend of increased farming in this semi-arid wheat belt. The settlers came mainly from humid lands in eastern North America and Europe. They sought to preserve soil moisture in the summer by leaving fields fallow – an idea widely promoted by professors and agronomists, but nevertheless unsuitable for the windy prairie. By the 1920s, this practice, combined with some dry years, led to serious wind erosion. As droughts brought dust storms, thousands of farm families gave up. An agricultural area the size of Belgium was completely destroyed. Social and economic distress was similar to the Dust Bowl of the American plains (c. 1931–1938).

What could have lessened the vulnerability of the farming population prior to this exodus? An impression of the long-term climate in this region may have lessened the hopeful flow of settlers during a few good seasons in the first place. Furthermore, knowledge that the transfer of farming methods from humid lands would favour soil erosion in the semi-arid, windy prairie would have been helpful. Farming families may have adapted their management practice and sustained fertility of their land enough to make a living. As it was, the ecosystem service *soil fertility maintenance* was compromised for the exploitation of the ecosystem service *food and fibre production*. The latter is the obvious target when farming, while the former, supporting service is just as vital. Vulnerability could have been lessened by an awareness and understanding of the interplay between these ecosystem services and agricultural management.

Pollination: What the bees do when no one is looking

Pollination, the transfer of pollen from one flower to another,[1] is critical to fruit and seed production. Insects and other animals pollinate flowers on their hunt for nectar, pollen or other floral products. In fact, wild and farmed animals provide pollination services to over three-quarters of the staple crop plants that feed humans (Nabhan and Buchmann, 1997). According to the US Department of Agriculture, the European honeybee alone adds $14 billion a year to US crops (Holden, 2004). However, both wild and cultivated populations of pollinators are declining (Buchmann and Nabhan, 1996). The commercially cultivated honeybee population of the US decreased by more than half, from 5.9 million colonies in 1947 to 2.6 million colonies in 2000 (Daily and Ellison, 2002), and continues to decline. Particularly worrisome is a new phenomenon, colony collapse disorder (CCD), which is currently little understood but causes great losses for many commercial bee-keepers in the US (Stokstad, 2007). The decline of pollinators overall is attributed to habitat loss, pesticide poisoning, diseases and pests (Ingram et al, 1996).

To take a regional example, California produces 80 per cent of the world's almond supply, with a $1.19 billion almond industry (Oberthur, 2004). The industry relies on honeybee cultures. Almond farmers rent hives from bee-keepers to be put in the blooming orchards. More than 1 million honeybee hives are needed to pollinate the almond groves in California's Central Valley alone. Serious bee shortages in the bee-keeping business are brought about by a number of diseases, such as bacterial foulbrood, fungal chalkbrood, nosema (caused by a protozoan), parasitic mites and, more recently, CCD. Another problem is the Africanized bee,[2] which breeds with managed honeybees and makes their offspring too aggressive to handle. For the first time in 1994, local bee shortages forced many California almond growers to import the bulk of the honeybees they needed from other states. The price to rent a hive for about five weeks climbed from $43 in 2003, over $48–53 in 2004 to $75–85 in 2005 (California Farm Bureau Association), and to $120 in the spring of 2007 (Stokstad, 2007).

Pollination is no longer a matter of course. Habitat loss and pesticides diminish the wild pollinators, while pests and diseases torment the cultivated honeybees. Commercial mass production and transport of honeybee colonies may have contributed to creating first calamities in the US bee-keeping business. Attempts to do without pollinators so far were as fruitless as unpollinated apple trees: giant blowers, helicopters and even mortar shells have been used in vain to spread pollen efficiently. Currently breeders try to develop 'self compatible' almond trees that require fewer bees. Alternative bee species are on trial for commercialization, such as the blue orchard bee. It remains hard to believe that any of these solutions will be able to effectively substitute pollination by wild and cultivated insects on a large scale.

To put the problem into ecological terms: we have compromised the ecosystem service *pollination* for the short-term maximization of *food and fibre production*. Hedgerows and wild habitat were eradicated to farm more land to increase the harvest, and thereby diminished the habitat that sustained pollinator abundance and diversity. Pesticides are used to the extent that their intended effect of increasing the harvest is counteracted by the lack of pollinators to produce a fruit in the first place.

In contrast, some organic farmers use no pesticides, but maintain hedgerows and wild habitat so successfully that they do not have to rent cultivated pollinators (Daily and Ellison, 2002). Given the new pressures described above, does organic farming still do better when it comes to pollination services? How much land do farmers need to put aside to maintain a sufficient wild pollinator community? This is one of the many questions that is currently investigated by applied ecologists (e.g. Kremen et al, 2004).

An awareness of the sensitivity of pollinator populations, wild and cultivated, could have prevented the rapid decline now known as 'pollinator crises' to the US Department of Agriculture. However, knowledge to support farmers in their efforts to overcome the pollination crisis is still sparse. The growing awareness of pollination as an essential ecosystem service facilitates research that can increase the adaptive capacity of farmers in this respect.

Ecosystem services and vulnerability in Europe: Projections into the future

What is the future of ecosystem service supply? The concern for global change and its effects on the supply of a range of ecosystem services during the present century motivated a recently completed European vulnerability assessment[3] (Schröter et al, 2005a; Metzger et al, 2008). This spatially explicit vulnerability assessment was based on multiple plausible global-change scenarios, a framework of ecosystem models, and a continuous stakeholder dialogue. The aim of this study was to help European stakeholders prepare for global change. The central question was: how much will the provision of ecosystem services in Europe change due to the combined effects of climate and land-use changes? In the following I describe the basic future scenarios for climate and land-use change we used. Then I highlight two examples in which ecosystem models were driven by these scenarios, to illustrate how future projections of ecosystem service supply can inform us of vital aspects of our vulnerability to global changes.

Scenarios of climate and land-use change

Plausible descriptions of socioeconomic and biophysical variables into the present century cover a range of possible futures, without assigning probabilities to any individual scenario. To deal with this uncertainty, the assessment was based on a set of multiple, internally consistent scenarios for the main global-change drivers (socioeconomic factors, atmospheric greenhouse gas concentrations, climate factors and land use). These scenarios cover Europe on a regional spatial scale through this century (EU15 plus Norway and Switzerland, henceforth referred to as EU15+, on a 10'×10' latitude/longitude grid resolution; time slices 2020, 2050, 2080 and baseline 1990).[4] The scenarios were developed from an interpretation for the European region of the global IPCC SRES (Special Report on Emissions Scenarios) storylines A1FI, A2, B1 and B2 (Nakicenovic and Swart, 2000).[5] By using these storylines as a common starting point, socioeconomic change relates directly to climatic change through greenhouse gas emissions, and to land-use change through climatic and socioeconomic drivers, such as demand and technology. Four different general circulation models (GCMs) were used to simulate plausible changes in European climate (Mitchell et al, 2004).[6] The analysis was then limited to seven priority scenarios out of all possible combinations of storylines and GCMs: A1FI, A2, B1, B2 calculated with the GCM HadCM3 (variation across storylines, 'socioeconomic options'), and A2 calculated additionally with the GCMs CGCM2, CSIRO2 and PCM (variation across climate models, 'climatic uncertainty'). All temperature-change scenarios in Europe showed high regional variation, but a clear trend towards warming. The projected temperature increase in Europe ranged from 2.1 to 4.4°C (across storylines) and from 2.7 to 3.4°C for the A2 storyline (across GCMs; 30-year averages from 2051 to 2080 compared with 1961 to 1990) (Schröter et al, 2005a). Changes in precipitation were more complex. In general, increases in winter precipitation and decreases in summer precipitation resulted in small overall changes when comparing annual averages. Regional variation between the results of the climate models was considerable (Mitchell et al, 2004). Generally, all scenarios agreed in decreasing precipitation in the south of Europe, as well as mostly increasing precipitation in the north (Schröter et al, 2005a).

A set of future land-use scenarios with the same spatial scale were developed based on the climatic and socioeconomic scenarios (Ewert et al, 2004; Kankaanpää and Carter, 2004; Rounsevell et al, 2005; Reginster and Rounsevell, 2006).[7] The variation across land-use scenarios based on different climate models, but on the same storyline, was very small, indicating that socioeconomic assumptions had a much greater effect on the land-use scenario results than climatic drivers. The general trends shown by the land-use scenarios were of reductions in agricultural areas for food production, partly compensated for by increases in bioenergy production and forests, as well as small increases in urban areas and areas protected for conservation and recreation (Schröter et al, 2005a). In the A ('economically oriented') scenarios the decline in agricultural land was especially pronounced. Here decreases of up to 21 per cent (absolute decrease in percentage of EU15+ area) in the surface areas of agricultural land used for food and fibre production (cropland and grassland) are caused primarily by the assumptions about the role of technological development (Ewert et al, 2005). Large parts of Europe become surplus to the requirement of food and fibre production, which allows extensification[8] and further provides opportunities for the substitution of food production by energy production through the cultivation of bioenergy crops (Rounsevell et al, 2005).

Biomass energy production: Where to plant the power plants

As described in the previous section, Europe may have some potential to grow bioenergy crops without compromising other ecosystem services such as food production or recreational value of a landscape. Since the European Commission's White Paper,[9] landowners, farmers and foresters have a great interest in biomass energy production, as we learned early in our stakeholder dialogue (see Chapter 11, this volume). In direct response to stakeholders we have therefore investigated potential global-change effects on the ecosystem service *biomass energy production*.

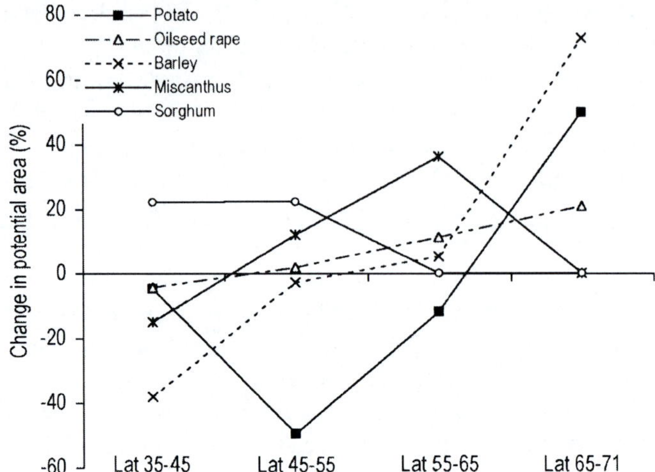

Note: Change relates to climatic conditions only; soil conditions are not taken into account.
Source: Results provided by Margaret Glendening and Gill Tuck, Institute of Arable Crops Research, Rothamsted, UK

Figure 6.2 *Percentage change in potential area for growth in different latitudinal bands in Europe in 2080 compared to baseline (1990) under the A2 scenario (climate by HadCM3)*

We assessed the distribution of 26 potential bioenergy crops under changing climate conditions (Tuck et al, 2006).[10] Under all scenarios the potential distribution of temperate oilseed, cereals, starch crops and solid biofuels was projected to increase in northern Europe due to increasing temperatures (high latitudes, Table 6.1), and to decrease in the most southern areas due to increased drought (low latitudes, Table 6.1). Hence, in southern Europe the choice of bioenergy crops available will be reduced in future. Different crop types show different trends. For example, climate change will reduce the area suitable for barley, miscanthus, oilseed rape and potato in the latitudinal band 35–45 (Figure 6.2), while the climatic conditions seem to be improved for sorghum. The climatic potential to grow barley, potato and oilseed rape increased by 2080 in the northern latitudes (Figure 6.2). Further agricultural considerations need to be taken into account when planning adaptive action based on these results, such as soil conditions.

Water supply: Growing demand and *changing climate*

Water supply is an environmental service; however, ecosystems are so vital for water purification, retention and storage that water supply may be called an *ecosystem* service. Water is an essential element for many vital processes within the human–environment system. Strictly speaking, it is a non-living renewable resource, even though living systems have a great influence on its production, consumption and regeneration. Water is a resource that connects all sectors within the human–environment system, since water is needed for energy production

Table 6.1 *Summary of main trends in impacts for Europe during this century*

Storyline GCM	A1FI HadCM3	A2 HadCM3	A2 PCM	A2 CGCM2	A2 CSIRO	B1 HadCM3	B2 HadCM3
Pot. distribution change, biofuels (%)[a]							
Overall	1	3	6	7	5	3	4
Latitude 35–45	−13	−8	−1	−3	−2	−7	−6
Latitude 45–55	−6	−2	4	8	−6	−1	0
Latitude 55–65	12	13	11	14	15	12	13
Latitude 65–71	32	23	19	16	34	18	22
Additional people living under water scarcity (10^6)[b]	44.3	15.7	7.5	11.7	5.8	44.3	25.8

Notes: a Change in potential distribution of 26 biofuel crops due to climate change, land area (%), 2080 compared to baseline (Tuck et al, 2006).

b Additional people (millions) living in watersheds with less than 1700m^3 per capita per year due to climate change in 2080 (compared with hypothetical case of no climate change) (Schröter et al, 2005a). Water-related resource problems are likely when water availability per capita falls below the threshold of 1700m^3 per capita per year (Falkenmark et al, 1989).

(e.g. cooling of nuclear power plants), agriculture, industrial production, navigation, domestic use and other living systems (forests, wetlands, etc.). Water is also linked to safety and the health sector in various ways (as beneficial and destructive force). Sustainable, transboundary water management hence is among the most difficult societal challenges.

The United Nations Environment Programme (UNEP) Global Environment Outlook-3 as well as the World Resources Institute estimated increases in the numbers of people living in water-stressed basins, due entirely to population growth (World Resources Institute, 2000; UNEP, 2002). To assess the added constraint of climate change on water supply we used a macro-scale hydrological model (Mac-pdm: Arnell, 1999 modified; Arnell, 2003).[11] By 2080, climate change may increase the number of people living under water scarcity by up to 44.3 million (Table 6.1). Reductions in 30-year mean runoff in parts of southern Europe may be as great as 30 per cent. The adverse effect of this scarcity is exacerbated since extractions per capita are higher in southern Europe due to irrigation. Furthermore, tourism results in substantial increases in water use, especially in summer. In addition to increasing the number of people served with water in a region, tourists' water consumption has been shown to be far in excess of that of local residents (World Tourism Organization, 2003). The variation in additional people living under water scarcity across different storylines (15.7–44.3 million) was higher than across different GCMs (for A2: 5.8–15.7 million, Table 6.1), stressing the potential to mitigate this impact by socioeconomic changes.

European vulnerability

Our European vulnerability assessment looked at a greater range of ecosystem services than presented here. We modelled ecosystem service indicators important to the agriculture, forestry, energy, nature conservation, water and tourism sectors. The uncertainty inherent in our estimates was large. Nevertheless, the direction of some problematic trends was common in all scenarios. Though some of the projected trends may be considered positive (e.g. increases in forest area and productivity), and others hold potential future opportunities (e.g. 'surplus land' for agricultural extensification and biomass energy production), most impacts were projected to have negative consequences for society (e.g. declining soil fertility, increasing risk of forest fires). These environmental impacts will add to our vulnerability to global change. In comparison between European regions, the Mediterranean seemed most vulnerable within Europe. Another area of great concern was the mountains.

The active participation and sustained interest of our collaborating stakeholders show that global change and ecosystem services are issues of concern to them, albeit among many others. The final product of the European assessment is a digital atlas of maps of changing ecosystem service supply and vulnerability (Metzger et al, 2004). Stakeholders have commented on the usefulness of the assessment with encouragement and criticism alike (de la Vega-Leinert and Schröter, 2005; de la Vega-Leinert and Schröter, Chapter 11, this volume). They were considerably more interested in information on ecosystem services and potential changes in supply than in generic indicators for adaptive capacity or vulnerability. As it stands, the European assessment has raised awareness and received ample media coverage. It has helped discuss the issues of climate change mitigation on a European scale. However, its goal to support specific stakeholders in their local decision making was rarely met. To increase the usefulness of our results for the development of local adaptation strategies, even finer spatial and temporal scales will have to be tackled in the future. Interactions between sectors and services have to be taken into account more fully.

Lowering vulnerability through sustainable management of ecosystem services

The basis for resilient (i.e. not vulnerable) human–environment systems is the sustainable use of ecosystem services without compromising one vital service over another. Ecosystem services can be private goods, such as the provisioning service *timber production* on privately owned land. However, the very same forest system also provides other ecosystem services, for example, the supporting service *primary production*, the regulating service *climate regulation*, and the cultural service *aesthetic appeal*. These services are public goods, whether recognized as such or not. The concept of ecosystem services holds the advantage that these private and public goods can be identified, acknowledged and managed as vital connections between ecosystems and humans in a more systematic way.

There seem to be three main reasons for unsustainable management of ecosystem services, one or more of which may apply in a particular case:

1 An ecosystem service is not recognized.
2 An ecosystem service is compromised to maximize profits at the cost of the public, because regulation and taxation set no limits.
3 An ecosystem service is used unsustainably, because of an immediate vital need and no alternatives.

The pollinator example described above may be a case of the first reason. Though certainly recognized by farmers, pollination was probably long taken for granted by most people – leading to the publication of a book with the meaningful title *The Forgotten Pollinators* (Buchmann and Nabhan, 1996).

Examples for the second case seem countless: exploiting one ecosystem service to the benefit of one actor, but to the cost of the public due to lack of regulation. This is known in game theory as the 'free-rider problem'. The complexity of the human–environment system leaves room for many free rides (Houck, 2003). The most obvious example may be using the atmosphere as a dump for greenhouse gases and thereby altering the global climate, which is likely to alter the majority of ecosystem services, as described in the European case study above.

The underlying cause of the Canadian dust bowl might be seen as farmers' immediate need to make a living, the third reason for unsustainable use of an ecosystem service. Soil erosion has accompanied human life on Earth in three big waves, each of which was followed by management efforts (McNeill and Winiwarter, 2004). Another example can be taken from the poorest country of the Western Hemisphere, namely Haiti. Haiti has undergone rapid deforestation, to increase arable area on marginal lands and to extract firewood. This was caused by the dire need of an extremely poor population that is not entitled to use the low-lying fertile lands. Only 20 per cent of the land is considered arable; however, 50 per cent is currently under agricultural production (Food and Agriculture Organization (FAO), 2001). Today less than 2 per cent of the land is forested. Deforestation has destabilized soils and altered the river basins, leading to soil erosion and increased risk of floods. In May 2004, heavy rains caused flooding and mudslides, killing 2665 people (Emergency Disasters Database (EM-DAT), 2005). Only four months later, Hurricane Jeanne again brought heavy rainfalls and caused yet another devastating flood, killing 2745 more people in Gonaïves, Haiti's third largest city, where hardly a house was left untouched by the flood waters (EM-DAT, 2005). While deforestation is widely acknowledged as a main cause of these disasters, reforestation is a slow and tedious task. Haiti is politically unstable and experiences violent outbreaks.

How can environmental science facilitate sustainable management of ecosystem services, and consequently decrease vulnerability? The first obligation is to raise awareness of the importance and complexity of ecosystems and the services they provide. In this respect, the Millennium Ecosystem Assessment (MA, www.millenniumassessment.org) has been a tremendous achievement. The MA was a global ecosystem study that represents a consensus of over 1300 scientists. One of its four key findings was that '[t]he degradation of ecosystem services could grow significantly worse during the first half of this century and is a barrier to achieving the Millennium Development Goals' (Reid et al, 2005). However, further studies are needed that specify and quantify the supply of ecosystem services under different management options, such as, for example, the European assessment described above (Schröter et al, 2005a).

If an ecosystem service is compromised to maximize profits at the cost of the public, because regulation and taxation set no limits, environmental scientists can sound the alarm and shed light on the causality. Research unravels how different ecosystem services work together. Ecosystem models can translate climate and land-use changes into changes in ecosystem service supply. One of the key ingredients to optimal use of ecosystem services is a reliable model of the ecosystem's response to different forms of use (Scheffer et al, 2000). Therefore, ecosystem models need to incorporate human actors and management. However, we have neither complete understanding nor control of the human–environment system. Scientists and policy makers have to work together to find useful regulations in the face of uncertainty. This leaves room for ill-willed manipulation, such as exaggerating the uncertainty of a finding to get away with complacency. For example, some ignore the consensus on anthropogenic climate change to avoid measures to reduce greenhouse gas emissions (Oreskes, 2004). How can society ensure that scientific knowledge and its limits are represented adequately to serve its people best? How can we ensure free media, an alert and well-informed public, as well as candid scientists and policy makers?

Finally, if ecosystem services are compromised to fulfil an immediate vital need, environmental scientists can ideally offer alternative and more sustainable technologies based on an understanding of the ecosystem. The implementation of alternative technologies itself requires social, economic and environmental resources. Therefore the key question remains: how to entitle and empower the poor to use their environment sustainably?

Conclusions

Human well-being depends on the sustained supply of ecosystem services – unsustainable use of ecosystem services increases vulnerability. Environmental scientists alone cannot provide the information and the tools that are needed to lessen the vulnerability of a region. However, they can make an essential contribution. They identify ecosystem services as vital links between humans and ecosystems. Moreover, they provide the best current understanding of the dynamics of the complex ecosystems that supply these services. Ecosystem models that include human management play an essential role in integrated assessment of global change. The uncertainty inherent in scientific knowledge leaves room for ill-willed manipulation. A sustained active dialogue between a free media, an alert and well-informed public, candid scientists and policy makers seems to be the best insurance against this. Sustainable management of ecosystem services thus requires abundant social, economic and environmental resources.

Therefore the key question remains: how to entitle and empower the poor to use their environment sustainably? This is a question that will not be answered by environmental scientists alone. It is a fundamental puzzle of humanity.

Acknowledgements

Parts of this chapter present work carried out within the EU-funded Fifth Framework project ATEAM (Advanced Terrestrial Ecosystem Analysis and Modelling, No. EVK2-2000-00075). Concepts were developed in discourse with all project members, especially T. Carter, W. Cramer, J. House, R. Leemans, A. C. de la Vega-Leinert, M. J. Metzger, I. C. Prentice, M. Rounsevell and M. T. Sykes. Some results presented here were taken from colleagues on the project; we specifically wish to acknowledge A. W. Arnell, M. Erhard, F. Ewert, M. Glendining, T. Mitchell, I. Reginster, J. Smith, P. Smith, G. Tuck, M. Wattenbach and D. W. Wilson. Part of this work was carried out while being hosted as a visiting research fellow by the *Science, Environment and Development Group* at the Center for International Development, Harvard University. Additional funding came from the project ALARM (Assessing LArge-scale environmental Risks with tested Methods, No. GOCE-CT-2003-506675).

Notes

1 More precisely, pollination is the process of moving pollen from the anthers (pollen-containing part of the floral stamens) of one flower to the stigma (receptive end of the carpel) of another.

2 Africanized bees arrived in Texas in 1990, after migrating steadily North since 1956, when African bees escaped from a geneticist's laboratory in Brazil. They interbred with local European honeybees and produced so-called Africanized bees.

3 ATEAM – Advanced Terrestrial Ecosystem Analysis and Modelling, www.pik-potsdam.de/ateam

4 The time slices represent 30-year averages; baseline 1990 (mean over 1961–1990), 2020 (mean over 1991–2020), 2050 (mean over 2021–2050) and 2080 (mean over 2051–2080).

5 The Special Report of Emission Scenarios (SRES) are narrative descriptions of plausible future worlds that were developed by a large group of experts in a long-term open review process as a function of major driving forces, such as population growth, economic development and technological change (Nakicenovic and Swart, 2000). They are structured in four major families labelled A1, A2, B1 and B2, each of which emphasizes a different set of social, environmental and economic ideals. These ideals are organized along two axes. The first major dimension focuses on 'material consumption' (dimension A; also referred to as 'economically oriented'), versus 'sustainability, equity and environment' (dimension B; sometimes referred to as 'environmentally oriented'). The second major dimension distinguishes 'globalization' (dimension 1) versus 'regionalization' (dimension 2). The narratives specify typical aspects and processes for each of the four quadrants identified by these dimensions. The A1 scenario was further elaborated by assuming different combinations of fuels

and technology development to satisfy energy demand. A1FI remains dominated by fossil fuels. Trajectories of greenhouse gas emissions were quantified using the integrated assessment model IMAGE 2.2 (IMAGE team, 2001). The A1FI socioeconomic scenario results in the highest emissions and consequently in the highest atmospheric concentrations of carbon dioxide (c. 960ppmv in 2100), followed by A2, B2 and finally B1 (870, 610 and 520ppmv, respectively; atmospheric CO_2 concentration in 2000 was c. 370ppmv).

6 Climate change scenarios with monthly values were created for five climatic variables: temperature, diurnal temperature range, precipitation, vapour pressure and cloud cover. The scenarios comprise all 16 combinations of four SRES emissions scenarios and four general circulation models (GCMs; PCM, CGCM2, CSIRO2, HadCM3), using GCM outputs from the IPCC Data Distribution Centre. The results were subsequently downscaled from $0.5° \times 0.5°$ to $10' \times 10'$ resolution. The climate scenarios of the 21st century replicate observed month-to-month, inter-annual and multi-decadal climate variability of the detrended 20th century climate. The full method is described in Mitchell et al (2004). The scenarios are known as TYN SC 1.0 and are publicly available (an advanced version is available from the ATEAM project).

7 The land-use categories we distinguished were: urban, agriculture (cropland, grassland and biofuels), forestry and designated areas (for conservation or recreation goals) (Ewert et al, 2004; Kankaanpää and Carter, 2004; Rounsevell et al, 2005, 2006; Reginster and Rounsevell 2006). The approach recognized three levels in the derivation of land-use scenarios that move from qualitative descriptions of global socioeconomic storylines, over European-sector driving forces, to quantitative projections of regional land-use change. For each land-use category the methodology broadly followed the same steps. First an assessment was made of the total area requirement (quantity) of each land use, as a function of changes in the relevant drivers. This was based on outputs from the global-scale IMAGE 2.2 Integrated Assessment Model on commodity demands at the European scale (IMAGE team, 2001). Second, scenario-specific spatial allocation rules were developed and applied to locate these land-use quantities in geographic space across Europe. Third and finally, the scenarios of the broad land-use types were post-processed to maintain the land-use constant in designated areas. This approach was implemented using a range of techniques that were specific to each land-use type, including reviews of the literature, expert judgement and modelling. Widespread consultation was undertaken with other experts in the field, as well as with stakeholders.

8 We refer to extensification as the transition of a land-cover or land-use type associated with high intensity of use to a lower intensity of use (e.g. improved grassland to semi-natural cover).

9 The European Commission's White Paper for a Community Strategy proposed a target of doubling the contribution of renewable energy sources to 12 per cent of the EU's total primary energy needs by 2010 (European Commission, 1997).

10 Bioenergy or biofuel crops are those annual and perennial species that are specifically cultivated to produce solid, liquid or gaseous forms of energy. Twenty-six actual or potential bioenergy crops were selected: oilseed rape, linseed, field mustard, hemp, sunflower, safflower, castor, olive, groundnut, barley, wheat, oats, rye, potato, sugar beet, jerusalem artichoke, sugarcane, cardoon, sorghum, kenaf, prickly pear, maize, reed canary grass, miscanthus, short rotation coppice and eucalyptus. Simple rules were derived from the literature for each crop for suitable climate conditions and elevation. The climate conditions were based on minimum and maximum monthly temperatures at various times of the year, and precipitation requirements. All crops

are assumed to be rainfed (not irrigated) and not protected from frost. The approach is described in detail in Tuck et al, 2006.

11 In general terms, the Mac-pdm model calculates the evolution of the components of the water balance at a daily time step (Arnell, 1999 modified; Arnell, 2003). Although the model was implemented at a scale of 10'×10', for most of the analyses, runoff was aggregated to the 0.5°×0.5° scale. Döll and Lehner's (2002) drainage direction map was used to link the 0.5°×0.5° cells together and enable the accumulation of flows along the river network. A total of 94 major river basins have been identified, based on currently proposed river basins and major topographic boundaries. Basin areas ranged from just over 10,000km^2 to 373,000km^2.

References

Arnell, N. W. (1999) 'A simple water balance model for the simulation of streamflow over a large geographic domain', *Journal of Hydrology*, vol 217, pp314–335

Arnell, N. W. (2003) 'Effects of IPCC SRES emissions scenarios on river runoff: A global perspective', *Hydrology and Earth System Sciences*, vol 7, pp619–641

Buchmann, S. L. and Nabhan, G. P. (1996) *The Forgotten Pollinators*, Island Press, Washington DC

Cohen, J. E. (2003) 'Human population: The next half century', *Science*, vol 302, p1172

Daily, G. C. (1997) *Nature's Services*, Island Press / Shearwater Books, Washington DC

Daily, G. C. and Ellison, K. (2002) *The New Economy of Nature: The Quest to Make Conservation Profitable*, Island Press / Shearwater Books, Washington DC

de Groot, R. S. (1992) *Functions of Nature: Evaluation of Nature in Environmental Planning, Management and Decision-Making*, Wolters-Noordhoff BV, Groningen, The Netherlands

de la Vega-Leinert, A. C. and Schröter, D. (2005) 'Vulnerability of human sectors to global changes', the 3rd ATEAM stakeholder dialogue workshop, 3–4 May 2004, Potsdam, Germany, 59pp

Döll, P. and Lehner, B. (2002) 'Validation of a new global 30-minute drainage direction map', *Journal of Hydrology*, vol 258, pp214–231

EM-DAT (2005) Emergency Disasters Database, www.em-dat.be

European Commission (1997) *Energy for the Future: Renewable Sources of Energy*, White Paper for a Community Strategy and Action Plan, 599, European Communities, Luxembourg

Ewert, F., Rounsevell, M. .D. A., Reginster, I., Metzger, M. and Leemans, R. (2004) 'Technology development and climate change as drivers of future agricultural land use' in McCarl, B. (ed) *Rural Lands, Agriculture and Climate Beyond 2015: Usage and Management Responses*, Kluwer Academic Publishers, Dordrecht

Ewert, F., Rounsevell, M. D. A., Reginster, I., Metzger, M. J. and Leemans, R. (2005) 'Future scenarios of European agricultural land use: I. Estimating changes in crop productivity', *Agriculture, Ecosystems & Environment*, vol 107, pp101–116

Falkenmark, M., Lundquist, J. and Widstrand, C. (1989) 'Macro-scale water scarcity requires micro-scale approaches: Aspects of vulnerability in semi-arid development', *Natural Resources Forum*, vol 13, pp258–267

FAO (2001) *The State of Food and Agriculture 2001*, Food and Agriculture Organization of the United Nations

Fraser, E. D. G. (2003) 'Social vulnerability and ecological fragility: Building bridges between social and natural sciences using the Irish Potato Famine as a case study', *Conservation Ecology*, vol 7(2), p9, www.consecol.org/vol7/iss2/art9/

Gunderson, L., Holling, C. S. and Light, S. S. (1995) *Barriers and Bridges to the Renewal of Ecosystems and Institutions*, Columbia University Press, New York

Holden, C. (2004) 'Consider the pollinators', *Science*, vol 304, p1592

Holling, C. S. (2001) 'Understanding the complexity of economic, ecological, and social systems', *Ecosystems*, vol 4, pp390–405

Houck, O. (2003) 'Tales from a troubled marriage: Science and law in environmental policy', *Science*, vol 302, pp1926–1929

IMAGE team (2001) *The IMAGE 2.2 Implementation of the SRES Scenarios: A Comprehensive Analysis of Emissions, Climate Change and Impacts in the 21st Century*, National Institute of Public Health and the Environment (RIVM), Bilthoven, The Netherlands

Ingram, M., Nabhan, G. and Buchmann, S. L. (1996) *Our Forgotten Pollinators: Protecting the Birds and Bees*, PANNA – Pesticide Action Network North America 6, www.pmac.net/birdbee.htm

IPCC (2001) *Climate Change 2001: The Scientific Basis; Impacts, Adaptation & Vulnerability; Mitigation*, Intergovernmental Panel on Climate Change Third Assessment Report, Cambridge University Press, Cambridge

IPCC (2007) 'Summary for policymakers', in Solomon, S., Qin, D., Manning, M., Chen, Z., Marquis, M., Averyt, K. B., Tignor, M. and Miller, H. L. (eds) *The Physical Science Basis*, Contribution of Working Group I to the Fourth Assessment Report of the Intergovernmental Panel on Climate Change, Cambridge University Press, Cambridge, UK and New York, NY, USA

Kankaanpää, S. and Carter, T. R. (2004) *Construction of European Forest Land Use Scenarios for the 21st Century*, Finnish Environment Institute, Helsinki

Kates, R. W., Clark, W. C., Corell, R., Hall, J. M., Jaeger, C. C., Lowe, I., McCarthy, J. J., Schellnhuber, H. J., Bolin, B., Dickson, N. M., Faucheux, S., Gallopin, G. C., Grubler, A., Huntley, B., Jäger, J., Jodha, N. S., Kasperson, R. E., Mabogunje, A., Matson, P., Mooney, H., Moore, B., O'Riordan, T. and Svedin, U. (2001) 'Sustainability Science', *Science*, vol 292, pp641–642

Kremen, C., Williams, N. M., Bugg, R. L., Fay, J. P. and Thorp, R. W. (2004) 'The area requirements of an ecosystem service: Crop pollination by native bee communities in California', *Ecology Letters*, vol 7, pp1109–1119

McNeill, J. R. (2001) *Something New Under the Sun: An Environmental History of the Twentieth-Century World*, W. W. Norton & Company Inc., New York, NY

McNeill, J. R. and Winiwarter, V. (2004) 'Breaking the sod: Humankind, history, and soil', *Science*, vol 304, pp1627–1629

Metzger, M., and Schröter, D. (2006) 'Towards a spatially explicit and quantitative vulnerability assessment of environmental change in Europe', *Regional Environmental Change*, vol 6, pp201–216

Metzger, M. J., Leemans, R., Schröter, D., Cramer, W. and ATEAM consortium (2004) *The ATEAM Vulnerability Mapping Tool*, Office C. T. de Wit Graduate School for Production Ecology & Resource Conservation (PE&RC), Wageningen, The Netherlands

Metzger, M. J., Schröter, D., Leemans, R. and Cramer, W. (2008) 'A spatially explicit and quantitative vulnerability assessment of ecosystem service change in Europe', *Regional Environmental Change*, vol 8, pp91–107

Millennium Ecosystem Assessment (2003) *Ecosystems and Human Well-Being: A Framework for Assessment*, Island Press, Washington DC

Millennium Ecosystem Assessment (2005) *Ecosystems and Human Well-Being: Synthesis*, World Resources Institute, Washington DC

Mitchell, T. D., Carter, T. R., Jones, P. D., Hulme, M.and New, M. (2004) 'A comprehensive set of high-resolution grids of monthly climate for Europe and the globe: The observed record (1901–2000) and 16 scenarios (2001–2100)', Tyndall Centre for Climate Change Research Working Paper 55, p25

Moss, R., Brenkert, A. and Malone, E. L. (2000) *Measuring Vulnerability: A Trial Indicator Set*, in Pacific Northwest Laboratory, Richland, MA

Nabhan, G. P. and Buchmann, S. L. (1997) 'Services provided by pollinators', in Daily, G. C. (ed) *Nature's Services: Societal Dependence on Natural Ecosystems*, Island Press, Washington DC, pp133–150

Nakicenovic, N. and Swart, R. (eds) (2000) *IPCC Special Report on Emissions Scenarios* (SRES), Cambridge University Press, Cambridge

Oberthur, A. (2004) 'Almond growers scramble for pollinating honey bees', *Indiana State Beekeepers Association Journal*, vol 124, p8

Oreskes, N. (2004) 'The scientific consensus on climate change', *Science*, vol 306, p1686

Palmer, M., Bernhardt, E., Chornesky, E., Collins, S., Dobson, A., Duke, C., Gold, B., Jacobson, R., Kingsland, S., Kranz, R., Mappin, M., Martinez, M. L., Micheli, F., Morse, J., Pace, M., Pascual, M., Palumbi, S., Reichmann, O. J., Simons, A., Townsend, A. and Turner, M. (2004) 'Ecology for a crowded planet', *Science*, vol 304, pp1251–1252

Parmesan, C. and Yohe, G. (2003) 'A globally coherent fingerprint of climate change impacts across natural systems', *Nature*, vol 421, pp37–42

Reginster, I. R. and Rounsevell, M. D. A. (2006) 'Scenarios of future urban land use in Europe', *Environment and Planning B: Planning and Design*, vol 33, pp619–636

Reid, W. V., Mooney, H. A., Cropper, A., Capistrano, D., Carpenter, S. R., Chopra, K., Dasgupta, P., Dietz, T., Duraiappah, A. K., Hassan, R., Kasperson, R., Leemans, R., May, R. M., McMichael, T. A. J., Pingali, P., Samper, C., Scholes, R., Watson, R. T., Zakri, A. H., Shidong, Z., Ash, N. J., Bennett, E., Kumar, P., Lee, M. J., RaudseppHearne, C., Simons, H., Thonell, J. and Zurek, M. B. (2005) *Millennium Ecosystem Assessment Synthesis Report*, Island Press, Washington DC

Root, T. L., Price, J. T., Hall, K. R., Schneider, S. H., Rosenzweig, C. and Pounds, J. A. (2003) 'Fingerprints of global warming on wild animals and plants', *Nature*, vol 421, pp57–60

Rounsevell, M. D. A., Ewert, F., Reginster, I., Leemans, R. and Carter, T. R. (2005) 'Future scenarios of European agricultural land use II. Projecting changes in cropland and grassland', *Agriculture, Ecosystems & Environment*, vol 107, pp117–135

Rounsevell, M. D. A., Reginster, I., Araújo, M. B., Carter, T. R., Dendoncker, N., Ewert, F., House, J. I., Kankaanpää, S., Leemans, R., Metzger, M. J., Schmit, C., Smith, P. and Tuck, G. (2006) 'A coherent set of future land use change scenarios for Europe', *Agriculture, Ecosystems & Environment*, vol 114, pp57–68

Sala, O. E., Chapin, F. S., Armesto, J. J., Berlow, E., Bloomfield, J., Dirzo, R., Huber-Sanwald, E., Huenneke, L. F., Jackson, R. B., Kinzig, A., Leemans, R., Lodge, D. M., Mooney, H. A., Oesterheld, M., Poff, N. L., Sykes, M. T., Walker, B. H., Walker, M. and Wall, D. H. (2000) 'Biodiversity: Global biodiversity scenarios for the year 2100', *Science*, vol 287, pp1770–1774

Scheffer, M., Brock, W. and Westley, F. (2000) 'Socioeconomic mechanisms preventing optimum use of ecosystem services: An interdisciplinary theoretical analysis', *Ecosystems*, vol 3, pp451–471

Schröter, D. (2001) 'Assessing vulnerability of European ecosystem services', Presentation at the workshop Methods and Models of Vulnerability Research, Analysis and Assessment, Sustainability Days, 28 September–5 October 2001, Potsdam, Germany

Schröter, D., Metzger, M. J., Cramer, W. and Leemans, R. (2004) 'Vulnerability assessment: Analysing the human environment system in the face of global environmental change', *Environmental Science Section Bulletin*, vol 2, pp11–17

Schröter, D., Cramer, W., Leemans, R., Prentice, I. C., Araújo, M. B., Arnell, N. W., Bondeau, A., Bugmann, H., Carter, T. R., Gracia, C. A., de la Vega-Leinert, A. C., Erhard, M., Ewert, F., Glendining, M., House, J. I., Kankaanpää, S., Klein, R. J. T., Lavorel, S., Lindner, M., Metzger, M. J., Meyer, J., Mitchell, T. D., Reginster, I., Rounsevell, M., Sabaté, S., Sitch, S., Smith, B., Smith, J., Smith, P., Sykes, M. T., Thonicke, K., Thuiller, W., Tuck, G., Zaehle, S. and Zierl, B. (2005a) 'Ecosystem service supply and vulnerability to global change in Europe', *Science*, vol 310, pp1333–1337

Schröter, D., Polsky, C. and Patt, A. G. (2005b) 'Assessing vulnerabilities to the effects of global change: An eight step approach', *Mitigation and Adaptation Strategies for Global Change*, vol 10, pp573–595

Smith, V. H., Tilman, G. D. and Nekola, J. C. (1999) 'Eutrophication: Impacts of excess nutrient inputs on freshwater, marine, and terrestrial ecosystems', *Environmental Pollution*, vol 100, pp179–196

Stenseth, N. C., Mysterud, A., Ottersen, G., Hurrell, J. W., Chan, K.-S. and Lima, M. (2002) 'Ecological effects of climate fluctuations', *Science*, vol 297, pp1292–1296

Stokstad, E. (2007) 'The case of the empty hives', *Science*, vol 316, pp970–972

Tuck, G., Glendining, M. J., Smith, P., House, J. I. and Wattenbach, M. (2006) 'The potential distribution of bioenergy crops in Europe under present and future climate', *Biomass & Bioenergy*, vol 30, pp183–197

Turner, B. L., Kasperson, R. E., Matson, P. A., McCarthy, J. J., Corell, R. W., Christensen, L., Eckley, N., Kasperson, J. X., Luers, A., Martello, M. L., Polsky, C., Pulsipher, A. and Schiller, A. (2003) 'A framework for vulnerability analysis in sustainability science', *Proceedings of the National Academy of Sciences of the United States of America*, vol 100, pp8074–8079

UNEP (2002) *GEO-3: Global Environmental Outlook Report 3*, United Nations Environment Programme

van der Leeuw, S. E. (2001) '"Vulnerability" and the integrated study of socio-natural phenomena', Update: *Newsletter of the International Human Dimensions Programme on Global Environmental Change 2*, article 2

Walker, B., Carpenter, S., Anderies, J., Abel, N., Cumming, G. S., Janssen, M., Lebel, L., Norberg, J., Peterson, G. D. and Pritchard, R. (2002) 'Resilience management in social-ecological systems: A working hypothesis for a participatory approach', *Conservation Ecology*, vol 6, p14

Walther, G.-R., Post, E., Convey, P., Menzel, A., Parmesan, C., Beebee, T. J. C., Fromentin, J.-M., Hoegh-Guldberg, O. and Bairlein, F. (2002) 'Ecological responses to recent climate change', *Nature*, vol 416, pp389–395

Waltner-Toews, D., Kay, J. J., Neudoerffer, C. and Gitau, T. (2003) 'Perspective changes everything: Managing ecosystems from the inside out', *Frontiers in Ecology and the Environment*, vol 1, pp23–30

Watson, R. T., Noble, I. R., Bolin, B., Ravindranath, N. H., Verardo, D. J. and Dokken, D. J. (eds) (2000) *Land Use, Land-Use Change and Forestry*, a Special Report of the Intergovernmental Panel on Climate Change (IPCC), Cambridge University Press, Cambridge

World Resources Institute (2000) *World Resources 2000–2001. People and Ecosystems: The Fraying Web of Life*, World Resources Institute, Washington DC

World Tourism Organisation (2003) *Climate Change and Tourism*, in The 1st International Conference on Climate Change and Tourism, Djerba, Tunisia, 55pp

Chapter 7

Assessing Vulnerability of Human Health

Hans-Martin Füssel and Kristie L. Ebi

Introduction

Anthropogenic climate change has major implications for the distribution and urgency of health risks around the world. In the last decade, a considerable number of studies have investigated how climate change may affect human population health, and how anticipatory adaptation strategies can reduce adverse health impacts of climate variability and change. In this chapter, we discuss how vulnerability and adaptation assessments can inform policies aimed at reducing climate-related health risks now and in the future.

The health of a population reflects, in a basic sense, their social and environmental living conditions. Many key determinants of human health, such as food availability, freshwater availability, physical safety and the microbiological environment, are strongly influenced by climatic conditions. Changes in climate are thus always associated with changes in health risks. Climate-sensitive health outcomes include: the direct impacts of extreme climate events, such as heatwaves, storms, floods and landslides; the indirect effects of climatic factors mediated through ecological systems, such as water- and food-borne diseases, vector- and rodent-borne diseases, pollen allergies and food and water shortages; and the health effects caused by the interaction of climatic and non-climatic factors, such as increased ground-level ozone (known as 'summer smog' in Europe). In fact, almost any impact of climate change may be associated with health effects, in particular in developing countries and in marginalized population groups that lack the capacity to cope with these impacts. For an overview of climate-sensitive health effects, see Table 7.1.

Table 7.1 *Summary of the known health effects of weather and climate*

Health outcome	Known effects of weather and climate
Cardiovascular respiratory mortality and heat stroke mortality	Short-term increases in mortality during heatwaves. V- and J-shaped relationship between temperature and mortality in populations in temperate climates. Deaths from heat stroke increase during heatwaves.
Allergic rhinitis	Weather affects the distribution, seasonality and production of aeroallergens.
Respiratory and cardiovascular diseases and mortality	Weather affects concentrations of harmful air pollutants.
Deaths and injuries	Floods, landslides and windstorms cause death and injuries.
Infectious diseases and mental disorders	Flooding disrupts water supply and sanitation systems and may damage transport systems and health care infrastructure. Floods may provide breeding sites for mosquito vectors and lead to outbreaks of disease. Floods may increase post-traumatic stress disorders.
Starvation, malnutrition and diarrhoeal and respiratory diseases	Drought reduces water availability for hygiene. Drought increases the risk of forest fires. Drought reduces food availability in populations that are highly dependent on household agriculture productivity and/or economically weak.
Mosquito, tick-borne diseases and rodent-borne diseases (such as malaria, dengue, tick-borne encephalitis and Lyme disease)	Higher temperatures shorten the development time of pathogens in vectors and increase the potential transmission to humans. Each vector species has specific climate conditions (temperature and humidity) necessary to be sufficiently abundant to maintain transmission.
Malnutrition and undernutrition	Climate change may decrease food supplies (crop yield and fish stocks) or access to food supplies.
Water-borne and food-borne diseases	Survival of disease-causing organisms is related to temperature. Climate conditions affect water availability and quality Extreme rainfall can affect the transport of disease-causing organisms into the water supply.

Source: Kovats et al, 2003a

Anthropogenic climate change constitutes a largely unfamiliar threat to human health and well-being. It will affect the urgency of existing health risks and introduce new health risks to currently unaffected regions. While health impacts can be both positive and negative, adverse impacts are expected to dominate in most regions (McMichael and Githeko, 2001; McMichael et al, 2003). Early impacts of climate change on population health include changes in the geographical and seasonal patterns of certain vector-borne and food-borne infectious diseases, increased heat stress, and changes in the health impacts from extreme weather events. As a result of complex relationships and competing explanations, it is still difficult to attribute observed changes in health outcomes to anthropogenic climate change. The most comprehensive assessment so far is the World Health Organization (WHO) Global Burden of Disease project (WHO, 2002; Campbell-Lendrum et al, 2003; McMichael et al, 2004). According to this assessment, anthropogenic climate change was responsible in the year 2000 for approximately 2.4 per cent of worldwide diarrhoea, 6 per cent of worldwide malaria, 7 per cent of worldwide dengue fever (predominantly in some industrialized countries) and 0.3 per cent of all deaths worldwide (see the section on Recent vulnerability assessments of human health for details).

In the following sections of this chapter, we present the main methods for estimating the health effects of future climate change; discuss how vulnerability assessments can facilitate planned adaptation; review the main approaches to vulnerability and adaptation assessment; present a generic framework for human health vulnerability and adaptation assessment; review selected human health vulnerability assessments, focusing on the framing of the assessment, the research methodology and lessons learned for future assessments; and draw some conclusions for future vulnerability and adaptation assessments of human health.

Methods for estimating future health impacts of climate change

The motivation for vulnerability assessments of climate change and human health is the expectation that past and future climate change already has or will aggravate existing health risks and/or introduce new health risks to a population. Estimates of current and future health risks from climate variability and change are derived by a variety of methods. The most common methods used for assessing the potential health impacts of climate change are expert judgement; analogue or historical studies; and biophysical modelling (Carter et al, 1996; Haines and McMichael, 1997; Parry and Carter, 1998). These methods can be used separately or overlap in an assessment.

Expert judgement includes extensive literature review and identification of comparable studies, in combination with the collective experience and judgement of a group of individuals with diverse, relevant expertise (Bernard and Ebi, 2001). Expert judgement can serve to rapidly assess the state of knowledge concerning a problem. Such analyses are largely triggered by policy needs.

The analogue approach uses recorded climatic regimes as analogues for the future climate of a given region (Glantz, 1996). Analogues include historical events or trends and geographic comparisons. For example, researchers use the climate anomalies associated with the El Niño Southern Oscillation to examine the potential effects of extreme climate variability on human health (Kovats et al, 2003b). Such analogue studies have limited applicability to populations with greater or lesser vulnerability to short-term variability than the historical reference population. Similarly, geographic analogues (such as using the current climate of a warmer low-latitude region to project the future climate of a colder high-latitude region) may be of limited value due to a lack of correspondence between the two locations on other important factors, such as living standards and behaviours. Finally, future weather patterns may vary from historical trends because of stochastic and non-linear processes (McMichael et al, 1996).

Biophysical modelling can be either empirical–statistical or process-based. An empirical model begins with the quantification of current associations between risk factors and disease outcomes. Estimates of future populations and potential exposures are then used to project quantitative relationships and to estimate statistical uncertainties. Process-based models begin with the integration of what is known about the system of interest. Theoretical and empirical information about the disease of interest are derived from epidemiologic, clinical and micro-level (molecular and genetic) studies. A mathematical model is then developed to estimate the association between climate and disease under a range of potential scenarios. A benefit of these models is that they allow for integrated consideration of the combinations of environmental, biological, ecological and social factors that influence health (although in practice few of these integrative analyses have been conducted); a drawback is that uncertainties accumulate (these, however, can be examined and made transparent) (Bernard and Ebi, 2001). Applications of this approach include integrated models of disease transmission for a variety of vector-borne diseases, such as malaria (Van Lieshout et al, 2004).

Planned adaptation to reduce climate-related health risks

Most climate-related health impairments can be avoided in principle by public health interventions. The range of suitable interventions includes technical, institutional, legal, educational, behavioural and medical measures. The considered measures are, in general, not new. For instance, vaccination against tick-borne encephalitis does not differ between newly affected regions and regions where the disease is already prevalent. Therefore, many measures aimed at reducing current vulnerability to climate variability would also reduce the health impacts caused by future climate change. However, adaptation to climate change may require action by people who have not considered climate an important factor for their decisions in the past and who are not used to dealing with newly emerging health risks (Willows and Connell, 2003).

Successful planned adaptation to a large extent depends on six preconditions (based on Last, 1998):

1 awareness of the problem and its causes;
2 availability of effective intervention measures;
3 information about effective and efficient intervention measures;

4 availability of resources to implement these measures;
5 cultural acceptability of these measures; and
6 incentives for actually implementing these measures.

For adaptation to be successful, all six preconditions have to be met to a certain degree. The main purpose of adaptation assessments is to raise awareness of the problem (1), to provide information about intervention measures (3) and to advise on the creation of incentives for actually implementing these measures (6). In some cases, they may also facilitate the provision of the necessary resources for adaptation measures (4), help raise the acceptability of certain measures (5) or trigger the development of new intervention options (2).

Since the main obstacles to successful adaptation vary from one decision context to another, scientific analysis and political efforts should be targeted on those elements that are most in need of improvement.

The design of effective adaptation strategies, policies and measures in public health needs to be based on an understanding of current health risks caused by climatic and non-climatic factors as well as of expected future risk changes. The assessment of future risks involves the combination of epidemiological knowledge about the relationship between health outcomes, climatic and non-climatic risk factors with future projections for these risk factors. Potential response strategies are then evaluated according to their effectiveness, efficiency and feasibility. This integrative task requires close collaboration across scientific disciplines, including climatologists, epidemiologists, public health managers and other experts. In addition, cooperation between public health experts from different regions can facilitate knowledge transfer from areas that already have experience coping with a particular climate-sensitive health risk to areas that may become affected in the future.

Main approaches to vulnerability and adaptation assessment

Assessments of climate impacts on human health and of suitable adaptations face a variety of challenges, such as: the diversity of climate-sensitive health impacts; the complex interaction of climatic, environmental, socioeconomic, demographic and behavioural factors in the causation of diseases; large uncertainties in regional projections of future climate change and socioeconomic conditions; and the scantiness of reliable epidemiological data on the current relationship between climatic factors and health outcomes, in particular in developing countries.

Most early studies of climate change and human health followed a hazards-based approach, such as described in the Intergovernmental Panel on Climate Change (IPCC) Technical Guidelines (Carter et al, 1996) and the United Nations Environment Programme (UNEP) Handbook on Methods for Impact Assessment and Adaptation Strategies (Feenstra et al, 1998). While these studies evaluated and extended the scientific knowledge about the relationship between climatic factors and human health and provided indispensable information on the scale of the problem and on particularly vulnerable regions, they offered only limited guidance to stakeholders concerned about adaptation. The main reasons are the mismatch in spatial and temporal scales between climate-impact projections and typical adaptation decisions, and the limited consideration of scientific uncertainties, existing climate-related risks and socioeconomic factors (Füssel and Klein, 2006).

Recognizing the limitations of the hazard-based approach to adaptation assessment in providing policy-relevant knowledge to adaptation decision makers, recent guidelines for adaptation assessment put a much stronger emphasis on bottom–up approaches, which integrate adaptation to future climate change with efforts to reduce vulnerability to current climate variability and non-climatic stressors. The most important of these guidelines are the United Nations Development Programme – Global Environment Facility (UNDP-GEF) Adaptation Policy Framework (Lim and Spanger-Siegfried, 2005) and the WHO-sponsored 'Methods of assessing human health vulnerability and public health adaptation to climate change' (Kovats et al, 2003a).

Given the diversity of decision contexts, climate-sensitive health outcomes, and regional socioeconomic and environmental conditions, no single methodological approach is appropriate for all human health vulnerability and adaptation assessments. The relative importance of hazards-based (top–down) and bottom–up approaches in a particular assessment context is determined by the objective of the assessment, the type of health effects considered, the level of existing knowledge about the climate–health relationship, the relative magnitude of expected changes in health risks caused by climate change compared to current risks, the confidence in projections of future climate change and associated health risks, the lead time of potential adaptations and the availability of resources for the assessment (Füssel, 2008). Top–down approaches are most useful if sufficient data and resources are available for the downscaling of climate scenarios from general circulation methods (GCMs), if the considered health outcome is a direct effect of exposure to climatic phenomena, and if effective adaptations take a long time to become fully effective. Examples include changes in regional planning, town planning and building codes aimed at reducing the adverse effects of more intense heat waves or floods in the future. In contrast, top–down approaches are of limited use if uncertainty about future risk changes is very large, if climatic stress factors are closely intertwined with non-climatic factors, if current climate-related risks are unsatisfactorily controlled, if the planning horizon of adaptation actors is short and if resources are limited. These conditions, which are particularly prevalent in developing countries, favour more qualitative bottom–up assessments. Their focus is on policies that provide short-term benefits by controlling health risks associated with current climate variability, and that are robust across the range of plausible climate change projections.

A generic framework for human health vulnerability and adaptation assessment

Guidelines for climate change adaptation assessment in human health are largely consistent with established risk management frameworks. A combination of the assessment approaches from the WHO Methods (Kovats et al, 2003a) and the United Kingdom Climate Impacts Programme (UKCIP) Climate Adaptation Framework (Willows and Connell, 2003) suggests the following major steps of the adaptation cycle (Füssel et al, 2006):

1. scoping the project;
2. screening of current and future risks;
3. examination of the adaptation baseline;
4. review of projected climate impacts in other sectors;
5. identification of key information needs for policy decisions;
6. analysis of future risk changes;
7. evaluation of future risk changes;
8. identification and evaluation of additional adaptation options;
9. prioritization and integration of adaptation options;
10. decision about adaptation strategy;
11. implementation of decision; and
12. monitoring and evaluation of effectiveness of adaptations.

When interventions for different climate-sensitive health risks are largely independent of each other, Steps 5 to 8 can be conducted along independent threads for each health risk considered. Some threads may use quantitative methods for assessing future health risks, such as mathematical models, whereas others may rely primarily on qualitative methods, such as expert assessment. The integration of these diverse sources of information in the formulation of an efficient and comprehensive adaptation strategy under resource constraints is one of the challenges facing the assessment team in Step 9.

The main steps of a climate change vulnerability and adaptation assessment for human health are presented above as a linear sequence of actions. This characterization, however, is a gross simplification of the progression of real assessments. The UKCIP Climate Adaptation Framework (Willows and Connell, 2003) highlights that a framework to support good adaptation decision making should be *circular* (emphasizing the importance of the adaptive approach to managing climate change problems and implementing response measures), *iterative* (so that the problem, objectives and decision-making criteria can be refined as new information arrives), and that certain stages are *tiered* (allowing the assessor to screen and evaluate certain risks and response options before embarking on a detailed analysis). The UKCIP framework further emphasized the importance of the comprehensive characterization of uncertainties and of a close collaboration with the stakeholders who will eventually implement the recommended adaptation measures in all assessments steps.

The ultimate goal of an adaptation policy assessment is to inform decision makers who should do what more, less, better or differently in the face of climate variability and change. Four factors are particularly important in this context (Füssel and Klein, 2004): the *magnitude* of expected health risks, the *familiarity* with the specific health risk, the *confidence* in projections of future risk changes and the *balance of risks* between acting early vs acting late. The development of an adaptation strategy for a particular health outcome in a specific region should thus be guided by the following questions (the respective steps in the adaptation cycle are given in brackets):

1 *How significant is the expected increase in a particular health risk due to climate change, compared to current risk levels and the effect of non-climatic risk factors (Steps 2 and 7)?*
The answer to this question largely determines the need for a detailed analysis. The larger the potential risk increase due to climate change, the more important is it to conduct a detailed assessment of this risk and of suitable adaptation actions.
2 *How familiar is the population with the particular health issue and with its effective control (Steps 3 and 8)?*
The answer to this question largely determines the need for new preventive measures. If the health outcome of concern is already prevalent in the region and if it is effectively controlled, additional adaptation measures can draw on existing experience or may not be necessary at all. In contrast, adaptation to new health risks will typically require significant additional efforts, and the development of response measures cannot draw on local experience. While learning from the experience of others who are already affected by this health risk can provide important lessons for the design of adaptation strategies, the transfer of response strategies from one location to another may be hindered by differences in social, economic, institutional, cultural or environmental conditions. If health risks are concerned that have long been prevalent in a region but are not yet effectively controlled, efforts should focus on the implementation of effective and feasible intervention measures that reduce current risks while being robust enough to accommodate future risk changes caused by climate change.
3 *How reliable are projections for future risk changes at the scale of potential adaptation measures (Steps 6 and 7)?*
The answer to this question largely determines the specificity with which interventions to reduce a particular health risk can be designed. If reliable projections about significant increases in regional health risk are available, *specific* adaptation measures can be implemented in advance. If future changes in regional health risks are very uncertain, a *generic* adaptation strategy (focusing on improved monitoring, surveillance, research etc.) is generally more appropriate.
4 *How large are the risks of acting late (in terms of additional disease burden) compared to the risks of acting early (in terms of additional costs) (Step 9)?*

The answer to this question largely determines the need for acting now. The larger the potential health risks in the near future and the smaller the expected reduction in adaptation costs due to additional information in the future, the more important it is to act sooner rather than later. In general, early action is particularly important if the measure is already effective under current climate conditions, if severe impacts are possible (e.g. high mortality from heatwaves), if decisions have a long lead time (e.g. epidemiological studies or changes in town planning), if decisions have long-term effects (e.g. building settlements in areas at risk of flooding), and to reverse trends that threaten future adaptive capacity. Delaying action can be a rational adaptation strategy if the risks are moderate, if response measures can be introduced quickly when needed, and if the cost of adaptations are exceedingly high compared to the expected health benefits. Balancing the risks of early vs late action cannot be done on a purely objective basis; it also needs to consider subjective value judgements, such as the risk attitude of the decision maker.

Recent vulnerability assessments of human health

Many countries have addressed health impacts in their national communications to the United Nations Framework Convention on Climate Change (UNFCCC); however, few of these constituted a formal assessment of the potential health impacts of climate change. Kovats and Menne (2003) reviewed vulnerability assessments undertaken for a national Ministry of Health or Environment that used formal assessment methods. A few large health assessments have been conducted as part of a comprehensive, multi-sectoral assessment, such as in the United States, Canada, the United Kingdom and Portugal. Assessments in developing countries have been undertaken primarily under the auspices of donor-funded capacity-building initiatives. The assessments undertaken ranged from comprehensive, well funded and well supported to assessments undertaken with little resources. Most assessments conducted to date have been first-generation vulnerability assessments (Füssel and Klein, 2006); their primary goals were identifying key vulnerabilities and research gaps. Some assessments also identified specific adaptation measures aimed at reducing vulnerability. The process of assessment often is not described in detail. In addition, only a few assessments reported the confidence or uncertainty surrounding the estimates of health risk reported (Kovats and Menne, 2003). Some selected assessments are reviewed below with respect to the framing of the assessment and research methods used.

US National Assessment of the Potential Health Consequences of Climate Variability and Change

The US Congress mandated regular assessments of the impacts of climate variability and change (US Global Change Research Act, 1990). The first national assessment was organized in multiple, overlapping layers of analysis, with teams from several geographic regions and from five economic or resource sectors (forestry, agriculture, water resources, coastal zone and human health). Three categories of products were produced: national synthesis documents, sectoral analyses and regional analyses. The assessment was intended to look at possible impacts of climate variability and change over the next 25 to 30 years, and over the next 100 years.

The goals of the health-impacts assessment were to investigate key determinants of climate–health interactions, to develop a research agenda and to identify appropriate current and future adaptation strategies (Bernard and Ebi, 2001). The assessment addressed the questions:

- How might climate change affect the country's health and existing or predicted stresses on health?
- What is the country's capacity to adapt to climate change, for example, through modifications to the health infrastructure or by adopting specific adaptive mechanisms?
- What essential knowledge gaps must be filled to fully understand the possible impacts of climate variability and change on human health?

The health assessment qualitatively used climate change projections developed for the National Assessment, and did not incorporate socioeconomic projections. The assessment focused on the potential impacts of climate variability and change on five health outcomes known to be associated with weather: temperature-related morbidity and mortality, injuries or illnesses from extreme weather events, air pollution-related health effects, water- and food-borne diseases, and vector- and rodent-borne diseases (Patz et al, 2000). The general approach was an integrated assessment across health disciplines, relying on a review of hundreds of peer-reviewed studies and government reports, the expert judgement of the panel members and those with whom they consulted, and incorporating some limited modelling of projected impacts of climate on health (Bernard and Ebi, 2001). Analyses of the roles of population vulnerability and adaptation were woven throughout the assessment with respect to each health outcome.

The assessment concluded that climate variability and change will probably increase risks for several climate-sensitive health determinants and outcomes, including morbidity and mortality attributable to high ambient temperatures and flooding. Although winter mortality rates are higher than summer rates, it was concluded that any ameliorating impact of increases in winter temperatures would not offset the expected mortality increase during periods of elevated temperatures. For the airborne pollutants, particularly ozone and particulate matter, the general conclusion was that it is uncertain how future pollutant concentrations will respond to climate change because ambient concentrations generally are the result of complex interactions between meteorological conditions, biophysical systems and human activities. An increase in the frequency and severity of extreme precipitation events could increase the risk of contamination events, which would increase the risk of water- and food-borne illnesses. The cumulative impacts of climate change on vector- and rodent-borne illness were uncertain. For mosquito-borne illnesses, it was concluded that an increase in average temperature will generally reduce the US population's susceptibility to epidemics, assuming increased amounts of time spent indoors in air-conditioned environments.

The health effects of climate change in the UK

In contrast to the US assessment, the UK assessment focused on delivering quantitative results for several health outcomes with respect to three time periods (2020s, 2050s, 2080s) and four climate scenarios derived by downscaled projections from a single GCM for different emission scenarios. The health outcomes considered were heat- and cold-related morbidity and mortality; cases of food poisoning; changes in the distribution of vector-borne diseases (tick-borne encephalitis, Lyme disease and *P. vivax* malaria) and of water-borne diseases (cholera, typhoid and cryptosporidiosis); deaths and injuries due to extreme weather events (windstorms, coastal and riverine flooding); respiratory diseases due to air pollution; and cases of skin cancer and eye cataracts due to stratospheric ozone depletion (UK Department of Health, 2002). The assessment involved spatial analogues, predictive modelling and expert judgement. The resulting report addressed the balance between the potential benefits and adverse impacts of climate change. The uncertainties surrounding the reported estimates were acknowledged to be large, with the main source of uncertainty being the future capacity to control these diseases in the future.

The assessment concluded that by 2050, climate change would have significant effects on health, both negatively and positively. It was estimated that excess cold weather deaths will decline significantly (by perhaps 20,000 cases annually). Heat-related hospitalizations and deaths, and cases of food poisoning, were projected to increase (about 2000 additional heat-related deaths and 10,000 additional cases of food poisoning annually). By 2050, the climate of the UK may be such that indigenous malaria could become re-established, but this was viewed as unlikely to be a major problem. It was considered that overall impact on water-borne diseases will be small. Health risks associated with severe winter gales and floods were projected to increase, with the level of increase depending on the effectiveness of adaptation. Air pollution-related deaths and illnesses were generally projected to decrease, but an increase in ozone concentrations was projected to result in several thousand extra deaths and a similar number of hospital admissions annually. Cases of skin cancer were projected to increase by about 5000 cases and cataracts by 2000 cases annually.

Climate change in Portugal: Scenarios, impacts and adaptation measures (SIAM project)

The Portuguese national assessment of climate change impacts and adaptation measures was conducted by a multidisciplinary research team of 50 Portuguese universities and co-funded by the Ministry of Science and a private research foundation (Santos et al, 2002). The SIAM project was divided functionally into ten groups and an integration team. Seven groups worked on climate change impacts and adaptation measures in specific sectors (water resources, coastal zones, agriculture, human health, energy, forests and biodiversity, and fisheries). The remaining groups worked on climate scenarios, socioeconomic scenarios and a sociological analysis of climate change issues in Portugal. All groups used the same suite of climate data (observations and scenarios) and socioeconomic scenarios. The assessment process included consultations with national and international experts as well as stakeholders (government, academia, media, etc.).

The SIAM health-impact assessment focused on heat-related mortality, air pollution-related health effects and vector-borne diseases. The health outcomes chosen were based on consultations with national and international experts, current level of concern and availability of suitable data. The following questions were addressed:

- What is the current (or historical) burden of the health outcome in Portugal?
- What is the climate–health relationship for this health outcome?
- Assuming the above relationship to be valid for all exposure scenarios, what climate change health impacts are anticipated for Portugal?

The current burden of diseases was obtained from national monitoring and control programmes as well as from the literature (Casimiro and Calheiros, 2002). Where there were sufficient health and climate data, such as in the heat-related mortality study, epidemiologic analyses were used to identify and quantify relationships between weather exposures and health outcome. These relationships were then used to estimate the burden of disease under different climate scenarios. The assessment specifically included identification of populations (distinguished by demographic factors, socioeconomic status, living conditions and other criteria) most vulnerable to climate change. It explored the uncertainty range of potential health outcomes through climate scenarios that represented plausible and internally consistent futures. The assessment also identified and evaluated strategies that might reduce potential health impacts, and identified knowledge gaps. The results were used to formulate the Climate Change National Program as well as in the Third National Communication to the UNFCCC.

The SIAM study projected the annual heat-related death rates in Lisbon to increase from between 5.4 and 6 (per 100,000) in 1980–1998 to between 8.5 and 12.1 by the 2020s and to a maximum of 29.5 by the 2050s, if no adaptations occur. The projected warmer and more variable winter weather was expected to result in better dispersion of nitrogen dioxide levels, thus reducing pollution-related health risks. Higher summer temperatures in contrast, were expected to reduce air quality by increasing ground-level ozone levels. Malaria and schistosomiasis, which are currently not endemic in Portugal, were projected to be more sensitive to the introduction of infected vectors than to temperature changes. Higher temperatures were projected to increase the transmission risk of zoonoses that are currently endemic to Portugal such as leishmaniasis, Lyme disease and Mediterranean spotted fever.

Climate change and adaptation strategies for human health (cCASHh)

The project 'Climate Change and Adaptation Strategies for Human Health' (cCASHh) was not a national assessment; it was funded by the European Commission and included many countries in the WHO European region. The overall objective of the project was:

- to identify human health vulnerability to climate change;
- to review current measures, technologies, policies and barriers to improving the adaptive capacity of populations to climate change;
- to identify for European populations the most appropriate measures, technologies and policies to successfully adapt to climate change; and
- to provide estimates of the health benefits of specific strategies or combinations of strategies for adaptation under different climate and socioeconomic scenarios.

Health-impact and adaptation assessments were carried out for several climate-sensitive health outcomes most likely to affect European populations: heat-related stress; floods; food-borne diseases; and vector- and rodent-borne diseases (leishmaniasis, malaria, hantavirus infections, West Nile virus, Lyme disease and tick-borne encephalitis). The applied methods included literature reviews, expert consultation, epidemiological modelling, integrated assessment modelling, review of current adaptation measures, and economic and policy analyses (Menne and Ebi, 2006).

The cCASHh project found that mortality due to heatwaves and floods has increased in Europe. Although there is considerable evidence that climate is an important determinant of the geographic range of vectors, data were insufficient to conclude that recent climate change has increased the incidence of vector- and rodent-borne diseases. Cases of salmonella were found to increase by 5–10 per cent for a 1°C increase in weekly temperature, for ambient temperatures above about 5°C. There was no evidence of a strong role of temperature in the transmission of campylobacteriosis.

WHO Global Burden of Disease

The Global Burden of Disease Study began in 1992 with the objective of quantifying the burden of disease and injury in human populations (Murray and Lopez, 1996). The goals were to produce the best possible evidence-based description of population health, the causes of lost health and likely future trends in health in order to inform policy making. The WHO Global Burden of Disease 2000 project (GBD) updated the 1990 study (Murray et al, 2003). It drew on a wide variety of data sources to develop internally consistent estimates of incidence, health state prevalence, severity and duration, and mortality for over 130 major health outcomes, for the years 2000 and beyond. To the extent possible, the GBD synthesized all relevant epidemiologic evidence on population health within a consistent and comprehensive framework, the comparative risk assessment. Twenty-six risk factors were assessed, including major environmental, occupational, behavioural and lifestyle risk factors. Climate change was one of the environmental risk factors assessed.

For climate change, the GBD assessed the total health impact caused by climate change between 2000 and 2030, and how much of this burden could be avoided by stabilizing greenhouse gas concentrations (WHO, 2002; Campbell-Lendrum et al, 2003; McMichael et al, 2004). The alternative exposure scenarios investigated were unmitigated emission trends (approximately following the IPCC IS92a scenario), emissions reductions resulting in stabilization at 750ppm CO_2 equivalent by 2210 (S750), and emissions reductions resulting in stabilization at 550ppm CO_2 equivalent by 2170 (S550). Climate change projections were generated by one GCM. The health outcomes included were chosen based on sensitivity to climate variation, predicted future importance, and availability of quantitative global models (or feasibility of constructing them). Specific impacts selected were the direct impacts of heat and cold, episodes of diarrhoeal disease, cases of dengue and *Falciparum* malaria, fatal injuries in coastal floods and inland floods, and prevalence of malnutrition.

In the year 2000, the mortality attributable to climate change was 154,000 (0.3 per cent) deaths, and the attributable burden of disability adjusted life years (DALYs) lost was 5.5 million (0.4 per cent), with approximately 50 per cent of the burden due to malnutrition (McMichael et al, 2004). About 46 per cent of the DALYs attributable to climate change were estimated to have occurred in the WHO South-east Asia Region, 23 per cent in countries in the Africa region with high child mortality and very high adult male mortality, and 14 per cent in countries in the Eastern Mediterranean region with high child and adult male mortality. For each health outcome, ranges of estimates were projected for relative risks attributable to climate change in 2030 under the alternative exposure scenarios (McMichael et al, 2004). The study concluded that if the understanding of broad relationships between climate and disease was realistic, then climate change was likely to cause significant health impacts by 2030 (Campbell-Lendrum et al, 2003).

Conclusions

Climate change vulnerability and adaptation assessments can provide indispensable information for the design and implementation of effective adaptation strategies. These assessments need to consider the broad range of climate-sensitive health outcomes, regional socioeconomic conditions, and potential adaptation actors. Key factors for the assessment and planning of adaptation strategies are the *magnitude* of expected health risks, the *familiarity* with the specific health risk, the *confidence* in projections of future risk changes and the *balance of risks* of early vs late action.

The climate-related health risks of concern are not new; they currently are associated with preventable morbidity and mortality. Therefore, most adaptation policies and measures will be based on current interventions with modifications to account for climate change, such as the implementation of heatwave early-warning systems in more cities or changing the location of surveillance activities in anticipation of vector-borne diseases changing their range. Whenever there is reliable information about future increases in health risks, public health should move from its current focus on monitoring, surveillance and response to a more proactive approach that includes prediction and effective prevention of climate-sensitive health determinants and outcomes.

The health-impact assessments conducted to date used a range of approaches from largely qualitative to quantitative. They found that climate change is likely to increase the incidence and intensity of a number of health determinants and outcomes, depending on the timeliness and effectiveness of suitable interventions. These assessments identified population health vulnerabilities, critical research gaps and key uncertainties. In doing so, they helped raise awareness of the potential health impacts of climate variability and change among scientists, policy makers and other stakeholders. The next round of assessments should be able to provide more specific and finer scale projections of impacts under a range of climate and socioeconomic scenarios to better inform adaptation planning.

The main problems encountered during all assessments of the potential health impacts of climate change included the scarcity of long-term health and environmental data, the limited number of published studies on the relationship between climate/weather and health outcomes, limited models to project how health outcomes might change under different climate change scenarios (given that such relationships are highly context-specific), and limited literature on climate change adaptation in the health sector (Patz et al, 2000; Scheraga and Furlow, 2001; Casimiro and Calheiros, 2002; Kovats and Menne, 2003; Ebi et al, 2006). An additional problem has been that some relevant literature (e.g. air quality studies) is published in non-health disciplines and therefore was difficult to identify for assessment teams lacking experts from that discipline. A major shortcoming of many health assessments has been the limited assessment of adaptive capacity and policy options.

A variety of lessons have been learned from the diversity of health-impact assessments mandated from an appropriate authority. First, the questions to be addressed need to be clearly framed, as should the expected outcomes (e.g. quantitative estimates of the burden of climate-sensitive diseases, recommendations to policy makers of adaptation measures to reduce vulnerability, etc.). Based on the questions to be addressed and the available resources, an interdisciplinary assessment team should be assembled. Second, the methods chosen for the collection and synthesis of information need to be appropriate to the data available and the outcomes expected. In many cases, qualitative assessments can provide as useful information as quantitative assessments to policy makers. Third, many assessments have found that stakeholder involvement throughout the process not only increased the value of the assessment, but also increased the relevancy of the results. Finally, since an entire policy community and infrastructure is already established to improve human health, it is important to link adaptation assessments related to global change with the existing policy context.

References

Bernard, S. M. and Ebi, K. L. (2001) 'Comments on the process and product of the Health Impacts Assessment component of the United States National Assessment of the potential consequences of climate variability and change', *Environmental Health Perspectives*, vol 109(Suppl 2), pp177–184

Campbell-Lendrum, D. H., Corvalan, C. F. and Prüss-Üstün, A. (2003) 'How much disease could climate change cause?', in McMichael, A. J., Campbell-Lendrum, D., Corvalan, C. F., Ebi, K. L., Githeko, A., Scheraga, J. D. and Woodward, A. (eds) *Climate Change And Human Health: Risks And Responses*, WHO/WMO/UNEP, Geneva

Carter, T., Parry, M., Nishioka, S. and Harasawa, H. (1996) 'Technical guidelines for assessing climate change impacts and adaptations', in Watson, R. T., Zinyowera, M. C. and Moss, R. H. (eds) *Second Assessment Report of the Intergovernmental Panel on Climate Change*, Cambridge University Press, New York

Casimiro, E. and Calheiros, J. M. (2002) 'Human health', in Santos, F. D., Forbes, K. and Moita, R. (eds) *Climate Change in Portugal: Scenarios, Impacts and Adaptation Measures - SIAM project*, Gradiva, Lisbon, Portugal

Ebi, K. L., Smith, J., Burton, I. and Scheraga, J. (2006) 'Some lessons learned from public health on the process of adaptation', *Mitigation and Adaptation Strategies for Global Change*, vol 11, pp607–620

Feenstra, J. F., Burton, I., Smith, J. B. and Tol, R. S. J. (eds) (1998) *Handbook on Methods for Climate Change Impact Assessment and Adaptation Strategies, Version 2.0*, United Nations Environment Programme, Nairobi

Füssel, H.-M. (2008) 'Assessing adaptation to the health risks of climate change: What guidance can existing frameworks provide?', *International Journal of Environmental Health Research*, vol 18(1), pp37–63

Füssel, H.-M. and Klein, R. J. T. (2004) 'Conceptual frameworks of adaptation to climate change and their applicability to human health', PIK Report No. 91, Potsdam, Germany

Füssel, H.-M. and Klein R. J. T. (2006) 'Assessing vulnerability and adaptation to climate change: An evolution of conceptual thinking', *Climatic Change*, vol 75, pp301–329

Füssel, H.-M., Klein, R. J. T. and Ebi, K. L. (2006) 'Adaptation assessment for public health', in Menne, B. and Ebi, K. L. (eds) *Climate Change and Adaptation Strategies for Human Health*, Steinkopff Verlag, Darmstadt, pp41–62

Glantz, M. H. (1996) 'Forecasting by analogy: Local responses to global climate change', in Smith, J. B., Bhatti, N, and Menzhulin, G. V. (eds) *Adapting to Climate Change: An International Perspective*, Springer Verlag, New York, pp407–426

Haines, A. and McMichael, A. J. (1997) 'Climate change and health: Implications for research, monitoring, and policy', *British Medical Journal*, vol 315, pp870–874

Kovats, R. S. and Menne, B. (2003) 'National assessments of health impacts of climate change', in McMichael, A. J., Campbell-Lendrum, D., Corvalan, C. F., Ebi, K. L., Githeko, A., Scheraga, J. D. and Woodward, A. (eds) *Climate Change and Human Health: Risks and Responses*, WHO/WMO/UNEP

Kovats, S., Ebi, K. L. and Menne, B. (2003a) *Methods of Assessing Human Health Vulnerability and Public Health Adaptation to Climate Change*, Health and Global Environmental Change Series No. 1, World Health Organization, Regional Office for Europe, Copenhagen, Denmark

Kovats, R. S., Bouma, M. J., Hajat, S., Worrall, E. and Haines, A. (2003b) 'El Nino and health', Lancet, vol 362, pp1481–1489

Last, L. M. (1998) *Public Health and Human Ecology*, second edition, McGraw-Hill, New York

Lim, B. and Spanger-Siegfried, E. (eds) (2005) *Adaptation Policy Frameworks for Climate Change*, Cambridge University Press, Cambridge

McMichael, A. J. and Githeko, A. (2001) 'Human health', in McCarthy, J. J., Canciani, O. F., Leary, N. A., Dokken, D. J. and White, K. S. (eds) *Climate Change 2001: Impacts, Adaptation, and Vulnerability*, Contribution of Working Group II to the Third Assessment Report of the Intergovernmental Panel on Climate Change, Cambridge University Press, Cambridge, ch 9

McMichael, A. J., Haines, A., Sloof, R. and Kovats, S. (1996) *Climate Change and Human Health*, World Health Organization, Geneva

McMichael, A. J., Campbell-Lendrum, D. H., Corvalan, C. F., Ebi, K. L., Githeko, A., Scheraga, J. D. and Woodward, A. (eds) (2003) *Climate Change and Human Health: Risks and Responses*, World Health Organization, Geneva

McMichael, A. J., Campbell-Lendrum, D., Kovats, S., Edwards, S., Wilkinson, P., Wilson, T., Nicholls, R., Hales, S., Tanser, F., LeSueur, D., Schlesinger, M. and Andronova, N. (2004) 'Global climate change', in Ezzati, M. Lopez, A., Rodgers, A. and Murray, C. (eds) *Comparative Quantification of Health Risks: Global and Regional Burden of Disease due to Selected Major Risk Factors*, World Health Organization, Geneva, pp1543–1649

Menne, B. and Ebi, K. L. (eds) (2006) *Climate Change and Adaptation Strategies for Human Health*, Steinkopff Verlag, Darmstadt

Murray, C. J. L., Ezzati, M., Lopez, A. D., Rodgers, A. and Vander Hoorn, S. (2003) 'Comparative quantification of health risks: Conceptual framework and methodological issues', *Population Health Metrics*, vol 1, p6

Murray, C. J. L. and Lopez, A. D. (eds) (1996) *The Global Burden of Disease: A Comprehensive Assessment of Mortality and Disability from Diseases, Injuries, and Risk Factors in 1990 and Projected to 2020*, Harvard University Press, Cambridge

Parry, M. and Carter, T. (1998) *Climate Impact and Adaptation Assessment: A Guide to the IPCC Approach*, Earthscan Publications, London

Patz, J. A., McGeehin, M. A., Bernard, S. M., Ebi, K. L., Epstein, P. R., Grambsch, A., Gubler, D. J., Reiter, P., Romieu, I., Rose, J. B., Samet, J. M. and Trtanj, J. (2000) 'The potential health impacts of climate variability and change for the United States: Executive summary of the report of the health sector of the U.S. national assessment', *Environmental Health Perspectives*, vol 108, pp367–376

Santos, F. D., Forbes, K. and Moita, R. (eds) (2002) *Climate Change in Portugal: Scenarios, Impacts and Adaptation Measures – SIAM Project*, Gradiva Publishers Lisbon

Scheraga, J. D. and Furlow, J. (2001) 'From assessment to policy: Lessons learned from the US national assessment', *Human and Ecological Risk Assessment*, vol 7, pp1227–1246

UK Department of Health (2002) *The Health Effects of Climate Change in the UK*, HMSO, London

US Global Change Research Act (1990) *Public Law 101-606*, 16 November 1990

Van Lieshout, M., Kovats, R. S., Livermore, M. T. J. and Martens, P. (2004) 'Climate change and malaria: Analysis of the SRES climate and socio-economic scenarios', *Global Environmental Change*, vol 14, pp87–99

WHO (World Health Organization) (2002) *World Health Report 2002: Reducing Risks, Promoting Healthy Life*, WHO, Geneva

Willows, R. and Connell, R. (2003) *Climate Adaptation: Risk, Uncertainty and Decision-Making*, UKCIP Technical Report, United Kingdom Climate Impacts Programme, Oxford

Chapter 8

Mapping Double Exposure to Climate Change and Trade Liberalization as an Awareness-Raising Tool

Robin Leichenko and Karen O'Brien

Introduction

Global climatic and economic changes are affecting the production conditions for many natural resource-based sectors, including agriculture, forestry, fisheries and tourism. Warmer temperatures, changing precipitation and wind patterns, and greater climate variability as a result of climate change can influence the biophysical environment, with either positive or negative results for sectors and regions. At the same time, globalization is creating economic, social, political and cultural transformations that interact with climate change to profoundly influence the vulnerability of some people and groups. While globalization has many facets, the liberalization of trade between countries and across larger international regions is among the most significant because it is transforming ecosystems, livelihoods and the capacity to adapt to all types of environmental change (Leichenko and O'Brien, 2008).

Both climate change and trade liberalization have uneven effects across spatial and temporal scales (O'Brien and Leichenko, 2003; Leichenko and O'Brien, 2008). Vulnerability to either process may be defined as a function of exposure, sensitivity and adaptive capacity (O'Brien et al, 2004). It is influenced by the dynamic context within which households, communities, regions or sectors experience changing conditions. Yet, understanding and addressing the vulnerability of people to one global process cannot be achieved without considering the impacts of other global change processes. Different processes interact at multiple scales to influence vulnerability, and static assessments of either climate change or globalization vulnerability are of limited use in a dynamically changing world (Leichenko and O'Brien, 2002).

In this chapter, we consider how climate change and trade liberalization together influence vulnerability to current and future environmental conditions. The concept of 'double exposure' refers to cases where a particular region, sector, social group or ecological area is simultaneously confronted by exposure to both climate change and globalization (O'Brien and Leichenko, 2000; Leichenko and O'Brien, 2008). It emphasizes the importance of considering the consequences of globalization when assessing vulnerability to climate change. The approach also highlights the uneven outcomes of both processes of change within a national context (Leichenko and O'Brien, 2008). Mapping vulnerability to both processes can serve as an awareness-raising tool that can guide responses and interventions for reducing vulnerability.

Vulnerability to climate change and global trade: State of the science

Vulnerability assessments of the impacts of climate change have been the focus of much attention in recent years. Earlier work in natural hazards (Cutter, 1996; Wisner et al, 2004) and food security (Bohle et al, 1994) has influenced vulnerability applications in climate change research. The methods applied to the empirical analysis of climate change vulnerability vary from regression techniques (e.g. Polsky, 2004) and composite indices and mapping (e.g. O'Brien et al, 2004) to more qualitative assessments (e.g. Adger, 1999; Eakin, 2006). One of the key points to emerge from all of these studies is that climate change differentially affects regions as well as social groups, and that these effects may change over time (Adger and Kelly, 1999; Leichenko and O'Brien, 2002).

Understanding vulnerability to globalization and trade liberalization is also a growing area of concern (Leichenko and O'Brien, 2008). Countries such as India and China play an increasingly prominent role in global trade, both in products and services. The impact of China's economic growth alone – as a supplier of low-priced exports and as a consumer of energy and resources – may have dramatic implications for both developing and developed countries (Shenkar, 2005). The regions and communities that are less integrated in the global system, or less able to compete for various reasons, may find that their livelihoods are eroded, at the same time as a shrinking public sector provides little support or relief to the distressed. Global trade policies may create new opportunities for some, but marginalize the livelihoods of others. As Jodha (2000, p297) notes, 'globalization brings new incentives, technologies, infrastructure, and support systems in response to high demand and profitability'. Yet it may also result in job losses, market collapses and erosion of existing comparative advantages. While some developing countries, which have increased integration in the world economy until the late 1990s, have achieved higher growth in incomes, higher life expectancy and better education, many other countries have experienced a fall in their trade to GDP ratio. As a result, the latter countries have experienced a contraction in economic output and an increase in poverty.

Despite the large number of empirical studies that have already been completed on the effects of climate change and trade liberalization, the development of vulnerability as a concept continues to advance. This includes efforts to develop more rigorous quantitative measures of vulnerability (e.g. Luers et al, 2003), as well as efforts to broaden the understanding to multiple stressors, including not only climate change but also economic and institutional changes such as price shocks, currency devaluations and the introduction of neoliberal resource management policies (Moss et al, 2001; Turner et al, 2003a, b; Eakin, 2003, 2006; O'Brien et al, 2004; Eriksen and Silva, 2007). Given the uncertainties in future biophysical and economic conditions (Eakin, 2006; Homer-Dixon, 2006), and the implications of this for the ability of people to respond to variable and changing conditions, new frameworks and methodologies for vulnerability assessments are needed that take into account the combined effects of climate change and trade liberalization on households, communities, regions or nations (Leichenko and O'Brien, 2008).

Indicator-based approaches

Indicator-based approaches to vulnerability assessments in climate change studies trace back to earlier work on poverty mapping and food insecurity (Downing, 1991; Ramachandran and Eastman, 1997; Henninger, 1998). Composite vulnerability indices were developed based on a linear combination of a set of standardized variables, either weighted or averaged, to create a single numeric index (Ramachandran and Eastman, 1997). Socioeconomic data, often derived from national or international standardized data sets, national censuses, or from aggregated household or community surveys, provide insights into the social dimensions of vulnerability. Spatial biophysical data sets, such as soils, vegetation or climate variables, can be combined with socioeconomic indices in a geographic information system (GIS) to produce a multidimensional index.

The selection of indicators is an important step in mapping vulnerability. Two very distinct approaches can be identified: inductive and deductive. The differences between these two approaches are described by Eriksen and Kelly (2007, pp19–20) as follows:

> *The deductive approach involves identifying a set of relationships on the basis of theory or some conceptual framework and selecting indicators on the basis of these relationships. Identifying the best possible indicators involves the 'operationalisation' of concepts. In deductive research, a hypothesis is tested by operationalising the concepts within it, collecting appropriate data and then examining the proposed relationships between the concepts.*

> *The inductive approach to selecting indicators involves relating a large number of variables to some measure of vulnerability or its consequences in order to identify the factors that are related to a statistically significant extent. The inductive approach involves a 'hoovering' of potentially relevant indicators then a winnowing based on a test of statistical significance to identify appropriate indicators.*

In reality, most indicator approaches to vulnerability are difficult to distinguish as either deductive or inductive because they often lack a clear conceptual and methodological framework and do not specify the criteria that lie behind indicator selection (Eriksen and Kelly, 2007). Data availability and data quality are concerns, and indicator studies may by necessity adopt a mixed and pragmatic approach.

Eriksen and Kelly (2007) also distinguish between indicators that describe a characteristic of a population or system, and those that measure a process that influences vulnerability. It can be argued that descriptive indicators of conditions provide only static snapshots of vulnerability, and do not capture the dynamics of processes that influence vulnerability (Leichenko and O'Brien, 2002; Eriksen and Kelly, 2007).[1] Processes such as climate change and trade liberalization may have the most severe consequences for vulnerable regions or populations, but they also contribute to vulnerability to future change. Capturing these dynamics is one of the challenges for indicator-based approaches.

Indicators that are commonly used in vulnerability assessments at the global level may include measures that represent the biophysical environment, or education, technology and other social characteristics (Yohe and Tol, 2002). Efforts to assess economic vulnerability to trade liberalization have focused on indicators such as the degree of economic openness, dependence on a narrow range of exports, dependence on strategic imports, and insularity, peripherality and remoteness (Briguglio, 1995). Indicator-based approaches have the advantage of being generalizable across multiple spatial scales even where data sources are limited. The indicator approach is also widely applicable and is able to capture the essence of the vulnerability problem. Indicators are also powerful tools for communicating research results to a broader audience. In the India example presented below, we develop and apply indicators of vulnerability to both climate change and trade liberalization.

Indian agriculture: Mapping multiple stressors

The double exposure framework emphasizes that both climate change and globalization are two interlinked processes that result in differential outcomes (Leichenko and O'Brien, 2008). In some cases, negative outcomes may co-occur and render it difficult to respond to shocks or long-term changes associated with one or both processes. Consequently, assessing the conditions under which vulnerability to both processes is relatively high can help to identify areas for intervention or support, and it can be used to highlight equity issues associated with both climate change and trade liberalization.

A three-step process was carried out to map the vulnerability of agriculture to climate change and trade liberalization at the district level in India (O'Brien et al, 2004). A fourth step, verification of the resulting maps and indicators by carrying out local level case studies, is described in O'Brien et al (2004). The methodology was based on the conceptualization of vulnerability described in the Intergovernmental Panel on Climate Change (IPCC) Third Assessment Report, namely that it is an outcome of sensitivity, exposure and adaptive capacity (McCarthy et al, 2001). The three steps, as outlined in O'Brien et al (2004), involved:

1 developing a vulnerability profile for climate change;
2 developing a vulnerability profile for trade liberalization; and
3 superimposing the profiles to identify 'double exposed' districts.

Vulnerability to climate change

The first step in the analysis entailed constructing a map of district-level vulnerability to climate change. The climate change vulnerability profile consisted of three components. First, an index of climate sensitivity was developed to identify areas that are likely to be affected by climate change. In the case of India, where a large part of the country is located in the semi-arid tropics and characterized by low and often erratic rainfall, and where much of the country relies on tropical monsoons for about 80 per cent of total annual rainfall, climate sensitivity can be measured by indicators of dryness and monsoon dependence. Second, exposure to climate change was considered. Assuming that climate change will influence climate sensitivity, either positively or negatively, the climate sensitivity index was recalculated taking into account the results from the HadRM2 regionally downscaled general circulation model (O'Brien et al, 2004). Third, adaptive capacity was represented by combining indicators that represent social, technological and biophysical factors (Bohle et al, 1994). A composite index for each of these factors was constructed using data from 1991 (O'Brien et al, 2004). Examples of the types of variables included in the social index include agricultural share of the labour force, literacy rates and gender discrimination (based on the proxy variable excess female mortality). Technological variables included irrigation rates, quality of transportation infrastructure, quality of banking facilities, and so forth. Biophysical variables included, for example, the quality and the depth of soil. The final index of adaptive capacity for each district was calculated as the average of these three indices.[2]

The three components of vulnerability to climate change were then combined, based on equal weighting, to create a map of climate change vulnerability. This map, shown in Figure 8.1, indicates the districts that can be considered currently vulnerable to future climate change. As indicated on the map, districts located in western and central India, including the states of Rajasthan, Gujarat and Madhya Pradesh, are most vulnerable to climate change.

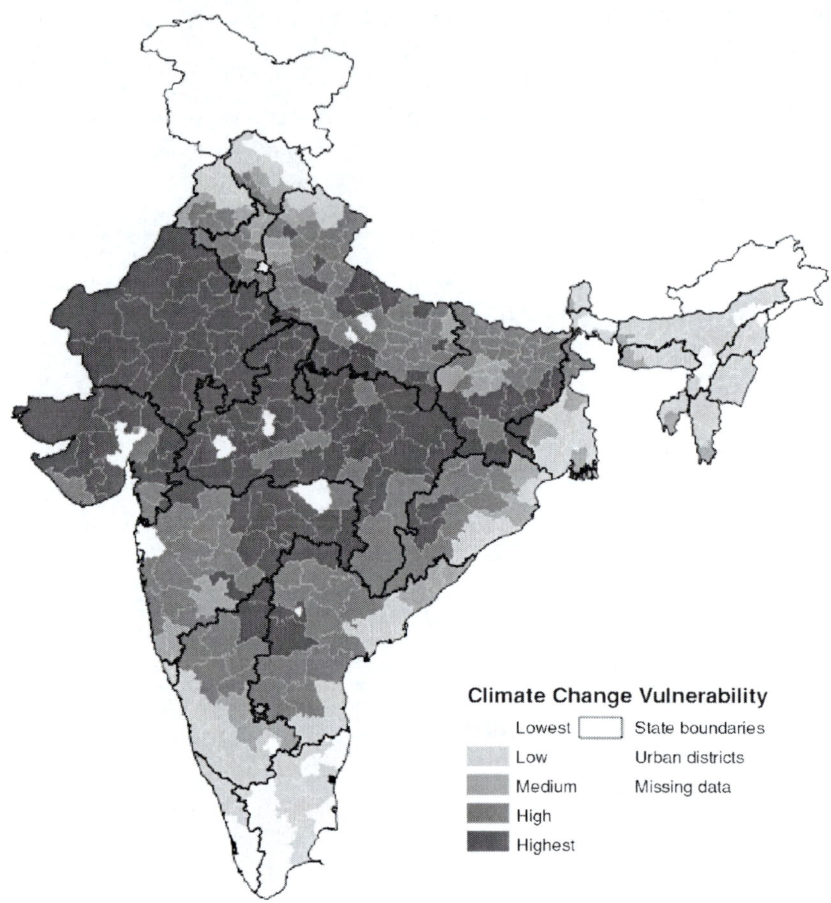

Note: Districts are ranked and presented as quantiles

Figure 8.1 *District-level mapping of climate change vulnerability, measured as a composite of adaptive capacity and climate sensitivity under exposure to climate change*

Vulnerability to trade liberalization

The next step entailed construction of a map of vulnerability to trade liberalization. The trade vulnerability profile illustrates which districts are sensitive to changes in international export and import prices based on a representative basket of either export- or import-competing agricultural products. Crops were selected for inclusion in the indices based on their importance nationally, whether or not the crop was internationally traded, geographical representativeness (i.e. crops that are grown throughout the country) and availability of district-level production area and yield data.[3] The export-sensitive crops comprise those that have been exported since 1991 and/or are expected to be export-competitive in the future: rice, wheat, sugar, tobacco and cotton. The import-sensitive crops comprise crops that have been imported since 1991 and/or are expected to face

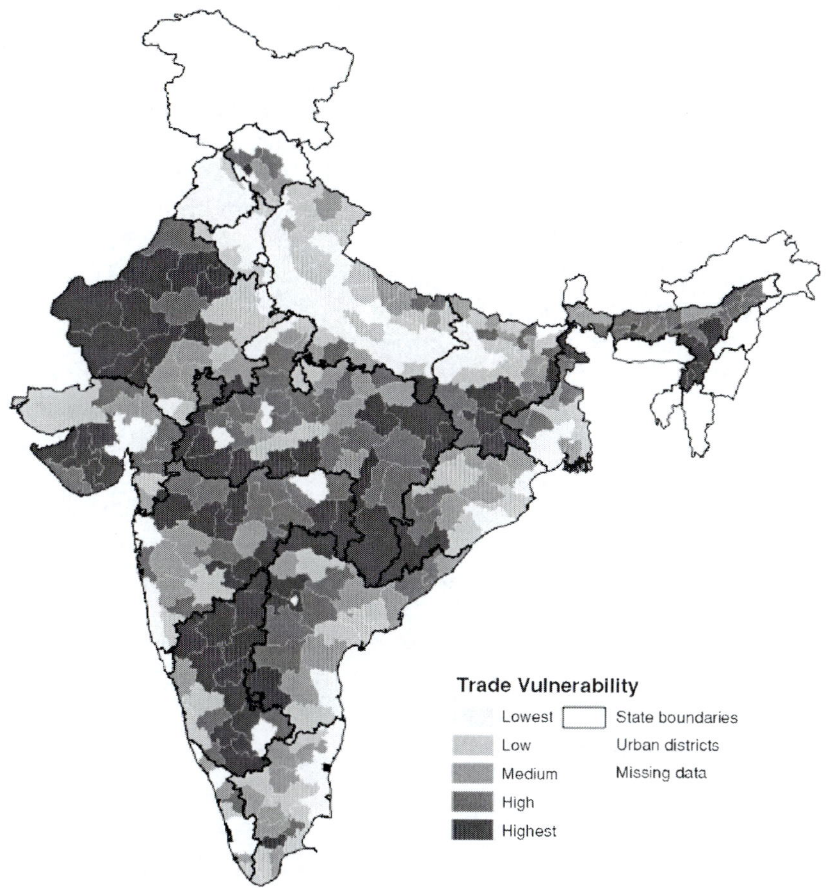

Note: Districts are ranked and presented as quantiles

Figure 8.2 *District-level mapping of trade vulnerability, measured as a composite of adaptive capacity and trade sensitivity (for a representative basket of import-sensitive crops)*

competition from international imports: rice, wheat, groundnuts, rape/mustard seed, gram and maize.[4] Export-sensitive areas may benefit from trade liberalization when terms of trade are favourable, but they may also be vulnerable to commodity price-related shocks. The vulnerability analysis presented above in Figure 8.2 focuses on import-sensitive crops.

The index of import sensitivity was based on productivity of representative import-competing crops in the district, the relative share of production area for the different crops and the distance of a district from an international port. District import productivity was calculated as the weighted sum of the normalized productivity of each import-competing crop, weighted by the share of the crop in the total area of import-competing crops grown in the district.[5] Accessibility was calculated based on the straight-line distance from the centroid of each district to the closest international port.[6] The import-sensitivity index identifies districts that may be vulnerable to price-related competition from international imports as a result of low productivity and/or proximity to an international port. Import-competing producers that are less productive and/or are closer to international ports are expected to face greater competition than producers that are more productive and/or located in more remote inland areas.

To adapt agriculture to changing economic conditions brought about by trade liberalization, the same biophysical, technological and social factors were considered to be important in determining adaptive capacity: soil conditions and groundwater availability influence the types of crops that can be cultivated, while literacy levels, gender discrimination, infrastructure and the availability of irrigation provide indicators of social and economic means of adapting to changing conditions of production. The percentage of farmers and agricultural wage labourers not only represents the importance of agriculture to the district, but also captures the presence or lack of alternative economic activities (O'Brien et al, 2004). The adaptive capacity index used in the climate change vulnerability map was combined with the trade sensitivity map for import-sensitive crops, to produce a map of vulnerability to trade liberalization. From this map, high vulnerability to trade liberalization is found in most of Rajasthan and Karnataka, as well as in substantial portions of Bihar, Madhya Pradesh, Maharashtra, Gujarat and Assam.

Double exposure: Vulnerability to both climate change and trade liberalization

To identify areas that are double-exposed to climate change and trade liberalization, the information from the climate change, trade liberalization and adaptive capacity maps were combined. Figure 8.3 illustrates the districts that exhibited high or very high vulnerability to trade liberalization, in addition to high or very high vulnerability to climate change. This map was created using the climate change vulnerability map (Figure 8.1) as the 'base' and then identifying via diagonal cross-hatching those districts that are in the high or very high vulnerability categories for both climate change and trade liberalization.[7] The double-exposed districts are concentrated in Rajasthan, Gujarat and Madhya Pradesh, as well as in southern Bihar and western Maharashtra. In these areas, both climate change and trade liberalization are likely to pose simultaneous challenges to the agricultural sector (O'Brien and Leichenko, 2000).

As discussed in O'Brien et al (2004) and Leichenko and O'Brien (2008), these double-exposed regions are likely to be areas where farmers are adapting to a variable and changing climate under conditions of economic stress. Reacting to two processes of change simultaneously will, of course, present challenges throughout India, but these districts are likely to feel disproportionately more stress, particularly if there is a mismatch between climate-compatible crops and market-driven demand for those crops. It is in these areas of double exposure where policy changes and other interventions may be most needed in order to help farmers to negotiate changing contexts for agricultural production.

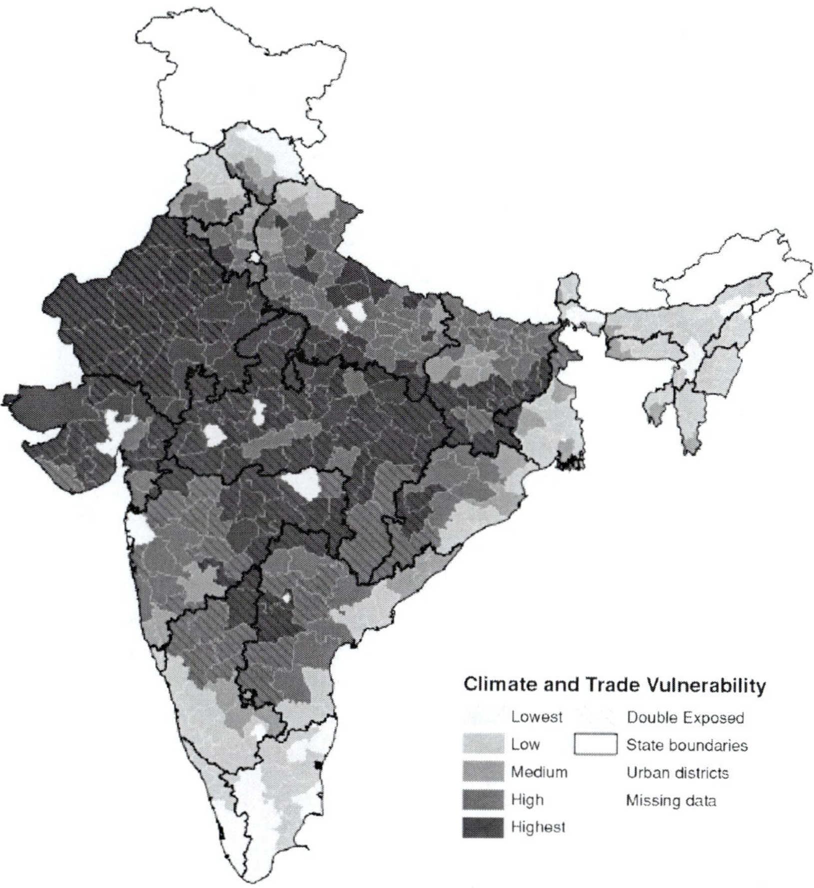

Figure 8.3 *Districts that rank in the highest two categories of climate change vulnerability and trade vulnerability are considered to be double exposed (depicted with hatching)*

Although policies, local institutions and other types of interventions and initiatives may have a notable influence on vulnerability, it is important to recognize that these factors are not captured in the indicators of vulnerability used to develop the macro-level profiles. To better understand the role that these factors play, it is necessary to shift to a more local scale. In this study, a series of local-level case studies carried out in vulnerable districts including Jhalawar, Chitradurga and Anantapur gave an improved understanding of the social and institutional dimensions of vulnerability that were not captured in the selected macro-level indicators. The results of these case studies, which are described in O'Brien et al (2004) and Leichenko and O'Brien (2008), demonstrated that both climate variability and changing economic policies are influencing production and cropping decisions at the local level. The case studies also showed that variation in state-level policies, particularly with respect to irrigation and marketing of export crops had a significant influence on the ability of farmers to adapt to both climate and trade-related pressures. More generally, the case studies confirmed that policies and initiatives originating at the national and state levels play a critical role in shaping vulnerability at the district, village and farm levels.

Conclusions

There is a growing body of literature on vulnerability science, which is seeking to increase the rigour and enhance the utility of vulnerability assessments for both researchers and policy makers (Turner et al, 2003a; Schröter et al, 2004). The results presented above demonstrate a method for mapping vulnerability that can be used to assess climate vulnerability in the context of a range of globalization-related changes. Mapping double exposure is an effective method to highlight differential vulnerability and to identify areas that are likely to be most vulnerable to multiple processes of global change. Rather than suggesting specific adaptation or mitigation strategies, the maps serve as a tool to raise awareness about the potential consequences of global changes for specific regions and districts. The maps may be particularly useful for decision makers at the state and national levels because they help to identify those areas that are likely to encounter significant hardship as the result of both processes of change. The approach also demonstrates that some regions may not be considered vulnerable to processes of change because of some combination of a) lower exposure; b) lower sensitivity; and 3) higher adaptive capacity. It raises the possibility that there may, in fact, be beneficiaries from both processes – at least in the short term, without consideration of the sustainability of benefits.

By demonstrating the differential effects of global change processes, the double exposure maps also raise issues of equity and justice that may not be apparent in other types of vulnerability analyses (O'Brien and Leichenko, 2006). Decisions and policies that drive or address climate change and trade liberalization typically originate at national and international levels. Yet the effects of these changes are not uniform across geographic regions, but may create benefits for some and losses for others (O'Brien and Leichenko, 2003). The double exposure maps identify those districts that are likely to be disproportionately negatively affected by these two simultaneous processes of change.

Acknowledgement

We thank Marthe Stiansen for assistance with the preparation of this manuscript.

Notes

1 An example of a static indicator of climate change vulnerability is life expectancy. In the case of Swaziland, average life expectancy in 2004 was about 35 years. A more dynamic representation would capture changes in life expectancy; that is, between 1991 and 2004, average life expectancy has decreased by 20 years. The process contributing to climate change vulnerability in this example is HIV/AIDS.

2 Each of the three indices is the average value of a set of normalized variables. The indices were weighted equally because we did not have an *a priori* reason to assume one set of factors was more important than others. This decision to adopt equal weighting was reinforced based on discussions and consultations with local experts on agricultural vulnerability in India (O'Brien et al, 2004). Concerning normalization, all of the variables in the vulnerability profiles are normalized based on the method in the United Nations Development Programme's Human Development Index. The values of each variable are normalized to the range of values in the data set.

3 Categorization of the crops as export-sensitive (i.e. have the potential for increased exports under liberalization) or import-sensitive (i.e. are vulnerable to competition from imports under liberalization) was based on current and past import and export data patterns from Food and Agriculture Organization data, as well as recent evaluations of the export/import potential of Indian agriculture (Gulati and Kelley, 1999; Gulati, 1999).

4 Note that two of the crops, wheat and rice, are categorized as both import- and export-sensitive because these crops are both imported and exported depending upon international prices and quantity produced within India in any given year.

5 For each import-competing crop, productivity for that crop $_{(c)}$ in district $_{(d)}$ was first calculated as total production/total area. Crop productivity by district was then normalized to a value between 0 and 100, such that high values for the index imply high productivity and low values imply low productivity. The minimum$_{c,I}$ and maximum$_{c,I}$ are the values of the lowest and highest productivity districts for that crop in India $_{(I)}$.

$$\text{Raw crop productivity index}_{c,d} = \frac{(\text{actual value}_{c,d} - \text{minimum value}_{c,I}) \times 100}{(\text{maximum value}_{c,I} - \text{minimum value}_{c,I})}$$

Next, the import crop productivity index was reversed so that high index values are associated with lower productivity and higher vulnerability to import competition: Import crop productivity index$_{c,d}$ = 1 – Raw import index$_{c,d}$

Finally, we calculated import productivity indices for each district as the weighted sum of the import crop index values for each crop, weighted by the area of import-competing production in that crop (Area$_{c,d}$) over the total area of production of the above import-competing crops in the district (Area$_{d}$):

$$\text{Import productivity index}_d = \Sigma \mathit{Area}_{c,d}/\mathit{Area}_d \times \mathit{Crop\ import\ productivity\ index}_{c,d}$$

6 Most raw agricultural products in India are shipped by truck and then via ship (in the case of exported products). Given the high density of roads in India, straight-line distance provides a reasonable approximation of the relative differences in travel costs between districts that are close to international ports and districts that are remote from international ports. We first calculated a raw normalized index using the distance of the district to the nearest port and the minimum and maximum distances to port of all districts in India.

$$\text{Raw distance index}_d = \frac{(\text{actual value}_d - \text{minimum value}_I) \times 100}{(\text{maximum value}_I - \text{minimum value}_I)}$$

We then reversed the index:

$$\text{Distance index}_d = 1 - \text{Raw distance index}_d$$

Low index values thus imply that the district has low accessibility (i.e. is farther from an international port) and is less vulnerable to competition from imported goods, while high values imply that the district has high accessibility (i.e. is closer to an international port) and is more vulnerable to international competition.

7 We used a quantile classification system for all of the vulnerability profile maps. Quantile classification creates classes that have the same number of features (districts) in each class. In our case, each of the five classes represents 20 per cent of the districts in India. Because the boundaries of the classes do not depend on the actual values (but rather on the number of districts), this method treats each data set similarly, resulting in comparable maps. For each of our maps, the 'highest' vulnerability class is determined by the top 20 per cent of districts with the highest vulnerability values; similarly, the lowest vulnerability class contains the bottom 20 per cent of the districts with the lowest vulnerability values. Using this method, one can compare the maps of globalization vulnerability to climate vulnerability and conclude that the classes of 'high' and 'highest' vulnerability are comparable, since each contain the same number of districts.

References

Adger, W. N. (1999) 'Social vulnerability to climate change and extremes in coastal Vietnam', *World Development*, vol 27(2), pp249–269

Adger, W. N. and Kelly, M. (1999) Social vulnerability to climate change and the architecture of entitlements', *Mitigation and Adaptation Strategies for Global Change*, vol 4(3–4), pp253–266

Bohle, H. G., Downing, T. E. and Watts, M. J. (1994) 'Climate change and social vulnerability', *Global Environmental Change*, vol 4(1), pp37–48

Briguglio, L. (1995) 'Small island states and their economic vulnerabilities', *World Development*, vol 23(9), pp1615–1632

Cutter, S. (1996) 'Vulnerability to environmental hazards', *Progress in Human Geography*, vol 20(4), pp529–539

Downing, T. E. (1991) 'Vulnerability to hunger in Africa: A climate change perspective, *Global Environmental Change*, vol 1(5), pp365–380

Eakin, H. (2003) 'The social vulnerability of irrigated vegetable farming households in central Puebla', *Journal of Environment and Development*, vol 12(4), pp414–429

Eakin, H. (2006) *Weathering Risk in Rural Mexico: Climatic, Institutional, and Economic Change*, The University of Arizona Press, Tucson

Eriksen, S. H. and Kelly, P. M. (2007) 'Developing credible vulnerability indicators for Climate Adaptation Policy Assessment', *Mitigation and Adaptation Strategies for Global Change* (forthcoming)

Gulati, A. (1999) 'Indian agriculture in an open economy: Will it prosper?', in Ahluwalia, I. J. and Little, I. M. D. (eds) *India's Economic Reforms and Development: Essays for*

Manmohan Singh, Oxford University Press, New Delhi, pp122–145

Gulati, A. and Kelley, T. (1999) *Trade Liberalization and Indian Agriculture: Cropping Pattern Changes and Efficiency Gains in Semi-Arid Tropics*, Oxford University Press, New Dehli

Henninger, N. (1998) *Mapping and Geographic Analysis of Human Welfare and Poverty: Review and Assessment*, World Resources Institute, Washington DC

Homer-Dixon, T. (2006) *The Upside of Down: Catastrophe, Creativity, and the Renewal of Civilization*, Island Press, Washington DC

Jodha, N. S. (2000) 'Globalization and fragile mountain environments: Policy challenges and choices', *Mountain Research and Development*, vol 20(4), pp296–299

Leichenko, R. M. and O'Brien, K. (2002) 'The dynamics of rural vulnerability to global change: The case of southern Africa', *Mitigation and Adaptation Strategies for Global Change*, vol 7(1), pp1–18

Leichenko, R. M. and O'Brien, K. L. (2008) *Environmental Change and Globalization: Double Exposures*, Oxford University Press, New York

Luers, A. L., Lobell, D. B., Sklar, L. S., Addams, C. L. and Matson, P. A. (2003) 'A method for quantifying vulnerability, applied to the agricultural system of the Yaqui Valley, Mexico', *Global Environmental Change*, vol 13(4), pp255–267

McCarthy, J. J., Canziani, O. F., Leary, N. A., Dokken, D. J. and White, K. S. (eds) (2001) *Climate Change 2001: Impacts, Adaptation, and Vulnerability*, Cambridge University Press, Cambridge

Moss, R. H., Breknert, A. L. and Malone E. L. (2001) *Vulnerability to Climate Change: A Quantitative Approach*, Pacific Northwest National Laboratory, www.globalchange.umd.edu/data/publications/Vulnerability_to_Climate_Change.pdf

O'Brien, K. L. and Leichenko R. M. (2000) 'Double exposure: Assessing the impacts of climate change within the context of economic globalization', *Global Environmental Change*, vol 10(3), pp221–232

O'Brien, K. L. and Leichenko, R. M. (2003) 'Winners and losers in the context of global change', *Annals of the Association of American Geographers*, vol 93(1), pp89–103

O'Brien, K. L. and Leichenko, R. M. (2006) 'Climate change, equity, and human security', *Die Erde*, vol 137(3), pp165–179

O'Brien, K. L., Leichenko, R. M., Kelkar, U., Venema, H., Aandahl, G., Tompkins, H., Javed, A., Bhadwal, S., Barg, S., Nygaard, L. and West, J. (2004) 'Mapping vulnerability to multiple stressors: Climate change and globalization in India', *Global Environmental Change*, vol 14(4), pp303–313

Polsky, C. (2004) 'Putting space and time in Ricardian climate change impact studies: Agriculture in the U.S. Great Plains, 1969–1992', *Annals of the Association of American Geographers*, vol 94(3), pp549–564

Ramachandran, M. and Eastman, J. R. (1997) 'Applications of GIS to vulnerability mapping: A West African food security case study', in *Applications of Geographic Information Systems (GIS) Technology in Environmental Risk Assessment and Management*, UNEP and the Clark Labs for Cartographic Technology and Geographic Analysis, Worcester, MA

Schröter, D., Polsky, C. and Patt, A. G. (2004) 'Assessing vulnerability to the effects of global change: An eight step approach', *Mitigation and Adaptation Strategies for Global Change*, vol 10(4), pp573–595

Shenkar, O. (2005) *The Chinese Century: The Rising Chinese Economy and its Impact on the Global Economy, the Balance of Power, and Your Job*, Wharton School Publishing, New Jersey

Silva, J. (2007) 'Trade and income inequality in a less developed country: The case of Mozambique', *Economic Geography*, vol 82(3), pp111–136

Turner, B. L., Kasperson, R. E., Matson, P. A., McCarthy, J. J., Corell, R. W., Christensen, L., Eckley, N., Kasperson, J. X., Luers, A., Martello, M. L., Polsky, C., Pulsipher, A. and Schiller, A. (2003a) 'A framework for vulnerability analysis in sustainability science', *Proceedings of the National Academy of Sciences of the United States of America*, vol 100(14), pp8074–8079

Turner, B. L., Matson, P. A., McCarthy, J. J., Corell, R. W., Christensen, L., Eckley, N., Hovelsrud-Broda, G. K., Kasperson, J. X., Kasperson, R. E., Luers, A., Martello, M. L., Matheisen, S., Naylor, R., Polsky, C., Pulsipher, A., Schiller, A., Selin, H. and Tyler, N. (2003b) 'Illustrating the coupled human–environment system for vulnerability analysis: Three case studies', *Proceedings of the National Academy of Sciences of the United States of America*, vol 100(14), pp8080–8085.

Wisner, B., Blaikie, P., Cannon, T. and Davis, I. (2004) *At Risk: Natural Hazards, People's Vulnerability and Disasters*, second edition, Routledge, London

Yohe, G. and Tol, R. S. J. (2002) 'Indicators for social and economic coping capacity: Moving toward a working definition of adaptive capacity', *Global Environmental Change*, vol 12(1), pp25–40

Chapter 9

An Agent-Based Framework for Assessing Vulnerability Futures

Lilibeth Acosta-Michlik and Mark Rounsevell

Introduction

The science of assessing vulnerability to global environmental change presents a great challenge because the study of 'human interactions with the global environment poses difficult problems of theory and method that [demands] new links among disciplines, theoretical constructs to deal with the complexities and the large spatial and temporal scales, and careful selection of research methods' (Stern et al, 1991, p6). A number of interdisciplinary studies dealing with the development of vulnerability concepts and frameworks have captured the complexities of human–environment interactions. Examples of these are the 'social vulnerability' of Adger (1999), 'double exposure' of O'Brien and Leichenko (2000), 'vulnerability-resilience' of Moss et al (2001), 'risk-chain' of Heitzmann et al (2002), 'vulnerability for sustainability' of Turner et al (2003), 'eight-step approach' of Schröter et al (2005) and 'security diagrams' of Acosta-Michlik et al (2006). However, the empirical application of these concepts remains a critical bottleneck for advancing the science of vulnerability in global environmental change because of the lack of appropriate methods. While mapping vulnerability using generic indices can potentially inform policy within or towards vulnerable regions, the approach does not capture the complexities of human–environment dynamics resulting from adaptation process. Hence, vulnerability maps are limited when identifying adaptation policies to help the most vulnerable people in vulnerable regions. Profiling vulnerability of vulnerable agents or communities is more useful for understanding the adaptive behaviour inherent in the human system. McLaughlin et al (2002) suggest that vulnerability profiles are a better alternative to indices because the former provide a clearer distinction of areas where one sub-index is dominant. In other words, indices can conceal differences in the relative strengths of individual variables. However, the temporal dynamics of human–environment interactions is difficult to capture in profiles because they can only describe the state of vulnerable people or places at a particular time. Only methods that explicitly consider both the complexities and dynamics of human–environment interactions can provide a comprehensive understanding of differential vulnerabilities and allow the projection of vulnerability estimates into the future (Acosta-Michlik, 2007a). This is also emphasized in the first chapter of this book, which explains that '[v]ulnerability is not a feature of how a system functions in the present, but rather about how it is likely to function in the future ...' (Patt et al, Chapter 1, this volume).

To fill these research gaps, this chapter aims to apply a method based on multi-agent systems and test its applicability for assessing vulnerability of farmers in the Alentejo region in Portugal. Unlike indicator-based approach, this method uses (generic) biophysical and socioeconomic indicators as the drivers, and not as a measure, of vulnerability. Moreover, the method using the agent-based approach makes use of the valuable information from vulnerability profiles, particularly those that describe the adaptive behaviour of agents to the changes in their biophysical and socioeconomic environment. A method based on multi-agent systems requires a novel framework that combines more global information from generic vulnerability indicators and more local information from static vulnerability profiles to generate an estimate of vulnerability futures, or an assessment of vulnerability condition in the future, that takes into account the dynamics of human–environment interactions. The framework was first introduced by Acosta-Michlik (2005) in the Intervulnerability Project, a pilot application of the framework in a case study in the Philippines, which was supported by the START Advanced Institute on Vulnerability to Global Environmental Change. The next section of this chapter presents the definition and description of the framework, which is referred to as 'intervulnerability'. In the discussion of methods in the following section, the empirical application of the agent-based framework and the steps for generating the input parameters that are required to construct and run the agent-based model are described. We then describe the case study area and present the computed model inputs and outputs including the estimates of vulnerability condition in the future. Issues concerning validation of processed-based models such as multi-agent systems and selected results of alternative validity checks are briefly presented. In presenting the conclusions, the chapter emphasizes that, while its current application for vulnerability assessment is at its early stage and thus serves the purposes of scientific research, the results of the model show that an agent-based framework has very good potential use for assessing vulnerability to improve adaptation.

Framework

Intervulnerability is a conceptual account of the dynamics of human–environment interactions in assessing vulnerability of local communities to global changes. The intervulnerability framework assists in merging the relevant socioeconomic and biophysical attributes of an agent's environment, and thus in assessing the differential vulnerability of local communities to interacting impacts of various global drivers such as globalization and climate change. It thus emphasizes the importance of considering the interaction of the impacts of global processes (i.e. multiple stresses) and the interconnection of global to local changes in assessing vulnerability. The core of the intervulnerability framework is the agents, whose adaptive decisions to the changes in their environment are influenced by their specific attributes or profiles, as depicted in Figure 9.1. While considering the global (or regional) drivers that cause changes in the local environment, the framework situates vulnerability not only within the locality of vulnerable people, but also by their individuality. Thus, the framework combines three levels of information to assess differential vulnerability:

1 at the global and/or regional levels, the drivers of global changes describing the current state of economic, social, institutional, physical and climatic environment as measured by (generic) indicators as well as the future changes in these indicators as represented by scenarios;
2 at the community level, the socioeconomic and biophysical environment that is directly influenced by the global drivers and their changes; and
3 at the agent level, the attributes or profiles that determine adaptive decisions of individuals (or group of individuals) in the community to the changes in their immediate socioeconomic and biophysical environment (details are presented in the section on methods).

By combining the above three informations, the framework does not ignore the existing conceptual thinking on vulnerability. In contrast, it makes better use of these ideas by putting them together in a mosaic designed to create a spatio-temporal structure with the agents at its core.

The spatio-temporal structure created in the framework captures both the changes in the global drivers and local environment and the shifts in the profiles of the individual agents. The latter is crucial because, like the environment, humans change. For example, as agents get older or acquire more knowledge, their attributes and thus their decisions and actions change over time. Because the outcomes of actions differ not only when the agents' profiles differ, but also when an agent's profile shifts, human vulnerability to its changing environment is never static. The dynamics of human–environment interactions is further reinforced in the framework by capturing the feedback effects of the outcomes on both the agents' profile and environment. Consider an agent whose actions to adapt to decreasing rainfall (e.g. adoption of drought-resistant crops) led to an increase in yield last year. The higher income generated from higher production will shift his

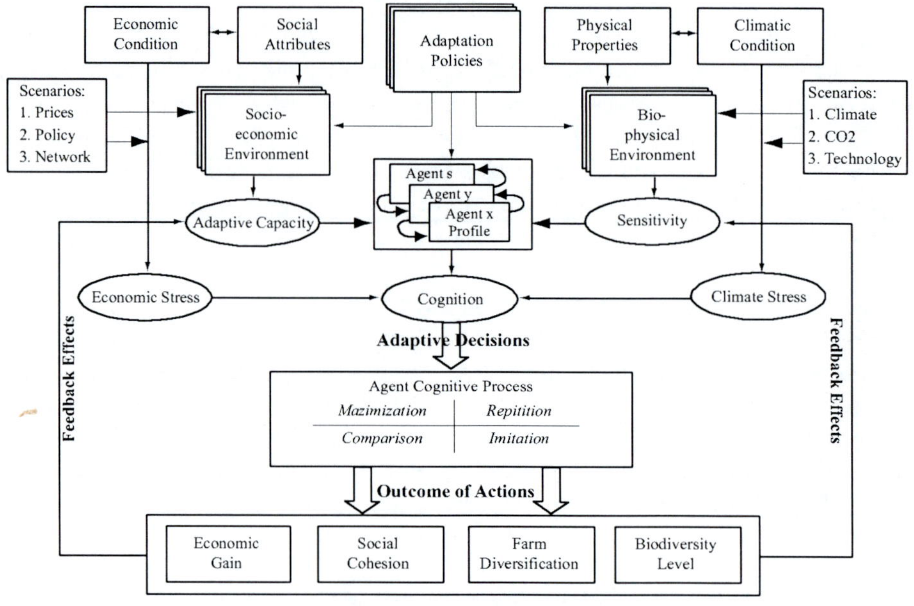

Figure 9.1 *Intervulnerability framework to assess dynamics of human–environment interactions*

profile from a low-income to high-income agent and enable him to improve his environment by investing on his land (e.g. developing or improving access to an irrigation system) this or next year. Through such feedback effects, the outcomes of the actions will continuously alter both the adaptive capacity of the agents and sensitivity of his environment, and ultimately the level of vulnerability. The framework assumes that the agents are not only heterogeneous, but also inherently proactive, possessing intelligent and autonomous behaviour. It thus places the agents that receive, perceive and process information from their environment in the core of vulnerability assessment, and not the information itself. The framework moves away from the current practice of assessing vulnerability in which information is extracted from the complex human and natural system and interpreted through the use of socioeconomic and biophysical indicators. Such indicator-based approaches limit analysis to generic information, which assumes a vulnerable population that is homogeneous, and neglects the vulnerable agents with cognitive abilities to adapt to changes in their environment. The intervulnerability framework thus suggests that agent's vulnerability to global changes is a function not only of his exposure, sensitivity and adaptive capacity, but also of his cognition. Cognition is an important determinant of vulnerability because it allows the agents to receive and exchange information, to perceive and evaluate risks, to identify and weigh options, to make decisions and perform actions, and to modify and update his profile according to the outcome of these actions. In the framework in Figure 9.1, agents' cognitions are represented in a behavioural model, which describes different cognitive strategies of agents with different profiles. Behavioural models should be both theoretically consistent and geographically relevant. The latter suggests that behavioural models should be developed from, or supported by, field investigations like survey, interviews and dialogue, whichever is most appropriate. In this chapter, four cognitive strategies (deliberation, repetition, comparison and imitation) based on the 'consumat approach' of Jager et al (2000) were used because they provide the most suitable representation of behavioural model in the case study area. However, this may not be the case in other case study areas with different socioeconomic and biophysical environments, so that alternative cognitive strategies need to be either developed or identified.

Based on the intervulnerability framework, vulnerability is measured by the outcome of the actions following the agents' adaptive decisions to the changes in their local environment. The set of outcomes to measure vulnerability is a range of economic, social or ecological 'variables' that have direct influence on the adaptive capacity of the agents (or community as a whole) and the sensitivity of their environment. As opposed to indicators, these variables are subject to variation resulting from dynamic characteristics of the human and environment system. As the level of assessment is very local, the outcomes are assumed not to have a significant impact on the global and regional drivers, which are the sources of stresses. Although exposure in this sense is something beyond the control of the local agents, it is something they can adapt to. Moreover, the framework assumes that exposure can be substantially altered only through global or regional mitigation. While mitigation measures can be made explicit in the framework by including alternative policy or impact scenarios, they remain exogenous to the system. In contrast, adaptation that results from either policy or agents' own decision is endogenous in as far as adoption of adaptation options depends on the profiles of the agents. For example, a risk-averse agent will adopt a different adaptive strategy from one that is not, a low-income agent will adopt a different measure from one with a high income, and so on. Consequently, actions will differ between agents, and so will the outcomes and the vulnerability. In theory, a wide range of economic, social and ecological variables can be used to measure vulnerability depending on the types and sources of exposure, the attributes of the agents and their environment, and the degree of complexity of human–environment interactions. In practice, however, the list of variables to be generated from the empirical application of the framework will be restricted not only by the limited information available as input to the model, but also by the need to balance between quantity of model inputs and manageability of model outputs. For these reasons, the measures of vulnerability for the case study area presented in this chapter has been limited to four sets of outcomes including economic gain, social cohesion, farm diversification and biodiversity level, which directly affects the agents' adaptive capacity and their environment's sensitivity to exposure, in particular to droughts. While the variables used to represent these outcomes (i.e. level of income for economic gain, trend in land abandonment for social cohesion, sources of income for farm diversification, traditional farming for biodiversity level) appear similar to indicators used in developing generic indices of vulnerability, they are not. The economic, social and ecological variables used to estimate vulnerability futures in this framework are outcomes of agents' adaptive decisions and their dynamic interaction with the immediate environment. Because agents have different profiles due to their heterogeneity, the different outcomes of their actions enable the representation of differential vulnerability within a community. An agent-based framework like that of intervulnerability thus shifts the foci of vulnerability assessment from generic indices to diversified adapting agents.

Methods

A framework that places adaptive agents as foci of vulnerability assessment requires a method based on multi-agent systems. The concept of multi-agent systems has its origin from the computer sciences (i.e. artificial intelligence research) in the 1970s, but has recently gained popularity in the social sciences. Axtell (2000) reviewed various motivations for agent computing in the social sciences with particular reference to computational economics. Economists have sought alternative tools to classical equation-based models (e.g. statistical techniques and mathematical programming) so as to move away from the restrictions imposed by rational agent and equilibrium assumptions. In geography, there is also growing interest in considering human decision making and non-rational decisions to understand changes in land use and land cover (e.g. van der Veen and Rotmans, 2001; Parker et al, 2003; Huigen, 2004; Acosta-Michlik et al, 2005). Others have applied agent-based modelling to explore the relationship between human activities and natural resources (e.g. Jager et al, 2002, Bousquet et al, 2005) and to evaluate policy support (e.g. Berger, 2001). The increasing application of agent-based models to answer research questions that link human to natural systems underpins their usefulness in assessing human vulnerability to global changes. Very few authors, however, have so far explored the application of agent-based models to vulnerability science with respect to global change processes (e.g. Ziervogel et al, 2005; Acosta-Michlik et al, 2007a). Ziervogel et al (2005) used an agent-based social simulation model to assess the impact of using seasonal forecasts among smallholder farmers. While they based their model on empirical evidence from fieldwork in Lesotho, the agent-based application is an abstraction of the real situation since the simulation model 'created a village' of 700 household-agents. The agents are thus artificial, with attributes extracted from the information collected from the socioeconomic features of the case study area. A similar level of abstraction was made in Acosta-Michlik et al (2007a), in which information from 99 surveyed farmers was used to model a case study village in the Philippines consisting of 500 farmers. Unlike Ziervogel's paper, however, Acosta-Michlik linked the socioeconomic attributes of the farmers to the spatial and biophysical features of their farms using high-resolution GIS maps, and thus the human interaction with its local environment is explicitly represented in the model.

Similar to Acosta-Michlik et al (2007a), this chapter assesses the vulnerability of farmers to the impacts of globalization and climate change and models the dynamics of human–environment interactions. Unlike Ziervogel et al (2005) and Acosta-Michlik et al (2007a), however, the agents presented in this chapter are 'real' and not artificial in the sense that the agent-based model is a representation of real socioeconomic attributes of the farmers and actual biophysical characteristics of the farms. Thus, the agent-based analysis captures both the spatial and temporal dynamics of real human–environment interactions and the actual adaptive behaviour (including interaction) of local people to the impacts of global processes such as globalization and climate change. The novelty of the model presented here lies in its ability to capture the heterogeneity of agents, the dynamics of their interactions and their behaviour in response to the geography of physical space. It combines the GIS-based biophysical maps with agent-based socioeconomic survey so that the social characteristics of a geographic location are made explicit in assessing vulnerability. This is important because both social and physical environments influence human adaptive behaviour. Moreover, by putting emphasis on the adaptive agents, the model allows vulnerability assessment that is variable not only in space, but also in time. To illustrate the empirical application of the intervulnerability framework using an agent-based model, the impacts of global economic and climate changes on the vulnerability of Portuguese farmers and agricultural community are evaluated in this chapter. To construct the model, the agents' attributes and information about their environment were generated through the following steps:

1 defining the biophysical and socioeconomic environment;
2 developing downscaled economic and climate change scenarios; and
3 building agent profiles and cognitive strategies.

Agents' biophysical and socioeconomic environment

The case study area, which has a total land area of 44km^2, is the agricultural village of Amendoeira da Serra in the municipality of Mèrtola (Figure 9.2). The municipality is located in the Alentejo region in south-east Portugal at 37°40' N, 7°47' E. The Alentejo region has a typical Mediterranean climate, characterized by very hot summers with up to five dry months and a very irregular distribution of rainfall during the wet season. It has in the past experienced frequent droughts, accompanied by a regular occurrence of wildfires and very intensive flood events. The soils are developed from schist and are mostly poor. The village is characterized by low, gently hilly land with average altitudes ranging from 200 to 250m above sea level and over 50 per cent bedrock or very thin soils, which have very little agricultural potential. Due to these extreme biophysical conditions and its peripheral location, the agriculture system is extensive.

The agents in the model are 28 farmers in Amendoeira da Serra cultivating approximately 4400ha. They represent about 60 per cent of the total number of farmers and account for 82 per cent of the total agricultural land in the village. Almost all of the farmers receive agricultural support including subsidies for

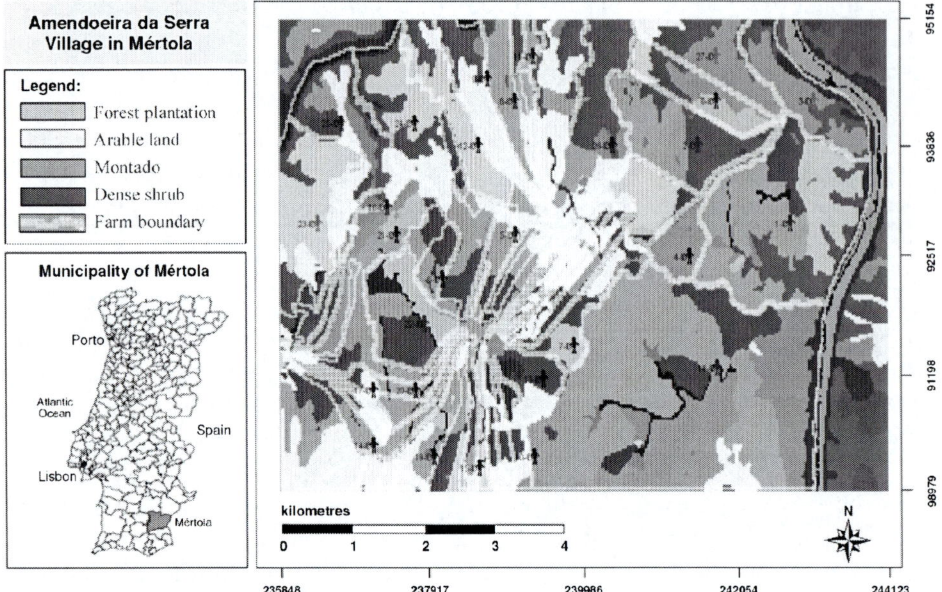

Figure 9.2 *Case study village in the municipality of Mèrtola in Alentejo, Portugal*

forest plantation, cereal and meat products; financial compensation for less favoured areas (LFAs); and agro-environmental measures. The farmers in the village have a very poor social network, which can be ascribed not only to the historical legacy of the peasant system, but also to their dependence on agricultural support. The village is thus characterized by both poor agricultural land and poor communal relationships. The productivity of farms, from which the farmers generate their income, is largely a function of the biophysical environment. The biophysical environment in the model is represented by natural and physical factors covering land use, soil properties, topographical features, water resources and climatic condition. The farms are characterized by a fragile physical environment (e.g. prone to erosion, poor soil quality) so they are very sensitive to climatic stress. In this model, the farms are represented by 25×25m resolution grid cells to capture the detailed biophysical factors that influence the land-use decisions of the farmers (Figure 9.2). Suitability maps for different land-use conversions were generated from binary logistic regression (Acosta-Michlik et al, 2007b). These maps are crucial for the model because a farmer's decision to cultivate a more profitable alternative crop depends on the crop's suitability to the biophysical features of his farm. Thus, as in real life, the farmers in the model are knowledgeable not only about the boundaries (i.e. given as white lines in Figure 9.2), but also about the crop suitability of their farms.

Economic and climate change scenarios

The impacts of global processes such as globalization and climate change are dynamic across space and over time. As a result, the agents' socioeconomic and biophysical environment has constantly changed in the past and will continue to change in the future. In this chapter, we assess the vulnerability of the farmers between the years 2000 and 2050 and so it is necessary to capture the future changes in the agent's environment resulting from global processes. To represent the future impacts of globalization and climate change, the A1FI SRES scenario was applied to the model. The SRES (Special Report on Emission Scenarios) framework (Nakicenovic et al, 2000) was used because the assumed socioeconomic changes relate directly to climate change through the emissions scenario. This ensures consistency in developing coupled globalization and climate change scenarios. Rounsevell et al (2005, 2006) describe scenarios for cross-cutting drivers in the European region. For example, in the A1FI scenario, which represents a global economic scenario, the economy is expected to experience very rapid economic growth. Moreover, the use of natural resources will increase as a result of growing material consumption and income/capital. Governments are assumed to be weak with a strong commitment to market-based solutions.

In assessing the vulnerability of farmers in Amendoeira da Serra, the impacts of globalization and climate change are translated through their effects on farm income, either at the level of prices or quantity of production. Farmers can engage in income maximization, which is represented in the model by the following equation:

$$\max \sum_{l}^{i} \left(Y_{i,t}^{k}\right) = \left[\left(P_{i,t}Q_{i,t}\right) \times \left(P_{j,t}Q_{j,t}\right)\right] \times A_{i,t}^{k} \tag{1}$$

$$\text{s.t. } S_{i,t}^{k} \geq \delta \tag{2}$$

where $Y_{i,t}^{k}$ is the income of farmer k at time t from crop i. $P_{i,t}$ and $P_{j,t}$ are the prices per unit of crop i and input j, while $Q_{i,t}$ and $Q_{j,t}$ are the quantities of crop i (i.e. expressed in terms of yield per hectare) and input j at time t. The total income of the farmer for crop i depends on the size of the area planted $A_{i,t}^{k}$ to this crop. The farmers in the model have a memory; they remember what happened in the past. If the income a farmer receives decreased continuously, say for the last three years, due to a decline in the price or yield of an existing crop, he adapts by looking for alternative crops that offer the highest possible income. However, the choice of alternative crops is restricted by the suitability $S_{i,t}^{k}$ of the farm of farmer k to the crop i, as measured by parameter δ. The value of this parameter was based on a binary logistic regression analysis of the historical land-use maps of the study area (Acosta-Michlik et al, 2007b). Land abandonment is also considered in the model as an adaptive decision.

Agents' profiles and cognitive strategies

By considering the agents' unique profiles and varying cognitive strategies, this chapter relaxes the homogeneity assumption in many existing frameworks and methods for vulnerability assessment. This is a relevant issue in vulnerability assessment because vulnerability depends on adaptive capacity, and the capacity to adapt varies among heterogeneous agents. For practical reasons, the heterogeneous agents have to be clustered based on common socioeconomic attributes. Cluster analysis was carried out to evaluate the farmers' socioeconomic attributes, which were collected through social survey. Cluster analysis is a fundamental data mining method that can be defined as the process of organizing objects into clusters (groups) such that objects within the same cluster have a high degree of similarity, while objects belonging to different clusters have a high degree of dissimilarity (San et al, 2004). After identifying the optimal numbers of clusters through the cluster analysis, a graphical representation of the attributes was used to facilitate matrix scoring. The matrix enabled the rapid labelling of clusters by a set of pre-defined labels and criteria that represent the farmer types in the case study area. The results of the cluster analysis and matrix scoring informed the development not only of the farmer profiles, but also of their decision rules and cognitive strategies.

Farmers belonging to a particular cluster are assumed to engage in similar cognitive strategies. As mentioned earlier, cognitive strategies can be summarized in behavioural models, which are developed through field investigations or computer-based simulations. Many behavioural models have been developed for the analysis of agent-based systems and tested using artificial agents with different degrees of intricacy (e.g. Rao and Georgreff, 1997; Anderson, 1996; Jager et al, 2000; Lewis, 2001; Ziervogel et al, 2005). For the purpose of vulnerability assessment, behavioural models based on field investigations are more appropriate to understand the particular attributes of the agents and the unique features of the local environment. Time constraints and data limitation did not allow development of such field-based models in the case study area in Portugal. However, by combining knowledge collected from the field survey and a literature review, an appropriate behavioural model was defined for the farmers in the village of Amendoeira da Serra. The behavioural model based on 'consumat approach' (Jager et al, 2000) was found to provide a good representation of the farmers' cognitive strategies – deliberation, comparison, imitation and repetition. In this chapter, farmers who possess information, money and motivation engage in deliberation or income maximization. Farmers who lack information and/or value the social norm engage in comparison, so they only use adaptation measures that are widely adopted in the community. Farmers' special relationship to a particular person encourages them to engage in imitation (e.g. neighbours). Farmers engage in repetition for various reasons including high level of satisfaction, low level of uncertainty, lack of knowledge or motivation, and so on. For the farmers to engage in appropriate cognitive strategies, they are provided in the model with a mental map through which they update the information and which serves as a memory to store information on abilities, opportunities and characteristics of other agents.

Results and discussions

Global changes and scenarios

Globalization, in particular through trade liberalization and technological development, affects the prices of crops as well as the prices of the inputs required to produce those crops. The market prices of cereal crops and livestock products in Portugal have experienced a substantial decrease in the past due to surplus production, which was brought about by the combined effects of the reduction in trade barriers and development of production technologies. Figure 9.3 shows that under global economic scenario (i.e. A1FI SRES scenario) the prices of these crops as well as major agricultural inputs, except labour, will continue to fall in the next four decades. At present, many rural areas in Portugal (including the Alentejo) are experiencing an increase in labour costs due to the rapid decline in the size of the agricultural labour force. Farmers find it increasingly difficult to find agricultural workers because of the availability of alternative employment outside agriculture and the opportunity costs associated with this. Only 40 per cent of the farmers employ agricultural workers in the village of Amendoeira da Serra. The globalization scenario assumes that this will not significantly change in the future because labour costs are assumed to continue to increase. However, significant changes are assumed in terms of the level of agricultural subsidies. In line with the current trade negotiations in the World Trade Organization, production subsidies for cereals and livestock are expected to fall significantly in the future. Forest subsidies will also decline, but not as rapidly as cereals and livestock due to the role of forest in climate change mitigation. Globalization will also affect crop yield through both climate and technological change. Technological development is assumed to result in a continuous increase in crop yield in the future (Figure 9.3). The changes in precipitation and CO_2 as a result of climate change are also expected to affect crop yield in Portugal, albeit in a minor way (see Ewert et al, 2005). The values in Figure 9.3 were used to introduce changes in the income from major agricultural crops planted and livestock raised in the case study area. The percentage changes in market prices (or subsidy) of farm output such as cereals, meat and forest as well as farm inputs such as fertilizer, pesticides and labour were used in the maximization function in equation (1), specifically for the variables $P_{i,t}$ and $P_{j,t}$. The percentage changes in yield due to the impacts of technology, climate and CO_2 enter into the same equation by altering the quantity of production.

Farmer profiles and strategies

The results of the cluster analysis suggest that the farmers in Amendoeira da Serra can be grouped into four clusters. Applying a matrix scoring approach, the following farmer profiles were identified from the attributes of the farmers in the four clusters: traditional, diversified, absentee and retired farmers (Table 9.1). Farmers in cluster 1 ('diversified') scored highly in terms of farm size, diversification of land use, number of employed workers, younger age and higher education.

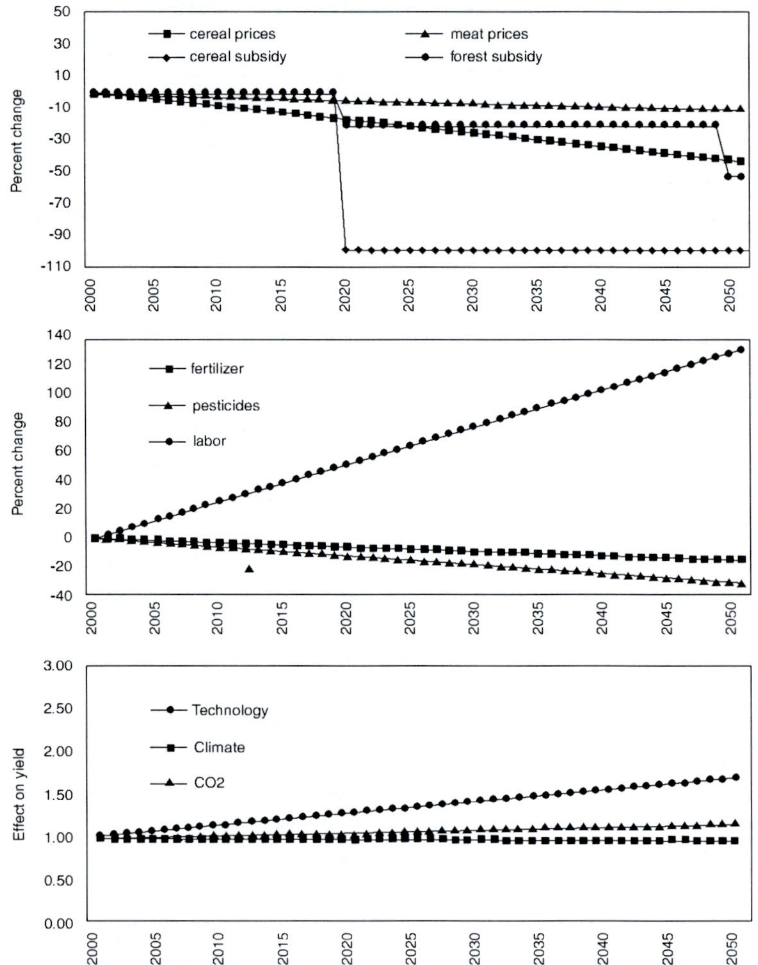

Note: Methods for computing technology, climate and CO_2 scenarios are based on Ewert et al (2005) and Rounsevell et al (2005)

Figure 9.3 *Trends in socioeconomic and climate-related variables, 2000–2050*

The main attributes characterizing the farmers in cluster 3 ('retired') are their old age and very low education. Farmers in cluster 3 ('absentee') are distinguished from farmers in other clusters by being resident outside the municipality and, as a result of this, their use of land for forest plantations. These farmers have high levels of education and acquired their farms through purchase. Farmers in cluster 4 ('traditional') are characterized by their inherited farms, the presence of successors and agricultural workers, small farms planted with arable crops and farmer residence located within the municipality. Due to their different profiles, the farmers belonging to the four clusters engage in different cognitive strategies. Diversified farmers will tend to engage in deliberation. Because deliberation

Table 9.1 *Matrix scoring of farmer attributes and typologies*

Attributes	*Cluster*			
	1	*2*	*3*	*4*
Traditional farmers				
Farm is inherited	+	+	+	++
Farmer has successor	+	+	+	++
Farmer does not employ worker	+	+	+	++
Farm size is less than 100 hectares	-	+	+	++
Land use is mainly arable	+	+	+	++
Residence is within the municipality	+	+	-	++
Diversified farmers				
Farm size is greater than 100 hectares*	++	+	+	-
Land use is diversified	++	+	-	-
Farmer employs worker	++	+	+	-
Age is less than 65 years	++	+	+	++
Education is more than 5 school years	++	+	++	-
Retired farmers				
Age is greater than 65 years	+	++	++	+
Education is less than 5 school years	+	++	+	++
Absentee farmers				
Residence is outside the municipality	+	+	++	-
Land use is mainly forest	+	+	++	-
Education is more than 7 school years	+	+	++	-
Farm is bought	+	+	++	-

*The median value of the farm size is 100 hectares.

Note: ++ cluster occupies the highest share, + a high share, and – no share out of the total attributes.

implies a certain degree of individualism, the decision of the farmers to maximize their income through land-use conversion or diversification is less dependent on contacts within the social network or the spatial location of the farmers. Attributes relating to efficient farm management (e.g. education, farm size, farm management, agricultural workers) are more important factors for engaging in deliberation. In the deliberation strategy, the diversified farmers compute income from alternative land uses and select the land use that yields the highest income. We thus use the term income maximization to represent a deliberation strategy.

A global economic scenario assumes a poor social network, and the social survey revealed that this is the current situation in Amendoeira da Serra. Hence, traditional farmers do not have the opportunity to compare their land-use decisions with the diversified farmers. The traditional farmers with larger farms, and hence greater investment capital, are assumed also to engage in income maximization. When their income is no longer profitable, in this case due to a reduction in subsidies and the low market prices of crops, traditional farmers with smaller farms, but higher education levels, are expected to migrate out of the village to look for alternative work in the city. The market value of agricultural land is low in a global economic scenario. Hence, out-migrating traditional farmers are assumed to abandon their lands. Note that in the past, land abandonment was widespread in the Alentejo region until farmers began to receive production subsidies through the Common Agricultural Policy (CAP). Retired farmers who receive a regular pension only engage in repetition because they become indifferent to the changes in their environment. They repeat their current land use irrespective of the social network and spatial location. Because the absentee farmers do not live in the village and their social network is limited to the owner of the neighbouring farms, they do not engage in social comparison. However, the neighbouring farms may influence their decisions, particularly if the neighbouring farmers also manage the farms of the absentee farmers. In Amendoeira da Serra this is often the case. This management arrangement assumes a good social relationship between the absentee and neighbouring farmers. In this case, the absentee farmers imitate their neighbouring farmer regardless of the neighbour's profile and update their income after engaging in imitation. However, a good social network does not exist in the global economic scenario so that imitation between neighbours is assumed not to exist. Acosta-Michlik et al (2007b) compare the effects of different levels of social network by taking into account scenarios other than a global economic scenario (e.g. global environmental scenario, regional economic and environmental scenarios).

The decision rules of the agents are important in agent-based models. In the application of an agent-based model in this chapter, the decision rules guide the agents' selection of appropriate strategies. The rules for the adaptive decisions of the farmers, which were identified from field survey and expert opinions, include the following:

- Change in income: when income declines, farmers with high levels of education and large farms adapt immediately by identifying alternative land uses or farming techniques to maximize their income.
- Suitability of land: farmers can only adopt alternative crops that are suitable to the physical characteristics of their farms.
- Availability of successors: farmers with family successors do not sell their land despite low profits from agriculture.
- Age of farmer: farmers that reach the age of 65 retire (those with over 80 years die in the model). Depending on the availability of successors, the farms are abandoned, sold or transferred to the successors.
- Level of education: with decreasing agricultural profitability, farmers with higher levels of education are more likely to abandon or sell their lands to seek employment outside the agricultural sector.
- Social interaction: exchange of information about alternative crops or farming techniques is only possible through good social networks. Interaction of farmers living outside the municipality is limited to the owners of neighbouring farms. (Note: poor social networks are assumed for A1FI scenario)

Vulnerability futures

As mentioned earlier, the four sets of outcomes used to measure vulnerability in this chapter are economic gain, social cohesion, farm diversification and biodiversity level. Figure 9.4 shows the results of the agent-based model with respect to these four measures of vulnerability for each type of farmers. The economic gain of the farmers is measured by ratio of their income to the average income of all the farmers in the village. Thus, with lower income ratio, the higher the farmer's level of vulnerability. The absentee farmers are expected to maintain a high level of income almost through 2050. This can be attributed to their large properties, which will remain mostly planted with forest. Unlike cereal and livestock, forest will continue to be subsidized under the global economic scenario. The average level of income of the retired farmers is lowest from 2001 to 2008, but increases significantly from 2009 when some farmers with large farms and high income retire. This shows the dynamic character of vulnerability because the profiles of the farmers change over time. Thus, the vulnerable group of people today may not necessarily be the vulnerable tomorrow. The erratic trend in the level of income of the diversified farmers is not only due to the impact of the retirement process, but also to their adaptive behaviour in terms of shifting to more profitable crops and diversifying their land use. The traditional farmers, who mostly cultivate cereals and raise livestock, will be affected the most by any reduction in subsidies as shown by the significant decrease in their income level. As a result, the model shows that some traditional farmers will decide to migrate out of the village and abandon their farms. Social cohesion, which supports knowledge transfer and thus adaptation, will be affected when farmers leave the village and abandon their farms. Hence, the higher the number of out-migration and land abandonment, the higher the level of vulnerability. Depopulation becomes even more problematic when the migrating farmers are young and educated because they are expected to have higher motivation and knowledge to adapt to global changes. In fact, Amendoeira da Serra is already experiencing the migration of young people out of the village, leaving the retired old people who have less capacity or motivation to adapt to global changes. The high number of land abandonments among retired farmers in Figure 9.4 represents the out-migration of their successors.

Farm diversification is a good adaptive measure because it offers alternative sources of income. Thus, farmers whose adaptive decisions result in higher levels of diversification are less vulnerable to global changes such as price fluctuations and/or climate extremes. Farm diversification is common among all types of farmers, with all farmers having almost the same number of income sources. Farm diversification is slightly higher among the diversified farmers because they do not only apply the traditional Portuguese 'montado farming system', which combines oak trees, cereals and livestock, but they also allow shrubs to grow for hunting purposes. The level of diversification among the diversified farmers will decline in the late 2010s when large-farm owners retire. Even after retirement, these farmers are expected to continue diversified farming because they can afford to employ agricultural workers. Certain types of farm diversification such

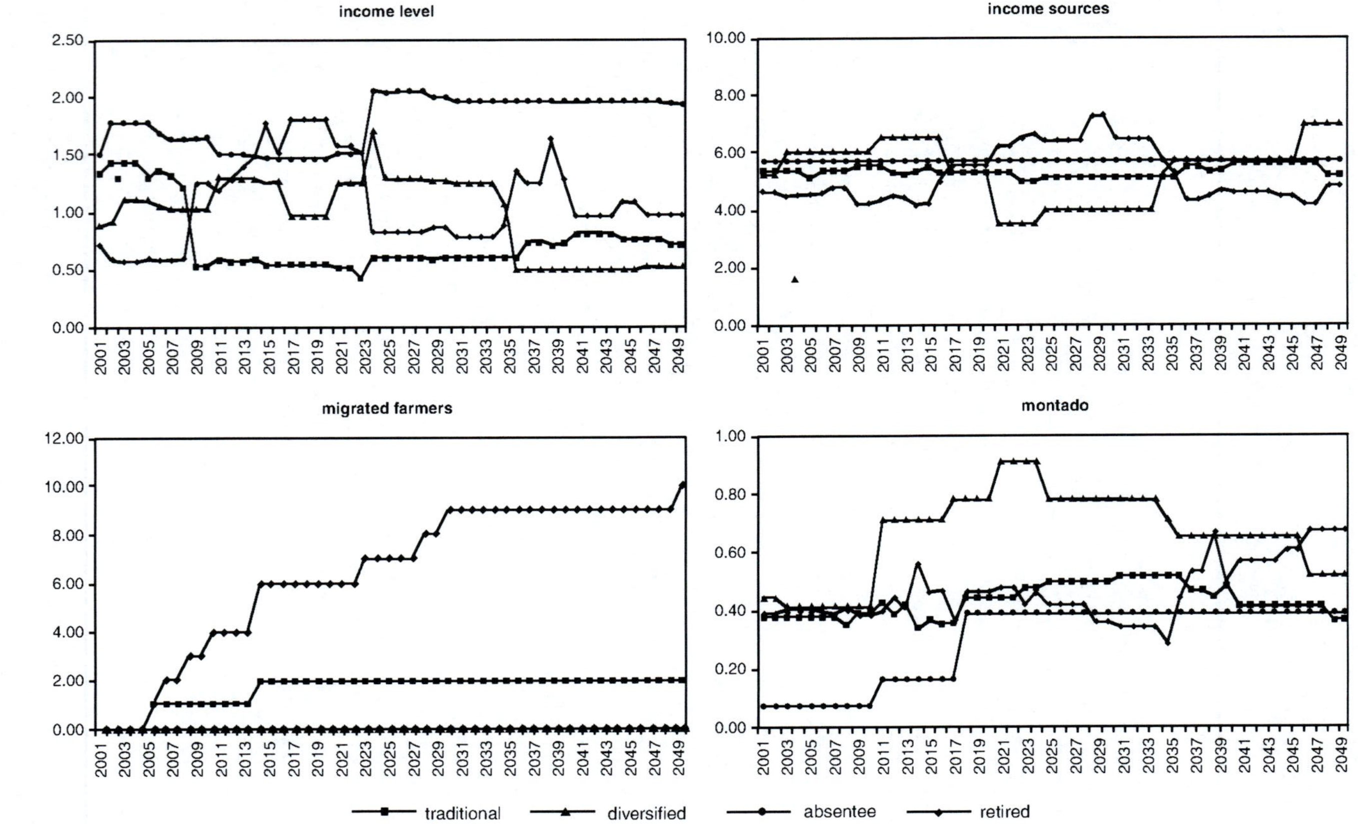

Note: Income level is the ratio of the average farmer income of a farmer profile to the average of all the farmers; migrated farmers are the number of farmers who have abandoned their lands; income sources are the number of different land uses, types of livestock, and non-farming activities; and the montado area refers to the ratio of the areas planted to montado and the total farm area.

Figure 9.4 *Trends in economic, social and ecological measures of vulnerability, 2001–2050*

as montado can improve biodiversity, which helps decrease sensitivity of the natural environment and promotes farm sustainability. Pinto-Correia (2000) argues that traditional landscapes in rural Europe, including the montado farming system in Portugal, represent a wealth of European historical and cultural patrimony heritage and maintain and enhance biodiversity, and hence they merit preservation. Moreover, Strijker (2005) explains that land abandonment is preferable to land intensification because the former leads to changes in biodiversity and provides options for positive developments. Hence, shrub growth resulting from land abandonment in Alentejo, Portugal could lead to improvement in the ecological environment in the region. In view of these, biodiversity level in the model is measured by the ratio of the area planted to montado and shrubs to the total farm area. The larger the area planted to montado and shrubs, the higher the level of biodiversity and the lower the level of vulnerability. Areas planted to montado are highest among the diversified farmers and lowest among the absentee farmers. Unlike the diversified farmers, the absentee farmers do not invest time and money to improve biodiversity and soil quality because agriculture activities are not the principal source of their income. As mentioned earlier, farms of absentee farmers are mostly covered by forest due to low land maintenance. However, forest plantations in the Alentejo region have even been detrimental to the natural environment not only because of forest fires in the drought season, but also because certain types of trees can further damage the already poor soil quality in the region.

The values of the four sets of vulnerability measures (i.e. economic gain, social cohesion, farm diversification and biodiversity level) in Figure 9.4 were standardized using linguistic value ranging from a very low to a very high level of vulnerability. These standardized values were then aggregated to present an overall overview of vulnerability in Amendoeira da Serra by type of farmers in Figure 9.5a. The same aggregated values are also presented in Figure 9.5b in percentage distribution to provide an idea of the average share of each type of farmers to the overall vulnerability in the village. The figures reveal that as a whole, the retired farmers will be the most vulnerable among the four types of farmers, followed by traditional farmers. If we were to distribute the burden of vulnerability among the farmers, the retired and traditional farmers will persistently share more than 60 per cent of this burden (Figure 9.5b). As mentioned above, the main source of vulnerability of the retired farmers is the lack of successors to manage their lands. The very low income is the main cause of vulnerability among the traditional farmers, which in turn is attributed to the low agricultural profitability in the village. As more and more low-income traditional farmers retire until 2050, the retired farmers will remain the most vulnerable group of farmers. Hence, to decrease the vulnerability of the retired farmers in the future, the condition of the low-income traditional farmers of today should be improved even before they retire. Computing the average vulnerability of all the farmers in the village, Figure 9.6 shows that poor economic gain is the main source of vulnerability in the village. Because vulnerability with respect to low income is not expected to decrease in a global economic scenario, more and more farmers will

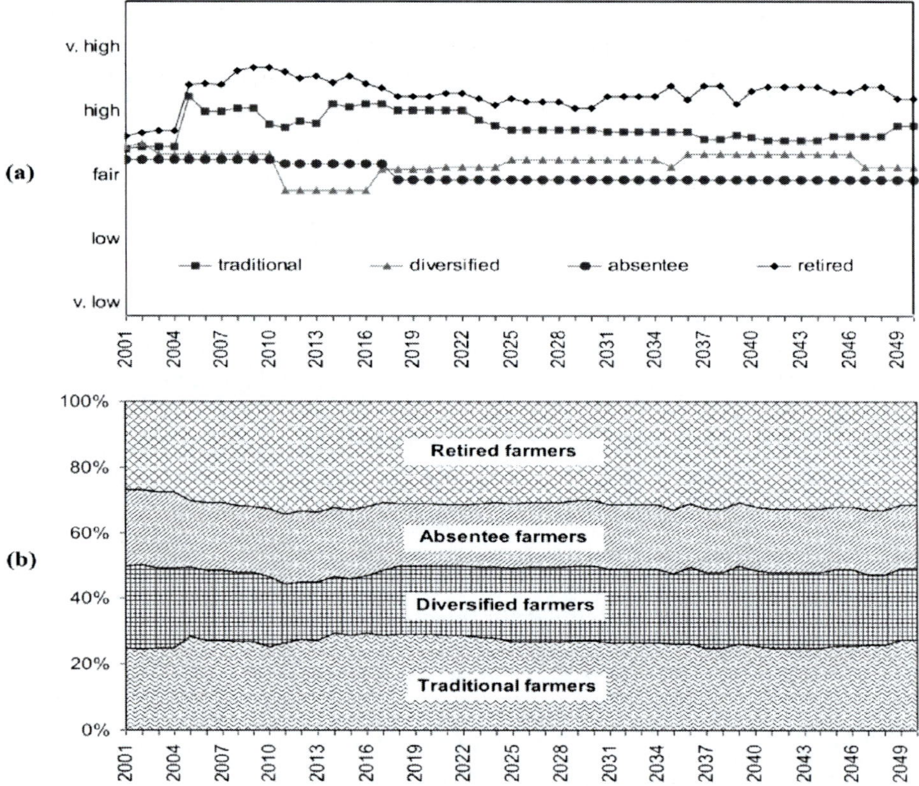

Figure 9.5 *Trend and distribution in vulnerability by type of farmers, 2001–2050*

abandon their farms, particularly the traditional farmers. Vulnerability with respect to lack of social cohesion will thus become an even more serious problem from the second half of the 2020s. Farm diversification will remain relatively stable, and thus will not contribute to any change in vulnerability because, as mentioned earlier, innovative farmers with large farm size will continue to maintain their montado farms even after retirement. The level of biodiversity will slightly improve, and thus result in a slight reduction in vulnerability in the village in the latter part of 2010. The improvement in biodiversity will be contributed by the increase in shrub land cover due to land abandonment. This implies that the decrease in ecological vulnerability could partly offset the increase in social vulnerability. Thus, the results of the model suggest that there are some trade-offs between different sources or causes of vulnerability. Hence, it is important to identify adaptation measures that could decrease vulnerability of one sector, without increasing that of another. For example, there are other ways to increase land cover of shrubs other than land abandonment. In the case study area, the farmers with large farms are allowing shrubs to grow in their land, not necessarily to improve biodiversity but to create space for hunting. Hunting can be a source of income through ecotourism. So with appropriate support from the government

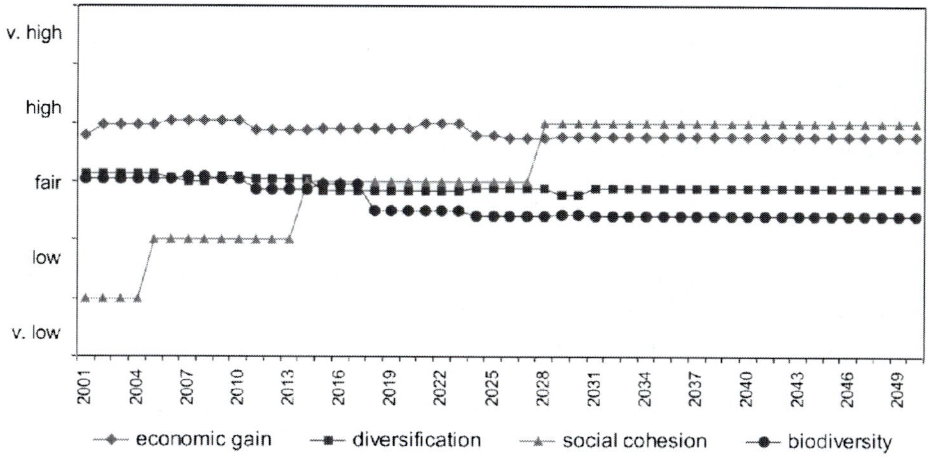

Figure 9.6 *Economic gain and vulnerability*

(e.g. promotion of and investment in ecotourism), for example, farmers with smaller farms like the traditional farmers can be encouraged to put their farms together to grow shrubs for hunting purpose. Such an adaptation measure could help solve not only problems related to social and ecological vulnerability, but also economic ones because it promotes income gain and farm diversification.

Model validations

The utility of empirically grounded models depends on their adequate validation and verification (Parker et al, 2003). The former checks truthfulness of a model with respect to its problem domain, and the latter checks the correctness of model construction. Models that seek to explore future scenarios are impossible to validate completely (Parker et al, 2003; Rounsevell et al, 2006). Moreover, an agent-based model is an assembly of different models, which the complex structure makes it difficult to validate as a whole. Alternatively, however, some parts of this structure can be individually validated to ensure that each of them represents real system behaviour. For example, the behavioural model of the agents was validated through expert judgement and supported by cluster analysis of farm typologies. Moreover, the statistical significance of the suitability maps of land-use conversions was also estimated. Model verification was undertaken in this chapter using sensitivity and uncertainty analyses. Incremental changes in the income parameters, including wheat prices, forest subsidies and labour wage, were mapped against the spatial land-use patterns that were generated from the model for the year 2050 to analyse the sensitivity of the model to the baseline values of the parameters. Results of 12 simulations based on ±25 per cent and ±50 per cent changes from the reference values show that there are more significant changes in land-use pattern when prices and subsidies decrease than when they increase. This is theoretically consistent with the decision rules that farmers adopt alternative land uses when their income decreases. Decision rules are important components of agent-based models, and these also require verification. Thus, a similar mapping procedure was applied to the decision rules (i.e. farm size, education level, land suitability) to verify the sensitivity of the model results to changes in these rules. Five simulation runs were made for each of the decision rules, with each run corresponding to certain incremental changes in their values. The decision rule on memory refers to the number of consecutive years in the past which the farmers consider in deciding whether or not to adopt alternative land use when their income continuously declines. The simulation runs represent 1 to 5 years. The five runs for the education level refer to the number of years the farmers spent in school (i.e. 0, 4, 6, 8, above 8 years). The values of the decision for farm size and suitability were changed by increments of 40ha and 20 per cent, respectively, with a starting value of zero. The results of the sensitivity analysis for these four decision rules are summarized in Figure 9.7. All the runs resulted in some changes in the land use, which implies that the model is sensitive to the changes in the decision rules. If this is not the case, then the model is not robust. Moreover, the direction of changes is consistent with the assumptions for all the rules. For example, the changes in land use decrease as the level of farm suitability decreases. Farm size and suitability have the largest impact on the changes in land use with number of affected pixels (25×25m) as high as 9000. Because the agent-based model uses GIS maps (e.g. land use), uncertainty analysis is important to verify possible errors and uncertainties in input maps. Such errors may have been generated from classifying land use through remote sensing, identifying farm boundaries through the global positioning system (GPS), and developing land

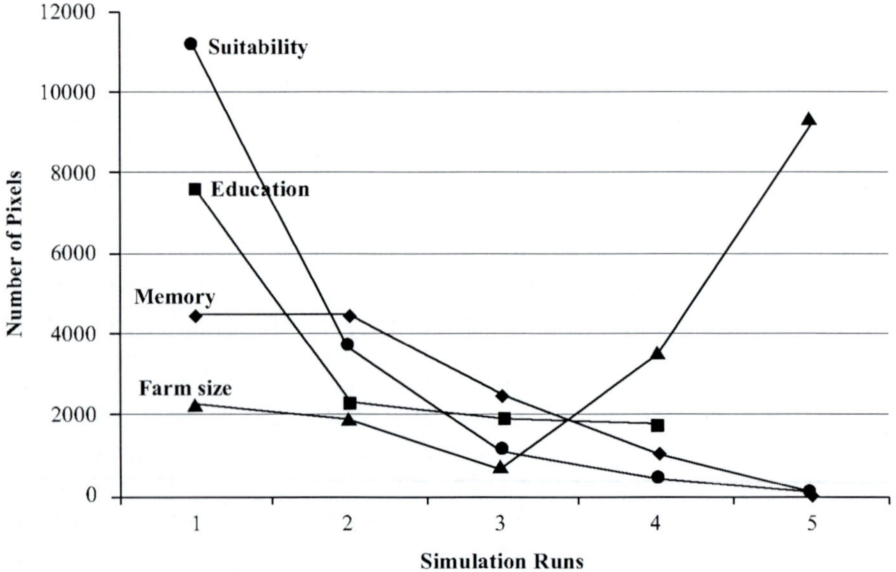

Figure 9.7 *Sensitivity analysis*

suitability through logistic regression. The degree of error propagation and uncertainty was investigated through random distortion of land use and suitability maps and systematic changes in farm size and boundaries. The results of the analysis verified the robustness of the model results to the relevant inputs.

Conclusions

This chapter presented an empirical application of a new vulnerability framework based on multi-agent systems to assess the vulnerability of Portuguese farmers to the combined impacts of global economic and climate change. A total of 28 farmers, who cover 60 per cent of the farming population and own 82 per cent of the farming area in a marginal agricultural village, represent the agents in the model. The results of the socioeconomic survey and cluster analysis reveal that these farmers can be grouped into four profiles (i.e. traditional, diversified, absentee and retired), each having different adaptive strategies to the changes in their socioeconomic and biophysical environment. The changes in the environment of the farmers were represented in the agent-based model through the inclusion of scenarios on prices, subsidies, technology, temperature and CO_2 from 2000 to 2050. Modelling the adaptive decisions of these farmers to these changes, the results of the agent-based model reveal the differential vulnerability of the farmers due to the variability in profiles and the erratic trend in the level of vulnerability due to the shifting in profiles. Among the four model outputs that were used to measure vulnerability (i.e. economic gain, farm diversification, social cohesion and biodiversity level), poor economic gain turned out to be the main source of vulnerability of the farmers in the village. The variables used to measure vulnerability in this chapter are rather limited in scope due to the lack of relevant survey data and tend to duplicate the indicators used for generating generic indices of vulnerability. As opposed to generic indicators, however, these variables capture the variation resulting from dynamic characteristics of the human and environment system. Future research on agent-based modelling to assess vulnerability should include a feedback dialogue with the farmers (or other relevant agents) to validate the results of the model. Such a dialogue will help review missing data inputs and identify unconventional model outputs, in particular with respect to the sources of vulnerability. Because the analysis in this chapter is only one of the very few initial attempts to explore the applicability of agent-based modelling to vulnerability assessment, its current application with all its limitations serves the purpose of scientific research. Further research is necessary to include additional variables that assess the sensitivity of environment to human action particularly in terms of land use and management, to consider various network analyses to assess the influence of social relationships in agents' adaptive decisions, to identify measures of vulnerability that are not similar to those used to generate generic vulnerability indices, and to include decision makers and/or planners as proactive agents in the model to capture the multi-scalar hierarchy in adaptation process.

At its current stage of application, however, the agent-based framework shows potential for assessing vulnerability to improve adaptation at the agent or community level because it is able to integrate cognition process, and thus consider adaptive decisions of human being to a constantly changing environment. Other useful features of the framework include its ability for simultaneous accounting of multiple stresses that influence the level of exposure through the use of scenarios, for combining different socioeconomic and biophysical factors affecting adaptive capacity and sensitivity to global changes, for capturing the dynamics of human–environment interactions, for placing the adaptive agents with different profiles in the core of vulnerability assessment, for putting together different vulnerability concepts to create both spatial extension and temporal dimension in vulnerability assessment, and for exploring different measures of vulnerability that are most relevant to the adaptive decisions and actions of agents at the community level. The framework recognizes that social systems are complex and strongly influenced by non-linear dynamics, which is an aspect of systems behaviour that indicator- and profile-based approaches alone cannot capture. While still in its infancy in the field of climate change, an agent-based approach is a very promising tool for vulnerability assessment in a changing global environment because it provides great potential for extending our understanding of complex social systems and how aggregate structures emerge from local rules of interaction. However, although an agent-based framework offers a good alternative to these approaches, models based on multi-agent systems are time-consuming and data hungry, which limit their application to well-documented case study areas. In this respect, indicator-based approaches have the advantage of being generalizable across multiple spatial scales even where data sources are limited. Future development of agent-based models could, therefore, usefully investigate how such approaches could be applied to broader geographic regions without losing the dynamic behaviour of interacting agents that underpins the concept. Because only then will an agent-based framework be able to meaningfully contribute to the development of global adaptation policy.

Acknowledgements

This chapter is an extension of the land-use model developed for the Vulnerability of Ecosystem Services to Land Use Change in Traditional Agricultural Landscapes (VISTA) project, which was funded by the 5th Framework Programme of the European Commission. The authors would like to thank their colleagues in the project, especially Anne van Doorn and Martha Bakker. They would also like to extend their gratitude to Marc Delgado and Montserrat Gómez Delgado for their support on the cluster and sensitivity analyses.

References

Acosta-Michlik, L. (2005) *Intervulnerability Assessment: Shifting Foci from Generic Indices to Adaptive Agents in Assessing Vulnerability to Global Environmental Change* (A Pilot Project in the Philippines), Project Report of the Advanced Institute on Vulnerability to Global Environmental Change www.start.org/Program/advanced_institutes_3.html

Acosta-Michlik, L., Rounsevell, M. D. A., Van Doorn, A. and Bakker, M. (2005) 'Modelling agent's socioeconomic and ecological environment: An agent-based approach for developing land use change scenarios', Crop Science and Technology 2005 Proceedings, Glasgow, 31 October–2 November 2005 www.bcpc.org/Congress2005/Congress2005_home.asp

Acosta-Michlik, L., Eierdanz, F., Alcamo, J., Klein, R. J. T., Kumar, K., Campe, S., Carius, A., Tänzler, D. and Krömker, D. (2006) 'How vulnerable is India to climatic stress? Measuring vulnerability to drought using the Security Diagram concept', *Climate Change and Human Security, Die Erde* Special Volume on Climate Change, vol 137(1), pp223–252

Acosta-Michlik, L., Espaldon, V., Ranola, R., Acosta, D. J., Anacta, V. J., Delgado, M. and Klein, R. J. T. (2007a) 'From generic indices to adaptive agents: Complementary approaches to assessing vulnerability to global environmental change', *Global Environmental Change* (submitted)

Acosta-Michlik, L., van Doorn, A., Bakker, M., Rounsevell, M. D. A. and Delgado, M. (2007b) 'An agent-based model of land use change in the traditional agricultural landscapes of the Alentejo, Portugal. Framing and modeling the agents' behavior', ABEAM Working Paper 06.2006, Département de Géographie, Université catholique de Louvain, Belgium, www.geo.ucl.ac.be/ABEAM/

Adger, W. N. (1999) 'Social vulnerability to climate change and extremes in coastal Vietnam', *World Development*, vol 27(2), pp249–269

Anderson, J. (1996) 'ACT: A simple theory of complex cognition', *American Psychologist*, vol 51(4), pp335–365

Axtell, R. (2000) 'Why agents? On the varied motivations for agent computing in the social sciences', Working Paper No. 17, Center on Social and Economic Dynamics, November 2000

Berger, T. (2001) 'Agent-based spatial models applied to agriculture: A simulation tool for technology diffusion, resource use changes and policy analysis', *Agricultural Economics*, vol 25, pp245–260

Bousquet, F., Trebul, G. and Hardy, B. (2005) *Companion Modelling and Multi-agent Systems for Integrated Natural Resource Management in Asia*, IRRI, Manila

Ewert, F., Rounsevell, M. D. A., Reginster, I., Metzger, M. and Leemans, R. (2005) 'Future scenarios of European agricultural land use. I: Estimating changes in crop productivity', *Agriculture, Ecosystems & Environment*, vol 107, pp101–116

Heitzmann K., Canagarajah, R. S. and Siegel, P. B. (2002) *Guidelines for Assessing the Sources of Risk and Vulnerability*, Social Protection Discussion Paper Series No. 0218, Social Protection Unit, Human Development Network, The World Bank, New York

Huigen, M. (2004) 'First principles of the MameLuke multi-actor modelling framework for land use change, illustrated with a Philippine case study', *Journal of Environmental Management*, vol 72, pp5–21

Jager W., Janssen, M. A., De Vries, H. J. M., De Greef, J. and Vlek, C. A. J. (2000) 'Behaviour in commons dilemmas: Homo economicus and Homo psychologicus in an ecological–economic model, *Ecological Economics*, vol 35(3), pp357–379

Jager, W., Janssen, M. A. and Vlek, C. A. J. (2002) 'How uncertainty stimulates over-harvesting in a resource dilemma: Three process explanations', *Journal of*

Environmental Psychology, vol 22, pp247–263

Lewis, R. (2001) 'Cognitive theory, SOAR', in *International Ecyclopedia of the Social and Behavioural Sciences*, Pergamon (Elsevier Science), Amsterdam

McLaughlin S., McKenna, J. and Cooper, J. A. G. (2002) 'Socio-economic data in coastal vulnerability indices: Constraints and opportunities', *Journal of Coastal Research*, Special Issue, vol 36, pp487–497

Moss, R.H., Brenkert, A. L. and Malone, E. L. (2001) *Vulnerability to Climate Change: A Quantitative Approach*, Pacific Northwest National Laboratory, www.globalchange.umd.edu/data/publications/Vulnerability_to_Climate_Change.pdf

Nakicenovic, N., Alcamo, J., Davis, G., de Vries, B., Fenhann, J., Gaffin, S., Gregory, K., Grübler, A., Jung, T.Y., Kram, T., Emilio la Rovere, E., Michaelis, L., Mori, S., Morita, T., Pepper, W., Pitcher, H., Price, L., Riahi, K., Roehrl, A., Rogner, H.-H., Sankovski, A., Schlesinger, M. E., Shukla, P. R., Smith, S., Swart, R. J., van Rooyen, S., Victor, N. and Dadi, Z. (2000) *Special Report on Emissions Scenarios*, Cambridge University Press, Cambridge

O'Brien, K. L. and Leichenko, R. M. (2000) 'Double exposure: Assessing the impacts of climate change within the context of economic globalization', *Global Environmental Change*, vol 10, pp221–232

Parker, D. C., Manson, S. M., Janssen, M. A., Hoffmann, M. J. and Deadman, P. (2003) 'Multi-agent systems for the simulation of land-use and land-cover change: A review', *Annals of the Association of American Geographers*, vol 93(2), pp314–337

Pinto-Correira, T. (2000) 'Future development in Portuguese rural areas: How to manage agricultural support for landscape conservation?', *Landscape and Urban Planning*, vol 50, pp95–106

Rao, A. S. and Georgreff, M. P (1997) 'Modeling rational agents with a BDI-architecture', in Huhns, M. N. and Singh, M. P. (eds) *Readings in Agents*, Morgan Kaufmann Publishers, San Francisco, CA, pp317–328

Rounsevell, M. D. A., Ewert, F., Reginster, I., Leemans, R. and Carter, T. R. (2005) 'Future scenarios of European agricultural land use. II: Projecting changes in cropland and grassland', *Agriculture, Ecosystems & Environment*, vol 107, pp117–135

Rounsevell, M. D. A., Reginster, I., Araújo, M. B., Carter, T. R., Dendoncker, N., Ewert, F., House, J. I., Kankaanpää, S., Leemans, R., Metzger, M. J., Schmit, C., Smith, P. and Tuck, G. (2006) 'A coherent set of future land use change scenarios for Europe', *Agriculture, Ecosystems & Environment*, vol 114, pp57–68

San, O. M., Van-Nam Huynh and Nakamori, Y. (2004) 'An alternative extension of the k-means algorithm for clustering categorical data', *International Journal of Applied Mathematics and Computer Science*, vol 14(2), pp241–247

Schröter, D., Polsky, C. and Patt, A. (2005) 'Assessing vulnerabilities to the effects of global change: An eight step approach', *Mitigation and Adaptation Strategies for Global Change*, vol 10, pp573–596

Stern, P. C., Young, O. R. and Druckman, D. (eds) (1991) *Global Environmental Change: Understanding the Human Dimensions*, Committee on the Human Dimensions of Global Change, National Research Council, www.nap.edu/openbook/

Strijker, D. (2005) 'Marginal lands in Europe: Causes of decline', *Basic and Applied Ecology*, vol 6, pp99–106

Turner, B. L., Kasperson, R. E., Matson, P. A., McCarthy, J. J., Corell, R. W., Christensen, L., Eckley, N., Kasperson, J. X., Luers, A., Martello, M. L., Polsky, C., Pulsipher, A. and Schiller, A. (2003) 'A framework for vulnerability analysis in sustainability science', *Proceedings of the National Academy of Sciences of the United States of America*, vol 100(14), pp8074–8079 van der Veen, A. and Rotmans, J. (2001) 'Dutch perspectives on agents, regions and land use change', *Environmental Modeling and Assessment*, vol 6(2), pp83–86

Ziervogel, G., Bithell, M., Washington, R. and Downing, T. (2005) 'Agent-based social simulation: A method for assessing the impact of seasonal climate forecast applications among smallholder farmers', *Agricultural Systems*, vol 83, pp1–26

Chapter 10

Assessing Financial and Economic Vulnerability to Natural Hazards: Bridging the Gap between Scientific Assessment and the Implementation of Disaster Risk Management with the CatSim Model

Stefan Hochrainer and Reinhard Mechler

Introduction

The number and losses of natural disasters have been increasing globally due to such factors as increases in wealth, population growth and migratory trends from rural to urban areas. Whereas more developed countries usually are able to cope with the impacts of natural disasters, in less developed countries often a large proportion of the population is severely affected and a substantial strain is put on a country's resources and ability to finance important social and economic programmes. Post-disaster, governments in addition to their responsibility for rebuilding public infrastructure, also have the moral or even explicit obligation to provide post-disaster emergency relief and assistance to affected households and business. Yet, in contrast to wealthier countries, developing country governments frequently face post-event liquidity crises in financing relief and reconstruction, leading to serious effects on their long-term development plans and their ability to finance needed and planned social and economic programmes. Typically, developing countries finance their post-disaster expenses by diverting from the budget or already disbursed development loans, as well as by relying on outside assistance from the international community. However, these sources can be insufficient, are often associated with longer time lags and will not provide incentives for risk reduction (Bayer and Mechler, 2005). Traditionally, the main emphasis in this context of disaster management has been on *ex post* approaches and relief, but recently the focus has been shifting towards *ex ante* measures taken before events. Realizing the unsustainability of after-the-event approaches in the long run, the proactive financing of disaster risks is slowly becoming an important cornerstone for tackling the substantial and increasing effects of natural disasters (Gurenko, 2004).

To reduce and manage disaster risks efficiently and systematically, one key technique of choice is risk modelling. Quantitative risk models have become important tools and are standardly required nowadays in the banking and insurance sectors for assessing high-probability and low-impact risk. The estimation of low-probability, high-consequence events by way of catastrophe models has only lately received more recognition via formalized algorithms and approaches (Embrechts et al, 1997; Banks, 2005). Catastrophe models typically generate probabilistic losses by simulating stochastic events based on the geophysical characteristics of the hazard, combining the hazard data with analyses of exposure in terms of values at risk and finally focusing on the vulnerability of people, assets and economies exposed.

Risk management and catastrophe modelling is prevalent within private sector insurance and reinsurance companies in order to better hedge portfolios and price risks. Within the public sector only recently have such approaches become more widely accepted, owing not least to the interest of donor institutions:

> *International aid and development funding agencies, besides sharing consternation at delays, disruptions, and increased costs, have the strong view that wisely planned hazard and vulnerability reduction efforts and funding before a catastrophe pay excellent dividends in reducing economic impacts. Mitigation expenditures are a very small fraction of the funds spent on reconstruction in the aftermath of catastrophes.* (Pollner, 2000, p44)

Yet, catastrophe modelling is complex and resource-intensive, to a large extent due to the fact that only a limited number of observations exist. Hence, one important step in modelling is to better help understand and inform if and to what extent agents are vulnerable to natural hazards now and in the future. Global and climate change are important topics which have to be considered within this process to minimize losses by adapting to ongoing or anticipated changes. Based on the risk bearer (e.g. households, business or the government), different dimensions of global and climate change are important for the decision-making process. From a government loss-financing perspective important variables include population growth, economic development and changes in the intensity of hazard events. There is an ongoing debate on these issues and its effects on the vulnerability of a country due to natural disaster events. For example, migration into hazard-prone areas will increase the likelihood that more people will be affected in the future by extreme events and this will also increase the losses the government has to finance to help the people. On the other hand, economic development usually increases the ability of the private sector and the government to handle natural disaster losses because more resources are available; however, in some cases vulnerability is increased as traditional coping mechanisms may not be known anymore and new ones are not effective yet (Benson and Clay, 2004). It is also likely that spatial and intensity patterns of extreme events will change due to climate change (Emanuel, 2005), which in turn could also effect the other two variables mentioned above. As can be seen, catastrophe modelling and risk management approaches have to incorporate a number of possible effects of climate and global changes on the system under study to arrive at sustainable solutions.

As with the translation of science into policy generally, it is usually not possible and effective for decision makers to try to grasp all the theory behind scientific results. There is a challenge to bridge the gap between the scientific assessment and risk management strategies, as well as policy-relevant and more practical issues. For issues of vulnerability and risk these issues are particularly pronounced, as it is often not evident who should manage vulnerability and risks. A number of research efforts on risk and vulnerability document this. For example, the research cluster 'Forest fire simulation system' of the German Research Network for Natural Disasters (DFNK) created an enabling atmosphere of multidisciplinary forest fire vulnerability and risk research in Germany through an integrative multidisciplinary approach (Merz et al, 2006). While such an integrated concept allows for developing comprehensive solutions that are not possible with disciplinary approaches (Merz et al, 2006), one of the problems encountered in this research was the heterogeneity of the user community which made it difficult to identify adequate users and their specific needs. Similarly, it has been experienced, that stakeholder workshops on vulnerability need not always be a success if perceptions of stakeholders and researchers are not reconciled (see for example the discussion in Schröter et al, 2004, p38).

In this chapter, we discuss recent work undertaken at the International Institute for Applied Systems Analysis (IIASA) (Hochrainer, 2006; Mechler et al, 2006) that aims at bridging this science–policy gap by using a systematic risk management approach informed by a catastrophe model with an interactive user interface. This approach combines important dimensions and their interrelationships in disaster risk management (DRM) and takes an integrative approach. We present some of the features of the IIASA CatSim (Catastrophe Simulation model) to outline one way how such an approach could look and gave indications of terms and concepts we found most useful as well as problematic in a stakeholder setting.

The chapter is organized as follows. In the next section, we introduce important concepts and the needs and problems of the disaster community, then outline a proposed solution for bridging the gap between catastrophe risk and vulnerability assessment and the policy making process. In the following section, the CatSim model, the methodology and risk measures used to visualize aspects of the risk and vulnerabilities governments are exposed to are explained in more detail and strengths and weaknesses of this approach are discussed. Based on a workshop held in the Caribbean in 2006 with key stakeholders the CatSim framework is presented and tested for its usefulness and practicability. The final section synthesizes the discussion and draws some conclusions related to modelling disaster risks and DRM.

Public sector risk and vulnerability

Need for planning

Developing country governments frequently lack the financial resilience to fully repair damaged critical public infrastructure or provide sufficient support to households and businesses for their recovery. In this context, resilience refers to the capacity of a social system to absorb economic disturbance and reorganize, or to 'bounce back' so as essentially to retain the same functionality (Walker et al, 2002). For example, following the 2001 earthquake in the state of Gujarat, India, funds for recovery from the central government and other sources fell far short of pledges, and actual funding only covered around 30 per cent of the state government's post-disaster reconstruction needs (World Bank, 2003). Such lack of financial robustness can also imply huge negative fiscal effects due to natural disaster events. As another example, in the case of Hurricane Emily on Grenada in 2005, the fiscal deficit in the years 2005–2007 increased by 12.7 million to 21.0 million Eastern Caribbean $ compared to the no-disaster scenario (see Figure 10.1).

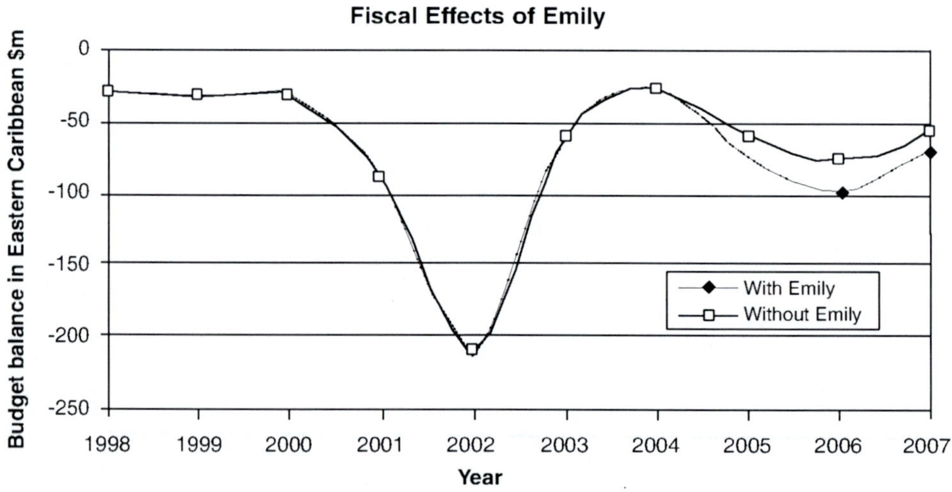

Source: Organisation of Eastern Caribbean States (OECS), 2005

Figure 10.1 *Fiscal effects of Hurricane Emily in 2005*

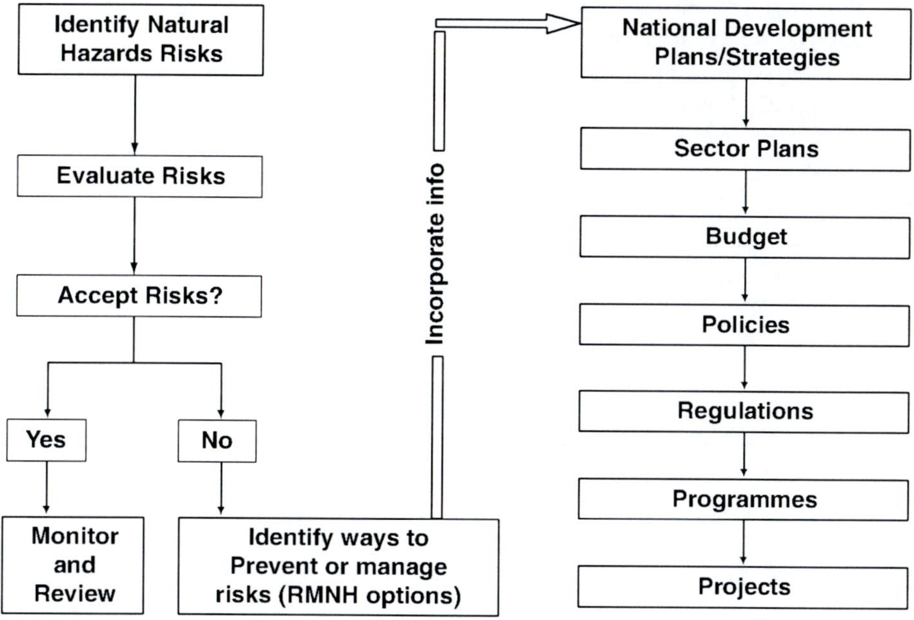

Source: Bettencourt et al, 2006

Figure 10.2 *Planning for disaster risks*

Government post-disaster liquidity crises and increasing fiscal deficits have sounded an alarm, prompting financial development organizations, such as the World Bank, among others, to call for greater attention to reducing financial vulnerability and increasing the resilience of the public sector (Pollner et al, 2001; Gurenko, 2004). To avoid negative (long-term) effects and be better prepared, natural disaster risks should be incorporated (e.g. mainstreamed) into the development planning process. The flow diagram in Figure 10.2 shows how each of the steps could be performed in a practical way.

First, the hazards to which a country or region is exposed should be identified. Then, risks are evaluated and acceptability considered. If not acceptable, analysts have to think about possible risk-management strategies including top–down as well as bottom–up approaches. As a next step, on various levels risks can be mainstreamed into strategies, programmes and projects in order to decrease risks to acceptable levels. Finally, risks need to be monitored, and reviewed continuously (e.g. on an annual basis). The last point is especially important in order to detect changes in the risk portfolio due to global and climate change which could result in altered risk-management strategies.

Assessing vulnerability and risk

The development of a viable risk-management strategy requires policy makers to consider a number of issues:

- Who assumes the risk – government or the commercial private sector, the rest of civil society and donors?
- What risk-reduction priorities support the broader goals of development planning? How do global and climate change issues fit into these goals?
- How can risk-financing instruments effectively encourage risk-reduction measures?
- How can the policy process for managing contingent liabilities be mainstreamed in fiscal and budget planning, and stakeholders included?
- What might be the respective roles of the public and private sectors as well as international financial institutions and other donors in disaster risk management?

Such considerations entail estimating vulnerability and risk and we focus on economic aspects in this chapter. In the literature, work on economic vulnerability to external shocks (often looking at small island developing states) has focused on the structure of an economy (e.g. commodity-based versus high-technology), the prevailing economic conditions (e.g. degree of inflation, economic recession) and the general stages of technical, scientific and economic development (Benson and Clay, 2004). Economic vulnerability is often assessed by a set or a composite index of indicators such as the degree of export dependence, lack of diversification, export concentration, export volatility, share of modern services and products in GDP, trade openness or simply GDP (Briguglio, 1995; Commonwealth Secretariat and World Bank, 2000).

This chapter focuses on the financial vulnerability of the public sector as a subset of economic vulnerability. We follow Turner et al's (2003) definition of vulnerability, which focuses on the degree to which a system or subsystem is likely to experience harm due to exposure to a hazard, either as a perturbation or stressor. Some communities suffer less harm than others from hurricanes, fires, floods and other extreme events because they can mitigate the damage and recover more rapidly and completely. As a case in point, Bangladesh has become less physically vulnerable to cyclones. Over the past four decades deaths from cyclones in Bangladesh have decreased by two orders of magnitude as people have learned to better heed warnings and use storm shelters. Moreover, the people in Bangladesh may become less economically vulnerable to the long-term economic losses from cyclones and other disasters as affordable micro-insurance and other financial hedging instruments become available (Bayer and Mechler, 2005). The latter relates to financial vulnerability and we define public sector financial vulnerability as the degree to which a public authority or government is likely to experience a lack of funds for financing post-disaster reconstruction investment and relief.

As illustrated in Figure 10.3, financial vulnerability depends on the asset risks the country is facing from natural hazards, which can be measured as a function of the *hazard* frequency and intensity, the public and private capital *exposure* and the *physical vulnerability* of public and private assets to the hazard. Climate change can be dealt with in this framework, for example increases in hazard frequency or intensity affect risk. Furthermore, global change and future changes

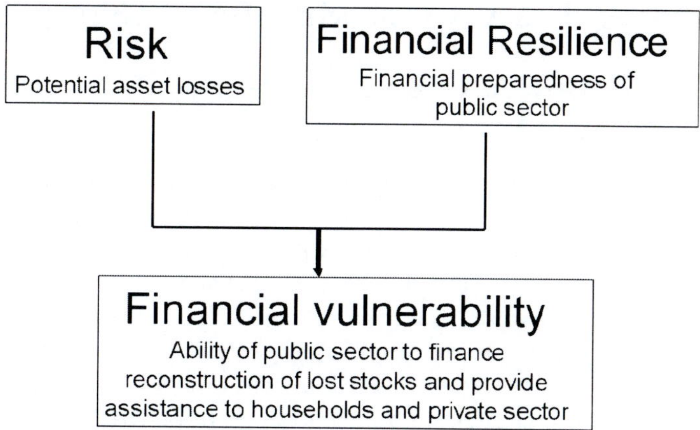

Figure 10.3 *Public sector financial vulnerability to natural hazards*

in exposure to hazards need to be considered when issues of future risk are addressed in the risk management process.

A second important component of public sector financial vulnerability – and introduced already above – is the *resilience* or financial capacity of the public authorities to cope with the losses. This can be measured by the available financial resources for meeting contingent government liabilities. If a government has sufficient budget, reserves or insurance cover to finance its post-disaster liabilities, or can easily raise capital through borrowing, then it is rather financially resilient to a disaster shock. In the opposite case, the government may not be able to cover the losses and a financing gap may occur. The potential for a *financing gap* is an important indicator among others of financial vulnerability.

Financial vulnerability to current exposure to hazard and future exposure as modified by climate change is only one aspect when it comes to assessing a country's vulnerability to natural hazards. Various other ecological or social perspectives can be taken, and definitions of vulnerability vary widely. Usually a line can be drawn between those approaches that use quantitative vulnerability-assessment techniques and those that are more qualitative due to a lack of data and less suitability for a quantitative understanding of the mechanisms. Both types of approaches are appropriate in their own right given the specific policy needs and the requisite policy-making processes. In the following, we present the risk modelling (quantitative) approach taken by us at IIASA using the CatSim model. We suggest that CatSim covers important aspects of the problem discussed above; in order to achieve a comprehensive understanding of the issues at stake, other aspects also have to be included. These aspects often cannot (or should not) be modelled in quantitative form, and we suggest addressing these on more conceptual levels. Links between the two approaches can be established on a procedural level by workshops or interdisciplinary collaborations. One option to be discussed in the following is the design and application of user interfaces, which establish an open environment for exchanging ideas across scientific or political borders.

Assessing disaster risk with the CatSim model

Scientific assessment of disaster risk: Catastrophe modelling

Catastrophic risk, compared to high-frequency, low-impact risk, forms a class of its own, which is characterized by specific signatures. It requires a special approach, specific modelling capabilities and a theory of its own (Johansen and Sornette, 2001). Extreme value theory (Embrechts et al, 1997) renders the theoretical basis for the assessment and prediction of catastrophic events such as natural disasters, financial crashes or large-scale ecological disruptions. Furthermore, in the last few decades the multidimensional nature of risk and dependence has been recognized (Malevergne and Sornette, 2006), leading to new developments to measure risk in a 'coherent' way (Artzner et al, 1999) and to represent the full dependence structure between assets by the use of copulas (Nelsen, 1998).

A myriad of problems remains when it comes to assessing extreme-event risks and vulnerability. The biggest problem still is data scarcity. Because of the low-frequency nature of extreme events, time series of past events alone are usually not sufficient to estimate distributions. Hence, engineering approaches also have to be used to simulate future events and their impact on the elements at risk. One additional problem is to estimate vulnerability functions to combine the impact level of the natural hazard with the losses it will cause. An important consideration here is the degree of uncertainty regarding both the probability and the outcome represented in the loss distributions. Another problem is the uncertainty of the risk measures as those are usually aggregates of many thousands of simulations. One possibility for the last two problems is to incorporate such uncertainty by the use of confidence regions in order to determine the bounds of risk measures (Kunreuther, 2002; Cullen and Small, 2004). Hence, it should be kept in mind that top–down estimates at this broad scale are necessarily rough; validating the model is rather difficult as a lot of simulations have to be done to arrive at aggregate risk measures as an output, which cannot be compared with single-loss scenarios in the past. One way to overcome this problem is to validate each piece of the catastrophe model separately. For example, the economic model can be calibrated by past experience of the macroeconomic behaviour of the country after significant loss events, and the loss distribution can be adapted by using past losses as baseline scenarios.

While these approaches and their limitations are important for studying catastrophic risk in a scientific manner, they may be less important when it comes to the task of providing decision support to policy makers on appropriate DRM strategies. Other techniques are becoming increasingly important and are discussed in the following.

The CatSim methodology

We now turn to explaining the CatSim model in some detail to provide a level of concreteness to the issues discussed so far, and highlight some features of this model which may be informative for guiding policy makers through the risk-management process. Due to the nature of natural hazard events, probability (risk)-based approaches are to be preferred to assess catastrophe risk and financial vulnerability. CatSim represents a stylized interactive model-based framework to assist public policy makers of financially vulnerable countries to design *ex ante* risk-financing strategies (Hochrainer, 2006; Mechler et al, 2006). CatSim analyses the risk-transfer decision in the wider context of a public investment decision by assessing both the direct financial as well as the opportunity costs in light of the government's fiscal and macroeconomic constraints. For representing the fiscal and macroeconomic context, CatSim builds on a simplified economic growth model with a focus on the public sector. An important modelling component is a detailed public finance module for analysing the ability of the state or central government to finance unexpected liquidity needs – referred to as the government's financial vulnerability. The model employs Monte Carlo simulation to generate random shocks to a state or country's capital stock. CatSim is equipped with a graphical interface that allows the user to interactively change default parameters, such as the probability of extreme events and the government's debt and other determinants of financial vulnerability, to assess the effects of uncertainties and/or global or climate changes. Since the user can interactively change important parameters and assumptions, risk-financing strategies can be examined in a transparent and iterative fashion. As a capacity-building tool, it can illustrate the trade-offs and choices the authorities confront in increasing their resilience to the risks of catastrophic disasters. The model has been constructed in close contact with stakeholders and was originally developed for the Regional Policy Dialogue of the Inter-American Development Bank, where this model was applied to case studies on Bolivia, Colombia, Dominican Republic, El Salvador and Honduras (see Freeman et al, 2002). It has been revised, extended and used with stakeholders in a number of hazard-exposed countries such as the Philippines, the Caribbean and most recently in Madagascar. The methodology consists of five stages as illustrated in Figure 10.4.

In stage 1, the risk of direct losses in terms of the probability of asset losses in the relevant country or region is assessed. Consistent with general practice, risk is modelled as a function of hazard (frequency and intensity), the elements exposed to those hazards and their physical vulnerability (for example, see Burby, 1991; Swiss Re, 2000). Based on the information on direct risks in the government portfolio, financial resilience can be evaluated by assessing the government's ability to finance its obligations for the specified disaster scenarios (stage 2). Financial resilience is directly affected by the general conditions prevailing in an economy; for example, the budget stance and changes in tax revenue have important implications on a country's financial capacity to deal with disaster losses.

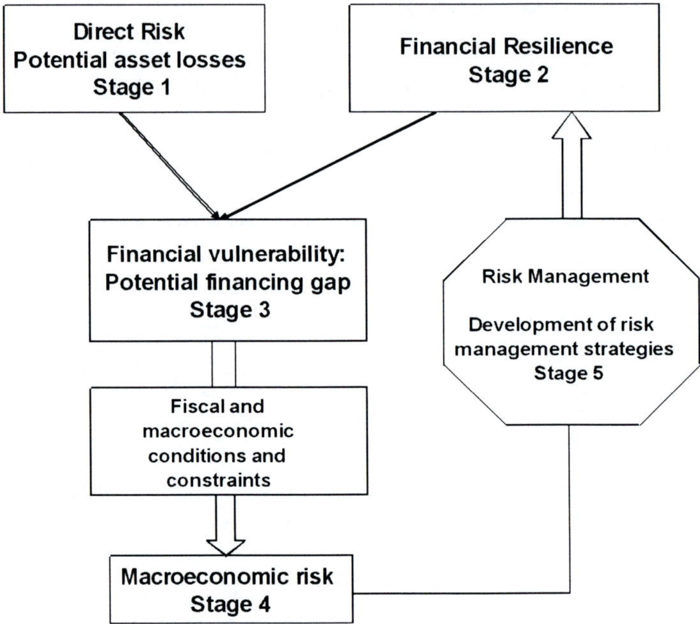

Source: Mechler et al, 2006

Figure 10.4 *Financial vulnerability and the CatSim methodology*

A main question underlying the CatSim tool is whether a government is financially prepared to repair damaged infrastructure and provide adequate relief and support to the private sector for the estimated damages. For this assessment (stage 3), it is necessary to examine the government's sources; both sources that will be relied on (probably in an ad hoc manner, *ex post* sources) after the disaster, and sources put into place before the disaster (*ex ante* financing). Comparing available financing with the government's post-disaster financial obligations yields an estimation of the potential *financing gap*.

To assess the possibility of a financing gap for a longer time horizon, there is also the possibility to attach probabilities to the financing gap – for example, one could find that in the current situation there is a 10 per cent probability that a financing gap will occur in the next ten years. This result can serve as a baseline to compare different risk-management strategies that would decrease this probability. Financial vulnerability can have serious repercussions on the national or regional economy and the population (stage 4). If the government cannot replace or repair damaged infrastructure, for example roads and hospitals, nor provide assistance to those in need after a disaster, this will have long-term consequences. The consequences for long-term economic development can also be illustrated by the CatSim tool. For example, trajectories of possible growth paths from the simulation can be shown and compared for the baseline as well as the proactive cases. The pros and cons of investing in the risk-financing instruments are shown in stage 5. Budgetary resources allocated to catastrophe reserve funds, insurance and contingent credit (as well as to preventive loss-reduction measures) reduce the potential financing gap, and thus can ensure a more stable development path. On the other hand, *ex ante* financing and prevention measures come at a price in terms of other investments foregone and will inevitably have an adverse impact on the growth path of an economy. The model assesses this trade-off by comparing the costs of selected *ex ante* measures with their benefits in terms of decreasing the possibility of encountering a financing gap. Four *ex ante* financing policy measures are currently considered in the CatSim tool: excess of loss insurance, contingent credit, reserve funds and catastrophe bonds. Also, one generic option for loss-reduction measures has been implemented in order to analyse the linkage with risk financing. The model is iterative: after strategies are chosen, it is possible to start again with stage 3, for example now with modified resilience and vulnerability variables, and assess risks and further options. Hence, an iterative process is started.[1]

Involving the stakeholders: User interfaces, implementation and policy issues

In the case of risk management, mainstreaming risk can be hampered due to a variety of reasons, including issues associated with (i) data, (ii), methodology, (iii) modelling, and (iv) the difficulties to put the results in a broader context in the decision-making process. While (i) and (iii) are more technical questions from a policy perspective, (ii) and (iv) are most important. If decision makers understand the methodology behind the results, it is easier to grasp the complex relationships between the various variables which constitute vulnerability and risk, while at the same time specific preferences can be incorporated into the whole risk-management process. From the authors' experience, policy makers expect a methodology that is based on sound scientific understanding and allows for interactions and stakeholder input. Furthermore, results have to be shown in such a way that they are easy to understand while complex enough to incorporate the main characteristics of the risk and vulnerability under evaluation. The core idea of the methodological approach for CatSim was that variables used to assess public financial vulnerability can be operationalized in such a way that they are directly linked to a catastrophe (risk-based) model. Graphical user interfaces (stand-alone application software) interactively guide the user through the methodology and outline crucial variables, parameters and results of the simulation, which can be modified to assess different kinds of strategies. The underlying philosophy is that policy makers actively assess ideas and strategies rather than being served with results. The methodology and user interfaces are directly connected, so that each step of the methodology is also represented by user interfaces with the corresponding variables and results.

Figure 10.5 may serve as an example, which shows the user interface for assessing the financial vulnerability of Grenada, a small island Caribbean country. The parameters that can be changed are listed at the top, while the graphical results are shown in the main part of the window. Without using any terminolo-

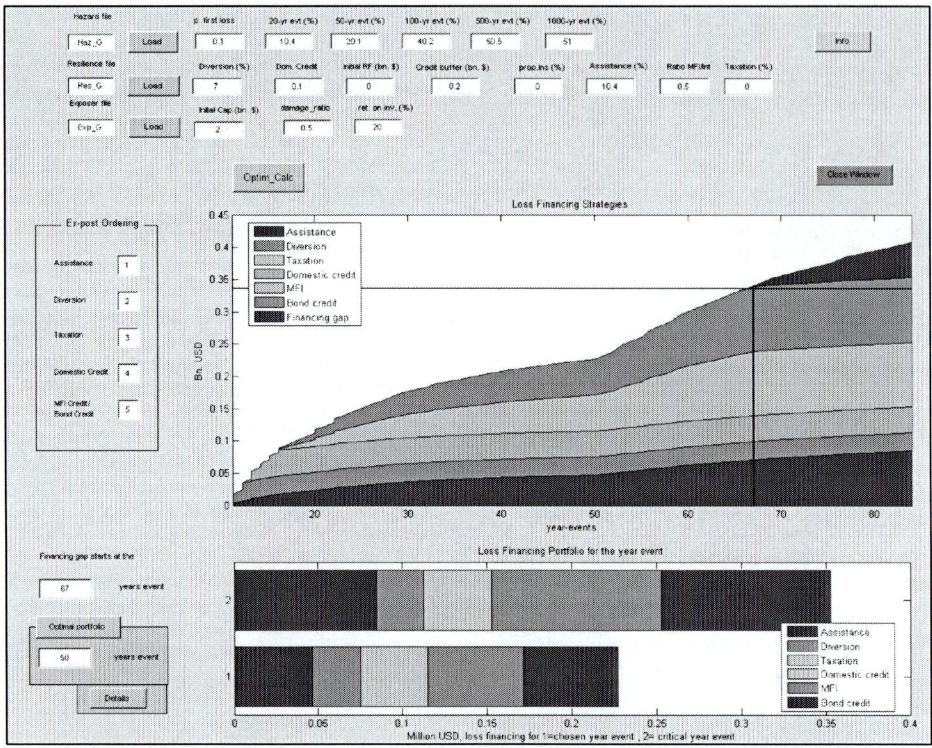

Figure 10.5 *CatSim user interface to determine the financial vulnerability for Grenada*

gies and modelling explanation, the user can easily understand the relationship between loss financing and the probability level of the disasters, if he knows that the x-axis is the graphical representation of the impact level of the disasters and the y-axis shows the damages due to disasters separated into different financing resources available. In the second picture, one can look at loss-financing strategies with all financial resources available and can compare those to types of events.

Issues of global and climate change can be assessed in this manner too, for example by shifting loss distributions or increasing the exposure over time. Yet, it is important to keep in mind that the model shows one dimension of the threat only, namely the financial vulnerability of the government and the implications for the future via a set of indicators. It is clear that other dimensions in the context of extreme events and global changes are equally important, such as environmental effects or protection of human lives, to name but a few; in the process of assessing financial vulnerability, such questions of adapting to global *and* climate change naturally arise because of the interrelationship of these different dimensions. The model can assist policy makers in assessing one piece of the problem, but results are not optimal in the sense that they solve the problems for all dimensions. Hence, an open process and discussion is always required when it comes to *decision making*.

Insights from using CatSim in a stakeholder setting

We now present experiences gained with using CatSim in a workshop on disaster risk bearing and financing with national policy makers from ministries and public authorities from the Caribbean. We discuss insights gained, the information and concepts found to be most useful for the respective audience, and problems and misunderstandings encountered.

There are at least three problems for Caribbean countries to efficiently bear or finance their natural disaster risk. First, due to the nature of small island states, spreading risks within their borders is not advisable and effective. Second, due to constraints on borrowing capacity in most Caribbean countries, there are limits to spreading risk over time, for example by post-disaster development loans. Finally, for insuring exposed government assets, international prices have to be paid which are subject to fluctuations caused elsewhere. For example, Barbados, one of the few countries in the region insuring public infrastructure, experienced a tenfold increase in insurance premiums after Hurricane Andrew in 1992 despite the fact that Barbados is not in the way of the major hurricane paths (Auffret, 2003). A formidable challenge facing insurance and other risk-financing mechanisms in highly exposed developing countries is thus rendering them affordable to middle- and low-income clients and governments. As a consequence, governments in the region affected by natural disasters have generally relied on outside assistance (aid) to finance their losses in the past.

On the other hand, regional initiatives have been created for tackling disaster risks in the region in a more concerted fashion. One option put forward in the 1990s within this cooperation was to create a regional Caribbean risk-sharing pool. Although concrete proposals had been put forward, implementation of such had not been achieved. After the severe hurricane season of 2005, where 30 cyclones of Category 5 made landfall, existing cooperation among the island states was rekindled and the regional pooling idea picked up again.

As one of the initiatives on risk mainstreaming and pooling, in late 2005 the Caribbean Development Bank (CDB) and the Inter-American Development Bank (IDB) established the Joint Initiative on Mainstreaming Disaster Risk Management in order to tackle the increasing disaster risk to the societies and economies of the Caribbean. The initiative strives to engage Caribbean countries to mainstream DRM in their planning and management processes. After a first phase that entailed a planning meeting of the permanent secretaries in finance and planning and heads of specialized agencies at the end of 2005, a need for more practical hands-on tools was recognized, and from 26 to 27 June 2006 the two institutions co-hosted a technical workshop on 'Management of Disaster Risk through Fiscal and Budget Planning' held at the CDB's headquarters in Barbados. The workshop assembled over 70 experts in disaster risk reduction and management from 16 Caribbean countries, including permanent secretaries, directors charged with budget and other planning in ministries of finance and planning, as well as national disaster authorities, and CDB, IDB and other staff from development organizations.

On the one hand, the purpose of the workshop was to improve cooperation and understanding for the risk-pooling options under discussion among the permanent secretaries of the ministries of finance and of planning and national disaster coordinators for better mainstreaming disaster risks. On the other hand – and related to this purpose – there was a desire for practical and usable tools for mainstreaming DRM into their national budgetary processes and fiscal strategies.

IIASA was asked to contribute to the two-day workshop by giving conceptual presentations on mainstreaming disaster risks and risk-financing instruments, and by preparing and leading a one-day technical, hands-on group exercise on risk management aided by CatSim. The main objective of the group exercise on the second day was to put into practice the workshop concepts and approaches to incorporate disaster risk management into fiscal and development planning as well as to explore the feasibility of using physical and financial disaster risk management options. Three reports ('notebooks') were developed with the help of IDB and CDB staff, laying out three stylized risk-management cases for three countries in the region. Questions brought up in the notebooks (CDB/IDB, 2007) and to be addressed with the help of CatSim are listed as follows:

- What are potential disaster impacts on the analysed countries and how can they be analysed?
- How can priorities be set for preventing disasters and transferring risks? What are the respective costs and benefits of preventive measures, and how do they compare with risk transfer? How much risk, thus, should be reduced and how much transferred?
- Do these priorities integrate with the broader goals of development planning?
- What are the pros and cons of different risk-financing instruments?
- How can risk-transfer instruments be effectively linked to risk-reduction measures?
- What might be the respective roles of the public and private sectors as well as international financial institutions and other donors in DRM?

Six breakout groups for the three hypothetical cases were formed in total, each to discuss and work through a country case. Two teams evaluated one country case with information on country disaster risk, fiscal position, and institutional capacity and programmes, in order to develop an integrated country risk management and financing strategy.

How did the participants experience the exercise?

CatSim was used in the exercises for identifying fiscal and economic risk and financial vulnerability (in terms of financing gaps for financing reconstruction and relief); furthermore, CatSim informed the evaluation of the pros and cons, costs and benefits of risk-financing instruments reserve fund, (re-)insurance or contingent credit. After discussions within the groups, each group prepared an integrated risk-mitigation and risk-financing strategy, and one of the two groups was asked to present the findings to the plenary while the other group commented. The presentations and commentaries provided an informative view of the country cases and the lively discussions within the groups during the exercise, and outlined for each country case the types of (additional) risk-financing options that may be desirable. Overall, the CatSim model approach was well taken up and the model found useful. It was repeatedly mentioned that the technical, model-based exercise was found to be the most useful part of the workshop. Comments elicited after the workshop included:

- 'Model should be used for the budgeting process';
- 'More training should be undertaken';
- 'Putting theory into practice ... provide model for use in countries ... pilot the model in selected countries and keep a priority at the top of the agenda'.

The groups also found the graphics containing the tool useful, and considered it of value in manipulating possible futures and selecting among the options. In general the discussion focused on the proactive nature of DRM and the need for sustaining efforts to reduce of risks to lives, property and the economies by an approach involving all major stakeholders.

In the following we want to discuss our – of necessity subjective – insights for a number of issues brought up in the workshop.

Understanding probability

One of the most important and challenging tasks of the workshop was to introduce to the audience the concept of probability of events and random outcomes. While most of the participants had basic knowledge about statistics, the notion of stochastic events (such as a 100-year hurricane event) and associated direct, indirect and macroeconomic losses, presented a challenge at the beginning. We used CatSim to suggest a shift from the predominant deterministic understanding of disaster events to a more probability-based risk management approach, where different outcomes such as probabilistic economic growth paths with and without proactive risk-management measures are studied and displayed. Our main intention was to focus the view of participants on more than one single outcome and the stochasticity of events. The focus on the most critical and debilitating events to be addressed by risk-management measures is a key issue in planning financially for disasters. By straight away showing the effects in a probability-based approach with the help of the graphical user interfaces (such as the one shown in Figure 10.5) rather than giving a theoretical explanation first, this important message seemed to have been understood relatively easily.

Assessing vulnerability and risk

After making the audience aware of the need for an understanding of probability within catastrophic risk management, we proceeded to give them a concrete concept to work with, and measure the vulnerability and risk of an event to a government and country risk portfolio. The financing gap concept (financial vulnerability) was used to address this issue. Again, instead of going into the theory first, we decided to work with a user interface where the relationship between probability of event and the financing options, as well as their limitations, are shown (see Figure 10.5). The probability concept introduced before thus was effectively embedded within a new framework (Figure 10.4). In this way, different strategies and their economic and financial constraints were assessed within the CatSim framework. In conjunction with a consideration of wider political and other constraints, to be assessed outside of CatSim, an interactive process was started where scientific and policy-relevant inputs were combined in an effective way.

The financing gap concept introduced at this stage still referred to the short term (usually to the following year) and the respective vulnerability (or risk) measures. The third step was now to expand this concept into a dynamic time horizon over several years. Most often the future time horizon chosen was between four and five years (a legislative period) or a ten-year time period. Adding more complexity to this process, for such time horizons, we introduced the financing gap now in probabilistic format – that is, the probability that a financing gap will occur in the future. As notions of probability and financing gap were understood before, this more complex approach could be used with greater ease. It was useful for most of the users to look back at the time where the different trajectories of possible futures were shown. The decrease in variability of all possible scenarios naturally led the audience to the conclusion that a trade-off between stability and growth had to be taken in the risk-management strategy assessment process.

Thinking about risk management

At this point, the fourth step – the design and analysis of risk-management strategies – was tackled. We now started analysing the different instruments and basic principles, explained in a more general way the day before, by assessing their impact on fiscal indicators (such as the budget stance and debt and economic growth, measured by the GDP impact). A number of strategies were assessed by including *ex ante* financial measures into the financial resilience module and comparing the new strategies with the old ones. A lively discussion developed within the breakout groups, and it is interesting to note that each group selected different risk-management strategies. To keep the assessment manageable, we did not look at mixed strategies (such as implementing insurance and risk reduction options) explicitly, but rather discussed some combinations verbally. Interestingly, because the policy makers knew their position in the process due to the concepts presented before, it was easier for them to adopt alternative perspectives as well, leading to a broader understanding of the problem within the groups.

Thinking about possible rather than optimal strategies

While different risk-management strategies were assessed in most of the groups with the same notebook, one specific instrument was favoured at the outset. This was due to the fact that the notebooks represented a simplified country case within the Caribbean and that some risk strategies where already under discussion for implementation in those countries, if only on the conceptual level. Hence, the hands-one exercise provided useful information to the audience on the effectiveness of this approach and on any other more desirable strategies. Finally strategies, advantages and limitations were discussed within a broader context, jointly assessed and compared, and then most promising ones chosen. Various participants were interested in optimal investment levels and risk-management portfolios (see the discussion below). We had to explain that, due to the multidimensional problem of natural disaster events, including ethical reasons and measurement problems, such a task is burdened with a number of problems and we would advise not to proceed in this fashion. We rather suggested analysis should be done within an integrated disaster management approach where non-quantifiable variables may be also have a role, and results and suggested policies can be discussed with a broader audience.

Finding consensus

An important issue brought up in the Caribbean, as well as other prior CatSim-based workshops in the Philippines, Madagascar, Honduras and elsewhere, was the nature of the interactive and group-based sessions, which were found to be amenable to improving the potential for finding consensus among various stakeholders. For the Caribbean, there were mainly two groups of stakeholders, representatives from finance ministries and DRM coordinators. Yet, one participant confirmed that the CatSim tool had facilitated the review of strategies and options within his group, and suggested that for implementation the required high-level decision making would depend on similar deliberations and consensus building among the main stakeholders in the economy. Another person suggested improvement to the model to incorporate very wide societal players and to build a team approach within government.

Problems encountered

Not surprisingly, a number of limitations of using the CatSim approach for the sessions were found and discussed during the workshop. One was that despite the focus of the exercise on graphical interfaces and information, the sessions would benefit from even more user-friendliness, and more training was generally seen as crucial. National studies with more in-depth country information were suggested in order to cater the model and results to the local needs. On the other hand, also *more* complexity was called for. For example, in each of the case studies only windstorm as the dominant hazard was looked at, and all other possible natural hazards were seen as less important and ignored in the analysis. The audience was very interested also in a multi-hazard analysis. Furthermore, additional to the focus on current exposure to hazards, the audience was also interested how or if climate change will affect their vulnerability and if it is incorporated in the model. While this would be possible with CatSim, for example by changing the parameters of the loss distribution, currently we feel that there is not enough evidence yet to quantify these changes in sufficient detail. A key issue of debate as discussed above was that the audience was interested in optimal portfolios of risk-management measures. We did not want to give some 'optimal' results, as optimality always has to refer to some objective function and this 'objective function' seemed not to have been clearly defined by the different participants. For example, while the finance specialists are most concerned with optimality in financial terms, the disaster coordinators may be more interested in preventing loss of life, which cannot feasibly be quantified and integrated into CatSim. Hence, the task was to explain to the audience that it is better to *simulate possible* strategies and discuss them instead of giving one answer that is only optimal in one dimension, say in financial terms. It should be noted that CatSim is able to give (local) optimal portfolios but this feature was disabled for the workshop. We feel that generally the possibilities as well as the limitations of 'science' have to be understood and discussed properly, and likewise made use of CatSim for the exercise.

It is difficult to say what concrete effects such workshops have on the policy-making process but some tentative comments can be given. First, if decision makers are not sufficiently aware of vulnerabilities and risk they will not incorporate it in their decisions. Second, if they do not know how to handle it in a rational manner, it is also likely that vulnerabilities and risks will not be incorporated in their decisions, as it is difficult to justify actions to the public. Third, putting the issue into the broader picture, for example into the development planning process, increases the chances of mainstreaming. CatSim tries to overcome these issues and provide a useful modelling tool for quantifying risk and risk-management options. In the Barbados workshop it seemed that at least these goals were fulfilled. Of the 100 workshop-evaluation questionnaires returned by the participants, 65 per cent found the workshop achieved its primary goal 'to enhance the understanding of the processes involved in the integration of disaster risk management in their national development strategies and to provide practical tools for use' very much, 26 per cent agreed and 7 per cent answered yes (4 per cent were unaccounted for). Seventy per cent stated that the information in this workshop will be of use for them in their daily work. Furthermore, 84 per cent appreciated the dynamic and interesting atmosphere. Finally, 88 per cent thought they mastered the notions which were presented in the workshop (CDB/IDB, 2007).

Conclusions

CatSim is an interactive model for catastrophe risk management supported by a graphical user interface to facilitate decision support for better assessing disaster vulnerability and risk, and planning the mainstreaming of DRM into economic planning and financial decisions. The authors have repeatedly used the model in interactive contexts such as the one in the Caribbean on mainstreaming hurricane risk into economic planning. In this chapter, we discussed the pros and cons of such an approach in order to more effectively inform the translation of scientific assessment of natural disaster risk and to *interactively* provide guidance to policy makers in the design and assessment of DRM strategies for bridging the gap between the scientific assessment and risk-management strategies, and policy-relevant and more practical issues. By discussing the CatSim experience, we outlined the benefits of a clear conceptual approach, corresponding good representation of modelling results and the possibility to interactively assess strategies within this approach. We find that rather than specific results, it is the *process* of assessing that may guide policy makers and stakeholders to more informed and mutually agreed decisions. While it is very difficult to determine the exact impact of CatSim on the thinking of users, and policies they need to adopt, the response of the participants was generally positive and leads us to believe in the usefulness of our approach.

It seems evident and intuitive that it is never feasible to provide all the information requirements of stakeholders for making more informed, holistic and state-of-the-art decisions, yet at a minimum, use can be made of computer-generated decision aids for analysing important dimensions of the problem under study. One possibility presented here to bridge the gap between the scientific assessment of risk, implementation and policy makers' needs is to utilize user interfaces, where the information is presented in a transparent way. At the same time, it is important to recognize and present the complex relationship of the variables under consideration, the assumptions of the model and the future consequences of the decisions made today.

Although, CatSim mostly addresses financial and economic vulnerability to natural disasters, issues of global and climate change can also be accounted for. For example, hazard frequency and intensity can be modified and the exposure to hazard or the physical sensitivity of residual buildings due to anticipated changes now and in the future can be altered. Yet, dimensions other than economic such as environmental or social concerns are not incorporated into CatSim. Nevertheless, we feel that the CatSim user interface can help to also bridge this gap between different dimensions by enabling an environment for open discussions. As well, it should also be kept in mind that an abundance of information may be counterproductive. It seems more expedient to focus on a more narrow, but flexible concept, which can be broadened over time, instead of irritating users by trying to capture 'everything'. As a consequence, it is very important also to explain model limitations and, instead of *black-box* models, give users the possibility to closely review various aspects within the modelling approach. All such issues lead to increased trust in the model and the associated process.

The need for cooperative, stakeholder-based approaches for disaster vulnerability and risk management certainly remains a crucial issue in the Caribbean with its diverse cultures and contexts, and the capacity for proactive management of disaster risks has been substantially improved over the last few years. As one milestone, in 2007 the Caribbean Catastrophe Risk Insurance Facility (CCRIF) was set up with support from donor institutions allowing Caribbean countries to better pool and share their disaster risks. The scheme basically constitutes a mutual insurance arrangement where risks and vulnerabilities are appropriately and transparently monitored and assessed in order to fairly calculate insurance premiums before an event and distribute disaster burdens post-disaster, issues that were at the heart at the 2006 Barbados workshop.

Note

1 More detail, equations, inter-module linkages and algorithms used in CatSim can be found in Hochrainer (2006).

References

Artzner, P., Delbaen F., Eber, J. M. and Heath, D. (1999) 'Coherent measures of risk', *Mathematical Finance*, vol 3, pp203–228

Auffret, P. (2003) *High Consumption Volatility: The Impact of Natural Disasters?*, World Bank Policy Research Working Paper Series No. 2962, The World Bank, Washington DC

Banks, E. (2005) *Catastrophic Risk: Analysis and Management*, Wiley Finance, Chichester

Bayer, J. and Mechler, R. (2005) 'Financing disaster risks in developing and emerging-economy countries', *Proceedings of OECD Conference on Catastrophic Risks and Insurance*, Paris, 22–23 November 2004

Benson, C. and Clay, E. J. (2004) *Understanding the Economic and Financial Impacts of Natural Disasters*, Disaster Risk Management Series No. 4, The World Bank, Washington DC

Bettencourt, S., Croad, R., Freeman, P., Hay, J., Jones, R., King, P., Lal, P., Mearns, A., Miller, G., Pswarayi-Riddihough, I., Simpson, A., Teuatabo, N., Trotz, U. and Van Aalst, M. (2006) 'Not if but when: Adapting to natural hazards in the Pacific Islands Region', Policy Note, East Asia and Pacific Region, Pacific Islands Country Management Unit, The World Bank, Washington DC

Briguglio, L. (1995) 'Small island developing states and their economic vulnerabilities', *World Development*, vol 23, pp1615–1632

Burby, R. (1991) *Sharing Environmental Risks: How to Control Governments' Losses in Natural Disasters*, Westview Press, Boulder, Colorado

CDB/IDB (2007) Report on the Technical Workshop: 'Management of Disaster Risk Through Fiscal and Budget Planning', 26–27 June 2006, Caribbean Development Bank, Barbados

Commonwealth Secretariat and World Bank (2000) *Small States: Meeting Challenges in the Global Economy*, Commonwealth Secretariat and the World Bank Joint Task Force on Small States, Washington DC and London

Cullen, A. C. and Small, M. J. (2004) Uncertain risk: The role and limits of quantitative assessment', in McDaniels, T. and Small, M. J. (eds) *Risk Analysis and Society*, Cambridge University Press, New York

Emanuel, K. (2005) 'Increasing destructiveness of tropical cyclones over the past 30 years', *Nature*, vol 436(4), pp686–688

Embrechts, P., Klueppelberg, C. and Mikosch, T. (1997) *Modelling Extremal Events*, Springer, New York

Freeman, P. K., Martin, L., Mechler, R., Pflug, G., Saldana, S. and Warner, K. (2002) *National Systems for Comprehensive Disaster Management: Financing Reconstruction*, Phase II background study, Regional Policy Dialogue Report, Inter-American Development Bank, Washington DC

Gurenko, E. (2004) *Catastrophe Risk and Reinsurance: A Country Risk Management Perspective*, Risk Books, London

Hochrainer, S. (2006) *Macroeconomic Risk Management Against Natural Disasters*, German University Press, Wiesbaden, Germany

Johansen, A. and Sornette, D. (2001) 'Large stock market price drawdowns are outliers', *Journal of Risk*, vol 4, pp69–110

Kunreuther, H. (2002) 'Risk analysis and risk management in an uncertain world', *Risk Analysis*, vol 22, pp655–644

Linnerooth-Bayer, J., Mechler, R. and Pflug, G. (2005) 'Refocusing disaster aid', *Science*, vol 309, pp1044–1046

Malevergne, Y. and Sornette, D. (2006) *Extreme Financial Risks*, Springer, New York

Mechler, R., Hochrainer, S., Linnerooth-Bayer, J. and Pflug, G. (2006) 'Public sector financial vulnerability to disasters: The IIASA–Catsim model', in Birkmann, J. (ed) *Measuring Vulnerability to Natural Hazards: Towards Disaster Resilient Societies*, United Nations University Press, Tokyo

Merz, B., Friedrich, J., Disse, M., Schwarz, J., Goldammer, J. G. and Wächter, J. (2006) Possibilities and limitations of interdisciplinary, user-oriented research: Experiences from the German Research Network Natural Disasters', *Natural Hazards*, vol 38, pp3–20

Nelsen, R. B. (1998) *An Introduction to Copulas*, Springer, New York

OECS (2005) *Grenada: Macro-Socio-Economic Assessment of the Damage caused by Hurricane Emily July 14th, 2005*, Organisation of Eastern Caribbean States, Castries, Saint Lucia, www.oecs.org/Documents/Grenada%20Report/GrenadaAssesment-Emily.pdf accessed 1 September 2008

Pollner, J. (2000) *Managing Catastrophic Risks Using Alternative Risk Financing and Insurance Pooling Mechanisms*, The World Bank, Washington DC

Pollner, J., Camara, M. and Martin, L. (2001) *Honduras. Catastrophe Risk Exposure of Public Assets: An Analysis of Financing Instruments for Smoothing Fiscal Volatility*, The World Bank, Washington DC

Schröter, D., Acosta-Michlik, L., Arnell, A.W., Araújo, M. B., Badeck, F., Bakker, M., Bondeau, A., Bugmann, H., Carter, T., de la Vega-Leinert, A. C., Erhard, M., Espiñeira, G. Z., Ewert, F., Fritsch, U., Friedlingstein, P., Glendining, M., Gracia, C. A., Hickler, T., House, J. Hulme, M., Kankaanpää, S., Klein, R. J. T., Krukenberg, B., Lavorel, S., Leemans, R., Lindner, M., Liski, J., Metzger, M. J., Meyer, J., Mitchell, T., Mohren, F., Morales, P., Moreno, J. M., Reginster, I., Reidsma, P., Rounsevell, M., Pla, E., Pluimers, J., Prentice, I. C., Pussinen, A. , Sánchez, A., Sabaté, S., Sitch, S., Smith, B., Smith, J., Smith, P., Sykes, M. T., Thonicke, K., Thuiller, W., Tuck, G., van der Werf, G., Vayreda, J., Wattenbach, M., Wilson, D. W., Woodward, F. I., Zaehle, S., Zierl, B., Zudin, S. and Cramer, W. (2004) *ATEAM: Final Report 2004*, Potsdam Institute for Climate Impact Research (PIK), Potsdam, Germany

Swiss Re (2000) *Storm Over Europe: An Underestimated Risk*, Swiss Reinsurance Company, Zurich

Turner, B. L., Kasperson, R., Matson, P., McCarthy, J. J., Corell, R., Christensehn, L., Eckley, N., Kasperson, J., Luers, A., Martello, M., Polsky, C., Pulsipher, A. and Schiller, A. (2003) 'A framework for vulnerability analysis in sustainability science', *PINAS*, vol 100, pp8074–8079

Walker, B., Carpenter, S., Anderes, J., Abel, N., Cumming, G., Jansen, M., Lebel, L., Norberg, J., Perereson, G. and Pichard, R. (2002) 'Resilience management in social-ecological systems: A working hypothesis for a participatory approach', *Conservation Ecology*, vol 6(1), p14

World Bank (2003) *Financing Rapid Onset Natural Disaster Losses in India: A Risk Management Approach*, The World Bank, Washington DC

Chapter 11

Evaluation of a Stakeholder Dialogue on European Vulnerability to Global Change

A. Cristina de la Vega-Leinert and Dagmar Schröter

Introduction

The ATEAM (Advanced Terrestrial Ecosystem Analysis and Modelling) project belonged to the 5th European research framework. It officially ran from 2001 to 2004 and was coordinated from the Potsdam Institute for Climate Impacts Research, Germany. Its overarching goal was to quantitatively assess the vulnerability of human sectors to global change. Its approach was centred on ecosystem modelling and based on the notion of ecosystem services, such as wood production and snow availability. The primary deliverables of the project were to be maps of European impacts and vulnerability to global change, explicitly conceived and implemented with policy makers and environmental managers in mind (Schröter et al, 2005; Schröter, Chapter 6, this volume). To this end a stakeholder dialogue initiative was embedded in the research process. This dialogue experience has affected the way participating scientists designed and performed their work and constitutes a milestone in integrated ecological modelling research for the purposes of global change impact and vulnerability assessments.

The underlying broad hypothesis of this initiative was that stakeholder dialogue, and participative methods in general, played a valuable role in the elaboration and evaluation of complex global change models, and in combining scientific credibility with social relevance. More specifically, it was hoped that by incorporating this activity within the overall project, scientists would have access to important sources of expertise on ecosystem management, which would act as a reality check for the vulnerability assessment to be produced.

A properly run participation process is, however, demanding of time and resources. Although it can substantially question the perspectives of participants, it may result in a difficult but inspiring collective learning exercise (Welp et al, 2006a). It has been argued that science–stakeholders dialogue processes may help to redefine positivist perceptions on the nature of scientific enquiry (Welp et al, 2006b; van den Hove and Sharman, 2006). This may also contribute to challenge the scientific construction of risk, which Wynne (2005) argues plays a significant role in establishing societal adaptation priorities. Dialogue initiatives can, therefore, become catalysts for reflection on the role and position of scientists as experts in society and by promoting different types of knowledge (Oels, 2006). Through an evaluation of the stakeholder dialogue within the ATEAM project we explore how this experiment contributed to enhance understanding of the challenges involved in reconciling the different priorities of participants, scientists and stakeholders alike.

We structure the chapter as follows: first, we present the specific goals and activities of the ATEAM stakeholder dialogue. We discuss the stakeholders targeted within the project with consideration of biases in the selection process and participating group. Second, we summarize the influence of stakeholders on the ATEAM research. Finally, the dialogue outcomes and process are evaluated and discussed in terms of their relevance for participating stakeholders and scientists.

Overall aims of the ATEAM stakeholder dialogue

ATEAM incorporated the participatory process of the stakeholder dialogue with the explicit aim of adjusting the project's results to better suit stakeholders' needs. From the stage of proposal writing, the research partners recognized that stakeholders were needed from the outset of the project in order to guide the direction of modelling. Stakeholders would then, later in the project, receive the results of the modelling, and be able to comment on their usefulness to them. The specific goals of the entire process thus included:

- identifying and evaluating indicators of change in ecosystem services;
- determining useful modelling scales (spatial and temporal) and units for these indicators;
- discussing adequate thresholds for these indicators, beyond which sectoral adaptive capacity could be exceeded;
- developing stakeholders' ability to use information derived from scenario analysis; and
- presenting, discussing and disseminating the project's results, as well as receiving feedback on format and content.

Stakeholder selection criteria

Potential participants were first identified using the snowball approach (see Biernacki and Waldorf, 1981), whereby relevant stakeholder contacts were pinpointed in iterative rounds within a progressively increasing network of contacts. To complement this, a systematic selection matrix was designed based on three main categories:

1. the human activity sectors considered in the overall assessment (e.g. 'Agriculture', 'Forestry');
2. the type and main interests of stakeholder organizations (e.g. private firm, public management, non-governmental organization); and
3. the scale of activity of the stakeholder organizations (i.e. from local to international).

The resulting stakeholder database and network included 204 identified stakeholders, 152 of which were approached and invited to our activities, with 58[1] deciding to participate in at least one activity (see Table 11.1).

We particularly targeted private agents, sectoral representatives, consultants and private businesses for 'Agriculture', 'Forestry', 'Water' and 'Tourism', since these stakeholders are predominant decision makers in these sectors. In contrast, for the sectors 'Biodiversity and nature conservation', 'Carbon storage potential' and 'Mountain environments', we approached stakeholders from public (academic/advisory/management) or independent sectors (NGOs, umbrella organizations). Here, the associated ecosystem services are often non-marketed (Reid et al, 2005), and are primarily relevant for national and/or European policy-making issues (e.g. climate mitigation, ecological directives). Government representatives or policy makers per se were not included in the stakeholder matrix. This was a deliberate choice as the project wished to focus on participants, such as scientific advisers, who were influential but nevertheless free to express their views rather than official policy lines. In the end, most targeted organizations had a European-to-global focus of activity, the scales at which the ATEAM results are the most relevant (spatial resolution of ATEAM results: c. 16×16km).

Selection bias

The stakeholder selection criteria included (inter-)sectoral expertise, some knowledge on climate and environmental issues, general interest in scientific issues and an open, curious and critical mind. Stakeholders' known or presumed views on global change did not, however, constitute a selection criterion to encourage multiple perspectives. The most effective ways to appraise to which extent stakeholders satisfied these criteria were through personal contact and experience of collaboration. This meant that after each stakeholder dialogue event, participants were short-listed for follow-up events, based on how well they 'fitted' the selection criteria according to the organizers. Rather than a public participation exercise, we pursued a focus group approach with selected participants. Therefore, a repre-

Table 11.1 *Targeted sectors[a] vs stakeholder organizational types[b]*

	Sectoral consultancy	*Sectoral rep.*	*Private business*	*Public body/ academic*	*Public body/ advise to policy*	*Public body/ resource management*	*NGO*	*Independent umbrella organization*	*TOTAL*
'Agriculture'	1 (2)	2 (10)	0 (2)	2 (2)	0 (0)	0 (1)	0 (0)	0 (1)	5 (18)
'Biodiversity and nature conservation'	1 (1)	0 (0)	0 (0)	4 (7)	2 (11)	3 (8)	1 (6)	0 (0)	11 (33)
'Carbon storage'	1 (5)	0 (0)	0 (5)	2 (7)	4 (17)	0 (0)	2 (3)	1 (5)	10 (42)
'Forestry'	2 (3)	7 (19)	0 (6)	3 (5)	4 (7)	2 (2)	1 (2)	0 (1)	19 (47)
'Mountain environments'	0 (0)	0 (1)	1 (3)	0 (2)	1 (1)	1 (1)	0 (0)	2 (10)	5 (18)
'Tourism'	2 (13)	0 (1)	0 (1)	0 (2)	0 (0)	0 (0)	0 (2)	0 (0)	2 (19)
'Water'	1 (5)	0 (0)	2 (6)	1 (2)	0 (5)	0 (0)	0 (0)	0 (1)	4 (19)
'Insurance'	0 (0)	0 (0)	0 (4)	0 (0)	0 (0)	0 (0)	0 (0)	0 (0)	0 (4)
Media	0 (0)	0 (0)	2 (5)	0 (0)	0 (0)	0 (0)	0 (0)	0 (0)	2 (5)
TOTAL	8 (29)	9 (31)	5 (32)	12 (27)	11 (41)	6 (12)	4 (13)	3 (18)	58 (204)
Total	Private	22 (92)		Public	29 (80)		Independent	7 (31)	

Note: Numbers indicate stakeholders who participated in one or more ATEAM dialogue activities; the total number of stakeholders identified for each category is given in brackets.

a Sectors targeted for the stakeholder dialogue do not correspond exactly to the ATEAM sectors per se which are 'Agriculture', 'Forestry', 'Carbon Storage', 'Water', 'Biodiversity and nature conservation' and 'Mountain environments'.

b The following organizational types were involved:

Sectoral consultancies: these can be commercial (e.g. DHI Water & Environment) or non-profit consultancies (e.g. Associazione Cultura Turismo Ambiente (ACTA)).

Sectoral representatives: include farmers' unions, cereal growers, land and forest owners, paper-agro industries etc.

Private business: from individual farmers to multinational corporations (e.g. IKEA, TETRAPACK, Gerling Reinsurance).

Public organizations whose main focus is to advise policy: these are directly involved in policy/decision making (e.g. Ministries of Environment, European Commission) or in advisory position (e.g. European Environmental Agency).

Public organizations whose main focuses are academic: research institutes who were not directly involved in ATEAM.

Public organizations whose main focuses are environmental resource management: e.g. forest, water and or natural park management.

Non-governmental organizations: from globally known organizations such as WWF, Greenpeace, to nationally important ones, such as Robinwood (Germany), to the Liga para a Protecção da Natureza (Portugal).

Independent umbrella organizations: these can be non-profit organizations focusing on awareness raising (e.g. Climate Network Europe, Commission internationale pour la protection des Alpes (CIPRA)) to organizations fostering trade (e.g. Organisation for Economic Co-operation and Development (OECD), Association of British Travel Agents).

sentative sample of society was not aimed at. However, repetitive attempts were made to engage as many different stakeholders as possible, although approached representatives of private companies and specific consumers/interest groups mostly chose not to participate.

Our selection criteria introduced a 'green' and 'scientific' bias in our stakeholder community, which was reinforced as stakeholders decided to participate or not. Stakeholders needed to be convinced that they would gain significant benefits before they committed any amount of time and effort into extra-professional activities. Communication skills and a feel for how to engage stakeholders and demonstrate the relevance of the dialogue process for their activities certainly helped to gain stakeholder support. However, in some cases the research topic was simply too disconnected from stakeholders' interests to secure their participation.

During the course of the ATEAM project, we held three general and three smaller scale sectoral stakeholder workshops. ATEAM scientists participated in 11 further stakeholder events organized within collaborating initiatives (see Schröter et al, 2004). Furthermore, multiple informal exchanges between scientists and stakeholders took place.

Evaluation of the ATEAM stakeholder dialogue

Methodology

At the main events, we asked stakeholders to complete a questionnaire on the project and workshop content and format. Informal feedback was collected during the events. External observers, moreover, evaluated the workshops in terms of content and process, and provided recommendations for future events (Jürgens, 2001; Vreugdenhil, 2003). Finally, we carried out semi-structured interviews with the project leader and coordinator, and one scientist per modelling team to explore their views on the impacts of the stakeholder dialogue on their research. The sections below summarize the main points made by participants, observers and scientists.

Stakeholders' influence on ATEAM research process and content

The project's aim to define and produce stakeholder-relevant results was a powerful coordination tool, which continuously steered the consortium's work. Beyond this, stakeholders themselves had a significant impact on the ATEAM research. This included:

1 thought-provoking perspectives and opinions on the research framework, the near final results and their meaningfulness for stakeholders' activities;
2 suggestions on ways to further improve result communication/ dissemination; and
3 contributions in shaping the future research agenda.

Table 11.2 *Examples of stakeholders' impacts on ATEAM's research*

Research teams	*Stakeholder impact*
Land-use scenarios	Evaluation and discussion of basic assumptions, sectoral drivers of change and of the decision rules guiding land-use prioritization. Reality check (e.g. importance of food quality vs quantity in the European context).
'Agriculture'	Supported the farmers' viability assessment (e.g. the future amount of land available for agriculture was more interesting than indicators for crop production). Supported and informed a detailed study of bioenergy crop suitability.
'Biodiversity and nature conservation'	Discussed the choice of indicator species. Supported the research team's preference for habitat vs the more commonly accepted species diversity and richness indicators.
'Carbon storage'	Research topic prioritization (e.g. a realistic land management rather than the originally planned nitrogen deposition module). Initiated a biomass energy case study not originally on the ATEAM task list (see above).
'Forestry'	Reality check on forest management and adaptation measures (e.g. time scales of planning in forestry; the importance of ownership and national and EU directives).
'Mountain environments'	Reality check on priorities in the tourism sector (e.g. infrastructure/ accessibility are more important aspects than aesthetics; links between characteristic species or landscapes and traditional local craft are highly attractive). Diverse perspectives on results for different mountain stakeholders (e.g. changes in water storage peak will affect differently the hydro electric and agricultural sectors).
'Water'	Discussion of scale issues. The ATEAM grid provides valuable information for national and supranational scales of decision making, but is not very useful for local and regional water managers who need information at catchment level (as provided in Alpine case studies).

Practically, stakeholders reviewed and evaluated the methodologies and assumptions used in developing the land-use scenarios and each sector-specific model (Table 11.2), as well as the temporal and spatial scales of the results. Stakeholders also helped to select and prioritize the indicators of ecosystem services to be used in the assessment framework. They further enthusiastically supported additional exploratory case studies, particularly that on biomass energy potential (Tuck et al, 2006) and agricultural adaptive capacity (Reidsma and Ewert, 2007).

Moreover, the dialogue process helped scientists gain a better understanding on how participants recognized and managed ecosystem services. Stakeholders provided invaluable information on the multiple facets and challenges of sectoral management practice and adaptation. Although ATEAM was predominantly grounded in the natural sciences, much effort was made to include ecosystem management in the vulnerability assessment. For example, decision making in a socioeconomic and policy context enters the assessment via the land-use scenarios and via ecosystem models that take into account agricultural and forest management. Nevertheless, a recurring theme during the dialogue was to learn just how complex human–environment interactions were in a context of EU, national and regional policies and under socioeconomic constraints, and to reflect on ways to better address this complexity in future modelling.

Finally, to ease the presentation, dissemination and analysis of the project results we developed a digital compilation of the project's most salient results, the ATEAM Atlas of European Vulnerability (Metzger et al, 2004; Metzger and Schröter, 2006). This tool allows users to select indicators of impact and vulnerability, using the socioeconomic, climate and land-use scenarios they are most interested in. The maps are placed in a fact sheet, which provides succinct information on the models, scenarios and indicators used, the main underlying assumptions and additional references. Aggregated results can be decomposed and both relative and absolute data can be viewed. Furthermore, simple queries can be performed and users can zoom on specific environmental regions or countries. Stakeholders' comments were instrumental in the improvement of early versions of the tool.

Stakeholders' evaluation

Content evaluation

Stakeholders generally found ATEAM's conceptual framework, the vulnerability assessment methodology, and the Atlas of European Vulnerability, interesting and innovative. The temporal and spatial scales of ATEAM analyses were, however, of unequal relevance. The 1990, 2020, 2050, 2080 time slices were for example useful for stakeholders in the 'Forestry', 'Carbon storage' and 'Biodiversity and nature conservation' sectors, and to a lesser extent in 'Mountains environments' and 'Tourism', for which long-term management was key. However, for the 'Water' and 'Agriculture' sectors short-term estimates for the next five to ten years would have been more useful. For many stakeholders the spatial scale of the assessment (the ATEAM 10'×10', i.e. c. 16×16km grid) remained too coarse, despite its exceptionally fine resolution in comparison to other global change assessments.

The identification and assessment of specific ecosystem services, which could be significantly impacted in future, were most relevant for the majority of stakeholders, since this information formed an appropriate basis for exploring adequate adaptation strategies at European-to-regional levels. In comparison, stakeholders judged the aggregated indicators for 'vulnerability' and 'adaptive capacity' per se of limited value (Schröter et al, 2005). Such concepts and indicators, therefore, seem to have more pertinence in the academic domain than in practical environmental management (Patt et al, 2005). Indeed, stakeholders are acutely aware of the opportunities and barriers to adaptation through management practice in their specific sectors. Since sectoral adaptation is often related to the necessity to run an economically viable activity, stakeholders critically review current policies, market fluctuations and environmental changes that may benefit or endanger their activity. They are thus continuously reappraising the vulnerability and adaptive capacity of their activity to changing conditions (albeit without using this terminology). ATEAM's macro-scale, generic index of adaptive capacity did not provide the specific information stakeholders wished and was thus of limited interest to them. For stakeholders, the missing link remains a sector-specific and risk-specific articulation of adaptive capacity with vulnerability. Scientists and stakeholders, therefore, agreed that the components of sectoral adaptive capacity, the interactions between macro and (inter-)sectoral adaptive capacities, and between these and vulnerability were, therefore, key areas for future research.

Within the land-use scenarios, stakeholders isolated particular driving forces, which should be better taken into account in scenario and model assumptions, in particular policy, market trends, sectoral management, consumer preferences and extreme events. Moreover, within the modelling of terrestrial carbon storage, stakeholders inspired a major research reorientation by prioritizing the implementation of more realistic forest management and land-use changes over the original plan for improved representation of the nitrogen cycle in dynamic vegetation models. Stakeholders further agreed that in disseminating research results, it should be clearly pointed out that scenarios represented alternative choices of society, rather than possible futures that unfolded independently from societal and individual decisions.

The significant agreement across modelling results and scenarios contributed to raise stakeholders' confidence in the project results. For example, in the ATEAM assessment, tree productivity increases in most North European scenarios but is limited by water availability in Mediterranean areas. Also all scenarios and results from all sectors agree on particular regional vulnerabilities, for example that of the Mediterranean and mountains regions (Schröter, Chapter 6, this volume). Stakeholders thus encouraged the development of comparative assessments of impacts of alternative policies across different economic sectors, which would allow decision makers to better choose between different future pathways.

Broad consensus was nevertheless that ATEAM results, or any vulnerability assessment, would not directly influence decision making and management behaviour due to the still too large temporal and spatial scales and associated significant accumulated uncertainty. Thus stakeholders, who await predictions or detailed quantified outputs to guide their decision making, will be disappointed by the lack of 'answers' integrated assessment can provide. Integrated assessment results should therefore not be viewed as a potential provider of predictions ('truth machines', see Shackley and Darier, 1998), but as a compilation of best current knowledge, and as food for thought and debate within a wider social discourse on global change. However, specific modelling tools produced to facilitate decision making may play an important role, such as decision support and expert systems, particularly targeted at a group of stakeholders. Efforts in this direction included the development of a tool for natural reserve selection that takes into account economic and ecological considerations (Araújo et al, 2002) and a comparison of the effectiveness of different reserve selection tools under climate change (Araújo et al, 2004).

Finally, stakeholders attached great importance to information on the economic cost and benefits of a specific policy (e.g. does it make economic sense to switch to biomass energy crops?). Thus linking ATEAM's vast information pool to economic valuation could have been one way to increase the meaningfulness of the project's results for stakeholders. Environmental and economic model coupling is a development that goes in this direction (Jaeger et al, 2002).

Process evaluation

An evaluation questionnaire was distributed to stakeholders at three events.[2] In total 22 stakeholders out of 58 completed the questionnaire. All numbers quoted below within brackets refer to respondents answering 'Yes' or 'Mostly' to questions out of a total of 22 respondents.[3]

Most respondents believed that the ATEAM workshops had been generally relevant to their work (19) and worth their time out of work (18). Most appreciated the workshop contents, the range of topics covered and found the presentations interesting (21). Most had gained some useful insights on the topics covered (21), and thought they would be able to integrate some of these in their work (19). For some, too many topics were covered during the events (2), which prevented in-depth discussions on the specific subjects they were interested in (e.g. local-scale impacts on biodiversity, downstream activities in 'Agriculture' or 'Forestry' sectors, sectoral adaptive capacity).

Most stakeholders felt comfortable enough to express their opinions (21) and believed that these had been adequately valued by all participants (19). Some emphasized the need for unbiased moderation to guarantee that all parties would be adequately heard. To address this critique in later events, stakeholders were offered the possibility to alternate with ATEAM scientists as discussion moderators. Overall, it appears that ATEAM managed to foster active participation and constructive criticism in an atmosphere of trust and friendliness. Moreover, stakeholders valued the opportunity to network with peers and scientists as a way to encourage synergies and collaboration. Many also believed that fellow participants were relevant to their own activity and considered keeping in touch with some of them independently from ATEAM (12).

Most respondents had been sufficiently interested in ATEAM to envisage participating in follow-up activities (17). Eventually 11 out of 58 stakeholders participated in at least two of the ATEAM dialogue activities. All respondents wished to receive further information on the project and its final results, and many had already talked about ATEAM to colleagues (18). It seems that for the respondents ATEAM had successfully engaged participants, raised interest in its research and provided a dynamic and stimulating discussion and dissemination platform.

The main criticisms on the dialogue process were the infrequency of the events, the long time between each event and the lack of regular and transparent feedback in between activities, especially on information on how stakeholders' comments had been taken into account. Some stakeholders expressed some frustration if they felt that their comments had not been adequately taken on board. This relates to a key issue in participative research. By asking stakeholders' opinion, ATEAM also raised the expectations that these opinions could and would be fully taken into account. However, the tight research plan and set list of deliverables the project had committed itself to produce meant that the margin of manoeuvre the project had in addressing stakeholders' comments was significantly narrower than stakeholders thought. This confirms the importance of clarifying as early as possible and as repetitively as necessary how far stakeholders may influence the research programme. Important stakeholders' concerns, nevertheless, did find their way into ATEAM research (e.g. the above-mentioned study on adaptive capacity of the 'Agriculture' sector). Other concerns, moreover, may only be addressed adequately through fundamental model developments (e.g. bridging gaps between global modelling scales and local management needs).

Stakeholders appreciated the role of the scientific community in formulating relevant societal questions regarding the causes and impacts of global change, and possible mitigation and adaptation options. They generally believed that ATEAM has succeeded in formulating strong messages on European vulnerability to global change, which provide some guidance in policy and decision making for a range of stakeholder groups (including landowners' and farmers' organizations, forestry and biodiversity managers, and environmental NGOs), and contribute to raising societal awareness on global change issues.

Both stakeholders and scientists agreed that the way results were framed, interpreted and communicated played a major role in how modelling outputs were used. Nevertheless, views on the best approaches to foster an informed use of scientific results differed. For scientists, the ATEAM Atlas should address issues of data clarity and comprehensiveness. Although stakeholders praised this initiative, some would have preferred meaningful user-targeted syntheses and policy recommendations, based on key mapped outputs. In trying to meet this request a delicate balance has to be found between honesty about the uncertainty of the results and clarity of the message conveyed.

Participating scientists' evaluation

Perception of the stakeholder dialogue experiment

Initially scientists' attitudes regarding the stakeholder dialogue and its meaningfulness in serving the research plan were mixed. Enthusiasm and interest about developing significant elements of applied and participative research, met scepticism on whether this activity would add substantially to the research in view of the costs involved (i.e. time, effort, resources), which could have been spent on the modelling itself. There was also anxiety about the potential failure to provide the information stakeholders sought.

The project incorporated elements of qualitative, participative social sciences in a framework otherwise centred on fundamental quantitative ecological modelling, and there was some uncertainty on how to perform this well. In the peer community some viewed this initiative 'at best' as a marketing trick to attract funding or 'at worst' as a 'non-scientific' goal, which would endanger the overall project's scientific credibility. This represented a significant risk and it required much effort to convince some project members and peers that the dialogue with stakeholders was a valid choice from a scientific point of view. The latter was achieved by not compromising in core parts of the research plan (e.g. the detailed modelling developments and the benchmarking exercise – see Morales et al, 2005), which were not presented to stakeholders. These formed the main scientific achievements per se of the project, and guaranteed scientific credibility in the ecological modelling peer community. As consensus was forged on the originality and feasibility of the overall methodology, including the generic adaptive capacity index, and the importance of the stakeholder dialogue component, the project achieved scientific recognition in the interdisciplinary global change assessment community.

Process evaluation

All interviewed scientists clearly took the need for consultation and transfer of scientific information to stakeholders seriously. They expected, however, to obtain valuable feedback from stakeholders on specific issues (e.g. thresholds of change in ecosystem service provision beyond which sectoral adaptive capacity would be endangered). This was not always the case, and some scientists felt somewhat frustrated at having invested substantial efforts into the dialogue for apparently little return. Like stakeholders, most scientists believed that the dialogue had been too fragmented. In terms of timing, moreover, the first workshops were simply too early for some scientists, who felt they had not had the time to become sufficiently familiar with new models, or to develop them to their satisfaction.

These critiques relate to the way the dialogue was designed and implemented: that is, few, far-apart, content-rich workshops. This format reduced the time available to explore some pertinent questions scientists and stakeholders had. Scientists and stakeholders alike would have welcomed more frequent, focused meetings, and to move away from the general 'presentation–feedback' mode, to a 'working group' approach. Some scientists thus pursued in-depth interactions with stakeholders outside the official dialogue activities.

Scientists generally felt comfortable during the dialogue interactions, since all stakeholders were science-literate and sympathetic to, or even experienced in ecological and/or global change modelling. Scientists found it easier to communicate with stakeholders who had a clear agenda (e.g. managers, scientific advisers, NGOs), than with some, who systematically focused on, or lobbied for, their own interests (e.g. a few private managers and consultants). A common language first needed to be established, which occasionally required long discussions to adjust the terminology to better suit stakeholders' opinions. For example, the term 'unprotected land' was renamed 'undesignated land' in the land-use scenarios, after some stakeholders insisted that all land management included some degree of protection. Even if terminology discussions take time and may appear tedious or frustrating, they are in fact necessary negotiation processes, which help to develop a broad consensus.

Scientists generally experienced stakeholders as understanding, curious and interested and some thus wondered if the lack of 'cultural shock' did not imply that the project had failed to find 'real' stakeholders. However, when some stakeholders insisted on their own agenda, even if this played a minor role in the wider scope of the project, some scientists experienced them as 'pushy' or 'narrow-minded'. This illustrates just how complicated the selection of the appropriate stakeholders for a given project can be. Indeed, within ATEAM, stakeholders needed to be able to understand the basic science, while being able to detach themselves sufficiently from their particular interests to contribute to a collective discussion.

Some scientists emphasized the challenges involved in communicating the usefulness of abstract, long-term exploratory research (e.g. scenarios of global change). Stakeholders appeared to be primarily interested in obtaining 'relatively certain' information on near-future sectoral impacts of global change at local scale. These seemingly irreconcilable expectations may have been prompted by the format chosen. Stakeholders were confronted with scenarios already largely developed, the assumptions and related value judgement of which, they were asked to comment upon. Initially, stakeholders reacted by pointing out driving forces, which were critical for them, sometimes only to hear that these were or could not be included at this stage (e.g. on the role of the agro-industry). Explicitly this activity opened the black box of scenario making to allow stakeholders to evaluate it. Implicitly, however, stakeholders were asked to accept and trust that the scenarios produced were as best as could be within current constraints. The ambivalent aims of the activity could explain the apparent mismatch in interests and expectations. Effectively, most stakeholders deal with uncertainty in their decision making and develop their own mental models and scenarios to perform their work (although they may not use this terminology). It is precisely these abilities that are funnelled into stakeholder-led scenario-making processes, within which stakeholders are given free rein to identify key driving forces and to elaborate narratives, which are then formalized and quantified by scientists (Shackley and Deanwood, 2003).

External observers' evaluation

Two external observers noted that stakeholders had little possibility to set the agenda of the meetings, to take an active part in the overall decisions on the research programme and outputs, or to be adequately informed on how their comments were incorporated within the research (Jürgens, 2001; Vreugdenhil, 2003). These are valid critiques. Indeed, more flexibility could have been built in to allow decisions and discussions to be steered more substantially by stakeholders. Stakeholders could have been brought in as early as the project proposal development stage. However, since the research plan was already largely set and agreed with the funding agencies before the first stakeholders were contacted, the methodology for modelling and scenario design and its implementation was only marginally influenced by interactions with stakeholders. Nevertheless, the work package on synthesis was left relatively open at the beginning of the project. Here, there was sufficient flexibility and resources to explore methods and tools in a learning-by-doing approach to best compile and communicate the results of the project and to adjust substantially to stakeholders' comments. It is within this part of the project that the ATEAM Atlas was developed (Metzger et al, 2004, 2006). The digital atlas was, however, also a solution proposed and developed by scientists with little contribution of stakeholders, apart from the feedback they provided during the final general workshop.

Discussion

A paradox in global change assessment research?

Global change models are increasingly being coupled to combine the insights of both biophysical and socioeconomic disciplines (Muetzelfeldt, 2003). More comprehensive results are thus produced, which help to uncover clear trends and/or a range of possible outcomes, while computer tools allow representing them in ever-finer resolutions (McCarthy et al, 2001). These results are, however, based on broad or generic assumptions, and even the finest models produce considerable uncertainty (Reilly et al, 2001). At the same time global change models such as those used in ATEAM, produce large amounts of interesting results, and browsing through them requires much dedication and understanding. For example, the ATEAM vulnerability atlas is a compilation of over 3000 maps, and many more summarizing charts (Metzger et al, 2004, 2006).

Despite the considerable achievement of producing these scientific results, there seems to be a paradox in presenting vast amounts of uncertain results in a format that inspires a high level of accuracy. A non-informed user will intuitively zoom into the region and sector that he or she is most interested in and overlook the broad simplifications and uncertainties attached to them. The potential for misunderstanding and misinterpretation of the results is thus large. ATEAM dealt with this serious issue by embedding all maps in succinct fact sheets. However, although clear flags can be built in to draw attentions to limits of modelling, these demand the users to commit the time and effort to understand them.

One way for future vulnerability assessment to tackle this paradox is to research methods to better assess and manage uncertainty in global change models (e.g. Rotmans and van Asselt, 2001). Another preferred by stakeholders is to produce targeted lay syntheses, with specific modelling outputs. This could be understood as the responsibility of scientists, since they would effectively take control of the whole scientific knowledge production, integration and communication process. However, few scientists are keen to perform all these tasks, while those who do are often considered as 'interpreters' or 'communicators' of science, rather than scientists per se. In ATEAM a further way was explored: to take the initiative and the risk to dedicate substantial resources to collaborate with stakeholders and to open with them the black box of modelling. If stakeholders did not obtain the precise results they were after, the dialogue gave them the opportunity not only to debate the possible implications of global change, but also to better understand global change modelling itself, including the attached uncertainty. This could be seen as a first step in developing participating interfaces promoting collaborative enquiry as proposed by van den Hove (2007).

Transparency as a basis for open negotiation

Participatory research is about creating the opportunity for confrontation and discussion of different worldviews and perceptions. By opening a window for interactions, scientists are inviting stakeholders to have a say on the research process and content, and are thus opening themselves to criticism as well as praise. This feedback is extremely valuable, but can be difficult to accept, if it does not correspond to the expectations scientists have. Different participants have different expectations about what the dialogue and research should be about. The scope, boundaries and desired outcomes of the research and the dialogue exercise should be either collectively discussed and agreed upon, or at least clearly stated so that stakeholders understand what is expected from them, and what they can expect from participating in the process. Indeed, participants, whether scientist or stakeholder, have an implicit and explicit agenda in engaging in a dialogue process. Explicitly, scientists may for example want to evaluate their research with stakeholders; implicitly, however, they may also seek their endorsement to push their method and results forward. Explicitly, stakeholders may want to obtain more information, and implicitly steer scientific research in specific directions suited to their particular needs. There is nothing wrong about these objectives if they are made transparent, so that participants are aware of the diverse motivations at hand.

The scientists involved in ATEAM felt a strong responsibility in supporting a transition to sustainability by producing meaningful information for European policy and decision makers. Improving the societal relevance of ATEAM's results was thus an explicit aim of the project. At the same time the project aimed to improve the state of the art of ecological modelling per se. Another explicit goal was thus to achieve scientific credibility and recognition among the scientific peer community. These two explicit aims were not incompatible but raised different, sometimes conflicting priorities – for example, on how to adapt the planned research programme to best tackle stakeholders' needs. Moreover, scientists faced substantial restrictions in terms of data availability and quality. Even if resources were unlimited, many interesting scientific approaches and stakeholders' suggestions could not have been addressed for simple want of appropriate data. The many, sometimes mutually exclusive research avenues possible needed to be prioritized. In this process, stakeholders provided valuable input to better balance purely scientific and socially relevant research questions.

Detecting, making visible and reflecting on different participants' expectations is therefore a critical part of the process of a science–stakeholder dialogue (Welp et al, 2006b). If the object of the dialogue is not simply to collect and document different expectations, but to develop bridges for collaborative research, then these must be explicitly addressed. To do this, scientists and stakeholders need to view each other as partners in the co-creation of knowledge. Each participant brings his or her own expertise and domain of knowledge, which should be considered respectfully without disguised power hierarchies (Oels, 2006). The dialogue in itself can then be seen as a political process, which seeks to level inequalities between partners and where disagreements and conflicting expectations may be addressed in open negotiations (Welp and Stoll-Kleeman, 2006). To best address different expectations, participants must therefore be ready to (re)define the collective goals of the research at hand and the most appropriate ways to achieve them. Essentially, this demands that scientists accept sharing decision-power on the research process with stakeholders (Reason and Heron, 1986).

Reconciling scientists' and stakeholders' expectations in global change research

The potential of numerical modelling as a guide for policy making relies primarily on its scientific credibility at disciplinary and interdisciplinary level, but also on the degree of societal relevance and acceptance that models achieve among policy and decision makers. Both are to a certain extent a negotiated social process rather than purely a scientific exercise (van den Hove, 2007). This is the fundamental challenge integrated assessments face, namely to achieve an acceptable level of simplification and associated uncertainty while at the same time still encompassing the key complexity of the simulated systems. In tackling this challenge vulnerability assessment research is being pulled by two opposing forces related to different interpretations of the role of scientific enquiry. Van den Hove (2007) thus distinguished issue-driven 'science for action' from curiosity-driven 'science for science'. The former fosters a user-oriented discipline focused on satisfying stakeholders' short-term information needs (where scientists may become commissioned consultants or advisers). The latter prefers a discipline in which the definition of research problems, priorities and methodologies remain primarily in the hands of scientists and where stakeholders play a peripheral role. A compromise between these visions thus needs to be found in vulnerability assessments research, so that societal relevance does not take precedence over scientific excellence and credibility, and vice versa. This compromise will have to be negotiated on a case-by-case basis from the design to the implementation stages. To this end, innovative approaches to move away from the perception of science as top–down production of expert answers to one of science as collective exploration of the plausible are required.

If global change research is to overcome the discrepancies between stakeholders' expectations from science and current capability to fulfil these, further and stronger bridges are needed to reinforce dialogue and collaboration between science, policy and society. To raise the visibility and meaningfulness of vulnerability assessments as critical means to better understand global change and its potential worrying impacts on society, two trends are being followed, the common denominators of which are science-based stakeholder dialogues. On the one hand uncertainty has emerged in the last decade as a major issue in global change modelling and in the vaster context of the so-called 'post-normal science' paradigm (Funtowicz and Ravetz, 1993).[4] Key issues identified here are how better to communicate scientific uncertainty to policy makers and society, and more generally how to facilitate decision making in face of uncertainty. These lines of reflection have fostered the development of a rich discourse, bringing together representatives of science, policy and society to contribute to a better understanding of modelling opportunities and limits (e.g. Dessai and Hulme, 2004). Science–stakeholder dialogue processes dedicated to debating uncertainty as perceived by scientists and lay people could help to solve significant misunderstandings about the potential and limits of modelling. This would provide valuable opportunities to reflect on constructive manners to communicate uncertainty, and to incorporate it in decision making. The ATEAM dialogue process can be understood as a further step in this direction.

On the other hand some assessments seek to explicitly target specific policy- and management-oriented questions at higher spatial resolution, in close consultation with interested stakeholders. The aimed products here are smaller, dedicated models, clear and targeted result syntheses, and self-explanatory information tools, which consider national and sub-national scales. Both avenues can feed each other, for greater benefits, in particular in bridging the gap in temporal and spatial scales relevant for scientists and stakeholders, and to create a more dynamic scientific agenda, better suited to the rapidly changing policy agenda. The ATEAM analysis also has a role to play in this second area of research. It has for example already served as a broad basis for downscaled assessments (Zebisch et al, 2005). The vulnerability atlas and the tool for natural reserve selection developed within ATEAM are, moreover, valuable initiatives towards a better communication of global assessment results (Araújo et al, 2002, 2004; Metzger et al, 2004, 2006).

Conclusions

The ATEAM stakeholder dialogue has been in itself an important part of the project's results. The project collaborated with an expanding stakeholder network and its assessment approach was reviewed and improved in view of the dialogue outcomes. The original research plan and the ecosystem modelling per se were not fundamentally changed by stakeholders. However, stakeholders provided healthy and constructive 'outsiders' views on the project's research questions and aimed results. Through this experience scientists considerably adjusted their thinking and work. They further gained valuable insights on stakeholders' perceptions on ecosystem services and global change, as well as on ecosystem management and sectoral adaptive capacity. Together scientists and stakeholders contributed to developing bridges between the generators of scientific knowledge and their users.

Stakeholders need to understand the roles and limits of scientific enquiry and modelling performances. It is vital to understand that scientists cannot provide predictions of future global change impacts and vulnerability; instead they make projections and explore multiple scenarios. Stakeholders should not expect reliable predictions, as large uncertainty is unavoidable since society is continuously shaping its future in a complex unpredictable manner. Similarly scientists should be cautious when committing themselves to produce results that are socially relevant over the short term. To achieve these results scientists may need to yield a substantial part of their decision power over to the targeted stakeholders, or at least to negotiate openly with them the main lines of the proposed research. At the same time, scientists may need to accept the challenge of better communicating their research in formats preferred by stakeholders, or to dedicate more time still to 'educate' stakeholders to understand and use scientific results, while stakeholders 'educate' scientists to produce more relevant and helpful information. Education is, after all, a two-way process, and the time of bearded authorities talking down to the normal mortals is long over – which should be a great relief to all dialogue partners.

Acknowledgements

The authors are in debt to all stakeholders, who offered their time and valuable comments during the course of the project. We would also like to thank particularly the project leader, Wolfgang Cramer, Bärbel Zierl and Uta Fritsch for their enormous contribution to planning, leading and evaluating the stakeholder activities, and all ATEAMers for their continuous support. Additional thanks go to Martin Welp and Carlo Jaeger for their valuable advice and to the European Commission, which funded the ATEAM Project (Project No. EVK2-2000-00075) under the 5th Research Programme 'Energy, Environment and Sustainable Development'.

Notes

1 These numbers strictly refer to the stakeholders identified, approached or participating within the ATEAM dialogue activities reported upon here. Many more stakeholders were less directly involved within ATEAM via: 1) additional dissemination and outreach activities carried out within the project; and 2) parallel stakeholder networks and activities developed within other projects or institutes, within which ATEAMers participated (for a complete report on these see Schröter et al (2004)).

2 These were the 2nd and 3rd general stakeholder workshops and the Mountain and Biodiversity sectoral stakeholder workshop.

3 For the full results of the evaluation questionnaires see: de la Vega-Leinert et al (2004), which is available from the corresponding author. A summary of this report is included in Schröter et al (2004).

4 For Funtowicz and Ravetz (1993) 'normal', positivist science, based on objective, deducible or observable phenomena, fails to address the challenges posed by co-evolving natural and human systems. For example global change and related policy issues are characterized by large uncertainty, complex ethical dilemmas and a plurality of perspectives and value systems. To deal with these important aspects the authors promote a re-evaluation of scientific enquiry, its goals and methods. In particular, science should be developed in dialogue with society to better address key environmental, social and ethical challenges.

References

Araújo, M. B., Williams, P. H. and Turner, A. (2002) 'A sequential approach to minimize threats within selected conservation areas', *Biodiversity and Conservation*, vol 11, pp1011–1024

Araújo, M. B., Cabeza, M., Thuiller, W., Hannah, L. and Williams, P. H. (2004) 'Would climate change drive species out of reserves? An assessment of existing reserve-selection methods', *Global Change Biology*, vol 10, pp1618–1626

Biernacki, P. and Waldorf, D. (1981) 'Snowball sampling: Problems and techniques of chain referral sampling', *Sociological Methods and Research*, vol 10(2), pp141–163

de la Vega-Leinert, A. C., Schröter, D., Fritsch, U. and Zierl, B. (2004) *Results of the Stakeholder Evaluation Questionnaires*, ATEAM report, Potsdam Institute for Climate Impact Research (PIK), Germany, available from the corresponding author

de la Vega-Leinert, A. C., Schröter, D., Leemans, R., Fritsch, U. and Pluimers, J. (in review) 'A stakeholder dialogue on European vulnerability', *Regional Environmental Change*

Dessai, S. and Hulme, M. (2004) 'Does climate adaptation policy need probabilities?', *Climate Policy*, vol 4, pp107–128

Funtowicz, S. O. and Ravetz, J. R. (1993) 'Science for a post-normal age' *Futures*, vol 25, pp739–755

Jaeger, C., Leimbach, M., Carraro, C., Hasselmann, K., Hourcade, J. C., Keeler, A. and Klein, R. (2002) *Community Integrated Assessment: Modules for Cooperation*, Nota di Lavoro, Milano, Italia. FEEM, PIK / PIK Publications, Potsdam Institute for Climate Impact Research, Potsdam, Germany

Jürgens, I. (2001) 'Climate change and the communication between scientists and stakeholders: Towards a participatory notion of communication', unpublished MSc. thesis, Lund University, Lund, Sweden

McCarthy, J. J., Canziani, O. F., Leary, N. A., Dokken, D. J. and White, K. S. (eds) (2001) *Climate Change 2001: Impacts, Adaptation and Vulnerability*, Contribution of Working Group II to the Third Assessment Report of the Intergovernmental Panel on Climate Change (IPCC), Cambridge University Press, Cambridge

Metzger, M. J. and Schröter, D. (2006) 'Towards a spatially explicit and quantitative vulnerability assessment of environmental change in Europe', *Regional Environmental Change*, vol 6(4), pp201–216, doi:10.1007/s10113-006-0020-2

Metzger, M. J., Leemans, R., Schröter, D., Cramer, W. and the ATEAM consortium (2004) *The ATEAM Vulnerability Mapping Tool*, CD-ROM publication No. 27, Office C. T. de Wit Graduate School for Production Ecology and Resource Conservation (PE&RC), Wageningen, The Netherlands, www.pik-potsdam.de/ateam

Morales, P., Sykes, M. T., Prentice, C., Smith, P., Smith, B., Bugmann, H., Zierl, B., Friedlingstein, P., Viovy, N., Sabaté, S., Sánchez, A., Pla, E., Gracia, C. A., Sitch, S., Arneth, A. and Ogee, J. (2005) 'Comparing and evaluating process-based ecosystem model predictions of carbon and water fluxes in major European forest biomes', *Global Change Biology*, vol 11(12), p2211

Muetzelfeldt, R. (2003) *Declarative Modelling in Ecological and Environmental Research*, AVEC Papers, www.pik-potsdam.de/avec/decmod_final8.pdf

Oels, A. (2006) 'Evaluating stakeholder dialogues', in Stoll-Kleemann, S. and Welp, M. (eds) *Stakeholder Involvement in Environmental Management, Policy Making and Research: Theory and Practice*, Springer Verlag, Cambridge, pp117–147

Patt, T., Klein, R. J. T. and de la Vega-Leinert, A. C. (2005) 'Taking the uncertainty in climate change vulnerability assessment seriously', *Comptes Rendus Geoscience*, vol 337, pp411–424

Reason, P. and Heron, J. (1986) 'Research with people: The paradigm of cooperative experiential inquiry', *Person-Centred Review*, vol 1(4), pp456–476

Reid, W. V., Mooney, H. A., Cropper, A., Capistrano, D., Carpenter, S. R., Chopra, K., Dasgupta, P., Dietz, T., Duraiappah, A. K., Hassan, R., Kasperson, R., Leemans, R., May, R. M., McMichael, T. A. J., Pingali, P., Samper, C., Scholes, R., Watson, R. T., Zakri, A. H., Shidong, Z., Ash, N. J., Bennett, E., Kumar, P., Lee, M. J., Raudsepp-Hearne, C., Simons, H., Thonell, J. and Zurek, M. B. (2005) *Ecosystems and Human Well-being*, Millennium Ecosystem Assessment Synthesis Report, Island Press, Washington DC

Reidsma, P. and Ewert, F. (2007) 'Assessing the adaptive capacity of European agriculture under different climate and management conditions', *Climatic Change*, vol 84(3–4), pp403–422

Reilly, J., Stone, P. H., Forest, C., Webster, M. D., Jacoby, H. D. and Prinn, R. (2001) 'Climate change: Uncertainty and climate change assessments', *Science*, vol 293(5529), pp430–433

Rotmans, J. and van Asselt, M. B. A. (2001) 'Uncertainty management in integrated assessment modelling: Towards a pluralistic approach', *Environmental Monitoring and Assessment*, vol 69(2), pp101–130

Schröter, D. and the ATEAM Consortium (2004) *Final ATEAM Report 2004. Section 5 and 6*, Potsdam Institute for Climate Impact Research, Potsdam, Germany, www.pik-potsdam.de/ateam/ateam_final_report_sections_5_to_6.pdf

Schröter, D., Cramer, W., Leemans, R., Prentice, C. I., Araújo, M. B., Arnell, N. W., Bondeau, A., Bugmann, H., Carter, T. R., Gracia, C. A., de la Vega-Leinert, A. C., Erhard, M., Ewert, F., Glendinning, M., House, J. I., Kankaanpää, S., Klein, R. J. T., Lavorel, S., Lindner, M., Metzger, M. J., Meyer, M., Mitchell, T., Reginster, I., Rounsevell, M., Sabaté, S., Sitch, S., Smith, B., Smith, J., Smith, P., Sykes, M. T., Thonicke, K., Thuiller, W., Tuck, G., Zaehle, S. and Zierl, B. (2005) 'Ecosystem service supply and vulnerability to global change in Europe', *Science*, vol 310, pp1333–1337

Shackley, S. and Darier, E. (1998) 'Seduction of the sirens: Global climate change and modelling', *Science and Public Policy*, vol 25(5), pp313–326

Shackley, S. and Deanwood, R. (2003) 'Constructing social futures for climate change impacts and response studies: Building qualitative and quantitative scenarios with the participation of stakeholders', *Climate Research*, vol 24(1), pp71–90

Tuck, G., Glendining, M. J., Smith, P., House, J. I. and Wattenbach, M. (2006) 'The potential distribution of bioenergy crops in Europe under present and future climate', *Biomass & Bioenergy*, vol 30(3), pp183–197

van den Hove, S. (2007) 'A rationale for science–policy interface', *Futures*, vol 39(7), pp807–826 van den Hove, S. and Sharman, M. (2006) 'Interfaces between science and policy for environmental governance: Lessons and open questions from the European Platform for Biodiversity Research Strategy', in Guimarães Pereira, Â., Guedes Vaz, S. and Tognetti, S. (eds) *Interfaces between Science and Society*, Greenleaf Publishing Ltd, Sheffield

Vreugdenhil, J. J. (2003) 'Stakeholder, scientists, scenarios and the skills of shaping dialogue: Evaluation of the scenario development and the stakeholder dialogue in the ATEAM project', unpublished MSc thesis, Wageningen University, Wageningen, The Netherlands

Welp, M. and Stoll-Kleemann, S. (2006) 'Integrative theory of reflexive dialogues', in Stoll-Kleemann, S. and Welp, M. (eds) *Stakeholder Involvement in Environmental Management, Policy Making and Research: Theory and Practice*, Springer Verlag, Cambridge, pp43–78

Welp, M., de la Vega-Leinert, A., Stoll-Kleemann, S. and Fürstenau, C. (2006a) 'Science-based stakeholder dialogues in climate change research', in Stoll-Kleemann, S. and Welp, M. (eds) *Stakeholder Involvement in Environmental Management, Policy Making and Research: Theory and Practice*, Springer Verlag, Cambridge, pp213–240

Welp, M., de la Vega-Leinert, A., Stoll-Kleemann, S. and Jaeger, C. C. (2006b) 'Theoretical approaches for science-based stakeholder dialogues', *Global Environmental Change*, vol 16(2), pp115–234

Wynne, B. (2005) 'Risk as globalizing "democratic" discourse? Framing subjects and citizens', in Leach, M., Scoones, I. and Wynne, B. (eds) *Science and Citizens: Globalization and the Challenge of Engagement*, Zed Books, London

Zebisch, M., Grothmann, T., Schröter, D., Haße, C., Fritsch, U. and Cramer, W. (2005) *Climate Change in Germany: Vulnerability and Adaptation of Climate Sensitive Sectors*, Report commissioned by the Federal Environmental Agency, Germany (UFOPLAN 201 41 253), Potsdam Institute of Climate Impact Research, Potsdam, Germany; in German and English, www.umweltbundesamt.de/index-e.htm

Chapter 12

Defining Dangerous Climate Change: The Beijing Exercise

Martin Welp, Antonella Battaglini and Carlo C. Jaeger

Introduction

The world is facing rapid climate change with potentially serious consequences for ecosystems, people's livelihoods and society at large. The ultimate objective of international climate policy, according to the United Nations Framework Convention on Climate Change (UNFCCC; United Nations 1992), is to avoid dangerous interference with the climate system. This is directly related to targets for long-term climate policies (cf. Hasselmann et al, 2003). To come up with a reasonable definition of warming levels that would qualify as dangerous is not a task that can be fulfilled by scientists alone. There is a need to create settings in which scientists and stakeholders can exchange views, agree or disagree and thus integrate factual knowledge and normative judgements.

We will present and discuss a recent qualitative vulnerability assessment process initiated by the European Climate Forum (ECF) and the Potsdam Institute for Climate Impact Research (PIK). The vulnerability assessment focused on the question 'What constitutes dangerous climate change?' The question was approached from a regional perspective and critical vulnerabilities in selected world regions were at the core of the assessment.

Climate change and the UNFCCC Article 2

Article 2 of the UNFCCC defines as the overarching goal of climate policy the 'stabilization of greenhouse gas concentrations in the atmosphere at a level that would prevent dangerous anthropogenic interference with the climate system'.

The UNFCCC is valid international law, ratified by even more states than the Kyoto Protocol, including the USA. With respect to the interpretations of the climate convention, most prominently Article 2, policy makers need the support of the research community in structuring and interpreting dangerous levels of climate change. The UNFCCC as such gives only preliminary hints at how the notion of dangerous climate change should be interpreted. For example, it states that a level that prevents dangerous anthropogenic interference with the climate system '... should be achieved within a time frame sufficient to allow ecosystems to adapt naturally to climate change, to ensure that food production is not threatened and to enable economic development to proceed in a sustainable manner'.

With Russia's ratification of the Kyoto Protocol in October 2004 the question of dangerous levels of climate change and the implications for emission reduction targets, in particular the second commitment period of the Kyoto Protocol, gained new momentum. No major policy shifts are possible for the first commitment period ending in 2012. However, policy making in view of the time period after 2012 is currently in its hot phase. Policies will be influenced by the Fourth Assessment Report of the Intergovernmental Panel on Climate Change (IPCC, 2007) and other assessments such as the Stern Review (Stern et al, 2006). These and the results of the Beijing exercise, which will be described below provide further input for the discussions about Article 2.

The ECF assessment process

The ECF is a non-profit association, which provides a platform for dialogues between scientists and stakeholders concerned with the climate problem. The members are some of the leading climate research institutes in Europe, companies and corporations (e.g. Deutsche Telekom, Munich Re, NEC High Performance Computing Europe), as well as non-governmental organizations, such as the World Wide Fund for Nature (WWF) and the European Business Council for Sustainable Energy. The board of ECF, set up both by scientists and stakeholders, decided in 2003 to carry out an assessment on key vulnerable regions and climate change. The aim was to identify thresholds for impacts and adaptation in relation to Article 2. A key part of this assessment was an international symposium that took place in October 2004 in Beijing, organized jointly by ECF, PIK, the Institute of Atmospheric Physics in Beijing and the Nansen-Zhu International Research Centre.

Thus far few assessments had explicitly approached the question 'What is dangerous climate change?' from a regional perspective. There was a considerable body of literature on projected regional and local impacts but few efforts had been made to synthesize this material and draw conclusions on what regions are the most vulnerable with respect to climate change (Hare, 2003). Even when regional assessments had been done, these had usually focused on specific drivers of change (e.g. sea level, drought), specific impacts (e.g. floods, famine) or ecosystem services (e.g. the ATEAM project in Europe, Schröter et al, 2005). The exercise can thus be regarded as one of the first attempts to qualitatively assess in a comprehensive manner the multiple drivers, impacts and affected systems at regional level.

In contrast to data-rich, heavily model-based approaches, ECF facilitated a dialogue with key people, whom we believed had important competencies. This way the participants could contribute to the creation of a broader picture. Instead of starting with the development of new models on climate change impacts, already existing regional studies were critically scrutinized and summarized. Hitherto vulnerability assessments had been largely disjointed.

Furthermore, the exercise was not primarily an effort to develop a certain social science methodology, such as the Integrated Assessment Focus Group method in the ULYSSES project (Kasemir, 2003). Rather it was a dialogue exercise embedded in a vulnerability assessment. It also differed essentially from the activities run by the United Kingdom Climate Impacts Programme (UKCIP), where the stakeholders influence or determine the research agenda by commissioning studies that could satisfy their needs (www.UKCIP.org).

Studies that have included stakeholders in assessing Article 2 include the HOT project – Helping Operationalise Article Two – conducted by the National Institute of Public Health and Environment (RIVM) in The Netherlands. Results of the HOT project, phase 1,[1] were presented in the opening section of the symposium in Beijing with the intention to inform the audience on precedent activities in this field of research.

Structure of the assessment

In line with the formulation of Article 2 the focus of the assessment was on ecosystems, food production and sustainable development. Not all regions are, however, equally vulnerable to climate change. This is partly due to differences in the adaptive capacity and partly due to variations in expected regional warming levels and impacts. In order to advance and structure the debate it seemed important to identify what regions are the most vulnerable and why, and at what temperature levels serious and even irreversible impacts are likely to occur. Thirteen world regions were selected as the focus of the assessment. The selected regions were weighted towards developing countries and highly vulnerable regions. The aim was to have a balanced regional and geopolitical coverage. The regions were: China, Sahelian Africa, Australia, Southern Africa, South Asia (Indian subcontinent), North-West Europe and Central Europe, Mediterranean – Maghreb and North Africa, USA, Amazon, Andean Region, Russia, High Arctic Region, and Small Island States in the Pacific and the Caribbean. Furthermore the symposium explored a number of cross-cutting issues including legal aspects and interpretations of Article 2 of the UNFCCC, the risk of rapid or abrupt changes in the climate system (changes in the thermohaline circulation, changes in the West Antarctic ice sheet), and consequences of climate change on human health and the spread of vector-borne diseases such as malaria.

Three scientists from each of the regions were contacted and invited to give a paper and presentation at the four-day symposium in Beijing. The scientists were regional experts on at least one of the key issues: ecosystems, food production and sustainable development. Besides scientists, at least one stakeholder was invited from each of the regions concerned. By stakeholders we mean people outside the research community, who have a stake or interest in the issue. In the context of this assessment they were actors who have an interest in climate issues or can significantly influence future climate or climate policies, such as climate negotiators; other government officials, such as the UK's Department for Environment, Food and Rural Affairs (Defra) and the German Environment Agency; NGO representatives, such as Greenpeace, Climate Action Network (CAN); and the Inuit Circumpolar Conference; and company representatives (Insurance Australia Group Limited). In total more than 60 participants took part in the event in Beijing.[2]

The discussions were fuelled by presentations given by scientists. These gave a state-of-the-art picture of our present knowledge base. The requirement was that the presented information should be sufficiently understandable to people with different educational and professional backgrounds, so that a meaningful dialogue could take place. Instead of an overload of indicators and data, the stakeholders were confronted with a synthesis presented by scientists from each region. Besides model-based results, images and anecdotes were used and taken note of. Each region was discussed in parallel breakout groups and the results were summarized in plenary sessions. Proper documentation of the discussions was a key element in this process. The role of the stakeholders was to comment on the scientific presentations and to ask 'difficult questions'. The use of common sense and ordinary language, instead of unnecessarily complex scientific jargon, was encouraged. The stakeholders and the moderators consciously spurred the scientists to identify temperature thresholds for impacts that are likely to take place as a consequence of climate change. Experienced moderators sought to tease out views that are shared by the participants, while wanting to document the variety of views. A rough estimate on critical thresholds or even a best guess was considered to be helpful at this stage of the debate.

Substance of arguments and consensus

A definition of what constitutes dangerous levels of climate change cannot be based purely on scientific reasoning. Science can, however, play a key role in structuring the debate on dangerous levels of climate change (Schellnhuber et al, 2006). Exemplary issues that were discussed jointly by scientists and stakeholders are presented below. By compiling conclusions from each region – there may be a need to modify these as science progresses – and from other world regions, a general picture of dangerous levels of climate change began to emerge. Some of the regional findings have been summarized in other contexts such as the IPCC report or the Arctic Climate Impact Assessment (ACIA, 2005); some were based on very recent research results and model runs. During the four days of intensive dialogues and follow-up discussions via email, some participants were inclined to endorse the view that a 2°C increase of global mean temperature over a long period of time can, considering our present knowledge, be regarded as being intolerable and dangerous. Some participants, in particular from Bangladesh and the Arctic region were extremely critical with regard to the 2°C threshold. Indeed for the Inuit culture the current warming is already considered to be dangerous and further increase in temperature to 2°C and beyond may cause irreparable damage. Except for a few exceptions, namely in the case of the small islands and Australia, the personal beliefs of scientists were not translated into a clear and straightforward scientific endorsement of a threshold, thus re-enforcing the difficulty scientists have in committing themselves to a clear threshold.

The argument created in Beijing was that the figure of 2°C may be somewhat higher or lower, but it is not an arbitrary one.[3] A 1°C increase is likely to have impacts, but these would not necessarily qualify as being dangerous in the sense of jeopardizing complete ecosystems such as the Amazon or significantly reducing food production in regions such as the Asian subcontinent or sub-Saharan Africa. In light of the vulnerability assessment conducted in Beijing there was some agreement to support the following line of argumentation: there is growing evidence for the view that an increase in global mean temperature of more than 3°C over a long period can reasonably not be regarded as being safe. At this point of time the option of keeping the 2°C goal should thus be kept open. The 2°C goal was not endorsed by all participants. As mentioned above, several participants considered this to be too high. Some participants held the view that the already observed warming of 0.8°C above pre-industrial levels must be regarded as dangerous climate change. Nevertheless all participants recognized the need for setting a threshold and having a political target, which helps to frame policies and provides directions for businesses. The discussions made clear that local and regional needs and vulnerability cannot be properly and legitimately represented by a global target. Moreover, a temperature level may not be the only relevant criterion for dangerous climate change. Changes in precipitation and drought patterns in particular are of high relevance for agriculture, especially subsistence agriculture and the safety of people as well as infrastructure in flood-prone watersheds. Participants were in full agreement in recognizing the need to have emissions reduction and temperature control in parallel with adaptation measures in order to minimize impacts in regions with high vulnerability. In the following sections conclusions from selected subgroups are presented in more detail.

The Arctic region

An exemplary issue that was debated in Beijing was summer sea ice of the Arctic region, which scientists consider to be threatened by climate change. Nobody, however, knows the exact threshold for this to happen – that is, how much global temperature increase is needed for the sea ice to melt. It was argued that a reduction or complete loss of sea ice would have serious consequences for the living conditions of the Inuit and for polar fauna, including polar bears, which are popular iconic species for climate change impacts (Sheila Watt-Clautier, personal communication; ACIA, 2005). Based on discussions among scientists and stakeholders as well as recent studies, in which the participating scientists were involved, a warming level was eventually defined. Some models support the view that a 2.5°C increase in global mean temperature is likely to cause a significant or even complete loss of the summer sea ice (ECF, 2004).

Sea-level rise

The participants, furthermore, identified sea-level rise as a further critical issue likely to result from dangerous levels of climate change. Some argued that in the long run this could be the single most important aspect in defining dangerous climate change. For example, scientists argued that a 3°C global warming above pre-industrial levels could cause the melting of the Antarctic and Greenland ice sheets and of glaciers, and thus cause a 3–5m sea-level rise by 2300 (ECF, 2004). Several metres of sea-level rise over a few centuries would result in widespread loss of coastal and deltaic areas (such as Bangladesh, the Nile, Yangtse and Mekong Delta regions), including their ecosystems and human settlements. Furthermore, many of the world's largest cities and considerable wealth would be seriously impacted. Such impacts would, according to the involved scientists and stakeholders, clearly qualify as dangerous interference with the climate system.

Small islands

Small island developing states have in the climate debate played a more prominent role than their size of population for example might suggest. These countries have a strong moral argument in claiming that high-emission countries threaten the very existence of their territory. In the Caribbean region the period between 1960 and 2000 witnessed an exponential increase in the occurrence, severity and intensity of disasters. For example, Grenada, which was hit by Hurricane Ivan in 2004, had according to government representatives damages amounting to €670 million, which is 200 per cent of the island's current gross domestic product (GDP). Sea-level rise, tropical cyclones and droughts make these areas some of the most vulnerable, and thus prominent symbols of dangerous climate change.

The Amazon region

Another key example was the danger that the ecosystems of the Amazon region may fundamentally change due to climate change. Over the next decades there is a risk of abrupt and irreversible replacement of forests by savannah. This would cause a total change in the precipitation patterns, loss of biodiversity and serious pressure on people's livelihoods. Few would argue that a radical ecosystem change of this geographical dimension would not qualify as dangerous, even if considered in global terms. A clear temperature threshold was harder to find than in the case of Arctic sea ice and the issue was identified as a key one requiring further research.

Follow-up from Beijing

After the Beijing symposium a series of other events were organized by various institutions which addressed the question: 'What is dangerous climate change?' The most prominent one was a meeting in Exeter (UK) in February 2005, which brought together 200 scientists and was organized by Defra (Schellnhuber et al, 2006). It is important to notice that in this case stakeholders did not play a role; rather the participants were from the scientific community.

The report of the Beijing event[4] can be regarded as a key contribution to the public debate on Article 2 and the start of ECF outreach activities on this topic. The report was published and well received at the 10th Conference of Parties (COP10) side event in December 2005 in Buenos Aires, Argentina.[5] The media took notice of the report: several articles were published in international and national newspapers and broadcast in radio. Summaries of the main results were translated into several languages including Arabic, Chinese, Dioula, French, German, Russian and Spanish, and published on the web.

A follow-up ECF event on energy issues and climate security took place in November 2005, again in Beijing. Furthermore, the question of how to stay below the 2°C benchmark was discussed from the policy point of view at a subsequent symposium, 'Climate Policy in the Coming Phases of the Kyoto Process: Targets, Instruments, and the Role of Cap and Trade Schemes' in February 2006, in Brussels. At the annual ECF event in March 2007 in Berlin the question how to stay below 2°C was embedded in discussions on how to finance a transition into a low-carbon economy.

Vulnerability assessment to support global climate discourse

Complying with long-term mitigation targets, which are in line with Article 2, and the interpretation that a 2°C benchmark is reasonable, requires far-reaching political decisions that have to be made soon. These decisions, as many other political decisions, have to be made under uncertainty. Climate scientists can at the moment often give only a range of warming levels which can cause dangerous impacts in different regions. In some cases scientists may additionally be able to give a probability distribution.

The public understanding of science is largely based on a view of scientific progress creating 'true' and 'objective' knowledge, rather than knowledge that is characterized by uncertainties. The climate system and its interrelation with social and natural systems are very complex. Uncertainties in climate change models, as well as in models of climate change impacts and economic costs, challenge the normal ways of doing and communicating science (Schackley et al, 1998). Advocates of post-normal science (see Funtovicz and Ravetz, 1992; Saloranta, 2001) point out that it is important to extend the group of reviewers to encompass also non-scientists.

Facts, values and post-normal science

Science–policy interfaces, such as the Beijing exercise, allow joint construction of knowledge with the aim of enriching decision making (van den Hove, 2007). The findings of the group of stakeholders and scientists that met in Beijing supported the 2°C target adopted by the European Union.[6] Tol (2007) criticizes the EU target and argues that it is not justifiable in scientific terms. The evidence on which the 2°C target is based is in his view shaky, often methodologically flawed and based on a narrow set of studies. Tol furthermore argues that the question 'What is dangerous climate change?' cannot be solved without making value judgements. It is exactly for this reason that the dialogue process in Beijing had the aim of integrating factual and value considerations, while being explicit with regard to underlying assumptions of the participants.

In our view both factual arguments and normative arguments play a role in defining dangerous climate change. So far, however, science has evolved by trying to avoid, rather than cultivate, such a combination. One reason for this is a deeply rooted view that the two domains of discourse (factual and normative) should be separated (cf. Putnam, 2002; Jaeger, 2003). According to this view only factual arguments belong to the domain of science, while normative issues are beyond rational argumentation. We believe, however, that as decisions are taken not only on the basis of factual arguments, it is therefore necessary and possible to have an exchange about normative arguments. It is good to keep in mind that all models in vulnerability assessments are based on value judgements, although these are not always made explicit. Economists typically measure danger – in our case the level of dangerous climate change – in terms of loss of GDP. Advocates of the strictly monetary approach often ignore the fact that a GDP figure is already value laden. The underlying assumptions – What is measured? What discount rate is chosen? – cannot be considered to be value free.

Extending the scope of how an issue is framed is a further justification for post-normal science. In order to define what dangerous climate change is, it is essential to consider also other factors than GDP. Estimates of global GDP impacts, especially if extended over a long period of time, deny daily human reality and the relevance of short-term human decisions. In terms of global GDP the possibility of having a great number of people in Bangladesh dying in floods and being displaced due to sea-level rise, or the Inuit culture disappearing, is of no value or interest, because GDP losses, especially over a long period of time, would equal zero. Similar and more extraordinary examples can be found in history: World War I, for example, can be deemed to have had no long-term impacts on global GDP and the genocide in Rwanda and the Darfur/Sudan crisis to have had no impact at all. But from a moral and value point of view they all have been terrible events in the history of humanity. Climate change impacts may have only small influence on global GDP over long periods; measured in tragedies at local and regional level, however, the picture is likely to look grimmer. It is therefore clear that different views will prevail and testing different arguments is part of the dialogue process and a necessary step in the political process.

The question 'What constitutes dangerous climate change?' is a challenging one for scientific enquiry exactly because of the many ways it can be framed. What people perceive or feel as danger is very subjective and it is intimately related to specific events and locations. The notion of 'dangerous' is thus influenced by people's perceptions, values and worldviews. The integration of the two domains of discourse – factual and normative – also requires reassessing what we consider to be facts and values. According to Putnam (2002) a sharp 'fact/value' dichotomy becomes harmful when identified with a dichotomy between the objective and the purely subjective. Putnam argues that we can share rational arguments about values as well. An extended peer community consisting of various stakeholders provides critical insights into the interplay between facts and values. In terms of policy, pluralism increases the likelihood that some of the approaches will turn out to be useful (Lindblom and Cohen, 1979). A risk assessment approach as was adopted in the Beijing exercise can increase the social relevance of vulnerability assessments and extend them to defining and supporting mitigation targets. Many other problems of the modern world, like genetically modified organisms, nuclear weapons or nuclear power generation, are viewed from the angle of risk assessment. There is a vast body of literature on how risk can be analysed and communicated to different publics (cf. Jaeger et al, 2001). Risk assessment typically results in a threshold level. The link between the setting of a threshold based on scientific assessment and its use in policy is, however, not a straightforward process. Lemos and Morehouse (2005) point to the time dimension: there may be a time delay between the production of knowledge and the time when stakeholders perceive this new knowledge as 'usable' for decision making. Joint production of knowledge is likely to shorten this delay and may provide us windows of opportunities to act.

The role of stakeholders

Numerous actors including policy makers, managers in corporations and individual persons in their everyday life perform climate-relevant decisions at different levels. The range of potentially relevant stakeholders is thus very broad. Who to invite to stakeholder dialogues depends on the objectives of the dialogues, on resources, and the networks of which the scientists are part. The selection of both scientists and stakeholders has obviously an impact on the outcome of a dialogue. A key criterion for the success of such an assessment is the variety of involved organizations and subsequently the variety of views and interests.

In the vulnerability assessment described above, so-called expert stakeholders were selected. Biases in the selection process can impact the outcome of the dialogues and therefore the list of invitees needs to be thought out carefully. In Beijing, for example, stakeholders did not include major producing companies or energy companies, which might have defended a different position and not subscribed to a statement such as the 2°C threshold. In other types of stakeholder processes it may be reasonable to engage, for example, randomly selected citizens (Kasemir et al, 2003).

It can be assumed, however, that in cases where a group of scientists, business representatives and NGO representatives do share a common view, this view is more likely to find broader resonance among the broader public. The ECF will, however, not try to enforce a consensus on the 2°C view of dangerous climate change among its stakeholder and scientist members or a broader public. Thus, disagreement may prevail. A shared understanding of the differences of views and even incompatibilities of problem definition is valuable for scientific progress and for policy making.

The involvement of stakeholders, at the preparatory phase, was of primary importance for the process. In the initial phase, potential private and public funders were consulted and their research and capacity-building interests screened. A frequently voiced criticism of studies sponsored by the private sector is that such funding corrodes the credibility and independence of scientific enquiry. In our experience private funders do not direct scientific enquiry more than public funders do. In this case the core scientific concept, which was to synthesize key vulnerabilities in selected world regions and thus advance the scientific and political discussions on what constitutes dangerous climate change, was not directed by any of the sponsors. Furthermore, the involvement of NGOs in this kind of assessment can be seen as an important balance for business engagement in joint studies and events. Due to Munich Re's competence in health issues this topic was included in the scope of the assessment. The main private sector sponsor of the assessment was eventually Munich Re, which is currently one of the key players in the international debate on climate impacts. Further sponsors included the German Federal Ministry of the Environment, Nature Conservation and Nuclear Safety, the German Technical Cooperation Agency (GTZ), and the Heinrich Böll Foundation.

The assessment process itself was relevant from the point of view of capacity building as well: many scientists from developing countries took part in the process and became part of a network analysing the question of 'What constitutes dangerous climate change?' Thus the research capacity on impacts in different regions was strengthened, which was for example important for the GTZ.

Emerging research questions

One objective of science-based stakeholder dialogues is to identify new socially relevant research questions (Welp et al, 2006). Future research needs (both in terms of substance and methodology) were identified in the Beijing process and addressed in ECF-related research. There were a number of issues that could not be discussed in necessary detail in Beijing due to time limitations. One such issue is the question of overshooting – that is, warming of more than 2°C over a period of time. In view of the research results presented in Beijing it seemed to be reasonable to avoid overshooting over a long period of time (several decades), since this would very likely cause sea-level rise, a phenomenon which can be considered irreversible at least in terms of a lifetime and which would impact numerous low-lying cities worldwide. Also the rate of warming plays a crucial role: various ecosystems are not capable of adapting to climate change that occurs at great speed (e.g. coral reefs). Further research on this issue is needed.

The attractiveness of the Beijing process and the conclusions is partly due to the fact that climate policy needs a clear and simple benchmark. But also business stakeholders engaged in ECF considered the target as being useful for arguing why climate protection is of high importance for sustainable businesses. The question business representatives expressed at one of the follow-up events was: 'What does the two degrees target mean for us, corporations and companies? How does it translate into concentration levels, emission reduction targets and strategies for mitigation?' There are no simple answers to these questions, and the overall regulatory framework as well as the business strategies of individual companies need to be addressed in climate research.

A further question was related to the fact that climate risks have to be put into perspective with present-day pressures on ecosystems caused by various socio-economic driving forces. For example, the possibility of the Amazon rainforest turning into a savannah ecosystem due to changing precipitation patterns was shown by one model. Although this risk has to be taken seriously, more scientific enquiry and runs with other models are required. At present, a combination of pressures caused by international trade (demand for timber, biofuels or food products such as soybean and beef), landownership issues and many others, cause a vicious circle of deforestation in the Amazon region. Climate change can exacerbate the situation and cause the system to shift to another state: from forest ecosystem to savannah ecosystem.

The dialogue exercise in Beijing showed that there is great need to develop scientific tools that can be applied to tackling the question 'What is dangerous climate change?' Probabilistic approaches play an important role in this context. Scientists are usually cautious, in some cases even reluctant, in expressing a threshold for certain impacts to take place. It can be viewed as a positive feature if scientists are clear about the uncertainties of their research and do not give the impression that precise figures can be expressed in all cases. However, expert judgements and probabilities of what could happen at different temperature levels are important for climate policies and the public understanding of science. Such probabilities do not need to be crisp numbers. Probabilistic statements of the kind of 'very likely, likely, less likely' are of value too and can be embedded in vulnerability assessments, for example by applying Bayesian learning (Welp and Stoll-Kleemann, 2006). For example expert elicitations using a probabilistic approach have been conducted at PIK to assess the likelihood of a slow-down or complete shut-down of the thermohaline circulation. A further probabilistic approach for estimating the impacts of floods in some of the world's large river systems under different climate scenarios has been recently introduced by Kleinen and Petschel-Held (2007).

Conclusion

We have outlined a process and the main outcomes of a vulnerability assessment to identify and support mitigation targets. The social relevance of the Beijing process can be seen as being high, as it relates closely to a piece of international law, namely the UN Framework Convention on Climate Change, and in particular Article 2. A strength of the exercise was that it contributed to the creation of shared images of what dangerous climate change may look like. The public debate urgently needs this kind of shared images. Images are created partly by the movie industry (Reusswig, 2004) and television, novels (Allen, 2005) and the printed media, as well as the marketing industry. Television and especially movies can use computer animations and simulations that look extremely realistic and which therefore makes them powerful. The media frames environmental issues usually from different angles than risk assessment (Sachsman et al, 2004) as adopted in our case. Scientists therefore should use the opportunity to take part in the process of creating images and also in communicating them directly. Publishing concise reports in ordinary language on the internet is one way of communicating with non-scientific audiences. The indirect way – via public media – often leads to attention given to best-selling stories rather than less dramatic or slow processes.

In the assessment process described above scientists and stakeholders came up with a shared view of what can be characterized as dangerous climate change. The main conclusion was that a warming of more than 2°C in comparison to pre-industrial levels over a long period of time may be considered dangerous. This was the conclusion of selected scientists and stakeholders from 13 world regions, and thus of a limited, although dedicated and well-informed group of people. The exercise can be considered as a social learning process, which resulted in a vision of what can be considered as dangerous climate change. What humankind is willing to cope with has to be debated in a broader setting, but this exercise provided an update of past assessments by including very recent research results and model runs. From the point of view of policy and business communication such a target is useful because it provides a clear benchmark to which policies can be related.

Deepening our understanding of the risks in different regions and at different temperature levels remains a task for the climate change research community. In our view future studies need to focus on three lines of research: first, vulnerability assessments that deepen our understanding of what constitutes dangerous climate change and what impacts will take place at different warming levels, with special focus on the 2°C warming level. Second, the socioeconomic implications of the 2°C goal need to be assessed in different regions. The third line of research is linked to the previous one: 'What investments are needed to avoid warming levels that are higher than 2°C?' Finding timely answers to the questions requires joint production of knowledge involving both scientists and stakeholders.

Acknowledgement

We thank William (Bill) Hare for having scientifically framed the Beijing symposium and pushed it forward. We also thank all participants and organizers of the symposium for their commitment and interest in the process (the full list of participants is available at www.european-climate-forum.net).

Notes

1 The HOT project was designed to take place in three phases. The first phase aimed at designing a dialogue process that facilitates the exchange of views by using questionnaires and workshops. The first phase of HOT was completed shortly before the Beijing Symposium.

2 The full list of participants is available at www.european-climate-forum.net.

3 The threshold can be compared to speed limits on roads and highways. For example, a 50km/h speed limit in cities is set at this level since there is strong evidence that higher speeds would cause significantly more accidents with pedestrians, cyclists and other cars. That the limit is not 48km/h or 53km/h is a matter of agreement.

4 A documentation of the event in Beijing and detailed summaries of impacts in different regions can be found in the ECF report (European Climate Forum, 2004). The report can be downloaded at www.european-climate-forum.net.

5 The side event was hosted by the European Union and the participants included the German Environment Minister Juergen Trittin, the elected Chair of the Inuit Circumpolar Council Mrs Sheila Watt-Cloutier, Munich Re and other key players in the international climate policy arena.

6 In June 1996 the EU's Environment Council declared a long-term target for CO_2 concentrations of 550ppm. The European Union later adopted the 2°C goal, based on scientific advice. Also the German Advisory Board on Global Change (WBGU) has in its assessment supported this goal. According to a report of this board, a warming of more than 2°C could lead to intolerable impacts for ecosystems and worldwide food security. The report notes however that a threshold cannot be determined precisely (WBGU, 2003). With regard to recent research results there is a contradiction between the two EU goals. According to present understanding of climate sensitivity, a CO_2 concentration level of 450ppm would be equal to a warming of 2°C. Thus the 550ppm target seems to be incompatible with the 2°C goal.

References

ACIA, (2005) *Arctic Climate Impact Assessment*, Cambridge University Press, Cambridge, 1042pp

Allen, M. (2005) 'A novel view of global warming', *Nature*, vol 433(7023), p198

ECF (European Climate Forum) (2002) *Climate Change and Paths to Sustainability*, Conference report, ECF Annual Conference, Berlin, 14–15 November 2002, www.european-climate-forum.net

ECF (2004) 'What is dangerous climate change?', initial results of a Symposium on Key Vulnerable Regions Climate Change and Article 2 of the UNFCCC, Buenos Aires, 14 December 2004, www.european-climate-forum.net

Funtowicz, S. O. and Ravetz, J. R. (1992) 'Three types of risk assessment and the emergence of post-normal science', in Krimsky, S. and Golding, D. (eds) *Social Theories of Risk*, Praeger Publishers, Westport, pp251–273

Hasselmann, K., Latif, M., Hooss, G., Azar, C., Edenhofer, O., Jaeger, C. C., Johannessen, O. M., Kemfert, C., Welp, M. and Wokaun, A. (2003) 'The challenge of long-term climate change', *Science*, vol 302(5652), pp1923–1925

Hare, W. (2003) 'Assessment of knowledge on impacts of climate change: Contribution to the Specification of Art. 2 of the UNFCCC', WBGU, Wissenschaftlicher Beirat der Bundesregierung Globale Umweltveränderungen, www.wbgu.de/wbgu_sn2003_ex01.pdf

IPCC (2007) 'Summary for policymakers', in Solomon, S., Qin, D., Manning, M., Chen, Z., Marquis, M., Averyt, K. B., Tignor, M. and Miller, H. L. (eds) *The Physical Science Basis*, Contribution of Working Group I to the Fourth Assessment Report of the Intergovernmental Panel on Climate Change, Cambridge University Press, Cambridge and New York

Jaeger, C. C. (2003) *A Note on Domains of Discourse: Logical Know-How or Integrated Environmental Modelling*, PIK report No. 86, www.pik-potsdam.de

Jaeger, C. C., Renn, O., Rosa, E. A. and Webler, T. (2001) *Risk, Uncertainty, and Rational Action*, Earthscan, London

Kasemir, B., Jaeger, C. C. and Jäger, J. (2003) 'Citizen participation in sustainability assessments', in Kasemir, B., Jäger, J., Jaeger, C. C. and Gardner, M. T. (eds) *Public Participation in Sustainability Science*, Cambridge University Press, Cambridge, pp3–36

Kleinen, T. and Petschel-Held, G. (2007) 'Integrated assessment of changes in flooding probabilities due to climate change', *Climatic Change*, vol 81(3–4), pp283–312

Lemos, M. C. and Morehouse, B. J. (2005) 'The co-production of science and policy in integrated climate assessments', *Global Environmental Change*, vol 15(1), pp57–68

Lindblom, C. E. and Cohen, D. K. (1979) *Usable Knowledge: Social Science and Social Problem Solving*, Yale University Press, New Haven and London

Putnam, H. (2002) *The Collapse of the Fact / Value Dichotomy and Other Essays*, Harvard University Press, Cambridge, MA

Reusswig, F., Schwarzkopf, J. and Polenz, P. (2004) *Double Impact: The Climate Blockbuster 'The Day After Tomorrow' and its Impact on the German Cinema Public*, PIK Report No. 92, www.pik-potsdam.de

Sachsman, D. B., Simon, J. and Valenti, J. M. (2004) 'Risk and the environment reporters: A four-region analysis', *Public Understanding of Science*, vol 13, pp399–416

Saloranta, T. M. (2001) 'Post-normal science and the global climate change issue', *Climatic Change*, vol 50(4), pp395–404

Schellnhuber, H. J., Cramer, W., Nakicenovic, N., Wigley, T. and Yohe, G. (eds) (2006) *Avoiding Dangerous Climate Change*, Cambridge University Press, Cambridge

Schröter, D., Cramer, W., Leemans, R., Prentice, I. C., Araújo, M. B., Arnell, N. W., Bondeau, A., Bugmann, H., Carter, T. R., Gracia, C. A., Vega-Leinert, A. C. de la, Erhard, M., Ewert, F., Glendining, M., House, J.I., Kankaanpää, S., Klein, R. J. T., Lavorel, S., Lindner, M., Metzger, M. J., Meyer, J., Mitchell, T. D., Reginster, I., Rounsevell, M., Sabaté, S., Sitch, S., Smith, B., Smith, J., Smith, P., Sykes, M. T., Thonicke, K., Thuiller, W., Tuck, G., Zaehle, S. and Zierl, B. (2005) 'Ecosystem service supply and vulnerability to global change in Europe', *Science*, vol 310(5752), pp1333–1337

Shackley, S., Young, P., Parkinson, S. and Wynne, B. (1998) 'Uncertainty, complexity and concepts of good science in climate change modelling: Are GCMs the best tools?', *Climatic Change*, vol 38(2), pp159–205

Stern, N., Peters, S., Bakhshi, V., Bowen, A., Cameron, C., Catovsky, S., Crane, D., Cruickshank, S., Dietz, S., Edmonson, N., Garbett, S.-L., Hamid, L., Hoffman, G., Ingram, D., Jones, B., Patmore, N., Radcliffe, H., Sathiyarajah, R., Stock, M., Taylor, C., Vernon, T., Wanjie, H. and Zenghelis, D. (2006) *Stern Review: The Economics of Climate Change*, HM Treasury, London

Tol, R. S. J. (2007) 'Europe's long-term climate target: A critical evaluation', *Energy Policy*, vol 35(1), pp424–432

United Nations (1992) United Nations Framework Convention on Climate Change (UNFCCC), http://unfccc.int

van den Hove, S. (2007) 'A rationale for science–policy interfaces', *Futures*, vol 39(7), pp807–826

WBGU (German Advisory Council on Global Change) (2003) *Climate Protection Strategies for the 21st Century: Kyoto and Beyond*, Special Report, Berlin, www.wbgu.de/wbgu_sn2003_engl.pdf

Welp, M. and Stoll-Kleemann, S. (2006) 'Integrative theory of reflexive dialogues', in Stoll-Kleemann, S. and Welp, M. (eds) *Stakeholder Dialogues in Natural Resources Management and Integrated Assessments: Theory and Practice*, Springer Environmental Sciences, Berlin, Heidelberg, pp43–78

Welp, M., de la Vega-Leinert, A., Stoll-Kleemann, S. and Jaeger, C. C. (2006) 'Science-based stakeholder dialogues: Tools and theories', *Global Environmental Change*, vol 16(2), pp170–181

Chapter 13

A Framework for Analysing Methodologies of Vulnerability Assessments

Jochen Hinkel

Introduction

Vulnerability assessment (VA) has become a widespread activity in global change research. Knowledge about the vulnerabilities of different people, regions or sectors enables scientists and policy makers to anticipate impacts of global change and to develop appropriate responses. The assessment of vulnerability is a transdisciplinary activity, meaning that knowledge from a number of scientific disciplines and also from outside of science (policy makers and other stakeholders) needs to be integrated in order to understand the complex interactions of the human–environment system that determine vulnerability. Being a young and transdisciplinary research field, VA faces terminological and methodological challenges.

There is confusion regarding the meaning of the concept of vulnerability in the global change scientific community. The Intergovernmental Panel on Climate Change (IPCC) Third Assessment Report defined vulnerability as:

> ... *the degree to which a system is susceptible to, or unable to cope with, adverse effects of climate change, including climate variability and extremes. It is a function of the character, magnitude and rate of climate variation to which a system is exposed, its sensitivity, and its adaptive capacity.* (McCarthy et al, 2001, p995)

The extent to which this definition can be made operational for assessing vulnerability is limited, because the defining concepts themselves are rather vague. Many alternative definitions have been put forward within the global change and related scientific communities.

The diversity in definitions is accompanied by a similar diversity in methodologies for assessing vulnerability. Each problem addressed, exhibits unique features and requires the design of its proper approach. To this end, participants from different scientific disciplines and from outside of science come together and spend a lot of time on discussing which knowledge is relevant and how to configure it into an appropriate methodology. Over the years, approaches have grown in complexity, developing from considering only single stresses to considering multiple stresses, from merely assessing impacts to also taking adaptation into account, and from static approaches to dynamic ones (Füssel and Klein, 2006). Today, methodologies comprise a multitude of participatory and analytical methods.

In spite of the lack of commonly agreed definitions and approaches, there is a great need to be able to compare the results attained with different approaches. In fact, comparability is key to the notion of vulnerability: policy makers often ask which country, region or sector is most vulnerable in order to prioritize efforts that need to be undertaken in order to minimize risks and mitigate possible consequences (Burton et al, 2002; Füssel and Klein, 2006). In addition, there is a need to learn from and build on past assessments for designing new approaches.

Efforts to address these needs have focused upon analysing theoretical definitions of vulnerability and proposing overarching conceptual frameworks (Brooks, 2003; O'Brien et al, 2004, 2006; Füssel and Klein, 2006; Füssel, 2007; Ionescu et al, 2008). These analyses, though useful for conceptual clarification, have limited practical relevance for comparing vulnerabilities or learning from past assessments, because in many assessments the theoretical definition put forward is far away from the methodology applied. Here, I approach the above-mentioned needs from the other side. Instead of analysing and comparing theoretical definitions, I analyse and compare the methodologies applied for assessing vulnerability. Methodologies are operational definitions of vulnerability, because they define what vulnerability exactly means in the context of the specific assessments. In particular, this chapter addresses the following two questions.

The first question addressed is: how can the analysis, communication and comparison of methodologies be facilitated? To this end a graphical framework for representing methodologies is developed. By representing methodologies in a graphical and uniform manner, I aim at making complex methodologies quickly accessible to a reader and, as a consequence, at facilitating the analysis, communication and comparison of methodologies, as well as the design of new methodologies. The usefulness of the framework is explored by applying it to analyse and compare the methodologies of two recent VAs. While the approach presented is specifically beneficial to the young field of VA it is not limited to this field and can be applied to other sorts of transdisciplinary research.

The second question addressed is: which features of a methodology are useful for which purpose? As pointed out in the first chapter of this book, the primary aim of VAs is to serve the purposes of the users of the assessment results (e.g. stakeholders or decision makers) rather than to advance scientific understanding in its own right. While different purposes, such as to raise awareness, to improve adaptation and to frame the global environmental-change mitigation problems are named in the literature (Burton et al, 2002; Füssel and Klein, 2006; O'Brien et al, 2006; Smit and Wandel, 2006), they are rarely related to the design of the assessments' methodologies.

The rest of the chapter is organized as follows. The next section discusses the concept of a methodology in the context of transdisciplinary research. A graphical framework is developed for analysing methodologies. The framework is applied to analyse the methodologies of two recent VAs carried out by the Dynamic and Interactive Assessment of National, Regional and Global Vulnerability of Coastal Zones to Sea-Level Rise (DINAS-COAST) and Advanced Terrestrial Ecosystem Analysis and Modelling (ATEAM) projects and these methodologies are compared. The final section of this chapter concludes and gives an outlook.

Methodologies

The way transdisciplinary assessments in general and vulnerability assessments in particular solve problems differs from the way of disciplinary research (Hinkel, 2008). Generally, there is no single or obvious method for solving a given problem, nor are there ready-made methods that can be taken 'off the shelf'. Each problem addressed has unique features and requires the ad hoc design of its proper approach. Relevant knowledge of people from different scientific and non-scientific domains must be identified, selected and configured appropriately. For example, the VA carried out by the ATEAM project (Schröter et al, 2005) involved the development of various scenarios, workshops to identify stakeholders preferences, statistical analysis of socioeconomic data and simulation experiments with various hydrological and ecosystem models. For general descriptions of VA approaches see Schröter et al (2004) and the IPCC *Technical Guidelines for Assessing Climate Change Impacts and Adaptations* (Carter et al, 1994).

In the context of transdisciplinary assessments, the specific configuration of methods, data and people involved in solving a problem is usually called the methodology, integrated methodology or methodological approach of the assessment. Note that in other contexts the term 'methodology' is used in different senses, either to refer to a system of methods followed in a particular discipline or to the branch of philosophy that studies such systems (Wordnet, 2005). In order not to create confusion, I will follow the usage of the term in transdisciplinary research. Note also that methodologies are not methods. A method is a specification of a process that makes the process reproducible by others and applicable to other cases, both of which is generally not possible for a methodology of a transdisciplinary assessment. Methodologies always include elements that are specific to the case addressed.

Methodologies of transdisciplinary assessments are generated reflexively, that is, they are developed, applied and evaluated in parallel (Euler, 2005). A significant amount of time is usually spent on the design of methodologies; methods are transferred from one discipline to another, composed from disciplinary methods, or developed from scratch. Often the problem perception changes during the course of applying the methodology and the methodology must be adjusted accordingly.

Methodologies are operational definitions.[1] Operational definitions define the meaning of a term by giving rules on how to measure it, while theoretical definitions define the meaning of a term on the basis of other theoretical concepts (Schnell et al, 1999; Bernard, 2000). This distinction resembles the distinction made in philosophy of science between observable and non-observable or theoretical concepts (Stegmüller, 1974; Carnap, 1995). Vulnerability is a theoretical concept while, for example, income or temperature are observable ones.[2] A theoretical definition tries to capture all relevant dimensions of the introduced concept. For example, the above-mentioned IPCC definition of vulnerability names the dimensions, exposure, sensitivity and adaptive capacity. Making a theoretical concept operational means providing a method (an operation) for mapping it to observable concepts. That method is then called the operational definition.

In this manner, the methodology of a VA is an operational definition of vulnerability; it defines the specific meaning the concept of vulnerability has in the context of the assessment. The results of VAs are statements that declare that, or to what extent, certain entities are vulnerable. However, how do we interpret these statements? Some idea on the meaning of such statements can be gained by our intuitive understanding of the concept of vulnerability or with the help of the theoretical definitions that are used within the scientific community. However, since different people have different intuitive understandings and use different theoretical definitions, the exact meaning of these statements can only be understood by looking at the methodology that has generated them.

One motivation for writing this chapter is that while great effort has been made in analysing and comparing theoretical definitions, little effort has been made in analysing and comparing methodologies applied for assessing vulnerability. Furthermore, the work on theoretical definitions is hardly connected to case studies that assess vulnerability. In most case studies, operational definitions are not derived systematically from the theoretical ones and the relation between the two often remains obscure. In my opinion, an improved analysis of methodologies of VAs is more likely to advance the field of vulnerability research and possibly also leads to more robust theoretical definitions than further theoretical work far away from empirical 'reality'. After all, the primary aim of VAs is to support action in the empirical world.

Another motivation for analysing methodologies is that it is generally the only way of judging the quality of the results of transdisciplinary assessments. Generally, the result statements produced by VAs cannot be verified, because the 'classical' means of verification – that is, testing results through experiments or in situ observations – are lacking due to the large spatial and temporal scales considered. As a consequence, only the quality of the process that generated the statements can be considered and the methodology is the specifications of this process. Similar reasoning underlies, for example, the introduction of the International Organization for Standardization (ISO) management standards 9000 and 14000, which certify business processes, rather than the products produced (ISO, 2005).

A framework for analysing methodologies

Building on the intuitive understanding of methodologies developed in the last section, this section introduces a more formal graphical framework for analysing methodologies. The goal of the framework is to present methodologies in a compact and concise manner, which allows for their quick communication and comparison.

A methodology of a transdisciplinary assessment is represented as a directed, simple diagram with four types of nodes: data, methods, actors and activities. The actor nodes denote the people involved in the application (not the design) of the methodology, that is, the scientific experts or other stakeholders. The data nodes denote data in the widest sense, which includes observed or measured data, as well as derived data. The method nodes denote specifications of activities. Note that this is a very general understanding of what a method is. Whether a specification is widely accepted is not of interest here, as this would normally be the case in scientific discourse. Data and method nodes will be subsumed under the label of knowledge nodes. The activity nodes denote the individual steps of the methodology.

The lines of the diagram connect the activities with their inputs and outputs. Possible inputs to an activity are data, methods or actors. Possible outputs of an activity are data (i.e. the activity is data collection) and methods (i.e. the activity is the development of a method). All paths of the diagram end with the final output or the product of the methodology.

Each activity has one special input that will be called its driver. The arc between an activity and its driver is printed bold. The driver is either a method or an actor and activities will be called either method-driven or actor-driven, respectively. Method-driven activities consist of the application of their driving methods. Method-driven activities are reproducible by others, while actor-driven activities are not, because no specification is or can be given for them. Instead, an actor or the actor's intention drives the activity. Besides the driver, activities can have any number of further inputs.

Figure 13.1 shows an example methodology consisting of three activities. Activity 1 is the development of scenarios, Activity 2 is the development of a model and Activity 3 is the application of the model on the scenarios to produce data on impacts. Activities 1 and 3 are method-driven activities. Activity 2, the development of the model, is an actor-driven activity, because it cannot be specified in the form of a method and is therefore not reproducible for others.

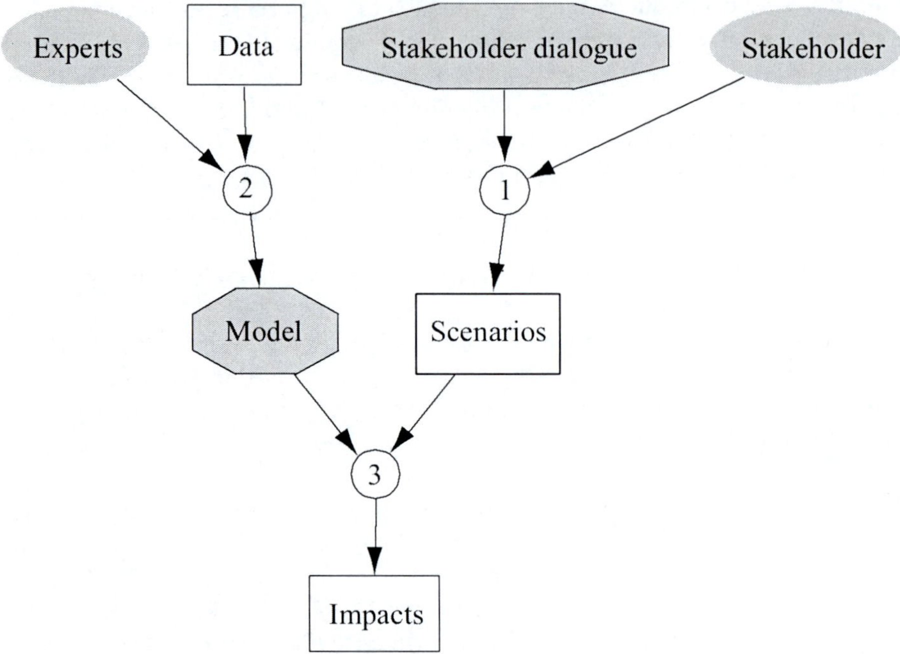

Note: The octagons represent methods, the rectangles data, the ovals actors and the numbered circles activities.

Figure 13.1 *Example of a methodology*

Activities that do not have any actor as input (no matter whether as driver or normal input) will be called objective, while those that do will be called subjective. It follows that all actor-driven activities are subjective. Objective activities are deterministic, that is, given the same input, they always yield the same output. Subjective activities are non-deterministic, even when driven by a method, because they are social processes that involve actors.

For example, in Figure 13.1, Activity 3 is an objective activity. The application of the model on the scenarios will always produce the same result no matter who runs the model. Therefore this activity does not have an actor as input. Activities 1 and 2 are subjective activities. Activity 1 is method-driven. It is based upon a method, the stakeholder dialogue, and therefore can be reproduced by others through applying the same method. However, even then the activity will most likely not yield the exact same scenarios. Activity 2 is actor-driven and therefore, by definition, not reproducible; the experts that develop the model represent their own knowledge without being guided by a method.

Note that it is difficult to establish a clear cut between objective and subjective activities. For example, the application of a model most likely involves some value judgements like setting model parameters. However, I am interested in the big picture and most of the time it is quite clear how to categorize an activity.

Knowledge nodes that have an incoming arc will be called derived and those that do not basic. Basic knowledge is fed into the methodology from the outside, while derived knowledge is produced within the methodology. For example, in Figure 13.1, the 'Data' and 'Stakeholder dialogue' nodes depict basic knowledge, while the 'Model', 'Scenarios' and 'Impacts' nodes depict derived knowledge.

Two test cases

The objective of this section is to test the practical applicability of the framework by analysing the methodologies of two recent VAs carried out by the EU-funded ATEAM and DINAS-COAST projects. The next section will then compare these two methodologies. The choice of these examples is motivated chiefly by the fact that I have first-hand knowledge of the two assessments.

Both projects have operationalized the IPCC definition of vulnerability as given in the Introduction to this chapter. The vulnerable systems regarded are regions, or more specifically the coupled human–environment systems of regions, that are exposed to certain climatic and socioeconomic changes. In both operationalizations adaptive capacity plays a major role. The way a region is influenced by climatic and socioeconomic changes depends not only on the magnitude of the exposure and its sensitivity to it, but also, to a great extent, on the capacity of the region's human system to adapt. Adaptive capacity is defined by the IPCC as the 'ability of a system to adjust to climate change (including climate variability and extremes) to moderate potential damages, to take advantage of opportunities, or to cope with the consequences' (McCarthy et al, 2001, p365).

ATEAM

The project ATEAM aimed at assessing the vulnerability of European regions relying on ecosystem services such as agriculture, forestry, carbon storage, carbon energy, water, biodiversity and mountains to global change. ATEAM's product is a digital atlas of vulnerability maps. See Schröter et al (2005) for a detailed account of the project.

Figure 13.2 shows the ATEAM methodology in terms of the framework. In Activity 1, general circulation models (GCMs) and the four emission scenarios of the IPCC Special Report on Emission Scenarios (SRES) (Nakicenovic and Swart, 2000) were used to produce climate scenarios. The climate scenarios were regionalized using data of observed patterns of regional climate (Activity 2). Experts of various disciplinary domains developed, also based upon the SRES scenarios, socioeconomic, land-use and nitrogen oxides (NO_x) deposition scenarios (Activities 3, 4 and 5, respectively).

After scenario development, the methodology proceeded along two parallel tracks. The first track assessed the potential impacts of the regional climate scenarios on the regions' ecosystem services. Therefore, the scenarios were fed into ecosystem and hydrology models (Activity 6). Stakeholders developed an ecosystem service indicator function that reduces the high-dimensional model output to a single dimension for each ecosystem service (Activity 7). The indica-

GCMs
SRES scenarios
1
Observed regional patterns
Climate scenarios
Regionalization method
2
Regional climate scenarios
Domain experts
EUROSTAT data
Multi-regression analysis
5
4
3
10
Ecosystem and hydrology models
NOx deposition scenarios
Land-use scenarios
Socioeconomic scenarios
Adaptive capacity index
6
11
Model output
Stakeholders
7
Adaptive capacity scenarios
Ecosystem service indicator function
8
Environmental classes of Europe
Potential impacts
Stratification method
9
Stratified potential impacts
Overlay function
12
Vulnerability maps of Europe

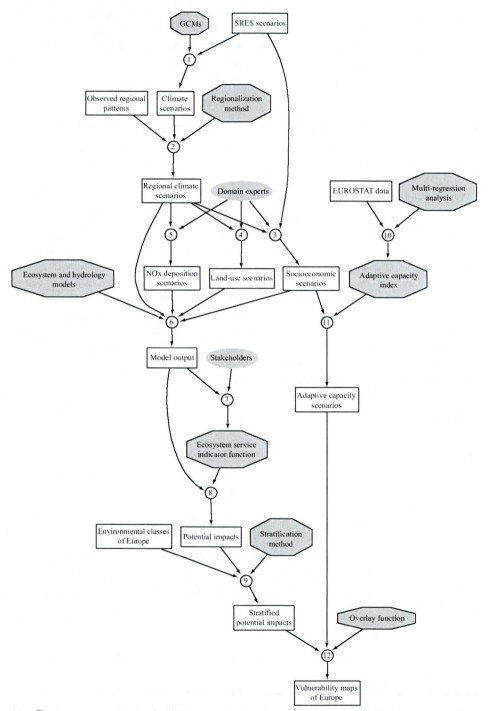

Note: The octagons represent methods, the rectangles data, the ovals actors and the numbered circles activities.

Figure 13.2 *The methodology of the ATEAM project*

tor function was applied on all model output to produce the 'potential impacts' data (Activity 8). This data was further processed by a so-called stratification method that normalized the regions' potential impact values to a scale between 0 and 1, based on the environmental class the regions belong to (Activity 9).

The second track assessed the regions' adaptive capacities. Detailed socioeconomic data of Europe was used to develop a statistical model, the adaptive capacity index, which represents the ability of the social system to adapt (Activity 10). The index was then applied on the socioeconomic scenarios to get future projections of the regions' adaptive capacities (Activity 11).

In a last activity, the data on potential impacts and adaptive capacities were combined into vulnerability maps (Activity 12). The maps display different magnitudes of potential impacts as different colours, and differences in adaptive capacities as colour saturation.

DINAS-COAST

The EU project DINAS-COAST aimed at assessing the vulnerability of coastal regions to sea-level rise. The product of DINAS-COAST is a user-friendly interactive tool called DIVA (Dynamic and Interactive Vulnerability Assessment). At its heart is an integrated model that enables its user to simulate the impacts of selected climatic and socioeconomic scenarios as well as adaptation strategies on the coastal regions of all coastal nations. See Chapter 5 for a comprehensive description of the project.

Figure 13.3 shows the DINAS-COAST methodology in terms of the framework. The methodology started with the development of climate and socioeconomic scenarios. The climate scenarios were produced with the climate model of intermediate complexity CLIMBER-2 of the Potsdam Institute for Climate Impact Research (Petoukhov et al, 2000) and the SRES scenarios (Activity 3). The climate scenarios were regionalized using the output of a GCM (Activity 4). Also based upon the SRES scenarios, socioeconomic scenarios were developed (Activity 5). A consistent global database (Vafeidis et al, 2008) containing information on coastal morphology, ecosystems and further socioeconomic characteristics was built up (Activity 2).

The main activity in terms of time and actors involved was the construction of an integrated model that represents the coupled human–environment system of the coast (Activity 6). Model development was based on an iterative method (Node 'DIVA Method') that enabled experts of different disciplines to integrate their knowledge about coastal subsystems in the form of computer modules (Hinkel, 2005). Since the goal of the project was to give the model directly to users, a graphical user interface (GUI) was constructed (Activity 1).

In a last step, the model, the scenarios and the GUI were combined into the DIVA tool (Activity 7). The DIVA tool allows its users to assess the vulnerability of different geographical entities (i.e. world regions, countries, administrative units and coastline segments) by choosing scenarios and adaptation strategies as inputs, running the model and comparing results achieved with different inputs.

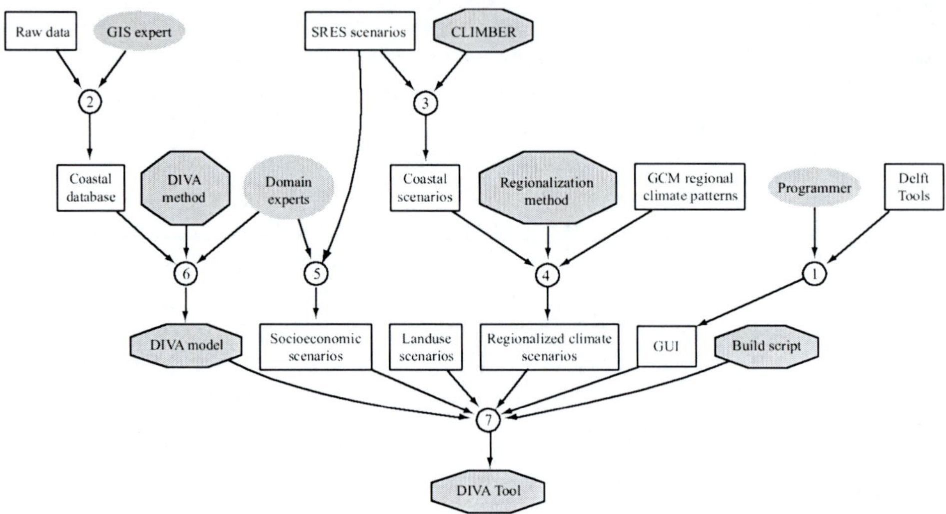

Note: The octagons represent methods, the rectangles data, the ovals actors and the numbered circles activities.

Figure 13.3 *The methodology of the DINAS-COAST project*

Comparative analysis

This section first compares the methodologies of ATEAM and DINAS-COAST, then compares the methodologies' products, and finally compares the user's perception of these products.

For the comparative analysis, it is important to note that the framework only captures the structure of a methodology and not its interpretation. Each activity of a methodology has a specific interpretation in the context of the assessment. For example, in the cases considered here, the activities stand for the dimensions of the theoretical definition of vulnerability, which are exposure, sensitivity and adaptive capacity (see also Methodologies section above). In order to effectively apply the framework for analysing methodologies and especially for comparing them, the structure and its interpretation have to be regarded jointly. In the following, I will use the term 'represent' to refer to the interpretation of the methodologies' activities.

Methodologies

In broad terms, the methodologies have a lot of commonalities. Computer models were used to represent the vulnerable systems. Climate and socioeconomic scenarios were developed to represent the exposures to which the systems' vulnerabilities were assessed. The models were then applied to scenarios to produce information on potential impacts. Last, model outputs were post-processed and converted into a form adequate for their potential users.

In both cases, the development of climate scenarios was a method-driven and objective activity, while the development of socioeconomic scenarios was actor-

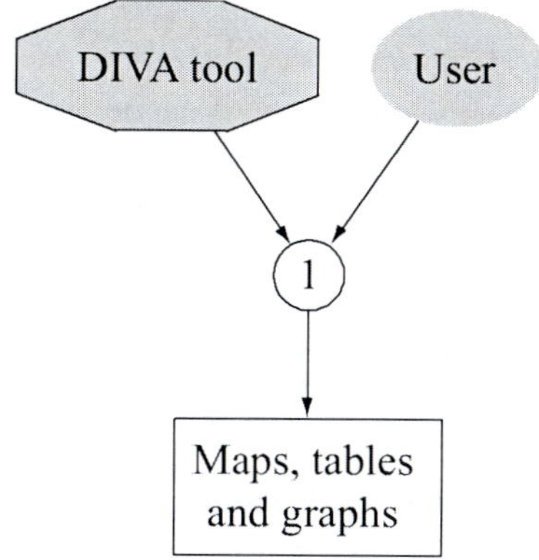

Note: The octagons represent methods, the rectangles data, the ovals actors and the numbered circles activities.

Figure 13.4 *The application of the DIVA tool*

driven. Existing methods (i.e. climate models) were used to produce scenarios of climatic change. However, no standard method existed for the development of socioeconomic scenarios and the corresponding activities were driven by domain experts.

The methodologies differ in the way the vulnerable system was represented. In ATEAM two separate models represented the vulnerable entity. Simulation models (Node 'Ecosystem and hydrology models' in Figure 13.2) represented the environmental system and some aspects of the human system, like the management of forestry and agriculture. A separate statistical model (Node 'Adaptive capacity index' in Figure 13.2) represented another aspect of the human system, namely the ability to respond to undesired impacts on the environmental system. This means that the impacts of the scenarios on the environment and the capacity of the human system to adapt to these impacts were assessed separately, without regarding the feedback between the two processes. In DINAS-COAST one integrated model represented the vulnerable entity. The impacts of the scenarios on the environment and the human system, as well as the human system's adaptation to these impacts, were assessed jointly.

In ATEAM the models that represent the vulnerable entity were, to the greater extent, basic knowledge while in DINAS-COAST they were derived. ATEAM built upon the knowledge and the resources previously invested by using already existing ecosystem and hydrology models in its methodology. Only the statistical adaptive capacity model had to be built from scratch (Activity 10 in Figure 13.2). DINAS-COAST built a new integrated model (node 'DIVA model' in Figure 13.3) as part of the project's methodology (Activity 6 in Figure 13.3), because one important aim of the project was to represent directly the feedback of the human adaptation actions on the coastal systems.

Another difference between the methodologies is that ATEAM involved stakeholders, while DINAS-COAST did not. In ATEAM, stakeholders developed an indicator function that reduces the high-dimensional output of the ecosystem models to one dimension for each ecosystem service (Activity 7 in Figure 13.2). This point will be picked up again in the next subsection.

A further difference between the two methodologies is that ATEAM produced data as its product, while DINAS-COAST produced a method. The product of ATEAM are maps that show the magnitudes of the potential impacts on the vulnerable regions and their adaptive capacities. The product of DINAS-COAST is the DIVA tool, which is a model of the vulnerable regions and a set of possible inputs for that model – that is, a set of scenarios and a set of adaptation strategies.

Methodologies and their products

Differences in methodologies translate into differences in their products, that is, the vulnerability statements produced through the application of the methodologies.

The difference in the type of product – data in the case of ATEAM and a method in the case of DINAS-COAST – is mirrored in the methodologies. While in ATEAM the application of the models that represent the vulnerable entities on the scenarios was part of the methodology (Activities 6 and 11 in Figure 13.2), in DINAS-COAST it is an extra activity to be performed by the user of the methodology's product (see Figure 13.4). Making the model available demands extra resources for tasks like making it platform-independent, documenting it, making it fast and developing an appropriate graphical user interface (Activity 1 in Figure 13.3).

The product of ATEAM, the vulnerability maps of Europe, is data in the form of a graph of a function. Disregarding the spatial and temporal dimensions, the project's methodology maps each of the four SRES scenarios to a scalar indicator representing the region's adaptive capacity and a vector indicator representing the impacts on the region. Symbolizing the four SRES scenarios as e_1, e_2, ..., e_4, the resulting adaptive capacities as a_1, a_2, ..., a_4, the resulting impacts as i_1, i_2, ..., i_4, and the methodology as $\rightarrow$, the result data of ATEAM can be depicted as the following list of statements:

$$\begin{aligned} e_1 &\rightarrow (i_1, a_1) \\ e_2 &\rightarrow (i_2, a_2) \\ e_3 &\rightarrow (i_3, a_3) \\ e_4 &\rightarrow (i_4, a_4) \end{aligned} \qquad (1)$$

Applying the DIVA tool to all combinations of scenarios and adaptation strategies also yields data in the form of a graph of a function, in which each combination of a scenario with an adaptation strategy is mapped to an impact indicator. Symbolizing the scenarios as e_1, e_2, ..., e_4, the adaptation strategies as u_1, u_2, ..., u_m, and the impact indicators as $y_{1,1}$, . . . $y_{4,m}$, the following matrix of statements is attained:

$$\begin{array}{llll}
(e_1, u_1) \rightarrow y_{1,1} & (e_1, u_1) \rightarrow y_{1,2} & \ldots & (e_1, u_m) \rightarrow y_{1,m} \\
(e_2, u_1) \rightarrow y_{2,1} & (e_2, u_2) \rightarrow y_{2,2} & \ldots & (e_2, u_m) \rightarrow y_{2,m} \\
(e_3, u_1) \rightarrow y_{3,1} & (e_3, u_2) \rightarrow y_{3,2} & \ldots & (e_3, u_m) \rightarrow y_{3,m} \\
(e_4, u_1) \rightarrow y_{4,1} & (e_4, u_2) \rightarrow y_{4,2} & \ldots & (e_4, u_m) \rightarrow y_{4,m}
\end{array} \quad (2)$$

In both cases, the result statements are similar in the sense that they relate (i) a value that represents a possible exposure (the e's), (ii) a value that represents the human response action (i.e. the a's in the ATEAM statements and the u's in the DINAS-COAST statements), and (iii) a value that represents impacts (i.e. the i's in the ATEAM statements and y's in the DINAS-COAST statements).

However, the statements are of different types. Whereas the human action appears on the right-hand side of the → (i.e. as output of the methodology) in the case of ATEAM, it appears on the left-hand side (i.e. as input to the methodology) in the case of DINAS-COAST. As a consequence, the interpretations of the two types of statements differ. The interpretation of an ATEAM statement $e \rightarrow (i, a)$ is of the form: 'When the world evolves according to scenario e, the impact on the vulnerable system will be i, if you don't do anything. At the same time your ability to adapt will be a.' The interpretation of a DINAS-COAST statement $(e, u) \rightarrow y$ is of the form: 'When the world evolves according to scenario e and you adapt according to strategy u, the impact on the vulnerable system will be y.'

The difference in the types of statements mirrors the different ways in which the coupled human–environment system was represented in the two methodologies. In ATEAM, the vulnerable system was represented by two separate parts of the methodology; hence, the impacts and the human response appear as separate parts in the result statements. In DINAS-COAST, the vulnerable system was represented by one model; hence, only one impact indicator which, however, already includes the adaptations to the impacts is produced.

A further difference lies in the level of aggregation of the indicators. In ATEAM, the indicators are of low dimensionality (one component for the adaptive capacity plus one component for each ecosystem service) and its components are normalized to a real-numbered scale between 0 and 1. In DINAS-COAST, the impact indicator is of high dimensionality and its components are not normalized. The indicator has roughly a hundred real-numbered dimensions, each of which stands for one aspect of the impact on a region (e.g. costs of flooding, wetlands lost, damage due to salinity intrusion, etc.). The level of aggregation determines the comparability of indicator values: the indicator values of ATEAM are intuitively easy to compare, while those of DINAS-COAST are not. Indicator values need to be compared for answering questions like: 'Which regions are most vulnerable?' or 'Under which scenario is a region most vulnerable?'

The differences in the level of aggregation and, as a consequence, comparability mirrors the different ways in which the preferences of the stakeholders were respected in the methodologies. The intuitive comparability of ATEAM's impact indicators is achieved by letting the stakeholders develop the 'ecosystem service indicator function' that reduces the high-dimensional output of the 'ecosystem and hydrology models' into one dimension for each ecosystem service (Activity 7 in Figure 13.2). The stakeholders selected and weighted the components of the model output that they valued as important for indicating the state of the ecosystem services. In DINAS-COAST stakeholders were not involved in the methodology. The high-dimensional output of the model is given directly to the users. However, a tool for facilitating the comparative analysis of the output in the form of graphs, tables and maps is also provided.

Products and their users

The previous two subsections were discussing methodologies and their products from the producer's perspective, that is from the perspective of the scholars designing and applying the methodology. This section considers the methodology from the consumer's perspective, that is from the perspective of the users of the methodologies' products. The discussion is based on published experiences gained from the ATEAM's final stakeholder workshop (Schröter et al, 2004) and on personal experiences gained from conducting user workshops with the DIVA tool.

One difference between the methodologies was that ATEAM delivered data and DINAS-COAST delivered a model as the product. The advantage of delivering a model is that users have a greater degree of freedom to produce results by manipulating model parameters, running their own scenarios, or even changing the model's code. A possible disadvantage is that users might be over-challenged by this great degree of freedom. In the DINAS-COAST workshops the users were generally positive about having received the model. The fact that the model was delivered to the users was perceived as giving the assessment extra credibility, because this way the users were able to conduct their 'own' VAs. In particular, the ability to run the model on updated data was welcomed. Many of the users discovered data inconsistencies when they zoomed into the region they knew best (a limitation due to the reliance on global data sources in the DINAS-COAST methodology) and thus appreciated the ability to change the data and rerun the model.

Another difference between the two assessments was the type of result statements produced – a measure representing the human system's capacity to adapt being the *output* of the methodology in the case of ATEAM (the adaptive capacity indicator) and the *input* to the methodology in the case of DINAS-COAST (the adaptation strategy). Stakeholders confronted with the results of ATEAM were less interested in the values of the adaptive capacity indicator, because they felt they could better judge their ability to adapt for themselves (Schröter et al, 2004). In the DIVA workshops, the users had trouble understanding the concept of choosing an adaptation strategy. While choosing a scenario is an accepted practice, choosing a strategy on how to adapt to the impacts of scenarios is not.

A third difference was the level of aggregation of the result statements. ATEAM produced rather simple, aggregate statements containing normalized adaptive capacity and potential impact indicators. These statements made the results accessible to a wide audience and generated a lot of media attention. ATEAM was invited by *Science* to write a paper (Schröter et al, 2005), which again generated further interest; within the first year after publication, the paper has already been cited 26 times (www.scopus.com, 13 June 2007). However, the stakeholders that had been involved in the methodology were less interested in these aggregate statements but rather in particular dimensions of the model output that related to their domain of interest (Schröter et al, 2004). DINAS-COAST produced more complex, less aggregate statements that contain multidimensional indicators. At the DIVA workshops, most users were, at first contact, overwhelmed with the many dimensions. However, after having understood how to run the model and analyse the multidimensional results by producing tables, graphs and maps with the GUI, many users expressed interest in having even more detailed information.

Conclusions and outlook

I argued that an essential part of a transdisciplinary assessment, such as a VA, consists in the ad hoc design of an appropriate methodology, which is a certain configuration of data, methods, actors and activities specifically tailored to the given problem. Supporting the communication and comparison of methodologies of assessments is therefore a crucial step in advancing transdisciplinary assessments. To this end, a graphical framework for representing methodologies of assessments was developed and applied for analysing and comparing the methodologies of two recent VAs carried out by the ATEAM and DINAS-COAST projects.

One major difference between the methodologies was that ATEAM produced data, while DINAS-COAST a method that is a model plus a set of input data. While delivering a model provides the user with more flexibility to produce results, it places an extra burden on the methodology in terms of adjusting the model to the needs of the users and developing a graphical user interface. It also places an extra burden on the users in terms of training required. In the case of DINAS-COAST, the users accepted the extra burden in return for the flexibility to run the model on their own data.

The methodologies also differed in the way the vulnerable system (i.e. the coupled human–environment system) was represented and, resulting from that, the type of result statements produced. While in the case of ATEAM different models represented the vulnerable entity without including the feedback of the human adaptation actions on the environment, in the case of DINAS-COAST one integrated model represented the vulnerable entity including the feedback. As a consequence, the ATEAM result statements consist of two indicators per vulnerable system, one indicating potential impacts and the other one indicating the capacity to adapt to these impacts. The DINAS-COAST result statements consist of one impact indicator per vulnerable system, which entails the assumption of a certain way to adapt. The users had trouble with both ways of handling adaptation. Further research is needed on how to handle adaptation methodologically and how to communicate results achieved to the users.

Both methodologies emphasized that the concept of vulnerability cannot be made operational by science alone; its meaning also depends on the preferences that the users of the methodologies' products have on the state of the vulnerable entities. While science provides knowledge in the form of models and data, it is left to the users to compare the model output (i.e. the impact indicators) produced.

However, the methodologies differed in the way the preferences of the users were taken into account and, resulting from that, the level of aggregation of the result statements produced. In the ATEAM methodology, stakeholders were involved in weighing the different dimensions of the model output, which led to aggregate result statements. In the DINAS-COAST methodology, no stakeholders were involved and less aggregate statements containing multi-dimensional indicators were produced. The users of the methodology's product, the DIVA tool, need to decide for themselves how to weigh the many dimensions of the model output. This activity is, however, supported by a graphical user interface.

Which level of aggregation is more useful depends on the type of user. In both assessments, the broader scientific and policy communities were more interested in aggregate statements, while those that actually make adaptation decisions were more interested in the specific dimensions of the model outputs.

The points made above exhibit a general trade-off between providing bold simple messages and providing detailed information for decision making. In terms of designing an assessment's methodology, this is the trade-off between reducing the complexity of the scientific knowledge to intuitively clear statements and delivering the complexity to the client together with tools to handle the complexity. It is hard to know beforehand which information is useful. The advice that can be given is to identify the users of the assessment's results at an early stage of the assessment and be flexible and able to adjust the methodology as the needs of the users become clearer.

The application of the framework to reconstruct methodologies is not trivial. A lot of people usually participate in an assessment, which makes it difficult to exactly reconstruct all the activities involved. The quality of the reconstruction depends on the available information sources in the form of literature and personal interviews. Furthermore, there is a danger in mixing three different views of a project's methodology: (i) the methodology originally designed at the beginning of the assessment; (ii) the methodology actually applied in the assessment; (iii) the methodology to be applied when one would repeat the assessment. Here, the focus lay on the second view.

One important aspect to note is that the granularity by which methodologies are analysed is arbitrary. Activities can be decomposed further into sub-activities or aggregated into super-activities. For example, in the case of DINAS-COAST, the activity of building the integrated model (Activity 6 in Figure 13.3) actually consisted of a series of sub-activities, such as specifying a shared language, programming modules and analysing the linkages between the modules (Hinkel,

2005). Presenting methodologies with different resolutions could be particularly beneficial for communicating and comparing them.

The framework could be extended in two directions. One direction would be to analyse the structure of the data and method nodes further, along the lines started in the subsection on Methodologies and their products. The individual dimensions of the data nodes could be distinguished and described. For such a deeper analysis it would be beneficial to adopt a mathematical notation, in which data are represented as sets, methods as functions or functors and the activities as function applications. The methodology would then be a composition of functions and functors.

Another direction of extension would be to attach information about the process of designing a methodology to the nodes. In a transdisciplinary assessment a lot of time is invested in discussing which methods or data to use. In order to learn from past assessments it would be interesting to know why certain methods or data have been selected. Alternative choices could be listed. Furthermore, methodologies are not static; changes are frequently made to them during the course of the assessment. It would be beneficial to know which changes have been made and why. Another interesting application would be to assess the structural uncertainties of methodologies by exploring how sensitive the methodologies' products are to the usage of other methods or data.

In order to prove its practical usefulness for communicating methodologies of VAs, the proposed framework needs to be applied to more cases. Most importantly, the framework should be beneficial to those who design and perform VAs. The application to other fields of transdisciplinary research, like sustainability or future research, will be explored.

Acknowledgements

The author thanks Klaus Eisenack, Paul Flondor, Mareen Hofmann, Cezar Ionescu, Malaak Kallache, Richard J. T. Klein, Rupert Klein, Antony Patt and Anne de la Vega for stimulating discussions and valuable insights. This chapter is a result of cooperation between the EVA project and the PIRSIQ activity at the Potsdam Institute for Climate Impact Research (PIK).

Notes

1 A methodology is not a particularly 'good' operational definition, because, as discussed above, it only holds for a small number of cases.

2 What observability means differs from discipline to discipline. For example, for a physicist temperature is observable, for a philosopher, however, it is not, because there is no direct sensory perception of it (only the position of a pointer can be observed). This means that observability is a convention: if the members of a discipline have agreed upon a simple or canonical way of measuring a concept, it is said to be observable. See, for example, Carnap (1995) for a discussion of observability.

References

Bernard, H. R. (2000) *Social Research Methods: Qualitative and Quantitative Approaches*, Sage Publications, Thousand Oaks, London

Brooks, N. (2003) 'Vulnerability, risk and adaptation: A conceptual framework', Tyndall Centre Working Paper 38, Tyndall Centre for Climate Change Research, Norwich

Burton, I., Huq, S., Lim, B., Pilifosova, O. and Schipper, E. L. (2002) 'From impact assessment to adaptation priorities: The shaping of adaptation policy' *Climate Policy*, vol 2, pp145–159

Carnap, R. (1995) *Introduction to Philosophy of Science*, Dover, New York

Carter, T. R., Parry, M. L., Harasawa, H. and Nishioka, S. (1994) *Technical Guidelines for Assessing Climate Change Impacts and Adaptations*, Report of Working Group II of the Intergovernmental Panel on Climate Change, Department of Geography, University College London, UK and the Center for Global Environmental Research, National Institute for Environmental Studies, Japan

Euler, P. (2005) 'Interdisziplinarität als kritisches Bildungsprinzip der Forschung: Methodologische Konsequenzen', in Schmidt, J. and Grunwald, A. (eds) *Method(olog)ische Fragen der Inter- und Transdisziplinarität Wege zu einer praxisstützenden Interdisziplinaritätsforschung, Technikfolgenabschätzung: Theorie und Praxis Nr. 2*, Forschungszentrum Karlsruhe, Institut für Technikfolgenabschätzung und Systemanalyse, Karlsruhe, Germany, pp63–68

Füssel, H. M. (2007) 'Vulnerability: A generally applicable conceptual framework for climate change research', *Global Environmental Change*, vol 17(2), pp155–167

Füssel, H. M. and Klein, R. J. T. (2006) 'Climate change vulnerability assessments: An evolution of conceptual thinking', *Climatic Change*, vol 75(3), pp301–329

Hinkel, J. (2005) 'DIVA: An iterative method for building modular integrated models', *Advances in Geosciences*, vol 4, pp45–50

Hinkel, J. (2008) 'Transdisciplinary knowledge integration: Cases from integrated assessment and vulnerability assessment', PhD thesis, Wageningen University, Wageningen, The Netherlands

Ionescu, C., Klein, R. J. T., Hinkel, J., Kavi Kumar. K. S. and Klein, R. (2008) 'Towards a formal framework of vulnerability to climate change', *Environmental Modeling and Assessment*, in press

ISO (2005) *Quality Management Systems: Fundamentals and Vocabulary*, International Organization for Standardization, Geneva, Switzerland

McCarthy, J. J., Canziani, O. F., Leary, N. A., Dokken, D. J. and White, K. S. (eds) (2001) *Climate Change 2001: Impacts, Adaptation and Vulnerability*, Cambridge University Press, Cambridge

Nakicenovic, N. and Swart, R. (eds) (2000) *Emissions Scenarios*, Special Report of Working Group III of the Intergovernmental Panel on Climate Change, Cambridge University Press, Cambridge

O'Brien, K., Eriksen, S., Schjolden, A. and Nygaard, L. (2004) 'What's in a word? Conflicting interpretations of vulnerability in climate change research', CICERO Working Paper 2004:04, Centre for International Climate and Environmental Research, University of Oslo, Oslo, Norway

O'Brien, K., Eriksen, S., Schjolden, A. and Nygaard, L. P. (2006) 'Why different interpretations of vulnerability matter in climate change discourses', *Climate Policy*, vol 7(1), pp73–88

Petoukhov, V., Ganopolski, A., Brovkin, V., Claussen, M., Eliseev, A., Kubatzki, C. and Rahmstorf, S. (2000) 'CLIMBER-2: A climate system model of intermediate complexity. Part I: model description and performance for present climate', *Climate Dynamics*, vol 16(1), pp1–17

Schnell, R., Hill, P. B. and Esser, E. (1999) *Methoden der empirischen Sozialforschung*, Oldenbourg, München

Schröter, D., Polsky, C. and Patt, A. (2004) 'Assessing vulnerabilities to the effects of global change: An eight step approach', *Mitigation and Adaptation Strategies for Global Change*, vol 10(4), pp573–595

Schröter, D., Cramer, W. Leemans, R., Prentice, I., Arajo, M., Arnell, N., Bondeau, A., Bugmann, H., Carter, T., Gracia, C., de la Vega-Leinert, A., Erhard, M., Ewert, F., Glendining, M., House, J., Kankaanpää, S., Klein, R. J. T., Lavorel, S., Lindner, M., Metzger, M. J., Meyer, J., Mitchell, T., Reginster, I., Rounsevell, M., Sabat, S., Sitch, S., Smith, B., Smith, J., Smith, P., Sykes, M., Thonicke, K., Thuiller, W., Tuck, G., Zaehle, S. and Zierl, B. (2005) 'Ecosystem service supply and vulnerability to global change in Europe', *Science*, vol 310(5752), pp1333–1337

Smit, B. and Wandel, J. (2006) 'Adaptation, adaptive capacity and vulnerability', *Global Environmental Change*, vol 16(3), pp282–292

Stegmüller, W. (1974) *Begriffsformen, Wissenschaftsprache, empirische Signifikanz und theoretische Begriffe. Probleme und Resultate der Wissenschaftstheorie und Analytischen Philosophie, Band II, Theorie und Erfahrung, 1*, Halbband, Springer, Berlin

Vafeidis, A. T., Nicholls, R. J., McFadden, L., Tol, R. S. J, Hinkel, J., Spencer, T., Grashoff, P. S, Boot, G. and Klein, R. J. T. (2008) 'A new global coastal database for impact and vulnerability analysis to sea-level rise', *Journal of Coastal Research*, vol 24(4), pp917–924

Wordnet (2005) http://wordnet.princeton.edu/, accessed 7 July 2005

Index